TEAM OF GIANTS

TEAM OF GIANTS

THE MAKING OF THE SPANISH-AMERICAN WAR

MATTHEW BERNSTEIN

UNIVERSITY OF OKLAHOMA PRESS : NORMAN

Publication of this book is made possible in part through the generosity of Edith Kinney Gaylord.

Library of Congress Cataloging-in-Publication Data
Names: Bernstein, Matthew, 1981– author.
Title: Team of giants : the making of the Spanish-American War / Matthew Bernstein.
Other titles: Making of the Spanish-American War
Description: Norman : University of Oklahoma Press, 2024. | Includes bibliographical references and index. | Summary: "Narrates how Theodore Roosevelt, Joseph 'Fighting Joe' Wheeler, and William Randolph Hearst, along with star reporters Richard Harding Davis and Stephen Crane, used political strategy, nascent US military might, and print media (mainly Hearst's San Francisco Examiner and New York Journal) to help ignite war with Spain over Cuba and the Philippines and ultimately establish the United States' offshore empire"—Provided by publisher.
Identifiers: LCCN 2024020284 | ISBN 978-0-8061-9471-4 (hardcover)
Subjects: LCSH: Spanish-American War, 1898—Causes. | Spanish-American War, 1898—Propaganda. | Roosevelt, Theodore, 1858–1919—Political and social views. | Wheeler, Joseph, 1836–1906—Political and social views. | Hearst, William Randolph 1863–1951—Influence. | Press and politics—United States—History—19th century. | Davis, Richard Harding, 1864–1916—Travel—Cuba. | Crane, Stephen, 1871–1900—Travel—Cuba. | BISAC: HISTORY / United States / 19th Century | HISTORY / Caribbean & West Indies / Cuba
Classification: LCC E721 .B476 2024 | DDC 973.8/9—dc23/eng/20240627
LC record available at https://lccn.loc.gov/2024020284

The paper in this book meets the guidelines for permanence and durability of the Committee on Production Guidelines for Book Longevity of the Council on Library Resources, Inc. ∞

1 2 3 4 5 6 7 8 9 10

To Jared Streets, Jarik Hille, and Chris Stewart

CONTENTS

MAPS

The United States, 1890. Courtesy of the Huntington Research Library, San Marino.

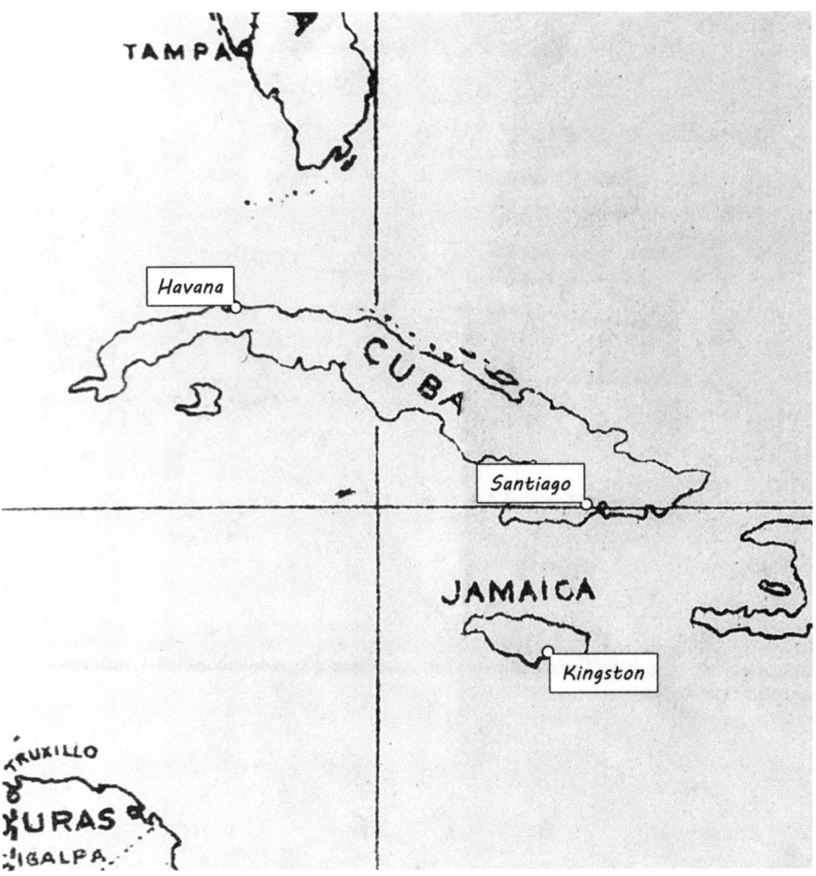

Cuba, 1890. Courtesy of the Huntington Research Library.

Havana, 1898, Scientific American Navy Supplement Map of Cuba, 1898. Courtesy of the Huntington Research Library.

PROLOGUE

The Battle of Las Guasimas

Lieutenant Colonel Theodore Roosevelt, while leading the 1st Volunteer Cavalry through the jungles of Cuba on the morning of June 24, 1898, was feeling particularly chatty. Unaware that Spanish soldiers were closer than Joseph "Fighting Joe" Wheeler anticipated, Roosevelt nonchalantly reminisced with *New York Journal* reporter Edward Marshall about a lunch they had shared at the Astor House with Marshall's boss, William Randolph Hearst.[1]

Suddenly something peculiar caught Roosevelt's eye. The barbed-wire fence beside him had been cut, and no rust showed on the ends.

"My God!" Roosevelt exclaimed. "This wire has been cut today."[2]

Moments later, a surgeon riding a mule blundered up to the front. Roosevelt shouted for him to be quiet, ironically making even more noise.

This was all the signal the Spanish needed.[3]

In an instant bullets began whistling around them. Richard Harding Davis, a star reporter for the *New York Herald* and one of Roosevelt's best friends, saw a soldier shot through the skull. Another star reporter, Stephen Crane, author of *The Red Badge of Courage* and a writer for Joseph Pulitzer's *New York World*, heard the commotion from the tail end of the column.

"The men marched noisily through the narrow road in the woods, talking volubly," Crane recalled, "when suddenly they struck the Spanish lines. Fierce fire was poured into their ranks."[4]

Because of the dense jungle and the smokeless powder the Spanish used, Roosevelt couldn't spot exactly where the bullets were coming from. And with Captain Allyn K. Capron commanding L Troop of the Rough Riders off to the right, Roosevelt didn't dare fire indiscriminately into the jungle and risk killing his own men. Scanning the mountainous jungle for the Spanish troops—his blue eyes flashing beneath his pince-nez glasses—Roosevelt was powerless to stop a fusillade of bullets that ripped into nine of his men.

Fortunately for Roosevelt, Richard Harding Davis was standing right beside him. "There they are, Colonel; look over there," Davis instructed, pointing. "I can see their hats near that glade."[5]

Looking at where Davis was signaling, Roosevelt spotted the Spanish. Calling for several of his best marksman, the lieutenant colonel directed them to return fire.

"There began a great fight in the thickets," Crane noted.[6]

These were the first shots fired in what would become known as the Battle of Las Guasimas, a key firefight in the Spanish-American War. The escalating war—a watershed moment in US history—exemplified the American zeitgeist of the late nineteenth century, encapsulating the growing power of the media, the hunger for heroic adventure, the Wild West's last hurrah, and the cauterizing of Civil War wounds.

Nowhere were these themes more evident than in the towering figures of the conflict, who grew more significant for their actions in helping set off the Spanish-American War and their roles during the war itself.

To Major General Joseph Wheeler, a former Confederate–turned-American general, the Spanish-American War was a shot at redemption. For rivals Stephen Crane and Richard Harding Davis, it was a chance for each to outdo the other in solidifying their claims as the greatest action reporter of their generation. For William Randolph Hearst, at that moment off the coast of Cuba on his chartered yacht *Sylvia,* the war was a three-ring circus through which he hoped to be recognized as the greatest newspaper proprietor on the planet. And to Theodore Roosevelt, the war was an opportunity to play Caesar in Gaul, demonstrating to the world his ability to lead the new American empire into the twentieth century if he played his cards right.

Although each man wanted different things, they formed the nucleus of a spectacular team.

— PART I —

THE PLAYERS

If you hesitate some bolder hand will stretch out before you and get the prize.

P. T. Barnum

1

DEPUTY SHERIFF ROOSEVELT

Theodore Roosevelt should have known better.

In late March 1886, Roosevelt and his closest ranch hands, Bill Sewall and Sewall's nephew Wilmot Dow, tramped through the Dakota Territory wilderness to a thicket of dwarf cedar trees. Roosevelt expected to find hanging from the high branches the carcasses of four deer Sewall and Dow had shot. With the deer safe from coyotes, Roosevelt noted that "game thus hung up in cold weather keeps indefinitely," and the weather certainly qualified as cold, having turned portions of the Little Missouri River to ice back in February.[1] But returning a fortnight later, they found only scattered remains of the deer.

Something had climbed the tree and eaten them. Examining the paw prints visible in the mud and snow, Roosevelt quickly put it together. The deer had been devoured by a pair of mountain lions.

"They had evidently been at work for some time," Roosevelt reflected, "and had eaten almost every scrap of flesh; one of the deer had been carried for some distance to the other side of a deep, narrow, chasm-like gully across which the cougar must have leaped with the carcass in its mouth."[2]

Determined that they would make the cats pay for poaching their kill, Roosevelt and the others followed the fresh tracks through deep ravines. Ultimately the tracks led to a gorge rimmed with cedar, where the hunters lost the trail. No matter. They planned on returning with a hunting hound the following day and set off for Roosevelt's Elkhorn Ranch.

Early the next morning Sewall checked on the clinker boat Roosevelt kept for crossing the Little Missouri. Sewall had firmly roped the boat to a tree, but he noticed that the rope had been cut, and the boat was gone. Investigating, Sewall discovered a red woolen mitten.[3]

First the deer and now the boat. Roosevelt was furious.

"We had no doubt as to who had stolen it," Roosevelt groused, "for . . . the only other thing in the shape of a boat on the Little Missouri was a small flat-bottomed scow in the possession of three hard characters who lived in a shack, or hut, some twenty miles above us."[4]

The leader of the trio was "Red" Finnigan, a brawny long-haired scoundrel who always wore a fringed buckskin coat and a broad-brimmed hat and was connected with several shooting scrapes. The previous summer Finnigan, smarting from a practical joke played on him, had shot up half the buildings in Medora with a buffalo gun. Finnigan traveled with Burnsted, a muscular ruffian, and Pfaffenbach, an old German with a penchant for violence. Word was that some of the local cowboys had recently discussed lynching them.[5]

Despite the reputation of the desperadoes, Roosevelt wanted to immediately saddle his horse Manitou and ride after them. The clinker boat had only been worth $30, but that wasn't the point. As a chairman of the Stockmen's Association, Roosevelt was technically a deputy sheriff, making riding after the outlaws his lawful duty. Plus, he had planned to use that boat to go after the lions who had eaten his deer. Also, Roosevelt knew that to allow thievery to go unchecked was to invite more theft.

"To submit tamely and meekly to theft," Roosevelt observed, "or to any other injury, is to invite almost certain repetition of the offense, in a place where self-reliant hardihood and the ability to hold one's own under all circumstances rank as the first of virtues."[6]

Finnigan and his bunch would have to be dealt with.

Sewall cautioned Roosevelt against riding out, explaining that his horse would struggle to cross the icy river and that he would have better odds of riding off a gorge than catching the thieves who, floating downstream on the current, would outpace any rider. The only thing to do was to construct a makeshift scow, and—because Finnigan likely thought no one was foolhardy enough to pursue them and was in no rush—they could possibly be overtaken.[7]

Roosevelt usually kept his own counsel, but he respected Sewall, a tough forty-year-old Mainer who had served as a guide in 1879, helping Roosevelt and their party to summit Mount Katahdin, Maine's high peak. Agreeing to his logic, Roosevelt sent to Medora, forty miles south, for provisions.

"I worked on the boat as fast as I could," Sewall recalled. "It took me about three days to build that boat."[8]

Roosevelt was pleased with the work.

"Seawall [*sic*] and Dow . . . were mighty men of their hands, skilled in woodcraft and the use of ax, paddle, and rifle," Roosevelt reflected. "They set to work with a will," and "in two or three days they had turned out a first-class bottom-boat."[9]

A powerful blizzard delayed the chase another three days. During that time Roosevelt wrote to a friend, Henry Cabot Lodge, that he was going "after some horse thieves." Once the blizzard subsided, on the morning of March 30, 1886, Roosevelt, Sewall, and Dow armed themselves with rifles and double-barreled duck guns and packed into the scow a fortnight's worth of coffee, flour, and bacon as well as warm bedding and a mess kit. To maneuver the boat, they took with them paddles, iron-shod poles, and heavy oars. Thinking ahead, Roosevelt also brought his camera, anticipating that the hunt could make a good article for *Century* magazine. With the Mainers' wives Mary Sewall and Elizabeth Dow—both five months pregnant—watching as they clambered aboard, the trio shoved off into the Little Missouri.[10]

"It was a strange, wild, desolate country of rough and barren bad lands that we passed through as we drifted with the current," Sewall recalled. An old hunter had warned them of the dangers of going down the river. One man had been abandoned by his fellows and was never seen again; another was eaten by a grizzly. But Sewall and Dow weren't afraid of the river, recollecting that "cowboys and hunters were mostly bow-legged and past-masters at riding, but they were not web-footed and used to riding logs and handling boats in rough waters the way Dow and I were."[11]

As for Roosevelt, with Sewall and Dow by his side he felt confident they would overtake Finnigan's band. "They were tough, hardy, resolute fellows, quick as cats, strong as bears, and able to travel like a bull moose," Roosevelt observed. "We felt very little uneasiness as to the result of a fight with the men we were after, provided we had anything like a fair show."[12]

At the same time, Roosevelt worried that they might not have a fair show. He noticed that the badlands surrounding the river were filled with gullies, steep walls, and hilltops crenellated with stone formations, the perfect place for an ambush.

That night when it grew too cold and dark to continue, Roosevelt, Sewall, and Dow beached the scow and camped ashore. The smattering of trees under which they slept afforded them little protection from the merciless wind. True to character, Roosevelt expressed that with their heavy jackets and great fur coats "we could bid defiance to the weather." In the morning they continued the hunt, but the only signs of life they saw were a cluster of abandoned tepees. That night the mercury plunged to zero. Roosevelt had brought *Anna Karenina* for reading material, and though the bitter cold must have brought Tolstoy's 1878 masterpiece to life, Roosevelt had always attributed the harsh Dakotas to an American author.[13]

"When one is in the Bad Lands," Roosevelt ruminated, "he feels as if they somehow *look* just exactly as Poe's tales and poems *sound*."[14]

For his part, Sewall allowed that the badlands were "perfectly named," for the treacherous river had perils he hadn't experienced in New England. He looked with trepidation at a great boulder up a steep bank, appearing as though it would fall at any moment. Just after they passed beneath it, the boulder plummeted, lifting the boat in a great wave. Later they caught sight of coal veins burning about seventy-five feet above the river. The wind may have been worst of all.[15]

"It was the crookedest wind in Dakota," Sewall grumbled.[16]

On the morning of April 1, the ice proved so thick that they knew it would be hours before they could launch the boat. Taking advantage of the break to hunt, they shot two deer, built a fire, and breakfasted on venison. Back in the scow Sewall acted as chief steersman, while Roosevelt and Dow watched the river and the surrounding cliffs for signs of the outlaws. In the downtime Roosevelt may have asked himself a pointed question.

What the hell was he doing here?

Roosevelt's path to hunting desperadoes in the Dakotas had begun innocently enough. Three years before on May 28, 1883, twenty-four-year-old Roosevelt—the youngest man in the New York State Legislature and the minority Speaker of the House—had aptly been made the guest of honor at a party at Clark's Tavern in New York City. Attending the party was Commander H. H. Gorringe, a retired naval officer who, like Roosevelt, believed in the expansion of the US Navy. Naturally, Gorringe wanted to shake hands with Roosevelt, who while attending Harvard had written the well-received but barely readable *Naval War of 1812*.[17]

Gorringe had just returned from a trip to the West and was in the early stages of opening up a hunting ranch. Roosevelt remarked that he would like to shoot a buffalo “while there were still buffalo left to shoot.”[18] Gorringe invited the New Yorker to accompany him on a trip in the fall to the badlands of Dakota Territory. Always up for adventure, Roosevelt accepted.

On August 31, 1883, Gorringe decided against the trip. But Roosevelt was still game. On September 3, kissing his pregnant wife Alice goodbye, Roosevelt loaded his duffel bag and gun case onto a westbound train and embarked on what for an ordinary man would be the trip of a lifetime.[19] Five days and about 2,400 miles later Roosevelt stepped off the Pullman in Little Missouri—about 200 miles north of Deadwood—composed of an assortment of small buildings in a ramshackle Dakota Territory town named for the nearby river. Derisively called “Little Misery” for obvious reasons, the town didn’t have much to offer. But Roosevelt, who longed to harden himself in the West as his heroes Daniel Boone and David Crockett had done, wasn’t about to complain. Roosevelt slept that night in a cot in the Pyramid Park Hotel and woke early the next morning, eager to explore this new world.[20]

Although Roosevelt hadn’t been aware of it when he decided to visit, Little Missouri was a bastion of lawlessness, with its nearest sheriff stationed 150 miles to the east, and was considered “the toughest town on the line” by the Northern Pacific. Everyone packed a pistol, and no one thought much of this dude from New York, at least at first. Roosevelt recalled that spectacles “were regarded in the Bad Lands as a sign of defective moral character,” and he received some hard stares by more than a few hard men.[21]

Irrespective of what people made of him, after more than a week of hunting and getting the lay of the land, on September 18 Roosevelt had a fateful conversation with two ranchers, Sylvane Ferris and Bill Merrifield. Sitting on logs outside Gregor Lang’s cabin after they’d taken supper, Roosevelt asked how much they thought it would cost to ably stock a cattle ranch. This wasn’t terribly far out of Roosevelt’s bailiwick; some time ago he had invested $5,000 in a beef company based out of Cheyenne. Roosevelt’s friend Hermann Hagedorn, hearing a retelling of the conversation between Roosevelt and the ranchers, recalled it like this:

“Depends what you want to do,” Sylvane answered, “but my guess is, if you want to do it right, it’ll spoil the looks of forty thousand dollars.”[22]

“How much would you need right off?” Roosevelt asked.

“Oh, a third would make a start,” Sylvane replied.

“Could you boys handle the cattle for me?”

“Why, yes,” Sylvane drawled, “I guess we could take care of ’em ’bout as well as the next man.”

"Why, I guess *so!*" Merrifield agreed.

"Well, will you do it?" Roosevelt offered.

"Now, that's another story," Sylvane explained. "Merrifield here and me is under contract with Wadsworth and Halley. We've got a bunch of cattle with them on shares."

"I'll buy those cattle," Roosevelt declared.

"All right. Then the best thing for us to do is go to Minnesota an' see those men an' get released from our contract," Sylvane explained.

"That will suit me," Roosevelt said, drawing a checkbook from his pocket. The ranchers watched with amazement as Roosevelt signed the check for $14,000 and handed it over, thus taking possession of the first cattle that would become the foundation of the two ranches—the Maltese Cross and the Elkhorn—that Roosevelt would own and operate.

"Don't you want a receipt?" Merrifield asked after a pause.

"Oh, that's all right."

On the morning of September 21, 1883, Gregor Lang watched Roosevelt disappear. "There goes the most remarkable man I ever met," Gregor told his son, Lincoln. "Unless I am badly mistaken, the world is due to hear from him one of these days."[23]

In late December, Roosevelt was back in New York's capital, Albany, 150 miles north of his home in New York City. When Roosevelt was renominated to the New York State Legislature on December 31, he also cemented the speakership. For a twenty-five-year-old, it was quite an accomplishment. But tragedy soon followed.

On February 13 assemblymen crowded around Roosevelt, shaking his hand and congratulating him on the telegram he had received that Alice had given birth to a healthy baby girl the night before. A second telegram followed, however. Reading it, Roosevelt rushed to the train station. When he reached 6 West Fifty-Seventh Street he found that the contents of the telegram were no exaggeration: both his mother and his wife were dying.

In horror, Roosevelt raced between the bedroom upstairs, where Alice was dying of Bright's disease, and the bedroom one floor below, where his mother Mittie was dying of typhoid fever. At 3 a.m. on Valentine's Day, Mittie perished.

"There *is* a curse on this house," Roosevelt declared. Eleven hours later Alice succumbed as well. In Roosevelt's diary he drew an X for February 14. Beneath the X he wrote, "The light has gone out of my life."[24]

Roosevelt attended the funerals as though in a fog. Then on March 9, 1884, he wrote to his friend from Maine, Bill Sewall, inviting him and his nephew to join him at the Elkhorn Ranch. "I feel sure you will do well for yourself by coming out with me. . . . I shall take you and Will Dow out next August."[25]

But before Roosevelt could escape to his ranch, he had politics to deal with. On April 23 he was in Utica, where he received the most votes for delegates at large, securing a prominent spot in the Republican National Convention in Chicago. Henry Cabot Lodge, who was running for the US House of Representatives and had recently published biographies on Daniel Webster and Alexander Hamilton, mentioned to a friend that Roosevelt was a "national figure of real importance." Lodge made a point to cultivate a friendship with young Roosevelt.[26]

The following day Roosevelt returned to Albany, where he was heartily congratulated. Spoiling the atmosphere was the rumor that the governor of New York, Grover Cleveland, was threatening to veto some of the regulatory bills Roosevelt had proposed.

"He mustn't do that!" Roosevelt exclaimed to William Hudson, a reporter for the *Brooklyn Daily Eagle* who sensed a juicy story. "I can't have that! I won't let him do that! I'll go up and see him at once."[27]

With Hudson trailing him, Roosevelt sprinted up the hill to New York's Executive Mansion. By the time Hudson caught up with him, Roosevelt was already banging his fist against Cleveland's desk in the Executive Office. To Roosevelt, Cleveland calmly explained that the bills were riddled with errors. Sentences were legally incomprehensible. A clause in the Tenure of Office Bill claimed two different terms. The bills needed to be repaired before they could be signed. Roosevelt bristled at this, stating that the "principle" was sound and the details were inconsequential.

"You must not veto those bills," Roosevelt blustered. "You cannot. You shall not. . . . I won't have it!"

Cleveland's patience was at an end. Drawing up his weight—just shy of three hundred pounds—Cleveland barked, "Mr. Roosevelt, I'm going to veto those bills!" As Cleveland's fist crashed onto the desk, Roosevelt retreated, muttering something about "an outrage." But the meeting was at an end.

Soon afterward Roosevelt managed to incite a disagreement with another future president, William McKinley. The matter was which horse Roosevelt would back at the convention in Chicago. Detesting James G. Blaine, while in the Windy City Roosevelt boomed George F. Edmunds for the nomination, even on June 6 when Blaine received 334½ votes on the first ballot to Edmunds's 93.

By the third ballot Blaine's lead had increased, putting him only 36 votes from securing the nomination.

Roosevelt never learned to be a gracious loser. Before the fourth ballot could be cast he started spiraling hurricane-like between various delegations, desperately trying to mount a defense against Blaine. When Roosevelt's ally Judge Foraker moved to adjourn, to permit Roosevelt time to stop Blaine's momentum, the motion was shouted down. Red-faced, Roosevelt leapt from his seat, demanding a roll call. The hall soon echoed with jeers and whistles. Despite this, Roosevelt launched into a bombastic speech until a New Jersey delegate commanded him to "sit down and stop your noise."[28]

"Shut up your own head, you damned scoundrel you!" Roosevelt shouted.

McKinley, a respected congressman from Ohio who had found his footing in Chicago as a peacemaker, quieted the hall.

"Let us have no technical objections. I am as good a friend of James G. Blaine as he has in this convention, and I insist that every man here shall have fair play."

When Blaine won the nomination, a great roar and a flurry of hats and handkerchiefs filled the hall, and McKinley—the unexpected kingmaker—was seen pushing happily through the crowd toward Roosevelt. Bending over the New Yorker's chair, McKinley asked him to second the nomination. Roosevelt shook his head no.

Once outside, Roosevelt groused to a *New York World* reporter, "I am going cattle-ranching in Dakota for the remainder of the summer and a part of the fall. What I shall do after that I cannot tell you."

On June 22 Roosevelt was back at the Maltese Cross Ranch. Soon afterward he took a clandestine trip with Antoine Amédée Marie Vincent Manca de Vallambrosa, a dangerous Frenchman who styled himself the Marquis de Morès and owned a neighboring ranch. Their purpose was to join a secret band of vigilantes, called "stranglers" because of their tendency to lynch the men they deemed too dangerous to live. But Granville Stuart, the vigilantes' leader, thought that Roosevelt and the marquis were too "socially prominent" and did not allow them to join their ranks.[29]

On August 1, Roosevelt was back at the Maltese Cross Ranch. Joining him that day were Bill Sewall and Wilmot Dow. At first they didn't think that the badlands would be good for cattle and preferred the river to anything else, but after a short time the Mainers became accustomed to the "desolate grandeur" of the place, as Sewall called it.[30]

Not long afterward Roosevelt was chasing after lost horses and found himself in Mingusville, thirty-five miles west of Medora. Stopping at Nolan's Hotel that evening, he entered the main room and immediately saw a man who looked like trouble.

"A shabby individual in a broad hat with a cocked gun in each hand was walking up and down the floor talking with strident profanity," Roosevelt recalled. "He had evidently been shooting at the clock, which had two or three holes in its face."[31]

As soon as he saw Roosevelt, the shabby individual jeered, "Four eyes is going to treat." Not looking for a fight, Roosevelt joined in the laughter, got behind the stove, and sat down. But the bully followed him. Although Roosevelt tried to laugh off the incident, the bully continued to curse him, leaning over Roosevelt with a pistol in each hand and demanding Roosevelt "set up the drinks."

"Well, if I've got to, I've got to," Roosevelt said, and looked past him.

The bully never saw it coming. Rising, Roosevelt punched the man in the jaw with his right, struck him with his left, and landed a third with his right.

"He fired the guns," Roosevelt remembered, "but I do not know whether this was merely a convulsive action, or whether he was trying to shoot at me. When he went down he struck the corner of the bar with his head. . . . I took away his guns, and the other people in the room . . . hustled him out and put him in the shed."

It was with satisfaction that Roosevelt learned the next day that the bully had been placed on a freight train. Having bested a western bad man, Roosevelt crowned his glory on September 13 by shooting a 1,200-pound grizzly bear between the eyes. On May 19, 1885, Roosevelt reached Box Elder Creek, where he assisted cowpunchers in the spring roundup. Roosevelt knew by now that if anyone called him "Four Eyes," he needed to deal with the situation quick. So, when a Texan addressed him as "Storm Windows," Roosevelt responded, "Put up or shut up."[32] The Texan deemed it best to thereafter censor his words around young Roosevelt.

"That four-eyed maverick," commented one grizzled cowboy, "has sand in his craw a-plenty."

"Roosevelt," Sewall reflected, "was afraid of nothing and nobody. . . . Theodore was not a big man—he was only of medium height, weighing about a hundred and fifty pounds, and was clear bone, muscle, and grit."[33] Sewall also reflected that Roosevelt often felt melancholy, confiding that he had nothing to live for. When Sewall brought up Baby Lee, Roosevelt allowed that his sister could care for the girl better than he could. Sewall argued that Roosevelt could still make his mark in politics. That and the vast wilds of Dakota seemed to hearten him somewhat.

Roosevelt's western adventures paid off in more than just cattle and renewed vigor. In July 1885 G. P. Putnam's Sons published Roosevelt's *Hunting Trips of a*

Ranchman, to favorable reviews in the United States and abroad. With the book selling for $15 a copy, Roosevelt was a man on the make. That summer he allowed himself a two-month break from the strenuous life, luxuriating with family in New York. On August 8, he was on hand to march as a National Guard captain for former president Ulysses S. Grant's funeral, proving closer to the action than when, at six years old, he'd watched Abraham Lincoln's funeral procession from an upstairs window.[34]

Roosevelt was back in Medora on August 25. With Sewall and Dow, Roosevelt discussed the arrest of the Marquis de Morès. That the marquis had killed Riley Luffsey two years earlier was common knowledge, but both times the justices of the peace had examined the case, they found the evidence thin. This time, however, they determined a chance of a conviction possible and placed the marquis behind bars in Bismarck while a grand jury was summoned. Then, on September 5, Roosevelt received an ominous letter that the marquis had penned from jail.

> My dear Roosevelt
>
> My principle is to take the bull by the horns. Joe Ferris is very active against me and has been instrumental in getting me indicted by furnishing money to witnesses and hunting them up. The papers also published very stupid accounts of our quarreling. . . . Is this done by your order? I thought you my friend. If you are my enemy I want to know it. I am always on hand as you know, and between gentlemen it is easy to settle matters of that sort directly.
>
> Yours very truly
> MORES
> Sept. 3, 1885.[35]

Roosevelt deduced that the marquis desired to shoot it out. But Roosevelt hadn't spread any gossip about the marquis. This was a perilous position to be in, for though Roosevelt hadn't caused the rift, personal honor demanded he not back down.

"I won't be bullied by a Frenchman. . . . What do you say if I make it rifles?" Roosevelt asked Sewall.[36]

Sewall agreed to act as Roosevelt's second but privately figured that his friend was smart enough to find a less deadly path. Roosevelt responded with a letter of his own, which he sent to the Marquis:

MEDORA, DAKOTA
September 6, 1885

Most emphatically I am not your enemy; if I were you would know it, for I would be an open one, and would not have asked you to my house nor gone to yours. As your final words, however, seem to imply a threat, it is due to myself to say that the statement is not made through any fear of possible consequences to me; I, too, as you know, am always on hand, and ever ready to hold myself accountable in any way for anything I have said or done.

Yours very truly
THEODORE ROOSEVELT[37]

The next letter from the marquis to Roosevelt was of a lighter tone. Evidently, having determined that Roosevelt was not his enemy and would fight if pressed, the marquis determined they would continue their relationship "*without trouble.*" This was good news for Roosevelt, for the marquis was acquitted of the charges on September 5 and was once more at large.[38]

Roosevelt was back in New York in October when he met with his old childhood sweetheart, twenty-four-year-old Edith Carow. All the old passions between them revived at once, and Roosevelt proposed on November 17, 1885. Edith happily agreed.

On Roosevelt, Edith commented, "Here was a person of refinement . . . and much sexual potential."[39]

But the nuptials would have to wait. In March 1886, Roosevelt returned to the Elkhorn Ranch. The hunting trip with his ranch hands, the discovery of the mountain lion tracks around the bloody deer scraps, and the theft of the boat all led inexorably to the morning of April 1. Roosevelt was playing a dangerous game. Trading barbed letters with the hot-tempered Marquis de Morès was one thing. Looking to throw down on the likes of Red Finnigan and his gang was quite another. One mistake and all of Roosevelt's life's ambition—a new beginning with Edith and his hat in the political arena—could be over in a sudden flash of gunfire.

The stolen boat appeared that afternoon, just as Roosevelt, Sewall, and Dow rounded a bend while laughing and talking. The boat lay beached against the right bank, seemingly empty. But just beyond, a campfire burned. In a moment the trio had their overcoats off (so their weapons would be easy to reach) and, after exchanging a few tense words, moored the scow.[40]

"As soon as it touched the shore ice," Roosevelt recalled, "I leaped and ran up behind a clump of bushes, so as to cover the landing others. . . . For a moment we felt a thrill of keen excitement and our veins tingled as we crept cautiously toward the fire."[41]

Soon they could see a solitary bandit near the fire, his weapons at his feet. It was the old German, Pfaffenbach. Suddenly surrounded by armed men, the German gave up peacefully. Upon securing Pfaffenbach, Roosevelt and the others crouched low, waiting for Finnigan and Burnsted to return. After more than an hour of waiting, Roosevelt and his posse heard the pair tramping toward the campfire and caught sight of their rifles glittering in the sunlight.

When Finnigan and Burnsted were only twenty feet from the camp, Roosevelt, Sewall, and Dow revealed themselves, their rifles cocked and pointed at the bandits.[42]

"Put up your hands!" Roosevelt demanded.[43]

Stunned, Burnsted did as bidden. Finnigan showed more sand.

"Finnigan hesitated for a second," Roosevelt recollected, "his eyes fairly wolfish; then, as I walked up a few paces, covering the center of his chest to avoid overshooting, and repeating the command, he saw that he had no show, and, with an oath, let his rifle drop and held his hands up beside his head."[44]

For the next week Roosevelt's posse marched Finnigan's gang 150 miles downriver. By April 6, their provisions all but gone, they were forced to mix the river water with the last of their flour to form wretched johnnycakes. During this time a strange sort of kinship overtook the captors and captives, possibly borne out of the fact that the lawmen hadn't executed the thieves on the spot and, concerned that their hands might freeze, did not bind them.

On April 7 Roosevelt and the others reached a cattle camp, restocking on coffee, sugar, and bacon. The following day, within the Killdeer Mountains, they reached C Diamond Ranch. There the party broke up. Sewall and Dow headed to Mandan, while Roosevelt placed his prisoners in a wagon, and while the rancher drove them forty-five miles to Dickinson, Roosevelt marched behind, his Winchester ready. Reaching Dickinson several days later, Roosevelt finally delivered the captives into the sheriff's custody.

For his trouble, Deputy Sheriff Roosevelt was paid $50.

In August, Roosevelt was back at the Elkhorn Ranch when Mary Sewall gave birth to a son. Less than a week later more happy news followed when Elizabeth Dow gave birth to a son as well. Fleeing from the increasingly domestic atmosphere, Roosevelt traveled to Mandan to witness Red Finnigan and Burnsted being convicted. As for Pfaffenbach, Roosevelt withdrew the charge, stating that "he did not have enough sense to do anything good or bad."[45]

Around this time word of the Cutting Affair circulated throughout the country, which threatened to launch the United States into war. A. K. Cutting, an American newspaperman, had been arrested in El Paso del Norte, Mexico, after publishing an article hostile to a rival newspaperman, Emigdio Medina. American politicians demanded Cutting's release, but President Porfirio Díaz didn't want to be seen bending to American authority. Talk of a second Mexican-American war was heard from Mexico City to Washington, D.C., and even in Dakota Territory.[46]

Wanting in on the action, Roosevelt envisioned raising "an entire regiment of cowboys" to ride across the Mexican border. He composed a letter to Secretary of War William C. Endicott notifying him that Roosevelt was "at the service of the government."[47]

To Lodge, Roosevelt implored, "Will you tell me at once if war becomes inevitable?"

To Roosevelt's chagrin, the Cleveland administration—with a bit of a nudge from Senator George Hearst, who didn't want the money made from his Mexican mines and cattle ranches disrupted—decided to handle the matter diplomatically.

"If a war had come off," Roosevelt reckoned, "I would surely have had behind me as utterly reckless a set of desperadoes as ever sat in the saddle."

Roosevelt's dream of leading a cowboy regiment into battle was closer than he thought, courtesy of a mischievous Californian whose tactics Roosevelt reviled but whose journalistic panache made him one of the most influential Americans of all time.

W. R., he was called.

2

HEARST'S FIRST NEWSPAPER WAR

William Randolph Hearst wanted more.

With a millionaire father, a quick wit, and a devil-may-care attitude, Hearst generally got what he wanted. Typically, he spent his father's money on flashy clothes, fast yachts, and whirlwind romances. But his most prized possession was his morning newspaper, made over to him by his father as a gift: the *San Francisco Examiner.*

Hearst, who would prove as instrumental as any man at fomenting the Spanish-American War, had become interested in publishing while at Harvard College. Along with keeping company with a Cambridge waitress, Tessie Powers, and a pet alligator, Champagne Charley, Hearst took over the literary *Harvard Lampoon,* expanding it from four to six pages. With a letter of introduction to the editor of the *Boston Globe,* Charles H. Taylor, Hearst observed the innerworkings of the East Coast paper, categorizing what could stand improvement.[1]

Vacationing in Washington, D.C., in 1885, typically taking a break from his professors' lectures, Hearst wrote to his father George Hearst, the mining tycoon and US senator from California. In his letter, W. R. Hearst implored his father to allow him to take over the *Examiner,* where he promised to create revolutionary changes.[2]

Despite Hearst being expelled from Harvard for lack of effort, George did give his son enough money to carry out his schemes. In February 1887 at twenty-three years old, W. R. Hearst sent a cable to James Gordon Bennett Jr., the editor and chief of the *New York Herald,* seeking to scoop some of the *Herald*'s juiciest articles before the *San Francisco Chronicle* and the *San Francisco Call* knew what hit them. When Bennett didn't respond, Hearst traveled to New York City himself. Finding Bennett gone, Hearst cabled a man in San Francisco: "Find Bennett and arrange for cable specials. He is in Paris, up the Mediterranean, at the Pyramids or going up the Nile. Hunt him."[3]

In short order, Bennett was located. By the first week of March, the words "Special to the Examiner" and "Copyright, 1887, by James Gordon Bennett" could be found throughout the *Examiner.* Splashing around even more of his parents' money, Hearst inked similar deals with the *New York Times* and S. S. McClure's syndicate. Subscribers to the *Examiner* were delighted to find inside science fiction from Jules Verne and W. C. Morrow. Then on March 4, 1887, signifying that Hearst had officially taken control of the *Examiner,* the words "W. R. Hearst, Proprietor" appeared on the rain-spattered second page.[4]

Naturally, Hearst took inventory. On the books, the circulation of the *Examiner* was technically 23,914. But Hearst knew that about one-third of these newspapers were giveaways—free subscriptions that Senator Hearst had offered to support his senatorial campaign. In actuality, the daily circulation was closer to 15,000, far less than the 37,500 subscribers boasted by the *Chronicle.* Considering the population of San Francisco was 350,000, this meant that more than 10 percent of California's most populous city subscribed to the enemy.[5]

Playing second fiddle was never W. R. Hearst's style.

To change the tune, Hearst hired the best talent he could buy. This included Arthur McEwen, a Scotsman who had cut his teeth as a journalist at the *Virginia City Evening Chronicle,* and McEwen's brother-in-law Charley Michelson, a master wordsmith who would decades later become a speech writer for Franklin Delano Roosevelt. Ernest Thayer and Frederick Harris Briggs, Hearst's friends from Harvard, were also on board, as was Edward Townsend, Senator Hearst's right-hand man. Townsend was supposed to rein in W. R. Hearst but quickly realized he'd have better luck lassoing a hurricane.[6]

With Hearst at the wheel, headlines became eye-popping. Stories on train wrecks, train robberies, fires, and floods dominated the front page. The March 19, 1887 *Examiner* headlines were emblematic.

> FIRE. A Crowded Hotel in Buffalo Becomes a Grave of Flames. Thirty Persons Burned to Death.

FLOOD. One Vast Sea Sweeps Everything Before It in the Northwest. Northern Pacific Trains Blockaded.
CHICAGO ANARCHISTS. The Supreme Court May Not Decide the Case Until September. Many Months Reprieve.
VIOLENT DEATHS. A Fatal Quarrel on Account of a Horserace in Madera. The Surgeon's Knife.[7]

Hearst also gave the paper a new moniker, printed boldly on the masthead: Monarch of the Dailies. On May 27 he traveled across the bay to Oakland, visiting the home of Ambrose Bierce, the irascible American Civil War veteran and newspaper wit.

Hearing a faint rap on the door, Bierce opened it to find a blue-eyed, blond-haired young man who stood about six foot, three when not slouching. As Bierce recalled,

> I did not ask him in, instate him in my better chair (I had two) and ask him how we could serve each other. If my memory is not at fault I merely said: "Well," and awaited the result.
>
> "I am from the *San Francisco Examiner*," he explained in a voice like the fragrance of violets made audible, and backed a little away.
>
> "O," I said, "you come from Mr. Hearst."
>
> Then that unearthly child lifted its blue eyes and cooed: "I am Mr. Hearst."
>
> His father had given him a daily newspaper and he had come to hire me to write for it.[8]

Under Hearst's direction, Bierce began writing venomous articles in the Sunday *Examiner* brimming with devilish wit. The result of Hearst's enterprise was the rapid increase of circulation. By the end of March, daily circulation at the *Examiner* was 26,475, a staggering gain of 2,561 in three weeks.[9]

Two days later, Hearst got some bad news on April 2 when the *San Francisco Call* and the *San Francisco Chronicle* scooped the *Examiner* on a fire that had destroyed the Del Monte Hotel in Monterey (Hearst knew the hotel well, incidentally; he'd there proposed to a former sweetheart, Eleanor Calhoun, before his mother, Phoebe, talked them out of it). Refusing to take that lying down, Hearst engaged a Southern Pacific train, filled it with *Examiner* men, and rattled to the scene. The next day the *Examiner* treated its readers to a stunning fourteen-page newspaper. The first two pages were filled with F. H. Briggs's illustrations of the fire's devastation.

Hearst even wrote the lead article himself.

> HUNGRY, FRANTIC FLAMES. They Leap Madly Upon the Splendid Pleasure Palace by the Bay of Monterey, Encircling Del Monte in Their Ravenous Embrace From Pinnacle to Foundation.[10]

In less than a month, the composition of the paper had changed dramatically. The fonts were bigger, the illustrations were grander and more frequent, and the placement of the articles, determined by Hearst, were artistic and eye-catching.

Furthermore, realizing the *Examiner* was moving beyond its printing capabilities, Hearst wrote to his father for assistance. The senator was directed to "see Mr. Hoe of Printing Press fame," to shop around for a "photographic instrument," and to determine a "routing machine for fine plates." When the senator did not respond, Hearst simply instructed Townsend to purchase the equipment, and Hearst paid for engravers and pressman to be trained in the new equipment. Soon the Examiner Building was installed with a Web Perfecting press, capable of printing, pasting, and folding fifteen thousand eight-page papers every hour.[11]

Hearst skipped supper, excited to see the new presses installed. A visitor to the building was surprised to see half a dozen men stripped to the waist, including Hearst, sweating over the machines. To fend off hunger, Hearst was eating cookies. He offered one to the stunned visitor. As the first plate was successfully cast, Hearst was so happy he danced a jig.[12]

"The *Examiner* was a madhouse inhabited by talented and erratic young men, drunk with life in a city that never existed before or since," recalled newspaperman George P. West. "They had a mad boss, one who flung away money, lived like a ruler of the later Empire and cheered them on as they made newspaper history."[13]

Charley Michelson was equally astounded but enjoying every minute of it. Recalled Michelson, "William Randolph Hearst, fresh from Harvard, had taken over the *San Francisco Examiner* and begun a whirlwind campaign to lift the paper from the sombre stodginess of a party organ. . . . I got two dollars for afternoon assignments and one dollar if they used me at night. My early run was the police courts, where a thousand interesting incidents, some of which really happened, brought me promotion to the regular staff at eighteen dollars a week."

Not everyone was amused. The other San Francisco newspapers had awoken to the fact that "Willie" was no flash in the pan. In mid-March the weekly newspaper *The Journalist* reported that "the *Examiner*'s enterprise has awakened a sleepless activity in the *Call* and the *Chronicle*. They have too much at stake to allow the *Examiner* to find them asleep in the future."[14]

The *Call* quickly dropped out of the unexpected circulation war, but Michael De Young was learning to play Hearst's game. If the *Examiner* could transform itself into a cosmopolitan paper, so could the *Chronicle*. De Young secured an exclusive cable agreement with Joseph Pulitzer's *New York World*, making Hearst and Pulitzer indirect competitors.

To his father in Washington, D.C., Hearst wrote, "The *Chronicle* is fighting very hard, and it does not hesitate to adopt any idea we bring out. . . . This gives us a hard road to hoe, but we are hoeing it vigorously and hope to keep advancing."[15]

In a subsequent letter to the senator, Hearst lamented, "We are having a hard fight with the *Examiner* against the other papers out here. . . . Right now is a crisis in the history of this paper. . . . Papa, you must do your best for us and you must do it immediately. Delay would be as fatal as neglect."[16]

In particular, Hearst was furious at the hand-in-coffer arrangement the *Chronicle* had with the Southern Pacific Railroad. Because the Hearst family opposed the Southern Pacific monopolistic hold on California, they couldn't get the same friendly rate as the *Chronicle*.

Things came to a boil after Hearst discovered that many of his father's business associates advertised in the *Chronicle*. Venting his frustration, Hearst wrote to his father, "As these sons of bitches are principally indebted to you for whatever they have, I think this is the god-damnedest low down business I have ever heard of. . . . Now if you will . . . withdraw all your business from these firms . . . and not give them anymore until they advertise in the *Examiner* and not in the *Chronicle*, I think we can accomplish something."[17]

Shortly thereafter Hearst acquired two special trains to deliver newspapers outside of the city. Citizens of San Jose, Santa Cruz, and Sacramento were delighted to see what new sensation young Hearst would report on next. On May 22, 1887, Hearst, Briggs, and Townsend even visited Santa Cruz personally, breakfasting with Mayor Robert Effey on chicken, trout, and rum omelets. Afterward, the mayor led Hearst and the *Examiner* boys to his private railroad car for champagne and celebratory speeches. The next Sunday, the amount of newspapers that the two trains delivered doubled, and a third train was added, traveling north through Sonoma. The *Examiner* confidently predicted its deliveries would double again the following week. By the end of May, the daily circulation for the *Examiner* was 30,768.[18]

On June 5, Hearst, Townsend, and McEwen were spotted at the Golden Eagle Hotel in Sacramento. The following day, readers of the *Examiner* noticed in the masthead a quote from the *Dixon Tribune*, a paper operating just south of

Sacramento: "The *Examiner* appears to have no end of surprises in store for the people. Its latest enterprise is special Sunday trains, conveying the *Examiner* . . . four to six hours ahead of the regular mail trains. The people appreciate such enterprise."[19]

Whether Hearst had spent time promoting the *Examiner* the previous day went unreported.

"Putting out a newspaper without promotion," Hearst commented, "is like winking at a girl in the dark—well-intentioned, but ineffective."[20]

The following day on June 6, men from the *Santa Cruz Sentinel* boarded one of the "lightning trains," bound for San Francisco and the *Examiner.* They were led to the fourth floor composing room. The room itself was sixty by seventy feet, the largest composing room west of Chicago. There the reporters chanced to meet Hearst, who, as the *Sentinel* observed the following day, "looks into every detail of the work, and is always to be found in one department or another. . . . [H]e exercises a generalship over them that makes his success positively certain."[21]

If the good press wasn't enough, two months later Hearst had more cause to celebrate. In August 1887, the *Examiner*'s daily circulation reached 37,805. It had taken Hearst only six months to dethrone Michael De Young, making the *Examiner* the most popular paper on the West Coast. There seemed no end in sight.[22]

Nor was there any end to Hearst's energy. In the autumn of 1887, Hearst lured away the New York *Sun*'s city editor, Allen Kelly, an outdoorsman and old friend of Arthur McEwen, making him the new city editor of the *Examiner.*

Allen Kelly's attractive young wife, Florence Finch Kelly, whom Kelly had met while they both worked at the *Boston Globe,* also came from New York to San Francisco. Like her husband, Florence Kelly began writing for the *Examiner.* The *Santa Cruz Sentinel,* praising her writing at the *Examiner,* described her as "slight and as dark as a Cuban. Her hair is intensely black and her eyes are deep grey." Through those deep gray eyes, Mrs. Kelly observed Hearst. She recalled Hearst's reaction when an *Examiner* editor told him how the president of the Spring Valley Water Company, which the *Examiner* was protesting for fixing water rates, had offered the editor a bribe to lay off the water company.[23]

"We must have them on the run if they are scared that much!" Hearst gloated. "What did you tell him?"

The editor related that he had cursed the man, scoffed at the bribe, and tossed him from the building.

"You're a fool!" Hearst said, laughing. "Why didn't you take the money and keep up the fight all the same? He would never have dared to say a word about it."

Florence Kelly never determined whether Hearst had been joking. That was his way. Periodically, he would amuse the staff by coming out of his office and dancing a jig but doing so with a solemn face. It may have been, as Irwin Stump noted, that Hearst "kept a real sympathy for the submerged man and woman, a real feeling of his own mission to plead their cause." Or it may have been, as future Hearst reporter James Creelman suggested, that journalism to Hearst was "an enchanted playground in which giants and dragons were slain simply for the fun of the thing."[24]

Indisputably, Hearst's actions garnered results. Because of the *Examiner*'s campaign, the Spring Valley Water Company reduced its rates by 16 percent. San Francisco businessmen suddenly had more money to spend on advertisements, and there was no question as to which newspaper generated the most customers.[25]

Celebrating his success, Hearst took his college sweetheart Tessie and some of the *Examiner* boys on various excursions, oftentimes to the theater or a vaudeville show. Other times he would invite them aboard his fifty-foot yacht *Aquila* and sail up and down San Francisco Bay or to his father's ranch in San Simeon, where they would ride horses, catch trout, and shoot quail.[26]

All of this cost money. When Phoebe caught a train to San Francisco to visit her son and speak with Irwin Stump, her husband's chief financial adviser, she was aghast. During 1887, Will had lavished $184,513 on the *Examiner* and $47,939 on himself. Phoebe may also have met with Tessie, whose presence she never pretended to enjoy. It was rumored that an arrangement was reached wherein Tessie agreed to leave her son and some of Phoebe's money found its way into Tessie's pocket. Meanwhile, Hearst promised to cut down expenses, and on February 12, 1888, he and McEwen boarded a train for the nation's capital.[27]

On February 14 two days before Hearst and McEwen reached Washington, D.C., President Grover Cleveland was informed of their imminent arrival. Acting quickly, the president and the first lady put together an invitation-only reception, inviting young Hearst and McEwen to the White House. Cleveland made it a point to shake Hearst's hand, confiding to him that he was fond of very young journalists: "It's these old fellows that I call the ghouls."[28]

Shaking hands with the president was all very well, but Hearst wasn't interested in mere accolades. He wanted to affect policy, to show Washington what he was capable of. To that effect, he and McEwen headed to the *Washington Post*. In a startling and innovative move, Hearst proceeded to rent the *Post*'s printing press and hired its staff for the day. With Hearst and McEwen running the show, they created a Washington edition of the *San Francisco Examiner*, commemorating George

Washington's birthday. Influential senators and congressmen were delighted and surprised to find the *San Francisco Examiner* on their doorsteps.[29]

During the spring of 1888, Hearst and his father were spotted in one of New York City's most luxurious hotels, the Hoffman House, located at 25th and Broadway. A reporter from the *New York Times* was on hand to hear a conversation between father and son. Senator Hearst had been griping to several friends about a jockey he suspected had thrown a race. "It cost me a pot of money," the senator complained, shaking his head.

"Of course it did," remarked W. R. Hearst. "Your racing stable will cost you half a million of dollars running it as you do now. It is too big and expensive for any man."

The senator raised his eyebrows thoughtfully. "I dunno," he said dryly. "It will cost a devilish sight less than the *Examiner*, after all."[30]

Back in San Francisco on June 3, 1888, the *Examiner* once again hit the ball out of the park. Hearst's Harvard friend Ernest Thayer published a baseball poem under his pseudonym "Phin" next to Bierce's "Prattle" column. The poem was titled "Casey at the Bat: A Ballad of the Republic, Sung in the Year 1888." Thayer had composed the comic poem in under an hour while sitting in the *Examiner*'s city room.[31]

Soon to be an American classic, the poem ended with "But there is no joy in Mudville—mighty Casey has struck out."

There may not have been joy in Mudville, but Hearst was having a ball.

By the end of 1888, however, it was clear Hearst wasn't content. At twenty-five, Hearst had gained recognition as the most resourceful and imaginative newspaperman on the West Coast. Yet, as with his father, simply being the best in the West wasn't enough for W. R. Heart.

Hearst yearned to buy a New York newspaper where he could demonstrate he was the most sensational newspaperman on the planet.

Even if he had to start a war to do it.

— 3 —

THE UNEXPECTED RISE OF RICHARD HARDING DAVIS

Even to the biggest story of the year, Richard Harding Davis could be fashionably late.

On May 31, 1889, the South Fork Dam burst, sending the entirety of Lake Conemaugh—all twenty million tons of water—roaring down the Allegheny Mountains. Pouring into Johnstown Valley, the flood ultimately killed approximately 2,209 people. At the time, Davis was on vacation from his job at the *Philadelphia Press*. But he quickly raced back.[1]

Recognizing the importance of being in the thick of it, the twenty-five-year-old rookie persuaded his bosses at the *Press* to give him the chance to report on the flood. By June 2, Davis was aboard a train on the Ohio Railroad traveling to Johnstown, Pennsylvania. The engine eventually arrived in Johnstown on the night of June 6, a biblical morass of mud, boulders, and swamp visible through the window.[2]

Disembarking, Davis found himself surrounded by droves of other reporters in what became known as the Lime Kiln Club, so called because an atmosphere of fellowship prevailed among the reporters, each of them feeling a kinship created by the shocking sights they witnessed, all except for Davis. Six feet tall, muscular, dignified in speech and manner with a dimpled chin, fair hair, and aristocratic blue eyes, Davis seemed more like a stage actor than a reporter. More than any other reporter, he was seen as a fish out of water.

One of Davis's first acts was to ask for directions to the nearest restaurant. Obviously, no restaurant had been left standing, and if its proprietors were still alive, they would be too busy grieving for their lost livelihoods and loved ones to serve Davis dinner.[3]

"The culinary department was taken charge of by Tom Keenan of the *Press,*" a reporter observed. "With an old coffee-pot taken from the debris at the bridge, some canned corned beef, a few boxes of crackers, a few quarts of condensed milk and a bag of unground coffee, he was soon able to get up a meal for his starving comrades."[4]

Crackers and canned corned beef were a far cry from the restaurants in which Davis was accustomed to dining. Davis's next question was even more senseless. He politely inquired where he might hire a horse and wagon. Finally, Davis amused the crowd by asking where he might find a boiled shirt.

"A boiled shirt," a reporter from the *New York Times* informed Davis, "is as rare here as a mince pie in Africa."[5]

Davis having just arrived, it may be that his shock at witnessing the ruins of Johnstown, where the only building left standing was the stone Methodist church, left him searching in vain for the ornaments of civilization: a restaurant, a horse and carriage, a clean shirt. Then again, it might have been Davis's way. After all, before gaining employment with the *Philadelphia Press,* Davis had lost his seven-dollar-a-week job with the *Philadelphia Record* over a sartorial matter.

In 1886 at the tender age of twenty-two, Davis was renowned for dressing like a dandy, as though he were just arriving from having tea with Queen Victoria. He sported a long yellow ulster—a Victorian overcoat that included a cape—with light green stripes and carried with him a heavy cane, called "the Davis railroad tie" by the wits in the newsroom. It was later reported by young ladies who knew him that Davis was "as clever with the needle as with the pen" and was "interested in having his own suit a little finer than his neighbors." Davis also wore white kid gloves. It was the gloves that put him in Dutch with James S. Chambers Jr., the city editor for the *Record.*[6]

One night, Chambers ordered Davis to remove his coat and gloves and start working on an overdue story. Davis removed his coat and pulled the story out of his pocket but neglected to remove his gloves. Chambers wasn't having it. He suggested an immediate extended vacation.

"Well, I guess I am fired. Is that it?" Davis asked.[7]

"Well, that's the English of it," Chambers agreed.

"Well, old chap," Davis said, extending his gloved hand, "I suppose I'll have to take my medicine."

In addition to having refined taste in clothing, Davis viewed food as more than mere sustenance. He was thoroughly displeased with the unappetizing scraps brought into Johnstown, particularly with its presentation.

"The act of feeding 12,000 a day lacks the easy grace of an afternoon tea," Davis airily noted, "and the way canned meats, sardine boxes, loaves of bread and bundles of tea fly through the air and are shoved into the baskets of the refugees would make a delicately organized nature lose its appetite for a week."[8]

What's more, one can be certain that the countless bodies and body parts strewn about the ruins of Johnstown were not to Davis's cultivated sense of decorum.

Despite Davis making a fool of himself immediately, he managed to redeem himself in short order. On the day he arrived in Johnstown, an argument broke out between a local deputy sheriff—who had lost his wife and baby in the flood—and a drunken 1st lieutenant in the National Guard. The local deputy attempted to quiet the intoxicated 1st lieutenant and stoically withstood the stream of abuse the lieutenant spat at him. This might have been the end of it had a muscular passerby not overheard the insults and, having less control over his emotions than the deputy, took a swing at the lieutenant.

Acting on instinct, Davis and his close friend and fellow reporter from the *Press,* Jennings Crute, intervened, keeping the passerby and the 1st lieutenant from each other. At this point, the drunken lieutenant reached for his pistol. Though the sheriff had declined the provocation, he acted with alacrity now that a firearm was in play. The sheriff wrestled the pistol from the lieutenant, ordering him to the barracks.

The next day the *Press* ran the story. In what became a signature for Davis, he was able to produce a sensational story on the very day he arrived at the scene.[9]

Davis also published in the *Press* an article about a man who, while celebrating Decoration Day, the original name for Memorial Day, overindulged with spirits. The man had been given a twenty-four-hour jail sentence. Unable to escape when the flood hit, the man drowned in his cell. Another report demonstrated Davis's eye for fashion, featuring a rescue worker whose hair and gown were as "carefully arrayed and . . . neat and fresh as if she had stepped that moment from the Quaker City's Rittenhouse Square." A further article urged families to adopt children who had lost their parents to the flood, stating that "no home in the Union was complete without a Johnstown orphan."[10]

Davis may have also been bemused by the undamaged poster advertising Augustus Daly's play *A Night Of,* and its "Intensely Funny" proclamation. After all, Davis's father, Clarke Davis, was close friends with Augustus Daly. But young Davis knew enough not to point out the sad irony. He had already cemented himself as a quick, hardworking reporter with his first sensational Johnstown article and strong subsequent pieces. There was no need to push his luck.[11]

Jennings Crute was not so fortunate. The veteran *Press* reporter caught a cold at Johnstown that turned into pneumonia. Crute died seven months later on December 3, the only press fatality at Johnstown. Other injuries sustained included John Ritenour of the *Post*, who fell twenty feet and sent home to recover; Clarence Bixby of the *Post*, who tumbled from a railroad bridge while attempting a crossing at 1 a.m. and was badly hurt; and Davis, who contracted sciatica, a lifelong condition that periodically inflamed the lumbar nerve of his right leg.[12]

In spite of the pain this caused, Davis was eager to prove he was still able. A man's man, he regularly punched a boxing bag. He'd been the only player to score a touchdown as part of a winless football team at Lehigh University in South Bethlehem, Pennsylvania, seventy miles north-northeast of Johnstown. He also fenced, raced boats, and one rainy Friday night was nearly arrested, becoming a hero for fighting a throng of sophomores who were attempting to coerce him into going along with the Cane Rush. The Cane Rush was a tradition at Lehigh wherein the freshman and the sophomores battled for who would possess for the year the ceremonial walking stick, usually through intimidation but sometimes through bloodshed. Davis would have none of it. Like Theodore Roosevelt, Davis believed in the concepts of manliness and heroism. It had been partially these beliefs that drove him to board a train to Johnstown, whatever the danger. And still burning within him was a fiery desire to prove himself.[13]

After ably covering the Johnstown Flood, Davis returned to Philadelphia. Hearing of an opportunity to travel to England and Ireland to cover the championship cricket team, he leapt at the chance. But he didn't leap high enough. The editors at the *Press* chose another reporter for the job. Undeterred, Davis saw to it that he was hired by the *Evening Telegraph* to report on the same cricket team.[14]

In London, Davis chanced to meet two men, an artist and an editor, both of whom would have a significant impact on his career.

The artist was Charles Gibson. Davis—wearing a brown suit, a soft hat, and a handkerchief about his neck—met Gibson while lounging in the smoking room of the Victoria Hotel. To Gibson's trained eye, he recognized that Davis was the very picture of youthful vitality and fashion. The two struck up a London conversation that would blossom into a New York friendship.[15]

The editor was Arthur Brisbane, a reporter for Charles A. Dana's *New York Sun*. Davis and Brisbane got along famously. Brisbane was six months Davis's junior but was rising in the ranks at the *Sun*, where Davis's career seemed stalled in Philadelphia. In other ways they were two of a kind. Like Davis, Brisbane was the sort who knew when to use a salad fork, dressed ostentatiously, and exuded confidence and ambition. To Davis, Brisbane spoke highly of New York City.[16]

Near the end of October, Davis too decided to gamble his future on Gotham. In antebellum America, Boston—considered by Bostonians to be the Athens of America—was where young writers made their name. But such was no longer the case. Sensationalism was the future, and its epicenter was New York City.[17]

"Make your mark in New York," Mark Twain gravely intoned in 1867, "and you're a made man."[18]

One morning in late October 1889, Davis entrained for New York City. At the railway station, he scribbled in pencil a letter to his mother, fifty-eight-year-old Rebecca Blaine Harding Davis, who lived in Philadelphia and was the most important person in young Davis's life.[19]

"I am not surprised that you were sad if you thought I was going away for good," Davis wrote. "I could not think of it myself. I am only going to make a little reputation and to learn enough of the business to enable me to live at home in the centre of the universe with you."[20]

It was no coincidence that Davis attempted to break into New York the same month that De Wolf Hopper, who had popularized Ernest L. Thayer's "Casey at the Bat" the previous year, was in New York City. Currently, Hopper was performing Davis's comic poem "The Limelight Man." Cunningly, Davis was looking to utilize some of that limelight to help land him a job at a New York newspaper.[21]

Park Row was where all the substantial newspaper buildings and offices were located. Davis could see the construction under way on Joseph Pulitzer's new World Building, which promised to dwarf the neighboring Sun Building and cast in shadow the *New York Tribune* and *Times* buildings just down the street.[22]

After Davis's first exploratory stroll down Park Row, it was looking like he had struck out. None of the papers were interested in hiring him, despite his sterling list of references. Discouraged, he took a seat on a bench in City Hall Park. It was there as the curtain seemed to be closing on his chances that the *Sun* reporter Davis had met in London, Arthur Brisbane, happened by, now managing editor of the *Evening Sun*. Brisbane offered Davis a job writing for the *Sun* at thirty dollars a week.[23]

Davis gratefully accepted the job offer. At thirty dollars a week, he made four times as much as he had in Philadelphia and twice as much as other cub reporters at the *Sun*. But it wasn't just the money that pleased Davis; he knew he had more opportunities in New York than anywhere else.[24]

Miraculously, Davis got his first big scoop on his first day on the job.

That morning while crossing City Hall Park on his way to the five-story Sun Building, Davis carried a hatbox and a bundle of canes. Suddenly a stranger in a beaver coat appeared before him.

"Mr. Williams," the stranger in the beaver coat greeted.[25]

"Mr. Norris," Davis corrected, giving a false name. Having taken a course in "con artistry," Davis was quick to spot that the stranger was not what he seemed and prudently gave himself an alias and a false identity, explaining that he was the son of a Philadelphia woolen goods manufacturer.

A few moments later a second stranger greeted Davis, this time calling him "Mr. Norris." The second stranger introduced himself as the nephew of "George Wanamaker," a Philadelphia businessman with a hand in the woolen goods manufacturer business. But Davis knew that Philadelphia's millionaire woolen goods manufacturer was John Wanamaker, not George Wanamaker. When the obvious bunco artist asked "Mr. Norris" if he would come with him to examine some woolen samples, Davis excused himself momentarily and walked into the Sun Building.

From 1811 to 1867 the unimpressive building overlooking the corner of Nassau and Frankfort was home to Tammany Hall. However, when Charles A. Dana and his backers bought it in 1867, recognizing that Nassau and Frankfort saw more pedestrian traffic than any street corner in New York City, Tammany Hall gleefully relocated, leaving behind its problems with the building. Over the years the building had been condemned by the health board on several occasions; it was infested with rats and gargantuan cockroaches and had been set on fire more than once. During the Charleston Earthquake of 1886, the Sun Building had swayed so violently that its reporters had fled into the street. Somehow after all this, the building was still standing.[26]

Davis raced up the metal spiral stairs to the third floor, where the newsroom was quartered. Finding an editor, Davis outlined his plan. The man outside was a con artist. Davis would let himself be conned and then capture the crook and write the story. Davis's superiors, impressed by their newest reporter's chutzpah, approved the assignment.[27]

Back on the street, Davis found "Wanamaker" waiting patiently. They left on a streetcar to a building on Mulberry Street, with the number 17 prominently displayed. Davis thought this odd, for the other numbers on that side of the street were even. The interior of the building had been done up to look like a railroad ticket office. After "Wanamaker" bought a "scalp ticket" from what appeared to be a ticket agent, he showed Davis a box filled with fabric.

While Davis was feeling the texture of the fabric, yet another man entered the scene wearing a sombrero and speaking with a strong southern accent. He claimed to be heading to Mobile, Alabama. Somehow a card game was struck up between "Wanamaker" and the southerner, who styled himself as a cattle king. "Wanamaker" won almost every hand. The trap was set. The cattle king appeared to be easy money. Davis was invited to play. Davis, as Mr. Norris, quickly won a thousand dollars from the cattle king. But the cattle king wasn't handing over any money yet. He wanted proof that the newcomer wouldn't have welched had he lost.

"How do I know you've got a thousand dollars about you?" the cattle king demanded.[28]

Davis admitted he hadn't the money on him but said that he had a trunk full of money at the Astor House, one of the finest hotels in the city. Somehow, Davis persuaded the cattle king to wait while he returned with the money.

"Wanamaker" escorted Davis to the Astor House and waited outside. Once in the lobby, Davis looked about desperately for a policeman. There wasn't one in sight. This meant Davis would have to do it the hard way.

Seconds later, Davis rejoined the con man outside the Astor House. Instead of showing "Wanamaker" the contents of his trunk, Davis showed him an illegal football hold, violently grabbing the con man around the neck and forcing him to the ground. A policeman quickly arrived and escorted them both to the station. There it was revealed that "Wanamaker" was actually Sheeny Mike, a nefarious con artist who preyed on wealthy out-of-towners. Davis was unable to relocate the ticket office, so the others escaped and with them the bulk of the evidence against Sheeny Mike. However, the judge—who along with most of the court laughed when he asked Davis his vocation and Davis replied "A reporter on the *Evening Sun*"—still gave Sheeny Mike six months in jail.

Back at the Sun Building, Davis wrote up the story. Brisbane was so delighted with it that he took it directly to Dana's partner, William Laffan. By the time Laffan finished the article he knew Brisbane had struck gold with their newest hire. It wasn't just that Davis had told a good story; Davis had *become* the story. The man was part reporter, part action hero, an anachronism the likes of which the world had never seen: a knight of the round table in 1889 New York City. Laffan gave Davis a front-page column, titling it "Our Green Reporter: He Locked Horns with a Bunco Man for Fun. They Met the Usual Way. Now the Bunco Man Is on the Island."

The next day, Davis was the toast of the town.

"From that day," recalled Edward Bok in 1894, "the name of Richard Harding Davis has been familiar to every New Yorker."

To his thunderstruck parents, Davis wrote, "I thought I would get on here after a while, but I really did not think I would have my name on the newspaper bulletins on the second day of my arrival."[29]

Davis was just getting started.

— 4 —

SOME KIND OF PREDATORY INSECT

Some people have a knack for landing in trouble.

On September 12, 1890, nineteen-year-old Stephen Crane left Claverack College in New York and began attending Lafayette College in Pennsylvania, ostensibly to study mining engineering. Crane had other ideas. In a flurry of activity, he joined the intramural baseball team, the Franklin Literary Society, the rival Washington Literary Society, and the Campus Club, a student-run organization that provided more affordable meals than those offered on the university's plan. A week after entering the campus, Crane also pledged at the fraternity Delta Epsilon. Without any clear goal in life, creating connections was a good idea. But it did make him a target for hazing.[1]

In late September, Crane was lounging in his room at 170 East Hall when a commotion came from outside his room. A pack of sophomores, with violence in mind, demanded that Crane open his door. Crane stoutly refused. No matter. The sophomores broke down the door and poured inside. But they were in for a surprise.

By the flickering light of a candle, the sophomores saw Crane standing in the corner, his face the color of ash and a pistol in his hand. Having lost their starch, the sophomores fled even as the pistol slipped from Crane's hand and fell to the floor.[2]

Although no further hazing incidents affected Crane, he never quite fit in at Lafayette. Before the semester ended, he determined mining engineering was "not at all to my taste." Impatient with his English professor Francis A. March, who insisted that classic texts be studied not just line by line but also word by word, Crane likened March and the other professors to "that incoherent mass of stage drivers and baggagemen" who harangued guests outside hotels. Crane recalled that such men engaged in "roaring and gesticulating, as unintelligible always as a row of Homeric experts."[3]

Crane's irritation at the classics and how his professors taught them likely had to do with his own experience working for his thirty-eight-year-old brother Townley (pronounced "Toonley"). Crane acted as a stringer for Townley's news outlet in the Crane hometown of Asbury Park, New Jersey. From Townley—a hard drinker and habitual cardplayer known as "the Shore Fiend" for his dogged reporting—Crane had a lot to learn. But "Townley's kid brother," as some reporters began calling him (a moniker young Crane was eager to shake), took to the business like a fish to water. Covering actual news stories, written with the purpose to inform and entertain the reader, was far different than classics. It was a cinch which style of writing Crane preferred.[4]

In late 1890 less than four months after he first began attending Lafayette, Crane quit the college, traveling eighty-five miles back to Asbury Park to the home of his mother, the widow Mary Helen Peck Crane. Mary, who had raised thirteen children, was naturally frustrated that her youngest child was more interested in smoking, chasing women, and playing baseball than studying. But she wasn't giving up. Using a family connection, she had young Crane enrolled at New York's prestigious Syracuse University, which had been cofounded by Crane's great-uncle, Jesse T. Peck.[5]

Enrolling on January 6, 1891, to please his mother, Crane initially stayed at the home of his great-aunt, the Widow Peck. But it didn't end well. His bohemian manner offended his great-aunt, and Crane was forced to move into a boardinghouse. Ultimately, he called upon his fraternal connections to move into Syracuse University's Delta Epsilon house. A friend later recalled that Crane arrived "in a cab and a cloud of tobacco smoke."[6]

Unlike Lafayette College, at Syracuse Crane was without a major. Although he excelled at English, he tended toward argument in class. In particular, he hated lugging about Alfred H. Welsh's *Development of English Literature and Language* for the class taught by Chancellor Sims.

Crane declared that the sentences found within were "ponderous, solemn and endless, in which wandered multitudes of homeless and friendless prepositions, adjectives looking for a parent, and quarrelling nouns, sentences which no longer symbolized the language form of thought but which had about them a quaint aroma from the dens of long-dead scholars."

Tired of Crane's complaints, one day Sims made an appeal to Scripture.

"Tut, tut—what does St. Paul say, Mr. Crane, what does St. Paul say?" Sims demanded.

"I know what St. Paul says . . . but I disagree with St. Paul," Crane replied.

In actuality, Crane enjoyed prose and poetry but liked his own much better than the classics. Afflicted (or blessed) with synesthesia, in his case where sounds seemed endowed with color, Crane's writing had the potential to be wholly unique.

More enjoyable than English literature to Crane was playing baseball. Shortly after joining Syracuse, he met with the head coach.

"What can you do?" the coach asked.[7]

"Not much," Crane answered, puffing on his pipe.

"Can you row?"

"Nop."

"Jump?"

"Nop."

"Swim?"

"Nop."

"Throw the hammer?"

"Nop."

"Play football?"

"A little."

"Humph! A little. That won't do here. Can you play baseball?"

"Betcher life!"

"What can you play best?"

"Catcher."

Crane joined the Syracuse College team, demonstrating himself to be the best player at the college. Along with being a deft catcher, sometimes even playing without a glove, he proved a good batter. Because he was not overwhelmingly strong—at five foot, seven, he was only 125 pounds—he mostly hit singles. But wearing the uniform of patent leather shoes, black stockings, beige trousers, and a crimson sweater, Crane was proud to be part of the team.

"The pitcher at the time was a rather large man, who threw a very swift ball," recalled a classmate and friend, Clarence Loomis Peasley, "and Crane was so light that he seemed to bound back with every catch. . . . He was the best player of the nine, and one of the best catchers that the University ever had."[8]

As for the city of Syracuse, Crane declared, "I expect to have some fun here."[9] Syracuse was a "dandy city" where he met some "dam pretty girls." A quick-witted baseball player who played guitar, flute, and melodeon and was invited to all the Delta Epsilon mixers, Crane proved mildly popular with the ladies. Unfortunately, he proved unpopular with his professors, who noticed in Crane raw talent but an unaccountable idleness.

After Crane fared poorly on a history exam and complained that the history book was inaccurate, Professor Little grew exasperated.

"Mr. Crane, what are you in this university for?" Professor Little demanded.

"Professor, that is a question I have been asking myself for some time," Crane admitted.

To Little's question of what Crane was interested in, Crane responded "Journalism."

"If that is the case, my neighbor, Eggleston, is an editor of the *Syracuse Standard*," Little mused, "and I should be very glad to ask him to give you a reporter's job, for until you get knocked about through contact with life, you will be wasting yourself at the university."

Between Little and Eggleston's resources, Crane landed a job not just at the *Syracuse Standard* but also as the Syracuse correspondent to Whitelaw Reid's *New York Tribune*. In particular, Crane worked for Willis Fletcher Johnson, who served as the day editor of the *Tribune* and had published the first full-length history of the Johnstown Flood in 1889. Johnson was also a family friend of the Cranes.[10]

It didn't take Crane long to make his first splash.

On June 1, 1891, the *Syracuse Daily Standard* ran Crane's article, which simultaneously appeared on the front page of the *New York Tribune*. The headline was eye-popping: "Great Bugs in Onondaga. They Swarm in a Quarry and Stop a Locomotive."[11]

The narrative centered around a locomotive, an "iron monster," swarmed by a breed of carnivorous insects outside Syracuse, New York:

> On the Lackawanna Railroad, are extensive limestone quarries, which have . . . penetrated deeply into the rock[,] . . . the track beneath the electric light completely thronged with strange insects of great size, some of them lying perfectly still in bunches, and some of them playing a sort of leapfrog game. . . . [I]nsects died with a crackling sound like the successive explosions of toy torpedoes. . . . [I]n the thick of the swarm the engine was brought to a stop. . . . [T]he bugs that had blocked the track were the issue

of a rare species of lithodome—a rock-boring mollusk—crossed with some kind of predatory insect.[12]

The article, read by hundreds of thousands of New Yorkers, caused ripples of shock and confusion. Can these bugs derail a train? If they can bore through rock, can they bore through flesh and bone? How many of them were there? billions? trillions? more?

As it happened, there were no insects at all. The whole thing was a hoax, one perpetuated by twenty-year-old Stephen Crane. Crane had gotten the idea after reading about how a swarm of caterpillars in Minnesota had caused a train to stop. Doubtless, Crane's own brief studies in Lafayette as a mining engineer played a part.

Whatever its genesis, readers of the *Tribune* were horrified to learn that predatory insects, trapped underground for millennia, had scrabbled to the surface and brought down a train. How long would it be before they invaded New York City?

The next day the *Tribune* ran a follow-up article about the Onondaga. Probably written by Johnson or Townley, the secondary article revealed the hoax. It described the Onondaga bugs: "While not so large as the light-house bug or the bonfire bug, the electric-light bug is nevertheless a formidable bug, and has even been known, when suffering from hunger, to attack and kill the great oil-warehouse fire bug, which frequently comes out and chases the firemen around the corner and devours the hose."[13]

Despite some indignant New Yorkers, Crane's first front-page article gave him confidence for further ventures.

Over the summer of 1891, Crane played a valuable role in Syracuse for the *Syracuse Standard* and the *New York Tribune*. Exploring urban Syracuse, he investigated the bordellos of Railroad Street (present-day Washington Street), the police courts, and the dark alleys where anything could happen. Although it would be two more years before Crane's first novel *Maggie* would debut, through these forays the plight of the downtrodden began to percolate in Crane's mind, and the idea that he could write a novel about a woman of the streets began to crystallize.[14]

As luck would have it, in August 1891 Crane drew the notice of one of the foremost members of the New York literati, Professor Hamlin Garland. Though Garland's first novel, *Main-Travelled Roads,* had appeared in print just two months beforehand, thirty-one-year-old Garland had gained fame as a lecturer and as a "Professor of Elocution and Literature" at Moses True Brown's Boston School of Oratory.

On August 17, 1891, Garland gave a lecture titled "The Local Novel." Among the young scholars in the Seaside Assembly at Avon-by-the-Sea, New Jersey, was Stephen Crane. The following day, the *Tribune* published an article titled "Howells Discussed at Avon-by-the-Sea." The article caught Garland's eye. In 1900, Garland reflected on the event in the *Saturday Evening Post:*

> The report of my first [Avon] lecture . . . was exceedingly well done in the "Tribune," and I asked for the name of the reporter. "He is a mere boy," was the reply of Mr. Albert, the manager of the assembly, "and his name is Stephen Crane."
>
> Crane came to see me the following evening, and turned out to be a reticent young fellow, with a big German pipe in his mouth. He was small, sallow and inclined to stoop, but sinewy and athletic for all—for we fell to talk of sports, and he consented to practice baseball pitching with me. I considered him at this time a very good reporter, and a capital catcher of curved balls—no more, and I said goodby to him two weeks later with no expectation of ever seeing him again.[15]

Little did Garland know.

With Crane spending more and more time as a reporter, his grades suffered. At first the dean of the college only admonished him for his apparent apathy. By the end of the semester, however, the dean was encouraging Crane to leave on his own.

"College life a waste of time. . . . Humanity is a much more interesting study," Crane decided. With a history of tuberculosis running in his family—most Crane experts believing that Crane had caught the disease as a child and knew it—Crane determined if he was doomed to die young, he would make the most of it.[16]

By the end of 1891 Crane dropped out of college, never to return. As such, when his mother died on December 7, 1891, her youngest child received no money from her estate. With few choices, Crane redoubled his writing efforts. For the next eight months, he continued to write newspaper reports for the *Syracuse Standard* and the *New York Tribune,* sketches and stories with middling success, and explore the seedy underbelly of New York City.

Despite Crane's talent, no one could have predicted that in the summer of 1892 he would create an uproar that, along with tipping the presidential election of 1892, would send him careening in a new direction. But against all odds, that was precisely what was about to happen.[17]

5

FIGHTING JOE

For Joseph "Fighting Joe" Wheeler, the election of 1892 was no Sunday picnic.

For the past year things had been going from bad to worse. The trouble had begun on April 27, 1891, in Augusta, Georgia—coincidentally where Wheeler had been born more than fifty-five years earlier—at a Veterans Day celebration where he had agreed to speak. Unfortunately for Wheeler, so too had South Carolina's Senator Wade Hampton

Hampton earned most of the ink by making a bellicose speech. Invoking Gettysburg and the ghost of Robert E. Lee, Hampton declared that they were "neither traitors nor rebels. . . . We . . . were fighting for God and our fatherland."[1]

When Hampton mentioned Wheeler it was only to try to steal Wheeler's thunder. Noting the eighteen thousand to twenty thousand Union men the Confederacy captured in 1865, Hampton espoused, "Wheeler said he whipped them, but it has been said that the infantry whipped them, and we caught them while they were running."

It was small wonder that Hampton was needling Wheeler in front of the crowd, for anyone who read the *New York World* knew Wheeler's real feelings that Wheeler thought Hampton a fool.

About a month before Wheeler and Hampton met in Augusta for the Veterans Day celebration, Frank G. Carpenter of the *World* got an exclusive interview with Wheeler.

"Wheeler . . . is a short, slim, nervous, wiry little fellow of about 125 pounds weight," Carpenter observed. "His black hair has become tinged with gray and white strands are creeping into his full black beard. His heart is still young, however, and though he has made a fortune since the war closed, as a planter, there is nothing snobbish about him."[2]

Describing the fifty-four-year-old as "the greatest cavalry leader of the South" and "one of the most popular congressmen in Washington," Carpenter jotted down Wheeler's comments about his escapades with Jefferson Davis and Wade Hampton in the Carolinas during the closing days of the American Civil War after they had fled Richmond.

"I knew that the war was over and I wanted Mr. Davis to fly," Wheeler recalled. "He did not seem to think as I did."

Instead, Davis held a cabinet meeting. There the president of the floundering Confederacy decided that Wheeler should move his command to Cokesboro, South Carolina. Wheeler expressed doubt that he could hold his men together, for they all considered the war over. That was when Hampton interrupted.

"Well, General Wheeler's troops may not obey," Hampton pompously declared, "but whatever I order mine to do they will do."

The bad light this put Wheeler in was made worse when he discovered his men had disbanded without orders. Still, Wheeler managed to scrape together an army of five hundred who pledged to stick to him. Heading south, Wheeler stopped at Yorkville, South Carolina, where he paid a call on Hampton's wife, Mary. From Mary, Wheeler learned that Hampton had just arrived. Visiting the lieutenant general, Wheeler saw that he was "as sad a man as I had ever seen." Apparently, the boast Hampton had made before Jefferson Davis had been hot air. Hampton had been forced to slink south with only one company, and by the time he reached Yorkville every man had deserted.

The interview proved popular and was soon disseminated throughout the country. That Hampton had read it was a certainty.

Taking the high ground, in Wheeler's own speech he declined to put the spurs to Hampton. After all, Wheeler needed all the support he could find in Washington. For that winter, in the first days of December 1891 Wheeler had one of the most coveted positions in Washington nearly in his grasp.

Under "Tsar" Thomas B. Reed's reign as Speaker of the House, Wheeler hadn't a rebel's chance of being appointed chair of the Committee on Military Affairs. But with a new Speaker set to be elected before the new year, Wheeler seized his opportunity.[3]

Fighting Joe Wheeler was in the US Capitol on December 6, 1891, when the voting commenced. The contest was between Roger Q. Mills of Texas and Charles Crisp of Georgia. Because both men were Democrats, Wheeler didn't initially know which horse to back. But nine years' experience in the House told him that Crisp was the likeliest candidate, and Wheeler figured if he could swing the speakership for Crisp, the grateful Georgian would reward him with the chairmanship. Determined, for the first twenty-nine ballots Wheeler championed Crisp with everything he had. But on the thirtieth ballot Wheeler switched horses, this time voting for Mills.

"Joe lost his head," remarked the *Buffalo Morning Express.*[4]

Belatedly recognizing that Mills didn't have the momentum and that Crisp would secure victory on this ballot, Wheeler quickly corrected the mistake before the vote could be tallied. Once all the votes were in, Crisp was named Speaker. Wheeler, confident that Crisp would shortly grant him the plum post, began to wheel and deal for certain congressman to become committee members.[5]

But Crisp had caught wise to Wheeler's double act. Although Crisp still appointed Wheeler to the Committee of Military Affairs, the Speaker gave the chair to Joseph H. Outhwaite of Ohio. Wheeler was stunned that Outhwaite, who had never served in the military, instead working as a high school teacher and a lawyer before being elected to Congress, had been given the prize.[6]

If this was embarrassing for Wheeler, the next act would be all but humiliating. On January 15, 1892, while debating the antisubsidy resolution on the House floor, Charles A. Boutelle of Maine incited laughter by describing Wheeler as "like a monkey on an elephant at the circus." Just as bad as being called a monkey, Boutelle was poking fun at Wheeler's stature; at five feet, two inches, Wheeler was hands down the shortest man in Congress.[7]

Wheeler was not in the Capitol building to hear Boutelle's comments but got an earful when he returned later that day. White with anger, Wheeler strode out of the chamber. The next day newspapers across the country reported that under the auspices of code duello, Wheeler had written Boutelle a formal challenge, a duel to the death. It proved only a rumor.

"I would never challenge a man who would not fight," Wheeler told a reporter for the *Atlanta Constitution* the following day.[8]

When asked if he would accept the challenge were it issued, Boutelle begged off while landing another blow. "A duel between General Wheeler and myself, with pistols, and without conditions, would not be fair on account of the difference in our size. I am a good deal bigger physically than he is, and, of course, afford just that much better mark to shoot at."

The argument soon blew over, yet interest in Wheeler remained high. In an article about Confederates in Congress, a reporter for Louisiana's *Times-Democrat* characterized Wheeler as perhaps "the most distinguished prisoner among the members of the House. . . . Gen. Wheeler was a graduate of West Point, and he entered the Confederate army as a lieutenant at the age of twenty-five. He was promoted again and again, and upon the death of J.E.B. Stuart he became the senior cavalry officer of the Confederate army. He was, in fact, the Phil Sheridan of the South."[9]

Wheeler's stint at West Point had been unremarkable. He graduated in 1859, ranked nineteen in a class of twenty-two. But none of his classmates had his war record. In early January 1861 Wheeler had been a twenty-four-year-old lieutenant serving in New Mexico when word came that his home state of Georgia was preparing to secede from the Union.

"Much as a I love the Union," Wheeler wrote his older brother William in Augusta, "and much as I am attached to my profession, all will be given up when my state, by its action, shows that such a course is necessary and proper. If Georgia withdraws and becomes a separate state, I cannot with justice and propriety to my people, hesitate in resigning my commission."

Georgia formally seceded on January 21, 1861, and Wheeler promptly resigned from the US Army. Joining the Confederacy, Wheeler fought at the Battle of Shiloh, the Siege of Corinth, and the Battle of Stones River, among others, ultimately rising to the position of major general. Captured shortly after the fall of Richmond, he was forced to share a room with the Confederacy's vice president, Alexander Stephens, aboard a steamboat heading north. To Stephens, Wheeler joked that he had been accustomed to traveling north every summer for his health, and it was "very kind" of the federal government to take him north by ship without expenses.

Reflecting on his one-month imprisonment in Fort Delaware, Wheeler remarked, "I did not grow fat on my diet. My breakfast was a piece of meat and piece of bread served on a tin plate, which was none too clean sometimes. For dinner I got a tin cup of soup, with a little piece of meat floating in it, and for supper I had a piece of bread. I had nothing in the shape of tea and coffee to drink, and I was watched very closely."[10]

Given his freedom, Wheeler remembered that he was "happy in the war being over and myself still alive."

It is small wonder that Wheeler was happy, for in 1866 he married the widow Daniella "Ella" Jones Sherrod, the daughter of a wealthy plantation owner. With Wheeler making money first as a lawyer and then a planter, the marriage proved fruitful, with Lucy born in November 1866. Annie, Ella, Joe Jr., Carrie, and Tom followed. Although baby Ella died as an infant, the rest thrived. In 1878, Wheeler became an Alabama state delegate for the Democratic Party. Two years later he ran for Congress as a Democrat against the Greenback, William M. Lowe. The election was contested, with both sides claiming fraud, but in the summer of 1882 Lowe was declared the winner, representing Alabama's Eighth District. Wheeler didn't lick his wounds for long. When Lowe died of tuberculosis in the fall of 1882, Wheeler won a special election to serve out his term, only to be replaced by the Democrat Luke Pryor in March 1883. In late 1884 Wheeler ran again and won. Since then Wheeler had handily bested his Republican challengers.

Despite his good humor, Wheeler's war record and his support for Free Silver rubbed some of his colleagues the wrong way. At the same time, Wheeler won praise in 1892 for helping shepherd through Congress a bill that provided a pension to veterans of the Indian Wars. Towing the party line, he also championed Grover Cleveland, the once and—if all went Democratic—future president in Cleveland's rematch against Benjamin Harrison. Theodore Roosevelt, who had moved from New York and the Dakota Territory to become commissioner of the Civil Service Commission in Washington, D.C., tacitly supported Harrison but privately didn't see much of a difference between the two.

"Frankly I think the record pretty bad for both Cleveland and Harrison," Roosevelt wrote to Henry Cabot Lodge on July 27, 1892, from Washington, D.C., "and it is rather Walrus and Carpenter work choosing between the records of the two parties, as far as civil service reform is concerned." Roosevelt went on to grouse that though Harrison's secretary of the navy, Benjamin F. Tracy, had made a "start" in the navy yards, "it is only a start, not permanent, and can not be until put under us."[11]

Unexpectedly, for Wheeler the presidential election soon took a back seat to Alabama politics. In the summer of 1892 Major E. C. Gordon, a millionaire cotton man, began making noise that he might replace Wheeler in Congress, forcing Fighting Joe into a primary battle. Knowing where their bread was buttered, several Alabama newspapers rushed to Wheeler's defense.[12]

"Little Joe is a wheel horse and we know he never balks, kicks, or cribs; besides, we are not trading horses just now," commented the *Florence Herald*. Wheeler took the challenge seriously. Returning to the "Heart of Dixie," he spoke before a large crowd in Bridgeport, just a few miles south of the Alabama-Tennessee line.[13]

Meanwhile, a different crowd of people in Asbury, New Jersey, 850 miles northeast of Bridgeport, soon captivated the country, courtesy of a tawny-haired college dropout with a talent for controversy.

On August 17, 1892, Stephen Crane was spending time with two friends: Arthur Oliver, a former classmate from Lafayette and a reporter for the *Daily Spray*, and Lily Brandon Munroe, a young lady with whom Crane desired an amorous relationship. Munroe was married to a topographer, but her relationship with her husband was strained, and Crane felt that the marriage shouldn't be a deterrent.

From the door of a billiards hall in Asbury Park, Crane, Oliver, and Munroe watched a parade take place consisting of the Junior Order of United American Mechanics. Crane thought that he detected a certain snobbery in the way the Asbury Park crowd watched the mechanics' parade because of the unprofessional way they marched, and he decided to lampoon the entire affair.

Townley had gone fishing, as it happened, but had instructed William K. Devereaux to look over the articles. Somehow Devereaux missed Crane's incendiary article. Due to the chaos of the Tribune Building being remodeled, the editors on Park Row also missed how the reading public would doubtless react to Crane's piece.

"Stevie . . . toyed with a boomerang," Devereaux later commented.[14]

Crane's anonymous article appeared in the August 21, 1892, edition of the *New York Tribune* under the innocuous-seeming title "On the New Jersey Coast."

"The procession was composed of men, bronzed, slope-shouldered, uncouth and begrimed by dust," Crane wrote. "Their clothes fitted them illy, for the most part, and they had no ideas of marching. . . . Such an assemblage of the spraddle-legged men of the middle class . . . had never appeared to an Asbury Park summer crowd, and the latter was vaguely amused."[15]

As it happened, no one was amused by Crane's article, least of all the Junior Order of American Mechanics.

On August 23 the Junior Order of American Mechanics formally complained to the *Tribune*, and the next day the *Tribune* published a letter from a member, E. A. Canfield, denouncing the "uncalled for and un-American criticism."[16]

Beneath Canfield's letter, an apology from the *Tribune* appeared: "We regret deeply that a bit of random correspondence passed inadvertently by the copy editor, should have put into our columns sentiments both foreign and repugnant to The Tribune."[17]

It might have ended there, but unfortunately for Crane and his brother Townley, the editor in chief of the *Tribune,* Whitelaw Reid, had been selected by President Benjamin Harrison as his running mate in the election of 1892. Naturally, Democratic papers gleefully used Crane's article to paint Harrison, Reid, and the entire Republican Party as antilabor.

Despite having already issued an apology, the *Tribune* conducted more damage control. For one, the *Tribune* editors explained that Whitelaw Reid had not overseen operations of the newspaper since becoming ambassador to France and couldn't have had anything to do with its publication. Townley also fired off a defense of his brother's article in the *Asbury Park Daily Press.* But by expressing ire at readers "who claim that the correspondents have no right to say anything about the town excepting in the way of praise," Townley may have inadvertently fanned the flames.[18]

When Reid heard of the brewing scandal, he was livid. With the White House at stake, Reid wired, "Discharge every man connected with that parade story."[19]

Although some of Crane's sketches would appear without a byline in the *Tribune* for the next month, young Crane was ignominiously fired.

When Crane asked Arthur Oliver what he thought of the sketch and Oliver replied that it was good but certainly not for publication, Crane grinned. "Especially not publication in the New York Tribune. . . . You see," Crane explained, "I seemed to have forgotten that my boss on the Tribune was running for Vice-President. Those jolly paraders read my story and annoyed him with a telegram. . . . So it was decided that the Tribune should eat its words."[20]

Soon afterward Crane once more ran into Hamlin Garland, lecturing again before the Seaside Assembly at Avon-by-the-Sea. Garland recalled that Crane looked distraught, relating how he had been fired from the *Tribune.*

"What did you expect from your journal—a medal?" Garland asked.[21]

"I guess I didn't stop to consider that," Crane replied.

Unlike Crane, Wheeler's chances were looking up, for that fall E. C. Gordon reconsidered entering the fray. In early September the major let it be known that he would not challenge the general for his seat.

This still left the Republican, Richard W. Austin, in the field. Going on the attack, on November 1, 1892, Austin spoke to a largely African American crowd in the Florence courthouse, declaring, "Wheeler has never done one thing for the farmers."[22]

Four days later Wheeler struck back. On November 5, Fighting Joe attended a barbecue a hundred miles southwest in Hartselle. Demonstrating himself as a fire-eater, Wheeler delivered a rousing three-hour oration, which the *Birmingham News* called "the ablest and most powerful speech that has been delivered in Alabama."[23]

On November 8, 1892, the United States went to the polls. The result, as the *San Francisco Examiner* reported the next morning, was a Democratic "Tidal Wave." Along with winning the popular by nearly four million votes, Cleveland won the electoral college by a vote 277 to 145, reclaiming the White House. Hearst himself was in good spirits. Not only had California helped return his father's old friend Grover Cleveland to glory, but also for the last year the *Examiner* had turned a profit. Never shy about self-promotion, that day the Hearst men also published on the masthead the circulation of the *Examiner:* 64,216.[24]

Whitelaw Reid, on the other hand, was less than thrilled. Half joking, Reid later lamented that he and Harrison would have won the election had it not been for Crane's write-up of the parade. Stephen Crane was "the man who beat me for vice-president. I don't know whether Grover Cleveland ever knew how much he owed him."[25]

Any other man, having lost his first big newspaper job, might have thrown in the towel. Instead, Crane decided to try to make his name in Gotham even without a big newspaper behind him. Trading the comforts of friends and family for the hardship of surviving as a starving artist, Crane finally shook the moniker of Townley's kid brother.

For better or for worse, Stephen Crane was heading to New York City.[26]

At the same time, the citizens of Alabama's Eighth District reelected Fighting Joe, who was in Washington on March 4, 1893, for the inauguration. Absent from Washington was Richard Harding Davis. This was a shame, for Davis—whose father was friends with Clarke and Grover Cleveland from Cape Cod, owning neighboring cottages—was naturally a great supporter of Cleveland. But Davis didn't let the mere fact that he was on a boat in the Mediterranean, on assignment for *Harper's Weekly,* stop him from celebrating in style.[27]

"Today Cleveland is inaugurated," Davis wrote to his mother, "and I took all the passengers down at the proper time and explained to them that at that moment a great man was being made president and gave them each an American cocktail to remember it by in which to toast him[.] I am getting to be a great speech maker."[28]

Meanwhile, Wheeler continued to use the press to shore up support from Montgomery to Washington. Along with supporting party policies in the Capitol building, Wheeler exerted some of his influence to land federal appointments for a few well-placed newspapermen. As it happened, Wheeler found himself awash in good press. His exploits were often retold, and in May 1893 his twenty-four-year-old daughter Annie was described by the *Montgomery Advertiser* as one of the most fearless and gallant equestrians around, always ready to help the needy or sick with "pleasant, encouraging words and sweet smiles."[29]

During the beginning of 1894, Wheeler and Ella wiled away their time canvassing relatives for information on their family tree. Their intention was to write it up as a book.

"I am greatly pleased to hear that this book is in progress," wrote the former mayor of Atlanta, George Hillyer, on February 6, 1894. This was in response to Wheeler seeking information on an ancestor of Ella's, Peter Early, who had served as both a senator and the governor of Georgia. "I want a copy of it as soon as it is published," Hillyer declared.[30]

Hillyer would have to wait, for by the summer of 1894 it was clear that Wheeler had a problem. Because Gordon had declined to face Wheeler in the primary two years earlier, the anti-Wheeler wing of Alabama's Eighth District Democrats coalesced around Judge William Richardson of Huntsville.

Having fought at Shiloh and Chickamauga with the 50th Regiment of the Alabama Infantry, Richardson currently worked as a probate judge in the Madison County Court but put more energy into supplanting "Little Joe" as the representative for Alabama's Eighth District. Of the seven counties Wheeler represented—Colbert, Lawrence, Lauderdale, Madison, Morgan, Jackson, and Limestone, totaling more than 150,000 people—Richardson was said to be very popular in Colbert County, just below the Tennessee River.[31]

In late August 1894, delegates were selected at county conventions throughout the Eighth District. On September 4, the delegates formally voted for Wheeler or Richardson at the Congressional Convention in Decatur. For the counties of Madison and Colbert, Richardson received a plurality of delegates. But in the other five counties, Wheeler had the numbers. Still, Richardson and his supporters felt they had drawn blood and that next time they might just unseat the wily general.

Shortly after the primary election, more rumors began to swirl that Wheeler's popularity in the press was due to him landing federal positions for several newspapermen. For some reason certain newspapers in particular leapt to his defense.[32]

"It takes a man with a big heart to refrain at times from saying something unkind about his persecutors," opined *the Scottsboro Citizen*. "Wheeler is too broadminded for little things. He is as magnanimous as he is brave."[33]

Wheeler may have won the battle with Richardson but still had to face the Republican challenger, Colonel Lee Crandall. Few people, however, thought that Crandall, who lived in Washington, D.C., would make any sort of showing.

"Mark the prediction, when Lee Crandall beats Gen. Wheeler for Congress in this district, frogs will be walking on stilts and ground hogs will be flying," remarked the *Alabama Enquirer*.[34]

Handily winning the election in November 1894, the following month Wheeler gladly resigned from the Committee of Military Affairs, trading it for the even more influential Committee of Ways and Means. There he kept a hand on the country's purse strings. Having won two elections that year and been given a promotion, Wheeler might have continued as he had—using the Alabama press to shore up his base, making the occasional speech at rallies in the Eighth District, and toeing the Democratic line in the House—but in the winter of 1894–1895 two momentous events took place, helping to create a sense of war fever in the United States.[35]

For one, on February 24, 1895, a small band of Cuban rebels in the eastern village of Baire declared that they would have "*independencia o muerte*" and that the Spanish would rule them no longer. The Spanish tried to put down the rebellion, but it soon drew the support of the Cuban poet José Julián Martí y Pérez; the exiled warrior Antonio Maceo Grajales, known as the "Bronze Titan"; the short-tempered Calixto García; and Máximo Gómez Baez, who had dedicated his life to Cuban liberation. Although most newspapers dismissed the uprising, the *Examiner* boys would soon predict that without American intervention, Spain would launch a campaign "of immediate subjugation of the island—and the portion of the rebels will be death."[36]

For another, the Bacheller syndicate in New York City began publishing excerpts of a colorful Civil War novel written by the hardscrabble, tubercular wordsmith Stephen Crane. Striking a chord with the reading public, concerned more with the feelings of the ordinary soldier than just the hard facts of who fought where—the utilitarian style that had previously dominated Civil War studies—Crane's excerpts were published in newspapers throughout the country.[37]

Wheeler, who was no slouch at using the press for his own purposes, sensed an opportunity. On March 12, 1895, he capitalized on the newfound Civil War interest, attending a meeting of the Confederate Historical Association in Memphis. When J. P. Young suggested that Wheeler speak, the crowd broke into applause. Cheers of "Wheeler! Wheeler!" filled the air.

Conducted to the front of the crowd, Wheeler described the awful magnitude of the war. Notably, he spoke of the bravery displayed by the soldiers, both Confederate and Union. Wheeler got another chance to reiterate this theme the following month at Shiloh before a vast crowd of ex-Confederate and ex-Union soldiers.

Of all the old soldiers who participated in the Shiloh reunion, the most famous of them all was Fighting Joe Wheeler, partially because by 1895 the most notorious generals—Ulysses S. Grant, Robert E. Lee, William Tecumseh Sherman, Phil Sheridan, Thomas "Stonewall" Jackson, and George Armstrong Custer—had died fighting or died in their beds. Only James Longstreet was alive but, having been made the goat of Gettysburg, was out of favor in the South. Furthermore, Wheeler's words had merit, for he had fought at Shiloh as a colonel in the 19th Alabama Infantry. Wheeler had his speech down pat.

"This is a very different sort of reunion, fellow soldiers," Wheeler opened. "North and South, from that which we held on this plateau thirty-three years ago, with the marshaling of hostile hosts, the roar of musketry and cannon, and the mingling of the blood of 23,000 killed and wounded men, friend and foe.[38]

"What, then, is the meaning of this joyous assemblage, in which the simple garb of the citizen has taken the place of the blue and the gray, and the gentle presence of woman means that one flag, with cordial acclaim, floats over our reunited country, and that peace has taken the place of fratricidal war, which had this merit—that from its ashes has sprung, I fervently believe, a broader patriotism than our country ever knew before."

This was certainly a different tack than the traditional Lost Cause narrative. While the crowd ate it up, Wheeler continued to conjure scenes of comradeship, peace, and charity.

Concluded Wheeler, "Shall I speak separately of the armies whose deeds have rendered this spot historic and sacred? Of the splendid onset from these hills of the Army of Mississippi—of the splendid resistance of the Army of the Tennessee, and of the coming of the Army of the Ohio, or Cumberland, as it is called, which I have loved as if it were my offspring? No! Today I banish these distinctions, and take each individual to my heart as my fellow-countryman."

Every member of the crowd—whether they had played "Dixie" or "John Brown's Body"—loved Wheeler's speech. It was cathartic, inspired, and certainly a little bit cunning. Like Crane, Wheeler had tapped into something the American public yearned for: a national sense of fraternity.

Unsurprisingly, as Fighting Joe Wheeler began planning further Civil War battlefield speeches that spring, Crane's *The Red Badge of Courage* grew in popularity.

The novel wasn't even fully out yet—not scheduled to be published in book form until the fall—but it had already caused Stephen Crane to be recognized as one of the most popular writers in New York City.

During that turbulent spring, New York City was alive with changes. Bicycles, also called velocipedes, became all the rage. Nikola Tesla's Fifth Avenue laboratory burned down, forcing the scientist to rebuild on East Houston Street. William Randolph Hearst, who was supposedly shopping for a New York newspaper, was frequently seen on Broadway. And Charles Delmonico, having tried an "alligator pear"—courtesy of Richard Harding Davis, back from Venezuela with a basket of them—instructed his restaurant to serve them. Through the influence of Delmonico's, avocados became popular throughout the country.

But perhaps the most significant improvement, which would dramatically alter the complexion of the city, was Mayor William L. Strong's decision to appoint as police commissioner a brilliant but unpredictable Harvard graduate, East Coast politician, and Dakota Territory rancher.

In April 1895, after six years of serving as the commissioner of the Civil Service Commission in Washington, Theodore Roosevelt returned to New York City.

—PART II—

THE TEAM

You furnish the pictures, and I'll furnish the war.
William Randolph Hearst

— 6 —

POLICE COMMISSIONER ROOSEVELT

Theodore Roosevelt was in a hurry.

On May 6, 1895, Police Commissioner Roosevelt met at City Hall at 10 a.m. with his fellow newly appointed police commissioners, Andrew D. Parker, a Democrat, and Colonel Frederick Grant, who, like his father Ulysses, was a Republican. They were soon joined by the fourth police commissioner, Avery D. Andrews, a Democrat and a West Pointer. At 10:30 a.m. the four men rounded a corner, marching toward New York's police headquarters at 300 Mulberry Street.

Roosevelt caught sight of forty-eight-year-old Jacob Riis, the veteran newspaper reporter, waiting outside. Roosevelt knew Riis well, having read Riis's groundbreaking exposé on life in the tenements, *How the Other Half Lives,* calling it "both an enlightenment and an inspiration." Delighted, Roosevelt broke into a run.[1]

Lincoln Steffens, a thirty-one-year-old investigative journalist from San Francisco who would soon have the term "muckraker" attached to his name, was also nearby. Steffens remembered the scene vividly:

> He [Roosevelt] came on ahead down the street; he yelled, "Hello, Jake," to Riis, and running up the stairs to the front door of Police Headquarters, he waved us reporters to follow. We did. With the police officials standing around watching, the new Board went up to the second story. . . . TR seized Riis, who introduced me, and still running, he asked questions: "Where

are our offices? Where is the Board Room? What do we do first?" Out of the half-heard answers he gathered the way to the Board Room, where the three old Commissioners waited like three of the new Commissioners, stiff, formal and dignified. Not TR. He introduced himself, his colleagues, with handshakes, and called a meeting of the new Board . . . [and] had himself elected President—this had been prearranged—and then adjourned to pull Riis and me with him into his office.[2]

"Now, then[,] what'll we do?"[3]

"It was all breathless and sudden," Steffens reflected in his autobiography, "but Riis and I were soon describing the situation to him, telling him which higher officers to consult, which to ignore and punish; what the forms were, the customs, rules, methods. It was just as if we three were the police board."

Roosevelt, who knew that Riis and Steffens had covered the police beat for years and understood the Machiavellian innerworkings of New York City better than anyone, listened to their advice.

These dire words caused clouds of tension within the police headquarters. On May 17 Arthur Brisbane, who like Roosevelt had been written up by Richard Harding Davis as one of the dashing "Young Men in New York" and had since left the *Evening Sun*, commented in the *New York World:*

When he asks a question, Mr. Roosevelt shoots it at the poor trembling policeman as he would shoot a bullet at a coyote. . . . His teeth are very white and almost as big as a colt's teeth. . . . They seem to say: "Tell the truth to your Commissioner, or he'll bite your head off."

Generally speaking, this interesting Commissioner's face is red. He has lived a great deal out of doors, and that accounts for it. His hair is thick and short. . . . Under his right ear he has a long scar. It is the opinion of all the policemen who have talked with him that he got that scar fighting an Indian out West. It is also their opinion that the Indian is dead. . . . One thing our noble force may make up its mind to at once—it must do as Roosevelt says, for it is not likely that it will succeed in beating him.[4]

One man who would have liked to have beaten Roosevelt, probably physically, was Chief of Police Tom Byrnes. Byrnes was seen as an untouchable in police headquarters. After fighting for the Union in the American Civil War, Byrnes had advanced with New York's finest from patrol to sergeant and then to captain and finally to chief. There Byrnes popularized the rogues' gallery of mug shots—including Big Jim Brady and Billy the Kid—and the weapons each criminal favored.[5]

Proving himself a deft hand at self-promotion, Byrnes authored *Professional Criminals of America,* published in 1886 by Cassell & Company, based on his own daring deeds. Sensing an opportunity, Nathaniel Hawthorne's son Julian began penning popular stories, purported to be "From the Diary of Inspector Byrnes." To his readers, Hawthorne described Inspector Byrnes as "Handsome[,] . . . large and powerful in every sense of the word. His head is well shaped, with a compact forehead, strong nose, and resolute mouth and chin, shaded with a heavy moustache. "His figure is erect, his step light, his bearing alert and easy.[6]

To the reading public of the United States, Byrnes may have been a paladin, keeping the citizens of New York City safe at night. But to the citizens of New York City, Byrnes was something else altogether.

Like a malevolent Hades, Byrnes ruled over the denizens of the underworld with absolute authority. Greengrocers paid $2 a day for the right to sell fruit and vegetables on the sidewalks. Gambling houses paid between $15 and $300 a month so as not to be raided. Saloons paid $10,000 for liquor licenses. Brothels paid $30,000 for the right to operate unmolested and allowed officers of the peace and their friends special dispensations. And in the Bowery, the East Side, and the Tenderloin, criminal gangs were permitted to operate unhindered so long as they stayed away from Wall Street. For this, Byrnes was rewarded by the upper crust. Criminals caught crossing the line, however, were given the "third degree," a term that Byrnes coined.[7]

Fearlessly, Steffens described Byrnes as "simple, no complications at all—a man who would buy you or beat you, as you might choose, but get you he would."[8]

By 1895 Chief Byrnes was said to be worth $350,000, not bad for a policeman's salary.[9]

Unsurprisingly, Byrnes permitted a corrupt and vicious element to operate within the police force, none so prominent as Inspector Alexander "Clubber" Williams, known as a ferocious head-cracker.

Captain Williams transferred from a quiet beat to the Tenderloin in 1876. Encompassing a square mile of vice, replete with bordellos, opium dens, gambling halls, and saloons, the Tenderloin encompassed both sides of Broadway, from Fifth to as far west as Ninth and from 23rd Street into the upper 30s. Williams found the area just to his liking. Legend had it that upon being transferred, he joked, "For some time now I've had to be content with the cheaper cuts of meat, like round steak. From now on, I'm sure I'll have a more generous diet of thick, juicy tenderloin."[10]

Promoted to inspector, Williams operated on the Lower East Side but held real estate as far away as Japan, courtesy of Byrne's system of graft.[11]

"I think I shall move against Byrnes at once," Roosevelt wrote Lodge on May 18. "I thoroughly distrust him, and cannot do any thorough work while he remains."[12]

Byrnes dismissed Roosevelt as a real threat, telling the new police commissioner as much.

"It will break you," Byrnes told Roosevelt. "You will yield. You are but human."

Roosevelt thought differently. On May 24 he and Police Commissioners Andrews, Parker, and Grant met behind closed doors at police headquarters. The press heard raised voices within. Soon after, Inspector Williams was summoned. The *San Francisco Examiner* reported that Williams was inside the room for less than a minute before stepping out and smiling grimly. Five minutes later Roosevelt appeared, addressing the waiting reporters.

"The board has nothing to say except that Inspector Williams has asked for retirement and the board has unanimously granted it," Roosevelt explained. "The law is mandatory."[13]

Shortly afterward, Williams removed his uniform coat and visited Chief Byrnes in his office one last time before leaving the police station. The *Examiner* printed a story indicating that Byrnes was next on Roosevelt's list, for although Grant stood by the chief, Roosevelt had convinced Andrews and Parker that Byrnes "had a demoralizing effect and was an obstacle to reform."

On May 28 with the threat of a public investigation hanging over him, Byrnes tendered his resignation. "Men stopped and stood to watch him go, silent, respectful, sad," noted Steffens, "and the next day, the world went on as usual."[14]

Apparently Grant had fallen into line, for the *Examiner* declared that the decision to oust Byrnes was "unanimous." Naturally, the *Examiner* gave Roosevelt the lion's share of the credit, remarking that "the shake-up in the New York police force was bound to come from the moment when Theodore Roosevelt accepted a place on the commission."[15]

Ten days later Roosevelt began his next campaign.

At 2 a.m. on June 7, 1895, Roosevelt met Riis outside the Union League Club on Fifth Avenue. Roosevelt wore a long black coat, had his collar turned up, and sported a soft bowler with the brim pulled down, partially concealing his face. Riis, wearing green-tinted glasses, looked like Riis. Quickly, the two men moved toward Third Avenue. Their mission was to spy on the New York City police.[16]

Roosevelt let Riis guide him on their early-morning patrol through the Lower East Side, for Riis had mapped out their clandestine route, having intimate knowledge of the city's slums. At dawn they were returning to headquarters, and Roosevelt was in high spirits. Of all the patrolmen they had tailed, only one had been at his post. The others had been seen chatting on the streets, carousing with prostitutes, and drinking in saloons. One had even been snoring on a butter tub.[17]

Roosevelt took a quick nap and then ordered six of the delinquent roundsmen and patrolmen brought before him. "A sorrier-looking set of men never came to police headquarters," Steffens wrote in the *Evening Post.* At 9:30, Roosevelt stood before the six luckless men. Instead of firing them, Commissioner Roosevelt warned them that further dereliction would cost them their jobs. The men obeyed, terrified. Lest he be thought of as a paper tiger, Roosevelt announced, "I certainly shall . . . deal severely with the next roundsman or patrolman I find guilty of any similar shortcomings."[18]

The next day Riis told his fellow reporters about his early-morning adventure with Roosevelt, and from there the story spread like wildfire, as Roosevelt intended. Headlines read "ROOSEVELT AS ROUNDSMAN" and "Policemen Didn't Dream the President of the Board Was Catching Them Napping." The *Sun* headline blazed "Roosevelt on Patrol: He Makes Night Hideous for Sleepy Patrolmen." Suddenly every police officer, from the newly instated Chief Conlin to the lowest roundsman, had to step carefully, for there was no telling where Roosevelt would show up next.[19]

"It may be in Harlem that the commissioner will strike like a bolt of lightning," commented the *Salt Lake Herald.* "Or it may be the far West Side, or the downtown slums of the East Side, or perhaps in the turbulent quarters of 'Hell's Kitchen.'"[20]

Roosevelt next met with Richard Harding Davis. The two had first met in late 1890, shortly after Scribner had published Davis's short story "Gallegher"; the city had gone nuts for it. Gallegher followed it up with a string of short stories featuring heroic young men who, like Davis, sought adventure. The reading public didn't just fall in love with the characters; they also fell in love with the author. Davis's fame had rocketed to new heights when the illustrator for "Gallegher," Charles Gibson—the artist whom Davis had befriended in London—put Davis on the cover of *Life* alongside his iconic "Gibson Girls."[21] Davis soon became the most famous man in New York City.

Booth Tarkington, who would win the Nobel Prize for Literature twice, recalled the thrill of catching sight of Davis while skipping a Princeton class: "When the Waldorf was wondrously completed, and we cut an exam, in Cuneiform Inscriptions for an excursion to see the world at lunch in its magnificence, and Richard

Harding Davis came into the Palm Room—then, oh, then, our day was radiant! That was the top of our fortune; we could never have hoped for so much. Of all the great people of every continent, this was the one we most desired to see."[22]

Over the years Roosevelt and Davis had grown as friends, reuniting in 1892 at a British Legation dinner. Personally, Roosevelt thought Davis "so entirely intelligent, it was difficult to argue with him. The man has the gift of narration, but when it comes to breeding, even Kipling could give him pointers."[23]

Similarly, though Davis liked and respected Roosevelt, he considered Roosevelt's table manners atrocious. At the 1892 British Legation dinner, Roosevelt's recent *Cosmopolitan* article was brought up, wherein Roosevelt took umbrage to Americans who demonstrated a "queer, strained humility" toward Englishman. Davis, who admired English culture and spoke in a Philadelphian accent crossed with an aristocratic brogue, minced words with Roosevelt on this issue.[24]

In a letter to Brander Matthews, the influential chair of dramatic literature at Columbia, Roosevelt remarked, "Davis . . . apparently considered it a triumphant answer to my position to inquire if I believed in the American custom of chewing tobacco and spitting all over the floor. . . . I did; and that in consequence the British Minister, who otherwise liked me, felt very badly about having me at the house, especially because I ate with my legs on the table during dinner."[25]

With Davis working as a correspondent for *Harper's Weekly*, Roosevelt asked the famous author to join him and Commissioner Andrews on their next early-morning patrol. Davis agreed. That night, the three men through the gas-lit ghettos of the Lower East Side. This time, all but one policeman was found doing his job. The men at their posts received congratulations from Roosevelt. Officer William E. Raith, caught in an oyster saloon on upper Third Avenue, was flatly told "Go to your post at once."[26]

Raith had been lucky. After a stop at Mikey Lyon's all-night restaurant in the Bowery for salads, steaks, and beer, the three companions toured the West Side precincts, which included the Tenderloin. There they discovered seven patrolmen away from their posts. Much later in the day Roosevelt handed their names and numbers to Chief Peter Conlin and said, "This time there will be no mercy." Roosevelt appeared as a complainant at the subsequent disciplinary hearing.[27]

"We would sit in a doorstep and take out our watches and time how long police talked to each other, or to citizens," Davis recollected. "Then R. would hurry up to them always asking first 'What is your post?' Before they recognized him [they] would always laugh or swear and say 'What the hell's that to you?' and then it was humorous for us to see their faces change as they recognized the spectacles and double rows of teeth. . . . Some of them were so frightened they could not answer his questions. One man couldn't remember his own name."[28]

Roosevelt's midnight beat resulted in more arrests than ever before. Shortly after he began his campaign, the *New York Press* recorded an unprecedented 2,437 arrests made that week.[29]

As for Roosevelt, his early-morning forays were personally doing him worlds of good.[30]

On June 16 Roosevelt wrote to his sister Anna, whom he called Bamie or Bye:

> Darling Bye,
>
> Twice I have spent the night in patrolling New York on my own account, to see exactly what the men were doing. My experiences were interesting, and the trips did good, though each meant my going forty hours at a stretch without any sleep. But in spite of my work I really doubt whether I have often been in better health. It is very interesting; and I feel as though it was so eminently practical; it has not a touch of the academic. . . . I have not tried to write a line of my book since I took office.[31]

Volume 4 of *The Winning of the West* was shelved while Roosevelt threw himself into his work. More night patrols followed, one with Lincoln Steffens, another with Stephen Crane's mentor Hamlin Garland, and more with Bob Ferguson, a family friend from Scotland, a fellow hunter and ranch partner, and a future Rough Rider. Though Roosevelt's tactics were effective, he was branded as "The Terror" and "Haroun el Roosevelt" after the Baghdad caliph Haroun el Raschid, known to stalk through the streets of the Round City at night a thousand years ago. Cartoons and editorials followed.[32]

Backfiring spectacularly, the press coverage meant to ridicule the new police commissioner helped make Roosevelt even more of a household name. Swinging greater political capital, het proved to be a highly capable police commissioner. During his watch, Roosevelt abolished police lodging houses, modernized the detective department, created the first bicycle squad, and ordered his men trained to use guns rather than simply being handed a deadly weapon and expected to learn how to use it on their own. He also improved positions for Jews on the force through his policy of meritocracy, punched holes in the glass ceiling by hiring a female secretary, and drew new recruits from New York City's underrepresented minorities.[33]

The citizens of New York City could accept these progressive changes. But when Police Commissioner Roosevelt decided to enforce the Sunday Excise Law—putting a cork in Sunday drinking—Gotham drew the line. The Sunday Excise Law had come about in 1857, a statute that forbade the sale of intoxicating liquors in saloons on the Sabbath. The law had only been slightly enforced and during the Civil War was almost completely forgotten. But in 1892 the Sunday Excise Law had been reaffirmed by a Democratic legislature on the strength of New York State's rural temperance vote. Certainly farmers, whose villages had exponentially more churches than saloons, were far removed from the realities of New York City's large and prosperous German population, with their Old World traditions of draining steins of lager after work. The law revealed a disconnect between rural and urban New York, with the New York City Police Department caught in the middle.[34]

Not wishing to gum up the machine, Chief Byrnes had largely winked at the law, at most using the threat of it as a means of extra leverage to extort money from saloon owners. But Commissioner Roosevelt was a different man altogether, as New York City came to realize.

On June 10, 1895, Roosevelt instructed his officers that from midnight Saturday to midnight Sunday they would "rigidly enforce" the Sunday Excise Law. "No matter if you think the law is a bad one you must see that your men carry out your orders to the letter," Roosevelt explained. To the press Roosevelt stated, "I do not deal with public sentiments. I deal with the law."[35]

Though it was not largely publicized, sentiment may actually have driven Roosevelt into waging such an unpopular crusade. The health of Theodore's brother Elliott—best remembered as the father of Eleanor Roosevelt—began to decline when he suffered his first seizure during puberty. Since then, seizures periodically wracked his body. Elliott inevitably found alcohol to be a helpful depressant if imbibed in prodigious quantities. Theodore never forgot one such drinking binge in Chicago; Elliott started with ale, switched to milk punch, then a mint julep, next a brandy smash, and ultimately sherry. Along with suffering from alcoholism, after an injury Elliott became dependent on morphine and laudanum.[36]

Several scandals followed, including the family paying $10,000 to a serving girl Elliott impregnated and Elliott being declared "insane" in the newspapers after leaving an asylum in Graz, Austria. On August 13, 1894, Civil Service commissioner Theodore Roosevelt received a telegram in Washington that his brother—who was once again drinking—was in New York City and very ill. Roosevelt did not respond. "He can't be helped," Roosevelt reasoned, "and he must simply be let go his own gait." The next day Elliott Roosevelt, suffering from delirium tremens, tried to "let go" out the window of his house. He suffered one final seizure and died.[37]

Eight months later, Theodore Roosevelt became the president of the Police Board of New York City. Less than two months after receiving the appointment, he decided to wage an uphill battle to enforce the Sunday Excise Law. Whether Roosevelt was motivated by guilt, grief, a sense of civic duty, a master plan to root out police corruption by putting the last dregs of the Byrnes regime at odds with the saloonkeepers, or an even more Machiavellian scheme to enforce an unpopular law passed by a Democratic legislature so as to force its repeal, as Roosevelt later claimed, was difficult to gage. However, in 1884 Roosevelt had been opposed to the Sunday Excise Law, calling it "entirely too strict." Eleven years later, less than a year after Elliott's death, Roosevelt seemingly had a change of heart.[38]

The result was that by the last day of June, 97 percent of New York City's saloons were closed. The following Sunday, many saloonkeepers and patrons had become barroom lawyers and were exploiting loopholes in the law. Because police had to witness alcohol being sold in order to make arrests, patrons suspiciously began carrying baskets and gripsacks in more prodigious numbers than ever before. Sodas and teas were also spiked with whiskey and gin. But on July 12 this practice was brought to a quick halt—at least in theory—when a Democratic judge handed down a shocking decision: taken literally, the Sunday Excise Law prohibited the serving of all drinks—alcoholic or not—on the Sabbath. Even milk, coffee, and apple juice were found to be against the law. "Only water to drink now," lamented the *New York Herald*.[39]

Roosevelt comment in a letter to Lodge dated July 14, 1895:

> For good or ill I have made an upset in New York politics; and with true parochialism, the average New Yorker regards the tariff, silver, and presidential nominees as all secondary to the Excise question.
>
> It is an awkward and ugly fight; yet I am sure I am right in my position, and I think there is an even chance of our winning on it.[40]

Two days later Roosevelt addressed a crowd of German Americans at 134 East 115th Street. There he heard the cries "He has not got any business to velcome us! Ve are here by right!"[41]

Flanked by Commissioner Parker and Commissioner Andrews, Roosevelt launched into his argument, stating that honestly enforcing an unpopular law was the best way to bring about its repeal and that it was Senator David B. Hill—not Roosevelt and his Republican allies—who reaffirmed the Sunday Excise Law with the goal of "keeping the saloons subservient allies to Tammany Hall." By the end of Roosevelt's speech, his audience was applauding.[42]

But the *World,* among the majority of New York newspapers, was "shrieking with rage," joined by Tammany Hall, which could not believe the temerity of the newest police commissioner. At least Byrnes had been predictable in his corruption. Roosevelt was proving to be as unpredictable as he was incorruptible.[43]

On August 3 the Liquor Sellers Association, which represented three-fourths of New York City's twelve thousand saloons, sided in favor of complete observation of the Sunday Excise Law. Moreover, the Liquor Sellers Association threatened expulsion to members who failed to comply. Its motives were the same as what Roosevelt had outlined in the speech he had delivered on July 16: to strengthen their case for the law's repeal. But the short-term effect was the continual observation of the detested law.[44]

Two days later on August 5, 1895, a post office clerk noticed an odd-looking package addressed to Roosevelt. The brave clerk tore the package open and was startled by "a puff of flame and smoke." A match fuse had exploded, causing the smoke. By some miracle, the live cartridge enveloped in gunpowder had not. Roosevelt was indifferent, calling the letter bomb "a cheap thing" and refusing to look at it. Roosevelt's eyes were fixed on weightier issues.[45]

Six weeks later on Wednesday, September 25, the newly formed United Societies for Liberal Sunday Laws staged a parade to protest Roosevelt and the Sunday Excise Law. More than 30,000 marchers paraded down Lexington Avenue. Along the parade route, 150,000 people cheered as they passed by. One of the men enjoying the parade was Commissioner Roosevelt, who "laughed louder than any one else" as he recognized his name on the placards and banners the protesters waved: "Rooseveltism is a farce and humbug" and "Send the Police Czar to Russia." A wagon titled "The Millionaire's Club" caught Roosevelt's eye. On the wagon were three men sporting tall hats and frock coats, one of whom bore more than a passing resemblance to Roosevelt. The trio sipped champagne while behind them a burlesque was taking place: a beer drinker was being arrested.[46]

"That is the best one yet," Roosevelt observed.

Spying one banner in particular, Roosevelt asked the bearer if he could keep it as a souvenir. "Certainly," the man replied, handing over a banner that read "Roosevelt's Razzle Dazzle Reform Racket."

It quickly became apparent that the crowd hadn't anticipated Roosevelt's presence and that Roosevelt's good spirit had won them over. Soon the words "Teddy, you're a man!" and "Bully for Teddy!" could be heard. The next day a Chicago newspaper captured with the headline, "Cheered by Those Who Came to Jeer" how completely Roosevelt had turned the tables on his opponents.[47]

Although the parade was a triumph for Roosevelt, no newspaper from New York to Chicago to San Francisco reported on the most significant event that occurred in New York and the world on September 25, 1895. Camouflaged by the razzle dazzle of the parade and kept secret from the press and the public through cloak-and-dagger negotiations, an agent working for a certain senator's son from San Francisco was in Gotham that Wednesday.[48]

W. R. Hearst was poised to invade New York City. The course of human events was about to radically change.

— 7 —

THE INVASION

In early October 1895, Hearst telegraphed the *San Francisco Examiner* office. He wanted Winifred Black, Homer Davenport, and Charlie Dryden to join him in New York City. On October 4 the trio boarded an eastbound train, speculating on Hearst's reasoning. Because Davenport was a gifted cartoonist, Dryden was a talented humorist and sports writer, and Black, writing under the name "Annie Laurie," was a specialist in stunt journalism, it was a certainty that Hearst needed them for more than the company.[1]

Years later, Black recalled the moment of epiphany in a magazine article:

> It all seems so simple now. But at that time we had no more idea of a Hearst newspaper in New York than we had of one established at the top of the mountains of the moon. When we reached Omaha, Dryden came into the car, and his face was as white as a sheet.[2]
>
> "I've got it!" he said. "The Chief's bought a New York paper. If I had known that, I wouldn't have stirred a step."
>
> "Neither would I," said Homer Davenport, who had left his young wife and brand-new baby at home in San Francisco.
>
> But of course that was all nonsense. We would have gone to the Fiji Island or to Greenland's icy mountains if the Big Chief had wanted.

By the time they reached New York, the word was out. Although John McLean—the publisher of the *Cincinnati Enquirer,* the German-language daily *Das Morgen Journal,* and the *New York Morning Journal*—had sought $400,000 for his two New York papers, Hearst had talked him down to $150,000, making the purchase on October 3. Although Hearst rented an office in the World Building, the *Journal*'s newsrooms constituted the second and third floors of the Tribune Building, located in the heart of Manhattan on the corner of Nassau and Spruce, part of the fabled Newspaper Row.[3]

As the publishers' journal the *Fourth Estate* reported, "W. R. Hearst Here. Has Come To Stay as Proprietor of the Journal. . . . The Young Californian Has Both Money and Brains—The Combination May Mean a Metropolitan Revolution."[4]

In other words, the invasion had begun.

Getting the lay of the land by taking an experimental flying machine over New York City, Hearst quickly realized that he had his work cut out for him. On the day he took ownership, the *New York Morning Journal* had a paltry circulation 43,000, each lackluster issue selling for a penny. Although this was far better than the *New York Times,* with its moribund circulation of about 10,000, Whitelaw Reid's literary *New York Tribune* had a stronger circulation of about 75,000. Charles Dana's *New York Sun* was better although it didn't top 100,000. The two heavyweights were James Gordon Bennett Jr.'s sensational *New York Herald,* with a circulation of about 200,000, and Joseph Pulitzer's even more outrageous *New York World,* leading the pack with a circulation of around 250,000, selling each copy for two pennies.[5]

No matter. Hearst enjoyed a little competition, so long as he came out on top.

Hearst left the running of the German paper in the hands of a German editor so that he himself could fully concentrate on the *New York Morning Journal.* Immediately dropping "Morning" from the title, Hearst sought to emulate and then outshine the bigger papers. To do this he employed a small army of reporters, editors, artists, copy boys, and clerks, bent over their rolltop desks in the main newsroom, the air choked with cigar smoke and the floor a maze of newspaper and spittoons. Samuel S. Chamberlain was transferred from the *San Francisco Examiner* to serve as managing editor. Henry R. Haxton, a mustachioed Englishman who in 1888 had jumped from a ferry into San Francisco Bay to report on how long it would take the Coast Guard to rescue him, traveled east to add action to the paper. To oversee the editorial page, Hearst hired Willis J. Abbot, a talented journalist from Chicago. After looking over the *Journal* headquarters, Abbot wrote to a friend that he had "secured very remunerative employment in a lunatic asylum."[6]

Overseeing everything was W. R. Hearst.

Black, who would become a Hearst fixture and ultimately write Phoebe Hearst's first biography, described W. R. Hearst as "tall, slender, good-looking, very blond, with a pink and white complexion and a little golden mustache, boyish . . . and still a bit under the influence of the impish high spirits of youth."[7]

Shaving his mustache in the first weeks of coming to New York, Hearst was looking to change more than just his appearance. Shades of the *Examiner*, throughout October and November the *Journal* evolved into a lively, entertaining newspaper.

When Charles Spencer-Churchill, Duke of Marlborough, was arrested for recklessly biking through Central Park, the *Journal*'s treatment made it a must-read. On October 27 Davenport lampooned former president Benjamin Harrison, whose chin whiskers were stroked by an elephant's trunk. On November 7 Hearst finally put his name on the masthead, the lead story the sensational wedding between the beautiful but reluctant Consuelo Vanderbilt and the hell-raising Duke of Marlborough. Three days later the *Journal* was the only New York newspaper to report on a fatal saloon shooting. And on November 23, Hearst hired none other than Richard Harding Davis—paying him a lordly price of $500—to cover the Princeton-Yale football game. Rivals who rooted for Hearst's failure, sniggering up their sleeves at the price, were astonished when the edition sold out. The result was the furious increase of circulation.[8]

Initially, Hearst rented a residence at the Hoffman House. This was where Hearst and his belated father had talked world affairs, George Hearst having died in 1891 from stomach cancer. Now unfettered except for his mother Phoebe, who held the purse strings but had just sold to the Rothchild interest a share of the fabulously lucrative Anaconda copper mine in Montana for $2.925 million and could rarely if ever deny her "darling boy" anything, Hearst lived large. After long nights at Broadway shows in the company of pretty women and his favorite newspapermen, he returned to the Tribune Building to put his stamp on the morning paper.[9]

Willis J. Abbot recalled the chief's inimitable style:

> [Hearst's] greatest joy in life was to attend the theater, follow it up with a lively supper and, at about 1:30 A.M., turn up at the office full of scintillating ideas and therewith rip my editorial page to pieces. Other pages were apt to suffer equally, and it was always an interesting spectacle to me to watch this young millionaire, usually in irreproachable evening dress, working

> over the forms, changing a head here, shifting the position of an article there, clamoring always for more pictures and bigger type.[10]

Only after he was satisfied did Hearst return to the Hoffman House like a lord returning to his manse. Hearst rose early, and a two-and-a-half-mile carriage ride deposited him once again at the Tribune Building, where he continued to work his magic.

Naturally, Hearst attracted attention. Even in the newsroom the young millionaire often wore straw hats with colored brims, checked suits from which dangled a gold watch chain, and high-laced shoes with mother-of-pearl buttons. He favored circus ties and loud, striped shirts. Once after bringing home a new collection of cravats, Hearst asked his Irish valet, George Thompson, for his verdict.

"I doubt these are any worse than your others," his faithful butler replied.[11]

Along with dining at Jim's Chop Shop on Broadway, Jack's on Sixth Avenue, and Martin's on University Place, Hearst often lunched half a mile south at Delmonico's. Whether he dined on tenderloin of beef with sweet potato croquettes, shrimp with alligator pear mousse, or Delmonico's steak went unreported. It was Hearst's naked ambition to out-sensationalize Joseph Pulitzer that made headlines.[12]

"No doubt it is to some extent at least the unparalleled success of the *World* under Joseph Pulitzer," commented M. I. Dexter in an editorial reprinted from coast to coast that October and November, "that has induced Mr. Hearst to try his luck in the New York field."[13]

When Hearst moved out of the Hoffman House, he initially settled across the street in the Worth House before moving into a four-story palace at 123 Lexington and 28th Street, once owned by President Chester A. Arthur. Adept at making hay, Hearst threw a grand ball in late November 1895, again hiring Davis. For a mere $250 Davis wrote up the affair in the *Journal*.[14]

Along with securing Davis, Hearst poached several talented members of Pulitzer's *World*. Among the most capable were Alan Dale, considered the wittiest drama critic in New York; H. Pruette Share, the *World*'s art manager; and Richard Welsh, who doubled as an editor for Harper & Brothers. By then every newspaperman knew that if they received a card saying "Mr. Hearst would be pleased to have you call," an offer was about to be made. Hearst also lured away from the *New York Recorder* Julius Chambers, one of the finest newspapermen in the city, and stole from the *Sun* the prolific author Julian Ralph, offering him more than the $100 a week Whitelaw Reid was paying and making Ralph his London correspondent.[15]

In early January—with the *Journal*'s circulation overtaking the *Tribune* and the *Sun,* cresting 100,000—Hearst asked for the *World*'s Sunday editor, Morrill Goddard, to meet him at his private suite in the Hoffman House. Along with treating Goddard to eggs, kidney sauté, and vintage wine, Hearst offered to double his salary if he traded the *World* for the *Journal.* Goddard had his reservations.

"Your proposition is tremendously interesting, Mr. Hearst, if you can carry out your plans. But some of the shrewdest men in the *World* claim that you can't possibly last longer than three months more in this town."[16]

Hearst smiled and pulled from his vest pocket a crumpled draft bill. It was from Wells, Fargo & Co. and was worth $35,000.

"That ought to convince you that I intend to remain in New York quite some time."[17]

Goddard divulged that he wouldn't be as effective without his staff of artists and writers.

"All right," replied Hearst. "Let's take the whole staff."

By the time Hearst's raid was over, only the office secretary, Emma Jane Hogg, was left. Legend has it that even the office cat deserted to Hearst.[18]

Pulitzer was furious to hear that Hearst had buffaloed him again. At six foot, two, thin as a rail, and nearly blind, Pulitzer still commanded the same respect at age fifty that he had when he was thirty-six after buying the moribund *St. Louis Dispatch,* which he'd turned into a gold mine. He ordered his business manager, Solomon S. Carvalho, to hire back his staff with pay raises. Carvalho succeeded for all of twenty-four hours. The next day from his ornately furnished office in the World Building, lined with California redwood, Hearst managed to lure the newspapermen back to the Hearst fold with the promise of even higher wages.

"I won't have my building used for purposes of seduction!" Pulitzer raged, ordering Hearst evicted from the premises.[19]

By now Pulitzer realized that Hearst was a serious threat. But while Pulitzer tried to marshal his resources, Hearst closed in for the kill. Pulitzer appointed city editor Richard Farrelly to replace Goddard, going so far as to arrange a banquet for Farrelly. The day before the feast, which Pulitzer was forced to cancel, Farrelly defected to Hearst as well. So too did cartoonist T. E. Powers. Naturally, Pulitzer lured Powers back with a better contract before Hearst roped him in with an ever greater one. This time Pulitzer decided to settle it in court, and Powers, the belle of the ball, was paid two hefty salaries while the case was litigated. When Hearst won the suit, Powers bought drinks at a Park Row watering hole. The incident was so comical that it inspired a friend of Farrelly's to paraphrase a line from *Uncle Tom's Cabin,* indicative of the new atmosphere in fin de siècle New York: "You can beat this poor old body but my soul belongs to William Randolph Hearst."[20]

Hearst next set his sights on Washington. Desirous to stop railroad baron Collis Huntington's funding bill in its tracks—believing that Huntington should repay the $65 million the Central Pacific owed rather than take out a loan for an equal amount—on January 18, 1896, Hearst sent a telegram in care of the *Examiner* from New York City to San Francisco. Its recipient was "Ambrose Bierce, Esq."[21] "Railroad combination so strong in Washington," Hearst wired, "that seems almost impossible to break them, yet it is certainly the duty of all having interests of the coast at heart to make most strenuous efforts. Will you please go to Washington for the Examiner? I will send Davenport from here, and the Journal will use whatever power it has to assist. Please answer quick."

Bierce wrote back that same day: "I shall be glad to do whatever I can toward defeating Mr. Huntington's funding bill and shall start for Washington on Monday evening next."[22]

The *Examiner* published the exchange, along with an accompanying article that alluded to "Casey at the Bat": "Ambrose Bierce knows the trail he is treading. He has blazed it with his own ax many times. And he knows the game he is hunting. He has chased it howling to its lair frequently. There will be no joy in the Huntington lobby when Bierce gets to Washington."[23]

Considering Hearst's newspaper savvy, the *New York Times* editorial writer Robert L. Duffus offered praise: "Here is journalism as large as the Rocky Mountains or the Painted Desert."[24]

"There is no man in our public life to-day who interests me so much as William Randolph Hearst," Upton Sinclair remarked in his 1907 study on America, *The Industrial Republic.* Sinclair noted that Hearst, rather than follow in his father's footsteps as a mining mogul as his father wished, was determined to "show the old man." Hearst recognized that by filling his newspapers with unadulterated life, he could attract more readers than anyone.[25]

"Give them big head-lines, and a shock on every page; give them royalty and 'high life,' scandal and spice, battle, murder and sudden death—and then they will buy your paper," Sinclair commented. "It was good fun for Mr. Hearst to do this. Watching his newspapers, what has struck me most is the sheer audacity of them. Audacity is his characteristic quality, and it is a characteristic American quality—it places him among our national treasures, along with Mark Twain, and P. T. Barnum, and Buffalo Bill."[26]

Although Hearst was called "Chief" by many of his newspapermen, he soon gained a new title. On January 21, 1896, while attending the annual election of the American Yacht Club at Delmonico's, Hearst was elected vice commodore.[27]

"Hearst . . . is a great clubman, and he owns a steam yacht, a luxury which few can afford," observed the *Saint Paul Globe*. "For his sake it is to be hoped that the Journal, instead of consuming an income after the fashion of a steam yacht, will turn in a handsome net profit."[28]

Hearst wasn't turning a profit, as it happened. Expanding the *San Francisco Examiner* had been pocket change compared to the cost of the *New York Journal*, said to be losing about $1,000 a day.[29] This was a fact not lost on Phoebe. But Hearst managed to convince his mother and her cousin, Edward Clark, serving as Phoebe's chief financial adviser, that there was method to his madness. At the same time, Hearst could brag to his mother that he was making great strides at the *Journal*, with the paper's circulation surpassing 150,000.[30]

If Phoebe doubted her son, she had only to read what the newspapers were saying about his success. Commented the *Buffalo Evening News* on January 23, "Since it became the property of Mr. Hearst of San Francisco the Journal has made a complete change in appearance and in scope as a newspaper. It has been broadened out on lines characteristic of the best journalism of San Francisco, and has interest for every class of reader. . . . The Journal now disputes with the Herald the leadership among the illustrated papers, and it leads all the big papers in popular interest."[31]

On February 10, 1896, in an attempt to slow Hearst, Pulitzer took Carvalho's advice and dropped the price of the *World* to a penny. The next day, the circulation of the *World* gained an additional 80,000 readers, rising to about 273,000 though at the expense of the *Advertiser* and the *New York Press*, not the *Journal*. Worse, after the initial circulation boom, circulation began to taper off. To balance the cost of lowering the price to a penny, Pulitzer raised his advertising rates. Wisely, Hearst kept his advertising rates the same, luring some advertisers to the *Journal*. All of this put a strain on Pulitzer's relationship with Carvalho.[32]

Pulitzer's troubles strengthened Hearst's resolve. Money be damned, Hearst initiated a campaign to buy as many billboards in the city as possible, advertising the *Journal*. He mailed out circulars to tens of thousands of women, drawing attention to the *Journal*'s "Woman's Page" and the ever-popular Julian Ralph's "London Letters." Hearst used every trick in the book and made up several on the spot.[33]

On February 22, Rochester's *Democrat and Chronicle* also heaped praise. "Hearst threw down the gauntlet and Pulitzer having picked it up we now have a battle such as journalism never saw before."[34]

Always interested in art, a habit picked up while crisscrossing Europe with Phoebe several times as a young man, on February 29, 1896, Hearst attended a party at 347 5th Avenue hosted by the artist and art collector J. Charles Arter. Along with looking over the Japanese paintings Arter had returned with from overseas, Hearst rubbed shoulders with the Russian consul general Alexander Olarovsky, Frederick Roosevelt Scovel (a cousin to Theodore), and Scovel's wife Vivien (Ulysses S. Grant's granddaughter). But it was the *Journal* that remained Hearst's true passion.[35]

"Put on a man wherever there is room," Hearst ordered the foreman of the composing room. "Don't let the copy wait. Let the men do the waiting."[36]

The newspapermen didn't mind, for along with trusting the Chief's instincts they were well compensated. In fact, any artist or reporter who produced work that Hearst felt particularly brilliant was rewarded with a liberal cash gratuity, and the gift of bicycles became commonplace.[37]

In March, the famous veteran reporter Murat Halstead returned from Cuba covering the Cuban revolutionaries' war against the oppressive Spanish Empire. Halstead's widely reprinted piece in the *Journal* was sympathetic to the Cubans, antagonistic to the Spanish, and ultimately called for not just American intervention and war with Spain but also annexation of the island itself.

"Why should Spain cling with a grasp as of despair to the last of her great American dominions? . . . Why should Cuba be the exception to all the rules, the one spot where the continuation of the logic of history of Spain must be forever regarded as a degradation—the land where the same fulfillment of fate as in the case of Mexico and Peru and all the rest should be associated with honor?" Halstead questioned.[38]

The reporter concluded that "as an American state Cuba would be worth her place in the splendid and immortal sisterhood, and as a prize of peace she would enter the Union with an endowment of the matchless prodigality of nature."

Wholeheartedly agreeing with the *Journal*'s position on Cuba was Police Commissioner Roosevelt. That month Roosevelt wrote to his sister Anna that "I wish our people would really interfere in Cuba, but the President . . . shies off."[39] Roosevelt was more belligerent in his 1913 autobiography: "The revolt in Cuba had dragged its weary length until conditions in the island had become so dreadful as to be a standing disgrace to us for permitting them to exist. . . . Spain attempted to govern her colonies on archaic principles, which rendered her control of them incompatible with the advance of humanity and intolerable to the conscience of mankind."[40]

To counter this sensation—wherein a respected Hearst reporter literally called for war with Spain to the purpose of adding another star to the flag—Pulitzer erected outside the World Building the largest thermometer anyone had ever seen, an eye-popping eleven feet tall.

"This is pretty smart," opined Rochester's *Democrat and Chronicle* on March 14, 1896, "but I should not be surprised if the Journal were to beat it, for Hearst is determined to teach Pulitzer a few more lessons before he is done with him."[41]

One such lesson involved a young hippopotamus housed in Central Park. The *Journal* conducted a voting contest to decide the name of the hippo. The contest proved popular, and a large force of *Journal* clerks were kept busy tabulating the results. "How did New York manage to get along without Mr. Hearst during the days when he was still in San Francisco?" asked John Smith in the *Buffalo Morning Express*. "He seems to have succeeded in striking the level of metropolitan intelligence even more accurately—that is, lower down—than Mr. Pulitzer of St. Louis has ever done."[42]

Carvalho agreed with this assessment. Finally breaking with Pulitzer, at the end of March Carvalho resigned as editor of the *World* and accepted Hearst's offer at the *Journal*.[43]

With everything rolling his way, Hearst pounced on another idea, possibly having germinated from speaking with Russia's consul general in February: to print the first report on the coronation of the new tsar. To that end, in April Hearst dispatched Richard Harding Davis to Moscow. To help Davis get the scoop, Hearst sent along Augustus Trowbridge, an assistant correspondent for the *Journal* who spoke English, French, German, Italian, and Russian.[44]

On April 20 the *New York Tribune* reported that Hearst was back in San Francisco. Speculating as to who the Republicans would nominate for president, Hearst commented, "McKinley seems to be the strongest candidate." Hearst also let slip the circulation of the *Journal*, an impressive 227,000, swiftly gaining on the *World*.[45]

Checking in on the *Examiner*, Hearst was pleased with Bierce's campaign against Huntington's funding bill. Along with artists Homer Davenport and Jimmy Swinnerton lampooning Huntington, Bierce's caustic articles had the desired effect. Through the *Journal* and the *Examiner*, Congress ultimately turned against Huntington, refusing his funding bill and demanding the return of the $65 million. Backed into a corner, the Central Pacific Railroad ultimately repaid the loan.

Over a decade later, Charles Edward Russell remarked in *Hampton's Magazine,* "These articles were extraordinary examples of invective and bitter sarcasm. . . . Mr. Bierce had the railroad forces frightened and wavering, and before the end of the year, he had them whipped."[46]

Hearst also had personal reasons for revisiting the Bay City. He was finalizing plans to have a $500,000 mausoleum erected in Cyprus Lawn Cemetery to house his late father's bones.[47]

Meanwhile, on May 25 nearly six thousand miles away in Moscow, Richard Harding Davis finally obtained the blue badge needed to attend the coronation. This was courtesy of Davis charming General Alexander McCook, whom President Grover Cleveland had sent to represent him at the Kremlin. The next day Davis was one of only a handful of Americans allowed to enter the Church of Assumption and witness the coronation of Nicholas Romanov and Alexandra Feodorovna.

Davis wrote to this brother that "it was the sight of the century."[48]

Naturally, rival newspapers were green with jealousy. Though the *New York Times* praised Davis's coverage, the *New York World* expressed mockery. On May 29, 1896, even the *Kansas City Journal* took a swing: "The indications were that the coronation of the czar would be quite a gorgeous event even before the arrival of Richard Harding Davis."[49]

On June 10 Hearst rattled into St. Louis, which would host the Republican National Convention between June 16 and June 18. It was there that William McKinley received 661.5 votes; Thomas B. Reed received only 84.5. McKinley would be the Republican nominee for president.[50]

Hearst was back in New York City on June 30, where he splashed some of his wealth around in the form of prize money at a bicycle parade to occur on July 18. In the meantime, on July 9, 1896, William Jennings Bryan delivered the "Cross of Gold" speech before the Democratic National Convention in Chicago, championing silver. The Boy Orator received thunderous applause and the party's nomination for president. Covering the convention, Abbot wrote a frenzied telegram urging Hearst to back Bryan.[51]

Having already received word of Bryan's nomination, Hearst gathered his top men around him, seeking counsel. As it happened, Hearst's entire inner circle, except for McEwen, pleaded with him to abandon the Nebraskan. In particular, Hearst's business manager Charles Palmer argued that backing Bryan would ruin the *New York Journal.* Bryan may have been beloved in the agrarian states, but in the financial capital of America the very concept of deflating gold engendered fear and hatred. Hearst certainly knew that if he stuck with the Democrats he was taking a great risk.

"I pondered all the day of Bryan's nomination and all that night upon what I should do. I had everything to lose and nothing to gain by supporting him," Hearst later reflected, "for I did not believe in free silver. . . . I came to the conclusion that the man might not be sound, but at least he was sincere, and that the cause he stood for was the people's cause."[52]

By backing Bryan, Hearst also recognized that he would further distinguish himself from Pulitzer. In other words, anyone in New York who wanted to see the McKinley versus Bryan battle from a different perspective would have to read the *Journal.*

To his men Hearst said, "Unlimber the guns; we are going to fight for Bryan."[53]

What Hearst meant, as his baffled editors came to understand it, was that both the *Examiner* and the *Journal* were to boom Bryan but avoid all mention of silver. Personally, Hearst thought the issue of bimetallism was a loser but wanted Bryan over McKinley at all costs. Eventually Abbot, struggling to plot a course between Scylla and Charybdis, explained the absurdity of his task with Hearst.

"At last with a sigh, he yielded," Abbot recalled, "called a conference of his editors, and informed them that although he personally disbelieved in free coinage, he had been convinced that he must subordinate his principles to those of the party."[54]

In other words, the *Journal* and the *Examiner* were now free to back Bryan *and* Bryan's chief platform. As for the *Das Morgen Journal,* despite being treated as an afterthought, its editor was in the room.

"Vy, Mr. Hearst," the editor stated with aplomb, "I haf been doing that already these three weeks!"

When on August 12, 1896, Bryan spoke before a crowd of forty thousand at Madison Square Garden, formally accepting the nomination for president, Hearst made sure the speech got a good write-up. Stephen Crane, covering the event for the *Evening Gazette,* was also in the crowd. The *New York Journal*'s action reporter, Henry Haxton, thought the *Journal* a better fit for the young author.

Crane was certainly in high demand, for the young author was at the height of his literary popularity that August. One year earlier *The Red Badge of Courage* had come out in book form to rave reviews. The book's success was partially due to the effect his own remarkable synesthesia had on the narrative—"a crimson roar," a "black procession of curious oaths"—which the reading public found poetic and novel. The book also benefited from Crane's refusal to use the familiar tropes of "Longstreet was on the right, Bragg on the left, Wallace's men on the ridge," and so on. To the reader's surprise, Crane never even named the battlefield wherein the story was set. Instead, Crane concentrated on the emotions of his main character, having Henry Fleming stunned and humiliated by his own cowardice early on, confident and self-satisfied by the book's end. The reading public ate it up and asked for more.

Crane delivered that August, publishing in *McClure's Magazine* a Henry Fleming follow-up, "The Veteran." Fleming, now an old man, recounted the battle (revealed to be Chancellorsville) before rushing into a burning barn to save a pair of colts. It was heroism on an emotional level. *Do what's right,* Crane seemed to be saying, *no matter the cost.*[55]

On September 10, 1896, Haxton happened to run into Hearst on a stairway of the Tribune Building and pitched that they hire Crane to write "novelettes based upon real incidents of New York life."[56]

Hearst, recognizing Crane's rare talent, approved the idea. Haxton wrote Crane about the good news that same day: "I am sure that if you read the police news in next Sunday and Monday mornings' papers and go to Jefferson Market Police Court on Monday morning, you will get the material for a good Tenderloin story to start with."

With Crane, they all got more than they bargained for. The next day, September 11, Crane lunched with Roosevelt, an admitted fan of *The Red Badge of Courage.* Three days later Crane observed the byzantine laws of justice at the Jefferson Market Police Court. The following evening, September 15, Crane was in the company of two prostitutes on Broadway when officer Charles Becker—a disciple of Alex "Clubber" Williams—arrested one of the ladies, red-haired Dora Clark, for soliciting. Becker would have arrested the other had she not claimed that Crane was her husband. Crane, despite Roosevelt trying to talk him out of it, decided to defend Clark at police court the following day, and Crane's testimony got her released with a warning. This caused a sensation throughout the city. Hearst made certain that Crane was extolled as a hero, a champion of the downtrodden, and most of the papers followed suit.

But Roosevelt was furious. Crane fanned the flames by sending Roosevelt a telegram stating that he would prefer charges against Becker for threatening to arrest him. With Crane the morning he sent the telegram was the *Journal*'s Frederick Lawrence, who had been part of the "Examiner's detective corps" in San

Francisco and as part of the *Journal* had traveled to Cuba to cover the rebellion before being thrown out. Lawrence reflected that after Crane sent Roosevelt the telegram, "an aroused and resentful police department bent all its unscrupulous energies to discrediting and making New York too hot for him to live in."[57]

Reflecting on his fluctuating reputation, Crane couldn't have been happy. A little less than a year earlier William Dean Howells had printed in *Harper's Weekly* a glowing review of *The Red Badge of Courage*. Favorable comparisons to Richard Harding Davis followed, and on November 19, 1895, Crane had bragged in a letter to his friend Willis Brooks Hawkins that he'd received from a Boston clipping bureau "forty-one new reviews of the Red Badge. And, oh, say, most of 'em were not only favorable but passionately enthusiastic." Crane had been on top of the world. Now it was all falling apart.[58]

Crane poured more oil on the fire by writing "Adventures of a Novelist," which the *Journal* published on September 20. In in it he detailed his side of the events that led to Dora Clark's arrest and his defense of her in court. Crane also excoriated Becker, painting him as a corrupt blackguard. The police raided Crane's studio apartment, turning up an opium pipe he'd kept as a souvenir, part of Crane's research in Chinatown and the Tenderloin for "Opium's Varied Dreams," syndicated the previous May. Allegations that Stephen Crane was an opium addict soon followed.

Crane ultimately decided not to press charges against Becker. Dora Clark pressed charges anyway. Feeling compelled to speak on her behalf, Crane testified in open court on October 15. But Becker's wily lawyer, Louis Grant, wasn't going to let Crane play the spotless hero. Referring to the scarlet lady who had claimed that Crane was her husband, Grant asked, "She is not your wife?"[59]

"No," Crane responded.

"Why did you say she was?"

"Because I know she was guiltless. It is impossible that she solicited, because she was under my protection. I felt bound to protect her."

Opium entered the picture when Grant asked if Crane smoked it. Despite Crane saying "No," some people believe there was hesitation before he denied it. Grant landed further points when he asked Crane if he ever lived at West 22nd. Dora Clark's lawyer, David M. Neuberger, advised Crane not to answer. Taking the attorney's advice, Crane said, "I refuse to answer."

"On what ground?" Grant asked.

"Because it would tend to degrade me," Crane admitted.

"Perhaps you think to answer this will tend to disgrace you. With whom did you live at such and such a place?"

Overwhelmed by the barrage of questions, Crane covered his face with his hands. Ultimately he admitted that the previous summer he had visited the prostitute Amy Leslie at her home at 121 West 27th Street. Damningly, the defense also produced a janitor, James O'Connor, who testified that the building Amy lived in was a brothel, the type where clients were commonly robbed, and that Crane had lived there for a month and a half. Although Crane's reputation was now mud, things went worse for Dora Clark. Under Grant's withering questions, she confessed to being a streetwalker, that her true name was Rubi Young, and that she was the mistress of a wealthy man staying at the Waldorf. Ultimately, at 2:30 a.m. on October 16, the court exonerated Becker.[60]

History took the side of Stephen Crane and Dora Clark, for Charles Becker's final act demonstrated himself to be one of the worst villains ever to call himself a New York City policeman. In 1912 Becker, promoted to the head of the Gambling Squad, and Herman Rosenthal, a notorious gambler, came to an agreement. Becker would turn a blind eye to the clandestine casino Rosenthal ran on West 45th Street and Broadway, and in return Becker would pocket 20 percent of the profits. Things went south after a man was killed during a raid on a dice game, prompting Rosenthal to spill to the *New York World* the details of the arrangement he and Becker had reached. Becker responded by hiring four gunmen to assassinate Rosenthal before the gambler could testify in court. On July 15, 1912, Rosenthal was gunned down on West 43rd Street and Broadway, just outside the Hotel Metropole. Before a month had passed all four assassins were captured and convicted, confessing that Becker had hired them. On July 30, 1915, Becker was placed in the electric chair. He was the first New York City policeman to be executed.[61]

None of that helped Stephen Crane. Despite newspapers all around the country largely taking his side, he knew that his name had suffered immeasurably. Even Roosevelt turned his back on Crane.

"I tried to save Crane from press comment," Roosevelt explained to Hamlin Garland, "but as he insisted on testifying I could only let the law take its course."[62]

Holding a grudge, after September 1896 Roosevelt never mentioned Crane's name in any of his writings, and no more invitations to lunch were ever sent. Roosevelt also let it be known that he was skeptical of Crane's story.

Crane didn't seem to blame Hearst for his troubles. Meeting with Hearst, Crane would later describe him in his novel *Active Service,* under the name

"Mr. Sturgeon" in his office: "He slid from the table and began to pace briskly to and fro, his hands deep in his trousers' pockets, his chin sunk in his collar, his light blue eyes afire with interest."[63]

As for his opinion of Hearst/Sturgeon, Crane wrote, "In reality he was some kind of a poet using his millions romantically."

Naturally, Hearst didn't hold the Dora Clark affair against Crane. On how to make a newspaper successful, Hearst later explained to an editor. "Get a lot of young people around you. Get rid of the blasé crowd. Get young people to whom it is not all dreary routine. Then GIVE THEM A CHANCE. Let them be young. Let them get excited. Do not repress them. Let them do things. Let them make a few mistakes. Maybe the public will LIKE the mistakes."[64]

Despite Hearst still liking him, Crane determined that things had become "too hot" for him in New York City. He didn't ask Hearst to transfer him to San Francisco, however. Instead, Crane took Irving Bacheller's offer, traveling a thousand miles south to Jacksonville, Florida, where the young author hoped to take a ship to Cuba. After all, war clouds were on the horizon.[65]

8

SILVER AND GOLD

Fighting Joe Wheeler strove to keep the good press going.

On September 19, 1895, four months after his electrifying speech at Shiloh, Wheeler delivered another oration at the dedication of Chickamauga Park at Chattanooga. He opened with a "patriotic prelude," as the *Scottsboro Citizen* recalled, honoring "American valor" and making clear that the soldiers "who once fought each other in deadly battle [are] now one people with one interest, one flag, one country and one ambition."[1]

The *Huntsville Argus*, the *Alabama Courier*, the *Chattanooga Times*, and the *Courtland Enterprise* all heaped praise on the congressman from Alabama, many reprinting the speech in full.[2]

The City of Atlanta went one better. When Atlanta opened the International Exposition that September, a bust of Wheeler was on display, furnished by the renowned sculptor William Rudolph O'Donovan, who had previously created statues of Ulysses S. Grant and Abraham Lincoln. But Wheeler knew that the sudden renewed interest in the American Civil War, courtesy of Stephen Crane's masterpiece, would only help him so much in next year's election. Rumor had it the Republicans might try something extracrafty this time. Instead of pitting a Republican against Wheeler, they were going to run a Democrat. The who of it was still cloaked in mystery, but the idea of it was dastardly enough to cause some to doubt whether Wheeler was up to the challenge.

Adroitly, Wheeler pivoted from making Civil War speeches to supporting the possibility of a future war, this one with Great Britain. The matter was the Venezuela Crisis, with both Venezuela and Great Britain claiming part of British Guiana as their own. Wheeler saw England's claim as a violation of the Monroe Doctrine and wasn't shy about saying so. In the November 1895 edition of the *North American Review,* Wheeler editorialized:

> We have always carefully abstained from any interference with these possessions of Great Britain, but to allow that nation to extend her territory on this hemisphere, either by treaty, or purchase, or conquest, or by the insidious encroachments which have characterized her dealings with Venezuela, the people of the United States should resist with all the power they possess. England fully understands that the principles announced by Mr. Monroe have become a settled policy of the United States, and as such must be considered and accepted as principles of international law.[3]

Wheeler went on to voice his belief that the United States should begin "the establishment of depots and naval stations" to protect American interests.[4]

The Venezuela Crisis escalated rapidly when on December 17, 1895, President Grover Cleveland—known as a stickler for law, however inconvenient—reaffirmed the Monroe Doctrine in an address to Congress, particularly in its relevance to the boundary dispute. "It is now incumbent upon the United States to take measures to determine . . . the true divisional line between the Republic of Venezuela and British Guiana. . . . When such report is made and accepted it will, in my opinion, be the duty of the United States to resist by every means in its power, as a willful aggression upon its rights and interests, the appropriation by Great Britain."[5]

Wheeler found unexpected allies in Hearst and Roosevelt.

Hearst's first foray into saber-rattling had occurred four years earlier, when he'd attempted to get the United States to choose a side during the Chilean Civil War. Hearst even went so far as to print on October 31, 1891, the bellicose headline "Chile Needs Whipping" alongside a front-page illustration of the entire US fleet. Of the twenty-three American ships, the most prominent included the *Oregon*, the *New York*, the *Texas,* and the *Maine.* With Hearst taking his show to New York City, on December 22, 1895, the *New York Journal* published an article (with illustrations) warning of where the Royal Navy might appear off Coney Island and—should the Venezuela Crisis hit a boiling point—shell Madison Square Garden.[6]

Roosevelt was equally belligerent.

"We are much interested in the outcome of the Venezuelan matter," Roosevelt wrote to his sister Anna's new husband, William Cowles, on the same day as Hearst's *Journal* article caused a stir on the East Coast. "I earnestly hope our government don't back down. If there is a muss I shall try to have a hand in it myself!"[7]

Roosevelt followed this up by writing to the editors of the *Harvard Crimson* on January 2, 1896. "If Harvard men wish peace with honor they will heartily . . . support the strictest application of the Monroe Doctrine; and will farther demand that immediate preparation be made to build a really first-class Navy."[8]

That Roosevelt, Hearst, and Wheeler advocated expanding the US Navy was largely due to the 557-page book *The Influence of Sea Power on History.* Published in 1890 by the president of the US Naval College, Captain Alfred Thayer Mahan, the treatise soon swept the world. Kaiser Wilhelm of Germany ordered a copy of the book placed aboard each ship in Germany's High Seas Fleet. Roosevelt devoured the book and became a devotee of Mahan, writing to the captain in early 1890 that "during the last two days I have spent half my time, busy as I am; in reading your book; and . . . have gone straight through and finished it. I can say with perfect sincerity that I think it very much the clearest and most instructive work of the kind." Hearst, whom the *Los Angeles Herald* called "a chip off the old block," followed in his father's footsteps, with the senator calling for an enlarged navy shortly after the publication of *The Influence of Sea Power on History.* Wheeler too saw wisdom in expanding the American fleet. Although he had always been a cavalryman—even writing the pocket-sized book *Revised System of Cavalry Tactics* in 1863—he recognized the importance of supremacy at sea.[9]

Unilateral negotiations ultimately allowed Venezuela, the United States, and Great Britain to save face, and the Venezuela Crisis simmered down later that January. But Wheeler, Roosevelt, and Hearst were not wholly appeased, continuing to push for a greater navy and a stricter enforcement of European encroachment in American waters.

With hostilities abating, Wheeler needed a different popular cause to champion. He found it through booming silver. Wheeler represented a largely agrarian population and was a plantation owner himself, sp this was a smart position for him to take. Although no one quite knew what would happen should silver join gold as the currency of the land, most financial experts believed that the elevation of silver would lead to the deflation of gold. This would have the dramatic effect of making farmers' loans—necessitated by the Panic of 1893—easier to repay. The cotton and silver states naturally cheered silver, while Wall Street viewed the Silverites and their champion, William Jennings Bryan, as exceptionally dangerous.

Even before the "Cross of Gold" speech rocked the Democratic National Convention in Chicago, Wheeler cast his lot with Bryan. This was a natural move, for along with the implementation of bimetallism rising in popularity in the South, Wheeler and Bryan were family friends. The day after Christmas 1895, Wheeler delivered his first major speech on silver on the floor of the Capitol building. He followed up that speech on February 6 and 13, 1896, and again on March 20. Although these orations made some noise in Washington, Wheeler knew they would have more effect in Alabama. Once again using the power of the press, he had thirty thousand copies of his March 20 speech distributed throughout the Cotton state, particularly in the Eighth District. Local newspapermen in particular loved both the speech and Wheeler's dash.

"We return thanks to Gen. Joseph Wheeler, the popular representative of North Alabama, for a copy of his excellent speech on the silver question," praised the *Hope Gazette.* "The people are with him on the question." Remarked the *National Tribune,* "Wheeler . . . is a favorite with the soldiers of both armies, and taken all in all, he enjoys a national reputation more enviable than that of any other member of the House."[10]

On April 4, 1896, Wheeler delivered another oration on the House floor, this one supporting the Cubans fighting the Spanish Empire.

"Spain, which at one time controlled two-thirds of this continent, and has been driven step by step till now she has only that beautiful island which to wreak her oppression—I believe that the sooner such a nation is driven from that island . . . the sooner Cuba becomes free and independent or a member of this great Commonwealth," Wheeler predicted, and "the sooner the cause of civilization and of Christianity receive the vindication to which it is entitled."[11]

Wheeler was not alone in his condemnation of the Spanish. Fred Lawrence's April 6 article in the *New York Journal,* detailing the butchery by Spanish soldiers of an all-female Cuban cavalry unit, dying bravely "amid bullets and machete strokes," inspired Wheeler's friend from Alabama, Senator John Tyler Morgan, to give a fiery speech in support of Cuba and the slain heroines. That Lawrence had made up the whole story was later pointed out by the *New York Herald*'s Cuban war correspondent, George Bronson Rea, but by then it was too late. Despite Rea calling Lawrence "deplorable" for this and other fakes, the stories gained momentum.[12]

Likewise, Murat Halstead's *Journal* articles advocating American annexation of Cuba had an effect. Calls for "Cuba Libre!" grew more and more prominent.

New York City's new police commissioner, Theodore Roosevelt, disagreed with Halstead on annexation but certainly favored military intervention. Beyond the fake news swirling around Cuba, Roosevelt recognized that the Spanish occupiers treated the Caribbean colony with wanton cruelty, implementing a program of *reconcentrado* (reconcentration). Under the Spanish reconcentration policy, hundreds of thousands of Cubans living in rural villages were placed into *reconcentrado* camps. The theory adopted by the Spanish general Don Valeriano Weyler was that sending swaths of the Cuban populace to the camps would impede the ability of the Cuban guerrillas to conduct an organized campaign against the Spanish. That thousands had starved to death in the camps did not weigh heavily on Weyler's conscience, but reports of such atrocities incited fury in the leading citizens of the United States.[13]

"We ought to drive the Spaniards out of Cuba; and it would be a good thing, in more ways than one, to do it," Roosevelt wrote to his sister Anna on March 30, 1896. "Congress ought to take more decisive action."[14]

Certainly by calling for American intervention, Wheeler was taking action. But President Cleveland had no wish to end his second term with a war, and with the vast majority of Congress seemingly unperturbed by rumors of Spanish atrocities against Cubans, the martial desire of Roosevelt, Wheeler, and Hearst fell on deaf ears. Suffering in Cuba continued unabated.

Josep Conangla i Fontanilles, a thirty-year-old native of Spain serving as a hospital assistant in the town of Aguacate, forty miles southeast of Havana, provided in his *Memoir of My Youth in Cuba* the clearest description of the misery of a *reconcentrado* camp.

> On the outskirts of Aguacate . . . there was a spacious, empty wood frame warehouse with a damaged, rotten roof. Half fallen down through neglect, it . . . may have served originally as a pen for cows or a storehouse for merchandise. . . . That warehouse, accordingly, was unsuitable for housing human beings, despite the fact that it was fitted out to take in a crushing jumble of unfortunate victims of the terrible reconcentration's first casualties.
>
> One afternoon, accompanied by other office workers, I wanted to see the real conditions of that appalling agglomeration of people all crammed together. And the shock of pity and indignation its horrendous scenes aroused in me was so intense that even now, sixty-two years later, my Christian soul still throbs with painful vibrations triggered by the same

> principled protests of moral indignation. That piling up of human beings was a scene out of Dante. Beaten down, weeping, half-naked and sick for the most part; some were dying, others lacking the most essential things for survival. Nonetheless, in brotherly fashion they shared the miserable victuals, clothes, blankets, or useful items that some of them had salvaged from their modest dwellings!
>
> Deeply affected in the presence of that horrible den of suffering—witness to the anguish of starving children and the cries of desperate mothers—from the depths of my conscience I cursed those responsible for such a detestable way of waging war. But then, feeling confused, pained, and humiliated in my human dignity by that inferno of barbaric cruelties, I left the horrendous building and walked with unsteady steps to the church/barracks.[15]

For red-blooded Americans who craved a war against an ancient empire with a medieval sense of morality, they had only to look ninety miles south of the Florida Keys.

But back in Alabama it was the silver issue that took center stage. The *Scottsboro Citizen* observed that Wheeler's distribution of his latest prosilver speech helped the prosilver Democratic gubernatorial nominee, Joseph F. Johnston, seize his party's nomination on April 13, 1896. If Johnston succeeded in winning the state election, which was exceedingly likely, having the new governor owing Wheeler a favor would be a nice feather in his cap.[16]

Beyond booming silver, Alabama farmers had another reason to appreciate Wheeler that spring. In January 1896 Julius Sterling Morton, one of the most hated agricultural secretaries in American history, abolished the practice of having seeds distributed gratis to farmers. Wheeler helped lead the popular charge against Morton, ultimately resulting in Congress passing a joint resolution that allowed for the distribution of seeds, though fewer than before. No matter. From Wheeler's own pockets he purchased $40,000 worth of seeds and had them sent to his constituents, ensuring that they had a good crop come harvest time.[17]

"The extreme norther tier of counties, called the Tennessee Valley, is one of the finest of farming sections," Wheeler bragged to the House on May 11, 1896. "It is watered by the Tennessee River. The farms are level and very fertile. Exceptionally fine."[18]

As for Wheeler's presence in Washington, having served in Congress for fourteen years, Fighting Joe was a common sight in the Capitol building, a particularly active member of the US House Committee of Ways and Means. Still spry at sixty years old, he walked as fast as he talked, as energetic as he had been during the Atlanta Campaign.

"Wheeler . . . is conspicuous for his rapid transit gait," lauded Carl Schofield in an article published in North Carolina's *Franklin Times* and various Pennsylvania newspapers. "Being a tireless worker and bubbling over with zeal, he dashes in and out of the House, through the corridors and into committee and office rooms with the speed of a record-breaking sprinter. So swift is his action that he has been nicknamed 'Maud S' after the famous trotter."[19]

As for Wheeler's southern drawl, there was no molasses in his delivery. In fact, Wheeler spoke so quickly that even the most experienced stenographers had difficulty taking down his remarks. Another characteristic of Wheeler was to address the House for "one minute" and then deliver an earnest and amazing barrage of words, filling pages of the *Congressional Record* in that "one-minute" oration. Rather than taking umbrage to Wheeler's eccentricities, most members of the House grew to enjoy his zeal. In short, Fighting Joe inspired amusement and respect rather than censure.[20]

Unfortunately for Wheeler, tragedy soon struck. In mid-May, Wheeler's wife of twenty years, Ella, took sick with appendicitis. The doctors performed an operation, but it became complicated by peritonitis. One comfort was that like Grant with his memoirs, Ella and Wheeler had finished the book they had lovingly crafted of their family tree before she grew too weak to continue. They dedicated the book to the only people likely to appreciate it: "To Our Dear Children." Wheeler also had copies of the book printed and distributed them gratis to libraries and historical societies throughout the South and the East Coast.

On May 19, 1896, Ella died in their Washington home at 1730 New Hampshire Avenue. She was only fifty-four years. Together she and Wheeler had raised six children to adulthood: Joe, Lucy, Annie, Julia, Tom, and Carrie. The funeral took place at the Wheeler home on May 21. In what must have been a particularly strange dichotomy of letter opening, the Wheeler household was subsequently inundated with letters of condolences and polite letters of acceptance from kind-hearted librarians.[21]

Wheeler had little time to grieve, for trouble was brewing back in Alabama. Once again he was facing a primary battle, Judge William Richardson having spent the last two years plotting how to best unseat Wheeler. Emulating Wheeler, Richardson now had support among a variety of newspapers, his chief party organ the *Huntsville Mercury*. Not since Wheeler called Jefferson Davis "president" had he such a fight on his hands.

With the election heating up, Wheeler finished his business in Washington. On the House floor he argued for lower taxes, called for six hundred thousand acres of public Alabama land to be set aside for schoolhouses, declared that the next president would be "a silver man," and added an appropriation to the River and Harbor Bill for $200,000 for the purpose of improving the rivers between Chattanooga and Riverton. Wheeler also claimed that only the Democratic Party was a "friend of farmers, laborers and bread earners." Traveling south, on July 4 Wheeler attended a picnic in Concord, attended by over a thousand people. Days later he debated with Richardson before a crowd of Democrats in Limestone County. Both Wheeler and Richardson delivered fine arguments, and though doubtless both men claimed victory, no one could be sure if the general or the judge would win the primary.[22]

On August 9, 1896, William T. Farley of Tuscumbia—thirty miles east of Wheeler's home, Pond Spring, in northern Alabama—gave him some advice in the form a handwritten letter. "Dear General! I think it would be well enough for now to spend another day in Tuscumbia, during the week—I believe Colbert is the battleground in this Contest."[23]

Farley's advice proved prophetic.

At 3 o'clock on the afternoon of August 21, 1896, the Colbert County Democratic Executive Committee met in Tuscumbia. Its purpose was to enroll delegates from several precincts to the County Convention, taking place the following day. But things went awry when twenty-six African American voters were refused being seated and have their votes counted. Richardson pounced, filing a protest that the African American votes needed to be counted.

If Wheeler thought this was bad, the events of August 22, 1896—election day—proved disastrous. Lawrence, Lauderdale, and Jackson went for Wheeler, and Madison, Limestone, and Morgan for Richardson. This was twenty-eight delegates for the judge and twenty-four for the general. But the primary wasn't over. It all came down to Colbert County, whose election seemed riddled with problems. Along with the twenty-six African Americans having been refused the right to vote, Richardson declared the elections in the nearby towns of Riverton, Leighton, and Cherokee illegal. In particular, Richardson claimed that he had proof that the election managers in Cherokee operated with no poll lists and no clerks and that a member of the county executive committee, Jasper Holseapple, traveled several miles from town and brought back in an envelope the names of twenty men, coincidentally all of whom voted for Wheeler.[24]

The result was complete chaos in northern Alabama.

As the weeks passed and lawyers and electors tried to figure out what happened and what to do, Wheeler and Richardson continued to battle each other in the press, each claiming victory. On September 1, Richardson proposed a new election. When Wheeler refused, Richardson's friends began calling for a "prorated" split rather than a "whole hog" winner-take-all election. In other words, Wheeler and Richardson would both battle the Republican challenger; should they win, they would share the congressional seat.[25]

Wheeler didn't like this, knowing that whoever the Republicans selected as the challenger would capitalize on the divided party. What's more, even should the Wheeler-Richardson ticket prevail, it was a certainty that if two congressmen from Alabama's Eighth District showed up to Capitol Hill they would both be made laughingstocks and sent home to get their elections in order. Recognizing this, the Wheeler and Richardson adherents decided that the only fair thing to do was to have one more election in Colbert County, may the best Confederate win. The election was scheduled for Saturday, September 26.

"The long continued agony is rapidly drawing to a close," commented the *Leighton News* on election day. "As we go to press the battle of ballots in the Richardson-Wheeler contest is raging fiercely all over the county. Ere this paper reaches many of its out-of-town readers, the battle will have been fought and victory be perching on the banner of Judge or the General."[26]

The next day all of the ballots were tallied, and victory was declared. Unless he lost the election to his Republican challenger, General Wheeler would be returned to Congress. The likelihood is that Colbert County remembered how earnestly Fighting Joe had fought for them.[27]

A few days later on October 2, 1896, the Democratic state senator of Alabama's Madison County, thirty-one-year-old Oscar Hundley, emerged as the Republican's champion to unseat Wheeler. Immediately, the newspapers predicted a tough fight.

"Gen. Wheeler has just emerged from a heated campaign with Judge Richardson for the Democratic nomination, and he is in no physical condition to engage in another joint canvas," commented Nashville's *Tennessean*.[28]

Hundley, who was a child when the Civil War began, didn't have Wheeler's recognition as a veteran on his side, but Hundley's father, Orville, had fought in the war. In fact, Orville had served as a colonel under Wheeler. Hundley himself earned a law degree from Vanderbilt University, which he put to good use, serving as an attorney for the Nashville, Chattanooga & St. Louis Railway. The Alabama House of Representatives and the Alabama Senate followed. Descended from a line of plantation owners, Hundley proved as wealthy as he was conspicuous, made more so when President Benjamin Harrison appointed him as a commissioner to the Chicago World's Fair. Then in 1896, with his sights on the Eighth District, Hundley joined with the Republicans. Along with having support among some Democrats, Hundley also had access to the Republican war chest. He made things especially lively by contributing $10,000 of his own money. Said to enjoy the support of both parties and being independently wealthy, Hundley promised to be a formidable adversary.[29]

For the next month Wheeler made a canvas of northern Alabama while his allies in the press continued to sing his praises. Jackson, Paint Rock, Hollytree, and Estill's Fork (present-day Estillfork) all witnessed Fighting Joe stumping for silver, Johnston, Bryan, and, of course, himself.[30]

Of these three candidates, all of them looked pretty good. Wheeler had a long track record of success, Johnston had his Civil War record and experience as president of the Sloss Iron & Steel Company, and Bryan had William Randolph Hearst.

With the *Journal* the only Democratic paper in New York supporting Bryan, Hearst pulled out all the stops. With Tammany Hall refusing to endorse Bryan, Hearst made the *Journal* newsroom Bryan's campaign headquarters. Hearst also printed a weekly "campaign extra," distributed gratis by free silver advocates. Furthermore, Hearst began a subscription drive, pledging to match each dollar raised with *Journal* money.[31]

The *New York Journal* painted Bryan as the country's only savior and William McKinley as a bloated capitalist and a clown. Appearing almost daily, front-page Davenport cartoons lampooned McKinley as a grotesquely obese puppet of the trusts, pulled by the strings of Republican boss Mark Hanna, festooned with dollar signs. When in August Hearst received communication from the German chancellor, Otto von Bismarck, Hearst published it for the world to see: "I hold to this very hour that it would be advisable to bring about between the nations chiefly engaged in the world's commerce, mutual agreement in favor of the establishment of bimetallism."[32]

Considering the campaign fourteen years later, Hearst reflected that the *Journal* was "like a solitary ship surrounded and hemmed in by a host of others, and from all sides shot and shell poured into our devoted hulk. Editorial guns raked us, business guns shattered us, popular guns battered us, and above the din and flame of battle rose the curses of the Wall Street crowd that hated us. . . . Advertisers called on me and said they would take out every advertisement if I continued to support Bryan, and I told them to take out their advertisements, as I needed more space in which to support Bryan."[33]

As for Theodore Roosevelt, the police commissioner looked at Bryan and his backers with trepidation. "If Bryan wins, we have before us some years of social misery," Roosevelt wrote on August 5 to his friend Cecil Spring Rice, "not markedly different than that of a South American Republic."[34]

Meanwhile, thirty-six-year-old Bryan cut a swath through the Midwest, politicking with inexhaustible energy. McKinley, on the other hand, conducted a "front porch" campaign from his home in Canton, Ohio. Bryan felt that his own strategy was more sound.

"I have no doubt of my election," Bryan wired Hearst in October, "and I base my confidence upon the fact that the free coinage sentiment is growing every day."[35]

Roosevelt felt differently. On October 8 he wrote Spring Rice: "I think the tide has turned here as regards Bryan. . . . The Bryanites have . . . the men who pray for anarchy . . . and who have been inflamed against the rich until they feel they are willing to sacrifice their own welfare, if they can make others less happy . . . but the higher class, including the immense mass of the railroad employees, are for us."[36]

In Alabama, Wheeler did his best to channel the flood of emotion the other way. On October 20 he distributed a circular on Washington, D.C., letterhead and addressed to "My Dear Friend." In it he declared, "The prosperity and welfare of this district for many years depends on our success. . . . [W]e must elect a Congress favorable to silver coinage. . . . I earnestly appeal to you to use your active influence in support of that noble champion of the people, WM. J. BRYAN, and also in support of myself in the election."[37]

On November 3, 1896, the nation went to the polls. Wheeler and Johnston had a good night. Despite Hundley running as essentially a Republican and a Democrat, his support proved insignificant to Wheeler's base, and Fighting Joe was reelected in strength. The Democrats also did well in New York City. According to poll analysis, 80 percent of German American voters traded the Republicans for the Democrats, resulting in landslide victories for Tammany Hall. Many members of the Grand Old Party narrowed their eyes at Police Commissioner Roosevelt, whose unpopular enforcement of the Sunday Excise Law did nothing to help their cause.[38]

As for Bryan, the *Journal* made sure that the election results were tallied in an entertaining manner for New Yorkers. Along with their standard morning issue, for election day the *Journal* put forth an evening edition as well. On its front page the *Journal* announced that "Colored Electric Lights from a Monster Balloon Will Flash the News to Greater New York and Jersey. If a Red Light Twinkles, Bryan is Leading; if Green, McKinley. Steady Red Glow Means Bryan Elected; Green, McKinley Wins. All Over the City Will Be the Journal's Bulletins, with Bands of Music, Stereopticons and Moving Pictures Showing Wonderful Views."[39]

"It was the most remarkable sight ever witnessed in New York," Richard Harding Davis wrote to his brother Charles.[40]

To Davis's delight, the *Journal*'s "Monster Balloon" ultimately glowed green. Bryan had carried twenty-two states—one of them Alabama—to McKinley's twenty-three. The states that went Republican had far greater populations, resulting in McKinley winning the popular vote 7,112,138 to 6,510,807 and the electoral vote 271 to 176. Most voters had concluded that they preferred the safety of gold to the insecurity of silver and therefore McKinley over Bryan.

By his own count, along with failing to launch the Boy Orator into the White House, Hearst lost $158,000 by booming Bryan. But newspapermen throughout the country agreed that it had been well worth the cost. Hearst's over-the-top election coverage—along with his patented brand of sensationalism, now called "yellow journalism" by the wits who knew they were seeing history being made—led to more people than ever buying copies of the *Journal.* On November 5, two days after the election, the *Journal* proudly trumpeted that by combining the circulation of Hearst's three New York newspapers—the morning *Journal,* the evening *Journal,* and the German *Das Morgen Journal*—the circulation had soared past 1.5 million. This was an accomplishment not even Pulitzer had achieved.[41]

As for Wheeler, the following year he found himself in the rare position of suffering bad press in Alabama. This occurred shortly after he introduced a bill that, if passed, would make it legal to sell homemade spirits without paying any tax. Poking fun, the *Bridgeport News* quickly dubbed him "Moonshine Joe," while the *Sheffield Record* commented that "Gen. Wheeler is now after the 'moonshine' support," and the *Bridgeport News* sniped that "the people who have been at a loss to know what excuse Gen. Wheeler will offer for his return to congress again can now satisfy their curiosity."[42]

The *Scottsboro Progressive Age* was much harsher.

"We are decidedly in favor of a change, just for the novelty of it," opined a Scottsboro reporter. "The General owns most of the newspaper organs which support him, or has a string of them, which gives him control of them. Hence they never tire of singing his praise." The reporter went on to say that by canvasing the Eighth District for a man of substance, the general could easily be defeated.[43]

With Wheeler's newspaper jiggery-pokery common knowledge and with Republicans controlling the House, Senate, and the Executive Branch, Wheeler must have worried that he'd be primaried once again and this time might just lose his seat. But if the momentum to support Cuba against Spain caught fire, as Wheeler, Roosevelt, and Hearst fervently wished, the midterm elections of 1898 would soon be subordinate to a different battle. And if all went just so, Fighting Joe Wheeler would be right in the thick of it.

— 9 —

SUNK

On November 28, 1896, Stephen Crane—going under the assumed name "Samuel Carleton"—registered at the St. James Hotel in Jacksonville, Florida. Famous for *The Red Badge of Courage* and crossing the New York City police, the young author evidently wanted to keep his presence out of the papers. But having just arrived in the city, he'd be damned if he didn't check out the waterfront saloons.[1]

Charley Michelson, on assignment for Hearst, took stock of Crane. Whereas the other would-be war correspondents could be found lounging around the hotel or talking shop in the cafés, Crane stuck to the seedier side of the street.

"Crane always disappeared on his arrival at a new town," Michelson recalled. "He dived into the deep waters of society and stayed under. Night after night Stephen loitered in the back room of a grimy waterfront saloon." Michelson figured that Crane preferred the waterfront because there his name would likely be unfamiliar to the "oilers, deck hands, sponge fisherman, wharf-rats and dock thieves, and all the rest of the human flotsam."[2]

The day after arriving in Jacksonville, Crane—anticipating that a filibustering vessel would take him to war-torn Cuba—wrote out a will and mailed it to his brother William. On the event of Crane's death, the brothers would split his money, one-third to William, one-third to Edmund, one-sixth to George, and one-sixth to Townley. Crane also sent $500 to his friend Willis Brooks Hawkins to take care of Amy Leslie's living and medical expenses. Amy, who had shared the train south with Crane as far as Washington, D.C., now claimed she was pregnant. Whether she was truly pregnant or whether she was angling for a marriage proposal or money for the abortion went unrecorded. Nor did Amy tell her tubercular lover about Isidor Siesfeld, another man with whom she was having a tryst.[3]

"There is not one man in three thousand who can be a real counsellor and guide for a girl so pretty as Amy," Crane wrote Hawkins.[4]

Amy stayed on the forefront of Crane's mind until one fall day when, having realized it would be some time before he could take ship to Cuba, Crane strolled down Jacksonville's bustling red light district and on the corner of Ashley and Hawk entered a popular bordello: the Hotel De Dreme. There Crane met the madame of the place, Cora. Bottle-blonde, sexually experienced, and six years older than twenty-five-year-old Crane, Cora proved just his type.[5]

As a token of his affection, on December 4 Crane presented Cora with a copy of Rudyard Kipling's newest book, *The Seven Seas*; his own *George's Mother*, which he inscribed to "an unnamed sweetheart"; and a further book, lost to history, on which he wrote

> To C. E. S. [Cora Ethel Stewart]
>
> Brevity is an element that enters importantly into all pleasures of life and this is what makes pleasure sad and so there is no pleasure but only sadness.
>
> Stephen Crane
> Jacksonville, Fla
> Nov 4th, 1896.[6]

That Crane wrote down the wrong month, switching December for November, perhaps an indication that amid the abundance of liquor, cigarettes, sex, and possibly opium, his senses were somewhat dulled in Jacksonville.

Cora, a Bostonian who had moved to New York City at age fifteen when her father died and was orphaned shortly afterward, was no stranger to fleeting romances. She became the mistress of Jerome Strivers, a notorious cad who lived off his father's carriage-manufacturing business, and the pair carried on a licentious four-year relationship, living in the London Club, an infamous Tenderloin gambling hall. After the relationship ran its course, twenty-one-year-old Cora married a dry goods merchant, Thomas Vinton Murphy, before trading Murphy for an English captain, Donald William Stewart, the two tying the knot in London.

Three years later having ended the relationship but not the marriage, Cora was back in Gotham, this time stroking the ego of Ferris S. Thompson, son of the founder of the First National Bank of the City of New York. Thompson and "Lady" Stewart traveled to Europe, luxuriating in Constantinople and living it up along the Orient Express. Things went rapidly south when Thompson began dallying with a Parisian actress, prompting Cora to stab Thompson in the arm. With Cora returning to the United States, Captain Stewart reentered the picture, suing Thompson for seducing his wife. The case was dismissed. Later that year Cora drifted to Jacksonville, where she began leasing the Hotel De Dreme, one of the ritziest bordellos in the city.[7]

"Sometimes I like to sit at home and read good books," Cora wrote, "at others I must drink absinthe and hang the night hours with scarlet embroideries. I must have music and the sings that march to music. These are moments when I desire squalor."[8]

Crane had found his soulmate.

Crane's newest love affair was interrupted when word came that Secretary of the Treasury John G. Carlisle had authorized the *Commodore* to set sail for Cuba. Gaining passage aboard the ship, on the afternoon of New Year's Day Crane watched seven African American stevedores load boxes of ammunition and bundles of rifles into the hatch while Cuban patriots looked on, singing patriotic songs. Crane, who had always tried to keep his own illicit actions from prying eyes, marveled at the lack of secrecy.

"Everything was perfectly open," Crane noted. "The Commodore was cleared with a cargo of arms and munitions for Cuba. . . . She loaded up as placidly as if she were going to carry oranges to New York, instead of Remingtons to Cuba. Down the river, furthermore, the revenue cutter Boutwell, the old isosceles triangle that protects the United States interests in the St. John's, lay at anchor, with no sign of excitement aboard her."[9]

A couple hours after sunset on New Year's Eve, the steamer was ready to launch. Between the crew and the Cuban filibusters, about twenty-five men populated the *Commodore*. Stephen Crane was listed as a seaman, supposedly earning $20 a month. The ship's captain was Edward Murphy, an Irishman who two months earlier had been tried in Philadelphia for violating the neutrality laws of the United States and Spain, that is, smuggling weapons from aboard the *Laurada* to Cuban rebels. Set free, Captain Murphy was looking to once again aid the Cuban cause. Although not listed officially, the steamer was laden with a number of Remingtons, three hundred machetes, two hundred thousand cartridges, and a thousand pounds of gunpowder, more than enough to accidentally blow the *Commodore* sky-high.[10]

After what Crane described as "a tumult of goodbys" in two languages and three long blasts from her steam whistle, the *Commodore* launched at 8 p.m., the lights of Jacksonville growing dim in the distance.

"Then at last we began to feel like filibusters," Crane recalled.[11]

It proved an inauspicious start. Rendered blind by a heavy fog off the St. James River, at Commodore's Point—less than two miles from the port—the steamer hit a sandbar, the hull running aground. The *Boutwell* soon arrived to drag the steamer out of the mud. It may be that because Captain Murphy was more familiar with the *Laurada* and had never been aboard the *Commodore* before, he failed to order a complete inspection of the hull. Attempting the journey once again, sometime after dawn on January 1 the *Commodore* once again ran aground, this time beaching at Mayport.

"The Boutwell was fussing around us in her venerable way, and, upon seeing our predicament, she came again to assist us," Crane recalled, "but this time, with engines reversed, the Commodore dragged herself away from the grip of the sand and again headed for the open sea."[12]

Seeing this, Captain Gilgore called out from the deck of the *Boutwell*, "Are you fellows going to sea to-day?"

"Yes, sir," Captain Murphy answered.

As the *Commodore*'s whistle saluted him, Captain Kilgore doffed his cap and said, "Well, gentlemen, I hope you have a pleasant cruise."

As the crew of the *Commodore* steamed south, smuggling weapons and ammunition to help the insurgent Cubans fight the Spanish army, Crane may have reflected on the conflict in Cuba. A student of the American Civil War, Crane was probably aware that Jefferson Davis, the US senator from Mississippi and future president of the Confederacy, had been an early proponent of an American invasion of the Caribbean island.

On May 5, 1848, Senator Davis had announced in the Capitol building that "Yucatán and Cuba are the salient points commanding the Gulf of Mexico, which I hold to be a basin of water belonging to the United States. . . . I am ready, for one, to declare that my steps will be forward, and that the cape of Yucatán and the island of Cuba must be ours."[13]

Davis's speech attracted the attention of Narciso López, one of the boldest filibusters on the planet. Born in Caracas, Venezuela, on November 2, 1797, López initially joined the *revolucionarios* in the Venezuelan War of Independence, fighting the Spanish. In 1814 López switched sides when pressed into the royalist forces, only to grow resentful of the Spanish after taking a Cuban wife and mixing with the oppressed Cuban populace. Before long "Cuba Libre" was on his lips and in his heart.[14]

After Jefferson Davis and Brevet Colonel Robert E. Lee declined López's request to lead an invasion of Cuba, López determined he would do it himself. In 1850 he attracted an army of six hundred southern adventurers, composed of Mississippians, Kentuckians, and Louisianans. The filibusters surprised the port city of Cárdenas, raising their flag over the Governor's Mansion but failing to rouse the Cuban populace against the Spanish. Reinforcement from Havana soon caused them to sail back to Key West, one step ahead of a Spanish man-of-war.[15]

In 1851, López tried it again. From New York City he cobbled together a 548-man army consisting of Germans, Irish, Italians, Poles, Scots, English, French, Canadians, Filipinos, Hungarians, and Colonel William Logan Crittenden, a veteran of the Mexican-American War and a West Pointer whose uncle served as the attorney general of the United States. López's second invasion proved even more disastrous. After López split the army, Crittenden and his forces were quickly captured. On August 16, Crittenden and thirty-nine other would-be liberators were shot to death in Havana before a crowd of twelve hundred.[16]

López wasn't captured until August 27. At 7 a.m. on September 1, 1851, López was seated in an iron chair in a Havana plaza, the metal collar of the garotte fitted around his neck. To the crowd of four thousand López declared, "My death will not change the destiny of Cuba." The executioner turned the screw twice, tightening the collar. News of Narciso López's execution by the Spanish quickly spread around the world.[17]

There was a message there that Stephen Crane could plainly read. Describing himself as an "inexperienced filibuster," he knew that his celebrity as an author wouldn't save him if he were caught aboard a ship smuggling weapons to Cuban revolutionaries. Like López and Crittenden, if captured Crane might very well end up garroted or shot to death before a Spanish firing squad.

Having had a sleepless night, Crane tried to sleep in the first mate's empty bunk. This proved fruitless, for every time the ship lurched, Crane imagined being shot. Eventually he visited the galley, inadvertently waking the cook, Charles B. Montgomery, who was resting on a bench.

"God," Montgomery said, "I don't feel right about this ship, somehow. It strikes me that something is going to happen to us. I don't know what it is, but the old ship is going to get it in the neck, I think."[18]

"Well, how about the men on board of her?" Crane asked. "Are any of us going to get out, prophet?"

"Yes," Montgomery answered. "Sometimes I have these damned feelings come over me, and they are always right, and it seems to me, somehow, that you and I will both get and meet again somewhere, down at Coney Island perhaps, or some place like that."

Crane next visited the pilothouse. Tom Smith, whom Crane recalled as an "old seaman" from Charleston with "weatherbeaten features," had the wheel.

"Well, Tom, how do you like filibustering?" Crane asked.

"I think I am about through with it," Tom replied. "I've been in a number of these expeditions and the pay is good, but I think if I ever get back safe this time I will cut it."

Crane was drowsing in a corner of the pilothouse when Captain Murphy entered. Shortly afterward the chief engineer burst in and told the captain that there was something wrong in the engine room. The crew quickly determined that the *Commodore* had not only lost power but was also taking on water. Having traveled one hundred miles south from Jacksonville, they were only about sixteen miles from the Florida coast, the nearest strip of land Mosquito Inlet, later renamed Ponce de Leon Inlet, but if they didn't act fast they'd never see land again.

Efforts to restart the engine failed. Murphy broke his arm, which was set in a sling. Crane joined in the line bailing water. When he began to slip on the wet, uneven deck, he took off his shoes and threw them into the sea.

"Well, Captain, I guess I won't need them if we have to swim," Crane said to Murphy.[19]

Before dawn on January 2, Captain Murphy gave the order to abandon ship. Three lifeboats were quickly launched. After taking a five-pound water jug from Murphy, Crane boarded a ten-foot dinghy, along with Murphy, Billy Higgins, the oiler, and Montgomery, the cook who had prophesized the *Commodore*'s doom. Things grew more dire when the third lifeboat foundered, forcing the four men aboard the lifeboat to return to the sinking *Commodore*. One of the men, crazed with despair, threw himself into the sea without a lifejacket. At 7 a.m. the *Commodore* sank and with it three more men. Efforts to save the men proved futile.

The dinghy and two surviving lifeboats paddled toward dry land. Aboard the dinghy Crane, Higgins, and Montgomery took turns rowing, as Murphy was unable due to his broken arm. All they had for nourishment was the five-pound jug of water. With the gunwales only six inches above the waterline, the threat of sinking was on everyone's mind. Nine hours after the sinking of the *Commodore*, at

4 p.m. the dinghy was only a few miles south of Daytona. But between rough seas, the wind, and the breakers, they knew they had little chance of making it to land before the dinghy capsized. Signaling their need for help, they fired a pistol into the air. Apparently the beachgoers mistook this for playfulness, for they sent no aid.

Things went better for the two remaining lifeboats. The first lifeboat, with twelve Cubans aboard, landed safely. Not long afterward the second lifeboat, carrying four Cubans, landed as well. Word quickly spread that the *Commodore* had sunk and that Crane was believed dead.[20]

"I am very sorry that I have no encouraging word to send you," a friend wrote to Cora on January 2. "The eleven men who were saved have arrived in town. . . . God save Crane if he is still alive."[21]

Crane and the other three men *were* still alive aboard the dinghy, but they knew that their strength would soon give out. On the morning of January 3, having given up on any chance of rescue, they decided to make a desperate push for shore. With only two lifejackets among them, Murphy decided the jackets should go to the weakest swimmers: Crane and Montgomery. Murphy likely thought that his own chances of survival, with his broken arm, were almost nil, deciding against wasting a lifejacket on himself.[22]

In the breakers of Daytona Beach, the dinghy capsized. A large wave caught Crane and threw him over the boat. Desperately, Crane swam for shore. A man on the beach recognized their peril. He first dragged Crane from the surf, then Montgomery and Murphy.

"Thanks, old man," Crane said. But the mood was spoiled when they caught sight of Billy Higgins.[23]

"In the low water, face down, lay the oiler," Crane recalled. Despite being the strongest swimmer, Higgins had evidently been knocked in the head when the dinghy capsized and had drowned.[24]

The news quickly spread that Stephen Crane had survived the sinking of the *Commodore*. Edward Marshall, the twenty-seven-year-old Sunday editor of the *New York Journal*, sent a wire: "Congratulations on plucky and successful fight for life."

Hearing on January 3 that her lover was still alive, Cora cabled Crane. "Thank God your safe have been almost crazy."[25]

Crane's response to Cora was poetical. "Love comes like the tall swift shadow of a ship at night. There is for a moment, the music of the water's turmoil, a bell, perhaps, a man's shout, a row of gleaming yellow lights. Then the slow sinking of this mystic shape. Then silence a bitter silence—the silence of the sea at night."[26]

Cora hungered for more than just poetry. Leaving the Hotel De Dreme to fend for itself, the next morning she caught a train for Daytona, arriving around noon. Stealing away to a private corner of the train station, Cora and Crane passionately embraced.[27]

With the front-page publication in the *New York Press* of "Stephen Crane's Own Story" on January 7, followed by "The Open Boat" in the June 1897 edition of *Scribner's Magazine,* Crane's reputation as a writer was once again on the rise. As happy as Crane was to have survived the shipwreck, he must have been equally jubilant to have undergone such a metamorphosis in the media. In a flash he'd gone from opium-addicted whoremonger to filibustering adventurer.

Crane was not unique in being able to transform himself, of course, for the 1890s was an age when personal transformations could frequently take place, made possible through the branching media—newspapers, magazines, books—becoming more prevalent and powerful than ever. The media mastery of the other pivotal figures in the coming war—Roosevelt, Wheeler, Davis, and Hearst—was evident.

Even while absorbed in the role of deputy sheriff in Dakota Territory, Roosevelt had brought along his camera, eager to shape his personal narrative as that of a hero. On a much grander scale, Roosevelt utilized a small battalion of writers to cast him as a great reformer and a larger-than-life police commissioner in New York City. Likewise, Wheeler transformed himself from a defeated Confederate, parroting the position of the Lost Cause, to a champion of a reunited America, trumpeted through the newspapermen he greased with favors and federal positions. Davis too, could have been stuck as the foolish Johnstown reporter. Instead, he remade himself into an action reporter in New York City, then kept the momentum going with a furious amount of publishing activity, exemplifying the adage "success begets success." And Hearst, who could have lived an easy life as a San Francisco playboy, transformed himself into a highly influential bicoastal newspaper proprietor, revitalizing and reshaping the newspaper industry in his own bombastic image.

That Hearst's addictive yellow journalism—light on the facts but filled with eye-popping narratives—signified danger was academically acknowledged, though mostly on an existential level. Sure, his compelling newspaper style helped blur the lines between truth and fiction, but few ordinary people seemed to care so long as the entertainment value was high.

After all, so long as Hearst didn't dream up a way of starting a war, what was the harm?

—10—

FURNISHING THE PICTURES

Coming to an agreement with Hearst—to report on the Cuban rebels for the *New York Journal* for one month, for the price of $3,000—Richard Harding Davis left for Key West on December 19, 1896. Although everything was bound to go wrong, to Davis it initially seemed like a lark.

"I have bought at *The Journal*'s expense a fifty dollar field glass which is a new invention and the best made," Davis wrote his family. "I have marked it so that you can see a man five miles off."[1]

Davis also met with two Hearst men: Charley Michelson, who remained one of the Chief's favorites, and Frederic Remington, among the finest living American artists.

"Already we are firm friends," Davis related.

The problem was lack of transportation to the island. A couple of days after Davis and the others reached Key West, Hearst attempted to remedy this issue by loaning the trio his own racing yacht, the *Vamoose,* a 110-foot-long vessel with a ten-foot beam.

"The *Vamoose* was scheduled to haul anchor the day after Christmas, but that day the crew went on strike, explaining that they were afraid they would be arrested. I don't know what they would have done had they known they were going further," Davis wrote home.

Finally, on the night of December 30 the *Vamoose* sailed south, manned by a new crew.

"A few hours after the *Vamoose* had left Key West a heavy storm arose—apparently much too violent for the slightly built launch," Charles Belmont Davis noted.

Remington provided different details. Clinging to the rail, Davis and Remington hung on for dear life. As they did so, they watched the Chinese cook construct a makeshift raft out of a door and some boxes. Davis suggested that they emulate the wily cook.

"Lie still," Remington told him. "You and I don't know how to do that. Let him make his raft. If we capsize, I'll throttle him and take it from him."[2]

At nearly three hundred pounds, Remington probably could have made good the threat. But as luck had it, the Chinese cook wasn't the only one convinced that the ship was about to sink. Despite the captain wishing to sail on, after only twenty miles the crew mutinied. Caught between the devil and the deep blue sea, the captain declared the *Vamoose* unseaworthy, allowing that they should return to the Florida Keys.

In frustration, Davis lay on the deck, tears filling his eyes.

"Guess I am done with the Journal forever," he wired his mother from dry land.[3]

Rebecca Davis prayed that would be the case. She was terrified that her son would suffer an untimely death as a war correspondent, shot to death or stricken with yellow fever. Davis had already told his mother in capital letters that "THERE IS NOT FEVER THIS TIME OF YEAR" and that "Santa Clara province . . . is no more Spanish than New Jersey and the Spaniards can't get in there." But as Charles Belmont Davis related, this did not curb the family's uneasiness. They became more troubled when they received Richard Harding Davis's New Year's day letter explaining Hearst's latest instructions.

"Now do cheer up and believe in the luck of Richard Harding Davis and the British Army," Davis wrote. "We have carte blanche from The Journal to buy or lease any boat on the coast and I rocked them for $1,000 advanced payment because of the delay over the Vamoose."

Even still, finding a ship proved an arduous task. While Michelson futilely scoured the docks, Davis whiled away the days. Davis would begin a typical morning by plunging shirtless into the bay. Afterward he dressed, ate a greasy breakfast, and then lit a huge three-cent Havana cigar while lounging on the hotel porch and having his shoes shined. Checking in at the cable office, Davis would find Michelson sending telegrams. Returning to the hotel, Davis studied Spanish. At three o'clock he rode a bicycle to meet the garrison's doctor and his wife, dining with the couple. Near sunset, Davis rode to the bay for another plunge. Freshening up and donning a dress suit, he took the launch to the US cruiser *Raleigh*, docked nearby. Admiring the fresh paint and brass, Davis smoked and played guitar on the quarterdeck. From aboard the *Raleigh* on the evening of January 1, 1897, Davis made a speech, with the crew happy to be spellbound by the famous author.

"The hero of our dreams was Richard Harding Davis," reflected H. L. Mencken.[4]

But Davis's celebrity wasn't helping him reach Cuba. Writing to his family on January 2, Davis complained, "I don't know when we shall get away, but it is no use kicking about it, Michaelson [*sic*] is doing all he can and the new tug will be along in a week anyway. I shall be so glad to get to Cuba that I will dance with glee."[5]

Soon after came the tragic news that the *Commodore* had sunk. Doubtless Rebecca added fear of her son drowning to the list of her Cuban worries. Shortly afterward, Davis ran into another of Hearst's employees in a barbershop: Ralph D. Paine.

Like Davis, Paine was the epitome of what a dashing newspaperman was supposed to be: six feet tall, muscular (having played football and rowed crew at Yale), and a brilliant wordsmith, paying for college through his early journalism in Jacksonville and Asbury Park. But Paine had struck out while working for Hearst. In early December 1896 Hearst had given Paine a ceremonial sword, worth $2,000, that the young millionaire had entrusted Paine to hand-deliver to General Máximo Gómez. Though Paine endured several adventures while on the high seas, he failed to reach Cuba. Ultimately he gave up and delivered the sword to a revolutionary with whom Gómez was friendly, José Alejandro Huau, who eventually shipped the sword to Gómez's wife in San Domingo.[6]

Davis found Hearst's tactics deplorable. "This new journalism is beyond my finding out," Davis wrote home on January 4. "It is not news they want. They send Gómez a two-thousand-dollar sword and two medicine chests and a keg of rum . . . and then the Journal publishes pictures of the sword and the *Vamoose* and the other fake freaks, and lets the news be written in the office or Key West."[7]

Adding to their aggravation, Davis and Remington scuttled their hopes of renting their own vessel to Cuba, instead booking passage aboard the *Olivette*, a passenger liner that traveled to Havana. At long last, the celebrated author and artist reached the Cuban capital.[8]

"They have segars to burn in this city and good food but it is not an interesting city," Davis declared of Havana.[9]

The day after they reached Havana, Davis and Remington met with the American consul general, sixty-one-year-old Fitzhugh Lee, who had served as a Confederate brigadier general and was a nephew of Robert E. Lee. Lee introduced them to the Spanish general Don Valeriano Weyler. Fresh from celebrating his men having killed General Maceo, the Bronze Titan, in a skirmish about a hundred miles east of Havana on December 7, Weyler was at his best around the famous and influential yanquis.

This was an act, of course. Weyler—a veteran of the Ten Years' War, the Carlist Wars, the Moorish War, and the uprising in the Philippines—knew the power of the press and took pains to keep Davis believing him to be merely an upright soldier. James Creelman, who knew Weyler better, described him as being "the most sinister figure of the nineteenth century," with cold gray eyes and "a smileless, cruel face." Other *Journal* reporters commonly referred to him as "El Coyote" and "Butcher" Weyler.[10]

Josep Conangla, still serving as a hospital assistant in Aguacate in January 1897, related a firsthand account in his memoir, demonstrating that if Creelman and the *Journal* exaggerated it wasn't by much:

> Within two days of learning about the death of Maceo . . . Captain-General Weyler suddenly arrived in the town preceded by a vanguard of cavalry. . . . Some of the flags raised because of Maceo's death were hurriedly raised again at the agitated instigation of the authorities. . . . Although Weyler's passage through Aguacate was brief, it prevented the majority of inhabitants from leaving their houses, nor did they appear at their doors, fearful that curiosity alone could provoke the well-known angry outbursts of the intolerant despot.[11]

Playing the considerate host, Weyler extended Davis and Remington an invitation to accompany him on his next campaign or to travel the island with his blessing so long as they didn't join the insurgents. Intending to clandestinely join the insurgents the first chance he got, Davis decided to visit a sugar plantation in Cienfuegos, 160 miles as the crow flies southeast of Havana.[12]

Around January 12, Remington determined that he'd had enough of this Cuban misadventure. The month they'd promised Hearst was up, after all.[13] According to Creelman in his 1901 autobiography, *On the Great Highway: The Wanderings and Adventures of a Special Correspondent,* Remington then cabled the Chief:

> W. R. Hearst, New York *Journal*, N.Y.:
>
> Everything is quiet. There is no trouble here. There will be no war. I wish to return. Remington.[14]

Hearst cabled back:

> Remington, Havana:
>
> Please remain. You furnish the pictures, and I'll furnish the war.
>
> W. R. Hearst.[15]

In 1907 a reporter for the *Times of London* read the passage in Creelman's autobiography and asked, "Is the Press of the United States going insane?" A newspaper proprietor sending sensational correspondents to cover a war was one thing; a newspaper proprietor starting a war was quite another. At least it was supposed to be.[16]

W. Joseph Campbell's terrific 2001 history *Yellow Journalism: Puncturing the Myths, Defining the Legacies* examined the legitimacy of the famous telegram. After extensive research Campbell concluded that though Creelman probably made up the exchange (that itself an example of yellow journalism), it is possible that the two telegrams were sent exactly as Creelman related.[17]

Hearst denied it, of course. The same year as the *Times of London* article appeared, Hearst referred to it as "clotted nonsense" and rolled his editorial eyes at the notion "that Mr. Hearst was chiefly responsible for the Spanish war." Naturally, Hearst's denial was met with derision. No newspaper had been so bellicose, arguing so passionately for war with Spain, than the influential *New York Journal.* From his cartoonists to his special correspondents, Hearst was having a powerful effect.[18]

As for Hearst's best biographers, W. A. Swanberg accepted Creelman's version of events without batting an eye, calling Hearst's response "Napoleonic." David Nasaw allowed that it was possible the telegrams were cabled. Kenneth Whyte contended that it was "probable" that the exchange, or something like it, took place, for Creelman was generally considered reliable. Perhaps the most sensational aspect of the legendary Remington-Hearst exchange was that after Creelman published it in 1901, for six years the literary world accepted the story verbatim. It may have shocked a London newspaperman, but to the American press the thought of W. R. Hearst telling Frederic Remington that he would soon kick off the Spanish-American War wasn't so far-fetched.[19]

While Remington left Cuba for New York, on January 12 Davis caught a train twenty-seven miles southeast to Jaruco, where he and his party slept in a barnyard. Davis jotted down that six poor Cuban insurgents died in Jaruco during his stay.

On January 14 Davis entrained for the port city of Matanzas, the capital of Matanzas Province, thirty-five miles east of Jaruco. Along the way he saw, in addition to fields of sugarcane, black smoke pouring from houses of the Cubans who had given shelter to the insurgents. They'd been set ablaze by the Spanish army. Records indicate that Matanzas was one of the hardest-hit provinces in Cuba, the Spanish destroying nearly all the farms and sugar mills and slaughtering nearly every chicken, duck, cow, and horse they could find.[20]

After six hours on the train Davis reached Matanzas, which he called "a beautiful little city" in a letter to his mother. Small wonder, for he booked a luxurious hotel room usually reserved for the "Capitan General," as Davis learned. Enjoying the view of the plaza from the balcony, with the palm trees swaying in the sea breeze, he reflected that he was "spending more of Willie Hearst's money than all of the officers spend in a week."[21]

Davis also dished to his mother how frustrated he'd become with Remington. "I am so relieved at getting old Remington to go as though I had won $5000," Davis wrote Rebecca, for Davis had grown to resent the petulant artist. Some of Davis's descriptions of the artist were so cutting that Charles, in his 1917 book *Adventures and Letters of Richard Harding Davis,* decided to leave them out. Nonetheless, they can be found in the Barrett Collection of the University of Virginia.

"Remington . . . always wanted to talk it over and that had to be done in the nearest or the most distant café," Davis complained, "and it always took him fifteen minutes before he got his cocktails to suit him. He always did as I wanted in the end but I am not used to giving reasons or to travelling in pairs."

In the next day's letter to Rebecca, Davis criticisms were even harsher. "Remington . . . is very excitable and a firebrand and makes the worst of everything. I would rather manage an Italian Opera Company than him."[22]

As for the war Davis was supposed to be covering, he saw plenty of evidence of it.

"The insurgents began first by destroying the sugar mills," Davis wrote Rebecca on January 16, "some of which were worth millions of dollars in machinery, and now the Spaniards are burning the homes of the people and herding them in and around the towns to starve out the insurgents and leave them without shelter or places to go for food or hide the wounded."[23]

Such barbarity typified the conflict between Spain and Cuba, though the roots of the strife were hundreds of years old.

In 1511 eight years before his conquest of Mexico, Hernán Cortés invaded Cuba seeking to pacify the local Taíno population through bloodshed. The guerrilla war raged for three years before the Taíno chieftain, Hatuey, was captured and burned alive. Along with founding a settlement in the region of Avan, which the Spanish called Havana, the Spanish turned Cuba into the largest slave colony in the Americas, importing eight hundred thousand African slaves between 1791 and 1867 to work the cane fields and sugar mills. Under cruel conditions, Cuba became the "sugar bowl" of the world, producing 42 percent of the global sugar supply, far and away the world's leading exporter of sugar. Then German chemist Franz Karl Achard developed a process of producing sugar from beets, which led to the establishment of the first German sugar beet refineries in 1801. By 1890 the sugar beet produced 59 percent of the world's sugar supply, causing exports to fall. As a result, Spain's treatment of Cuba grew more barbaric.

Some, such as Narciso López, fought against Spain's oppression. That López had been executed in Havana in 1851 for leading two failed revolutions against the Spanish put a lid on Cuban freedom for seventeen years. But in 1868 the conflict—which would become known as the Ten Years' War—boiled over. In 1869, the Congress of the Republic of Cuba adopted López's personal flag as the Cuban national banner. When gun-running Americans were captured and hanged by Spanish authorities in 1875, Secretary of State Hamilton Fish warned Spain to either work toward reconciliation with the Cuban populace or prepare for American intervention.[24]

By the time the Ten Years' War ended in 1878 with the Pact of Zanjón, 80,000 Spaniards and 250,000 Cubans were dead. Spain had made concessions—a Cuban representative would be allowed into Spanish parliament, and slavery would eventually be phased out (occurring in 1886)—but the Spanish also implemented a policy of malicious neglect, resulting in crippling poverty. Roads deteriorated. No new rail lines were built. The construction of schools was discouraged, the Spanish believing that education would only lead to revolution. By the 1890s, Cuban *insurrectos,* or *mambises*—commonly referred to as "insurgents" by the yanquis—were preparing to rise again. In 1894 as banditry spread across Cuba, military leaders met to discuss the uprising from Havana cafés to eastern villages. From the time independence had been declared in Baire, it had been bloody war. Of the four most distinguished Cuban leaders, two had fallen. Along with Maceo, killed on December 7, 1896, José Martí had been shot dead in the Battle of Dos

Rios on May 19, 1895. But Calixto García and Máximo Gómez still lived and with them the dream of a free Cuba.[25]

Davis learned to love the island, with its "great waterfalls and mossy rocks and grand plains and forests," but despised the war.

As David wrote to this mother,

> Only man here is vile, and it is cruel to see . . . the houses with roofs gone and gardens burned. . . . [E]very church but one that I have seen was a fortress with hammocks swung from the altars and rude barricades thrown up around the doorway—If this is war I am of the opinion that it is a senseless wicked institution made for soldiers, lovers and correspondents for different reasons, and for no one else in the world and it is too expensive for the others to keep it going to entertain these few gentlemen—I have seen very little of it yet and I probably won't see much more, but I have seen all I want.[26]

Sickened by what he witnessed, it seemed to Davis that the soldiers were the victims, regardless of the side or the cause, and the men who fought the wars from the sidelines were the villains. Furthermore, he saw the startling truth of modern warfare, as discovered during the American Civil War, that most soldiers died not by gunfire or cannon fire but by disease:

> The men who wear the red badge of courage, I don't feel sorry for, they have their reward in their bloody bandages . . . but those you meet coming back sick and dying of fever are the ones that make fighting contemptible—poor little farmers, poor little children with no interest in Cuba or Spain's right to hold it. . . . As soon as the rains begin the yellow fever and smallpox will set in and all vessels leaving Cuban ports will be quarantined and the island will be one great plague spot. The insurgents who are in the open fields will live and the soldiers will die for their officers know nothing of sanitation or care nothing.[27]

Davis was correct in his assessment. With terrible sanitation, Spanish records indicated that of the nearly 200,000 Spaniards on Cuba, 41,288 would succumb to malaria, typhus, dysentery, pneumonia, or yellow fever. The fever was the worst, with victims dying in terrible agony bleeding from ears, noses, rectums, and genitals and vomiting up blood and tissue. So far Davis had been lucky, but his mother's worries weren't for nothing.[28]

Planning to visit the insurgents, Davis used the pass Weyler had given him and traveled 160 miles southeast to Trinidad. There he witnessed the Spanish army executing thirty Cuban insurgents by firing squad, each one shot individually. Finally finding a juicy story worthy of the *Journal,* Davis focused on the execution of Adolfo Rodriguez, a twenty-year-old farmhand from Santa Clara Province sentenced by a military court for joining the insurgents. "The Death of Rodriguez" became the first article Davis wrote for the *Journal* as a war correspondent.

Allowed to kiss the crucifix held by a watching priest, Rodriguez was given a last cigarette. He was still smoking it when the Spaniards fired at the condemned man.

"The Cuban's head snapped back almost between his shoulders," Davis wrote, "but his body fell slowly, as though someone had pushed him gently forward from behind and he had stumbled. He sank on his side in the wet grass without a struggle or sound, and did not move again."[29]

Walking by, Davis noticed "the cigarette still burned, a tiny ring of living fire, at the place where the figure had first stood."

Still hoping to interview the rebels, Davis enlisted Cuban escorts. Suspicious that they were being observed by Spanish spies, Davis's would-be escorts backed out twice. Refusing to give up, Davis met in Cienfuegos—fifty miles northwest of Trinidad—with two twenty-seven-year-old reporters, George Bronson Rea of the *New York Herald* and Sylvester "Harry" Scovel of the *New York World.*[30]

Aware that he was being "systematically shadowed," as Rea put it in his 1897 history *Facts and Fakes in Cuba,* Davis registered under his own name at the hotel. The next morning they planned to travel together to join with General Máximo Gómez and his band of rebel insurgents. But when Rea and Scovel caught sight of a copy of the January 17, 1897, edition of the *New York Journal,* having just arrived aboard a mail steamer from Havana, they could hardly believe their eyes.

"It contained a full-page illustration of Richard Harding Davis, mounted on a charger, (?) and loaded down with cartridge-belts, repeating-rifles, and other war-like trappings," Rea recollected, "and the readers were given to understand that this was he as he appeared traveling around the country of Cuba with the insurgents."[31]

"Your paper has queered you, Davis," Scovel told Davis, holding up a copy of the *Journal.*[32]

Looking it over, Davis read with disgust a full-page story declaring that Davis and Remington had "reached the insurgent army on the island of Cuba." Davis knew this was a bald-faced lie. Remington had returned home, and Davis, for all his attempts, hadn't managed to locate the insurgents. Nor would Rea and Scovel help him do that. They apologized but informed Davis that he couldn't join them; he was far too conspicuous, particularly with the Spanish believing he'd previously joined the insurgent army.

"If I had been an escaping cashier of the *Journal*'s," Davis complained to Charles, "they could not have queered me better."

Convinced that Weyler would soon have him expelled from the country, Davis also suspected that his mother would be more worried than ever.

"I am torn between coming home and making your dear heart stop worrying and getting one story to justify me being here and that damn silly page of the Journals," Davis wrote Rebecca. As for Hearst, Davis had some choice words. "All Hearst wants is my name and I will give him that only it will be signed to a different sort of story from those they have been printing."[33]

Eventually it all became too much. Quitting Cuba, in February Davis sailed from Havana aboard the *Olivette*. It was at the ship's dinner table that, once more demonstrating the luck of R. H. D., Davis scored the biggest scoop of the trip.

Meeting young Clemencia Arango—a highly intelligent and cultured Cuban woman who could speak three languages and whose brother commanded a band of insurgents near Havana—Davis learned how outrageously she had been treated by the Spaniards. Before being allowed to board the *Olivette*, Spanish detectives had forced Clemencia to undergo two strip searches conducted by a matron. Clemencia's sister and two other young ladies were given the same treatment.

In the article he quickly composed, Davis failed to mention that it was a woman who conducted the strip searches, leaving the reader to believe they must have been administered by one or more of the Spanish men. Once in Tampa, Davis filed the story with the *Journal*, in the last lines appealing to Grover Cleveland, still president for the next three weeks, to punish Spain for these outrages. Hearst knew he had something special. On February 12, 1897, Hearst wrote up the bellicose, front-page headline himself, "Does Our Flag Shield Women?," printing Davis's article below it. Hearst also included a Remington illustration of three rough-looking Spaniards menacing a naked Cuban senorita. For some reason that issue of the *Journal* sold like hotcakes.[34]

With the *Journal* once again hitting it out of the park and the reading public incensed by the lecherous treatment of Clemencia and the other Cuban women by the Spanish rogues, an ambitious *World* reporter located Clemencia in Tampa for a follow-up article. When the reporter learned it had been a woman rather than a knot of men who conducted the strip searches, he realized he had a red-hot story.

Details soon appeared in the *World*: "Association for a few short weeks with the Journal has led Mr. Davis to write over his signature an atrociously exaggerated story of an alleged Spanish outrage upon a woman. . . . Mr. Davis and Mr. Remington should be well quarantined before they are allowed to mingle with reputable newspaper men."[35]

Despite criticism in the *World*, Hearst expressed pride in Davis and Remington. In 1940 Hearst reflected that he'd "sent Richard Harding Davis and Frederic Remington to Cuba to describe and depict the atrocities which the cruel Spaniards were inflicting upon the courageous Cubans, struggling for their liberties. These correspondents did their work admirably and aroused much indignation among Americans against 'Butcher' Weyler, the bloodthirsty general."

Davis, on the other hand, was mortified. Rather than blaming himself for being purposefully vague about who had actually stripped and searched the young ladies, he blamed Remington. On February 16, 1897, Davis wrote from Philadelphia a letter to the editor of the *World*. In the letter, which was published by the *World* the following day, Davis wrote, "Mr. Frederick Remington, who was not there, and who drew an imaginary picture of the scene, is responsible for the idea that the search was conducted by men. Had I seen the picture before it appeared, I should never have allowed it to accompany my article."[36]

Deciding never again to work for Hearst, Davis quickly found employment at the *New York World* when disturbing news came from Cuba: Harry Scovel had been captured by the Spanish and imprisoned for aiding the Cuban insurgents. At Pulitzer's behest, Davis wrote an open letter for the February 18, 1897, edition arguing that Scovel was not part of the military and that if he were to be killed "His Death Will Free Cuba." Remington also wrote a letter, which the *World* published three days later. The letters had an effect. To avoid provoking the American eagle, on March 9 Scovel was placed aboard a ship bound for American waters.[37]

Growing no moss, Davis next inked a deal with *Harper's Weekly*, agreeing to sail to Great Britain. It was in London that Davis ran into Stephen Crane.[38]

Although thirty-two-year-old Davis was far more famous than twenty-five-year-old Crane, nothing Davis had written had quite the impact as *The Red Badge of Courage*. Furthermore, Davis had been impressed by the book. "Stephen Crane seems to me to have written the last word as far as fighting or battles are concerned," Davis had written Charles after finishing Crane's Civil War novel. Meeting Crane in London, Davis found himself well-disposed toward the young author.[39]

"Crane . . . is very modest sturdy and shy," Davis wrote Charles.

Davis was probably unaware that Crane held a grudge against him. After Davis declined a celebratory dinner for the bohemian author back in December 1895,

Crane had written to a would-be lover that "Davis . . . has, I believe, all the intelligence of a saw-log."

On March 27, 1897, Davis treated Crane to lunch at the opulent Savoy Hotel, inviting along three other writers: Anthony Hope, Harold Frederic, and James Barrie. Barrie, who would go on to author *Peter Pan,* remarked that he'd enjoyed Davis's *Soldiers of Fortune* so much he was thinking of adapting it for the stage.[40]

Barrie's opinion flattered Davis, though this was the opinion shared by much of the literary world. First appearing as a magazine serial in early 1897, *Soldiers of Fortune* would be Davis's most enduring book. Epitomizing the hypermasculine Yankee, the main character Robert Clay worked as a mining engineer in a banana republic but proved equally skilled with a pistol. After corrupt politicians and rogue military leaders launched a coup that threatened his mining outfit, Clay fought back. With American pluck, Clay conducted a countercoup while carrying on a relationship with the pretty tomboy Hope Langham. Exhibiting plenty of dash and high spirit, the novel became one of the top-selling books that year.[41]

"Love-making and fighting constitute all the action, and the book is one that makes you sit up until you finish it," the *Buffalo Morning Express* praised that spring. "The men are marvelously well-favored by the Fates as usual, and their manners are irreproachable; and the women are simply Gibson girls made flesh. If this world were all like the world of Mr. Davis's books, what a nice world it would be."[42]

That Davis's newest book was an example of jingoistic American imperialism wasn't something reviewers openly spoke of; nevertheless, *Soldiers of Fortune* bolstered the argument of American intervention in Cuba.

Another man invited to the Savoy luncheon was Sir Evelyn Wood, a veteran of the Zulu War and the First Boer War. But instead of appearing himself, Wood sent a lance sergeant on horseback to the hotel with a large envelope marked "On Her Majesty's Secret Service," delivering it to Davis.

While Davis meticulously wrote out a receipt for the envelope, the entire hotel was on pins and needles thinking that war had been declared and that Davis was being sent to cover it. The contents were revealed to be less deadly for the denizens of London. Davis was being offered a job with the *London Times* serving as a war correspondent in Greece, for Athens and Constantinople were embroiled in the Greco-Turk War of 1897.

"Everyone in London thought it an enormous compliment," Davis wrote to his family, in particular mentioning Harold Frederic, Julian Ralph, and Ballard Smith. Davis may have left Crane off the list because Crane—whose celebration this was supposed to be—was heading to Athens as well, working as a war correspondent for Hearst's *Journal*. Whatever the case, Davis gave the "Her Majesty's Secret Service" envelope to Crane as a souvenir.[43]

On April 1, Davis and Crane crossed the channel together. At times Davis spotted Cora—whom Davis described as "a bi-roxide blonde"—with the luggage, but Crane did not introduce them, and Davis did not press. That Crane and Cora were living as man and wife did not escape the seasoned reporter. Davis may have camouflaged mild jealousy with a few biting comments to his brother. "Lady Stuart [*sic*] has run away from her husband to follow Crane. She is a commonplace dull woman old enough to have been his mother and with dyed yellow hair." Charles might have been tickled to note, now that his brother knew Crane better, that Davis was no longer describing Crane as "modest and shy."[44]

The pair of authors separated when Davis traveled to Florence, Italy, to see Charles.

"Of the many happy days we have spent together, I do not believe there were any much more happy than the three weeks Richard remained with me," Charles remarked.[45]

Noting that he was somewhat "envious" of the pile of money Davis made gambling in Monte Carlo, Monaco, Charles eventually parted company with his brother, with Davis heading for war-torn Greece.

The catalyst to the Greco-Turkish War of 1897 (there would be a much bloodier Greco-Turk War fought between 1919 and 1922), centered around the island of Crete. Controlled by the Ottoman Empire, the large Greek population on the island was in open revolt by early 1897, and when Athens sent a regiment to support the rebellion, Constantinople determined this an act of war. Although Athens responded by attempting an invasion, so far early maneuvers revealed the Greek military to be overmatched and unprepared.

Naturally, Davis rooted for the underdog.

Although the *Times* wished him to join the Turks and Ioannina, Davis instead endeavored to join the Greeks at Arta. For a week he searched for action along the northern border, sometimes in Greece, sometimes in Turkey. He caught one bombardment before following the Greeks into Turkey and then backtracked with the retreating Greek forces across the Gulf of Arta. Compared to Cuba, it all seemed very well-mannered to Davis.

"I never met with strangers anywhere who were so hospitable, so confiding and polite," Davis wrote to his family on April 28, 1897, from aboard a steamer on the way to Patras. "After that slaughter-yard and pest place of Cuba, which is much more terrible to me now than it was when I was there, or before I had seen that war can be conducted like any other evil of civilization, this opera bouffe warfare is like a duel between two gentlemen in the Bois."[46]

As for Davis himself, he was getting along splendidly.

"I live on brown bread and cheese and goat's milk and sleep like a log in shepherds' huts," Davis declared. "It is so beautiful that I almost grudge the night."[47]

In Athens, Davis reunited with Crane. To Rebecca, Davis wrote that "Crane . . . is writing for the *Journal* poor devil. He has not seen as much as I have either for several reasons but when a man can describe battles as well as he does without seeing them why should he care."[48]

Joined by John Bass, the leader of the *Journal*'s team, the correspondents traveled from Athens to the village of Velestino, which the Turkish army had attacked the week before. Davis was surprised to learn that Crane had managed to get the *Journal* to hire on Cora as a war correspondent as well and blamed her for distracting Crane. When on May 3 all the correspondents but Davis and Bass left Velestino, Davis wasn't sorry to see Cora leave. Harry Scovel of the *World* thought more highly of Cora. To his wife Frances, Scovel wrote, "I was afraid that she would ruin him, but really her influence has, so far, been the reverse." Scovel praised Cora for inspiring in Crane "such good work."

That night with the Greeks having abandoned Velestino, Davis and Bass broke into the mayor's residence.

"It was like 'The Swiss Family Robinson,'" Davis recalled in a letter home, "and we rejoiced over the discovery of soap and tablecloths and stray knives and forks, just as though we have been cast on a desert island."[49]

They awoke on the morning of May 4 to the sound of cannon fire. They had guessed right; there would be a battle.

Outside, Davis witnessed the six mountain guns constituting the Greek battery firing on the Turkish forces, advancing on an open plain toward the village. Rushing to the Greek trenches, Davis and Bass lay face-down as shells burst above them and bullets whizzed overhead. One shell struck three feet away, knocking Davis down. A hail of pebbles spilled into his mouth.

"At times the firing was so fierce," Davis wrote home, "that if you had raised your arm above your head, the hand would have been instantly torn off."[50]

About five minutes later the firing slackened, signaling that the Turks were retiring for the night. Crane soon returned from Volo, twelve miles north, himself suffering from dysentery and a toothache. Davis noted that Crane wrote up a 1,300-word article on the battle but, suffering so bad, was nowhere near the front.

Hence, Crane missed the Greeks retreating and the Turks seizing the abandoned village. Davis's conduct during the battle, on the other hand, garnered acclaim. When Bass told Davis he wished to write an article on Davis's conduct under fire, Davis flatly told him not to.

"In the first place they would probably have said I was there for the Journal and made silly pictures," Davis related to this family, "and then as I pointed out to him why should he describe how the Times correspondent acted and say nothing about Crane who was there for the Journal. But there was nothing to be said about what Crane did except that he ought to be ashamed of himself."[51]

As for Davis's war correspondence, the articles he wrote of the two-day battle were some of his finest writing. But they came at a cost. His sciatica, which periodically flared up ever since he'd contracted it in Johnstown, was so bad that he had to be carried on a donkey. Afterward, Davis boarded a hospital ship for Athens along with 116 wounded Greeks.

"They groaned all night and so did I," Davis admitted. "Then when the sun rose they sang, which was worse."

After two days in bed Davis boarded USS *San Francisco* for Florence. The war didn't last much longer, officially ending on May 20, 1897. Although the Turks had demonstrated military superiority, sympathy was still with Greece, and the following year international pressure would cause Crete to be liberated from Ottoman rule. Davis could take some pride in that.

Despite Davis's criticism, Crane too found a degree of success in the war. The boy who'd written a best-selling Civil War novel without having experienced a battle had finally "seen the elephant." The *New York Journal* happily printed in large print his articles on the Greco-Turk War under the byline "Stephen Crane," adding to the prestige of the correspondent and the newspaper. Hearst was happy as well, having printed in 1897 exclusive war correspondence from his fearless action reporters, Davis and Crane.

Possibly Hearst was a little too happy. In the summer of 1897, he came up with a sensation—an almost mythical quest—that if successful was sure to make headlines across the globe. With the stakes high, Hearst would send one of his reporters to rescue from a Spanish prison a Cuban damsel in distress and bring her back to the United States.

It was a plan so crazy it just might work.

11
FURNISHING THE WAR

The Hearst papers celebrated Theodore Roosevelt's appointment as assistant secretary of the navy in April 1897. Roosevelt would be missed as police commissioner, but as the author of *The Naval History of 1812* he would be more effective with the navy, the *San Francisco Examiner* editorialized. As for solving sensational crimes in New York City, William Randolph Hearst and the boys at the *New York Journal* had that covered.[1]

At about 3 p.m. on June 26, 1897, two teenagers—James McKenna, age thirteen, and John McGuire, age fourteen—were swimming in the East River near an old dock on Eleventh Street when something caught their eye. It looked like some sort of package floating in the river. Excitedly swimming to it, they found the object wrapped in red oilcloth. With each boy taking a hand, they brought the package to dry land. There, a curious crowd gathered to see what they had discovered, and someone loaned McKenna a knife to cut it open. Inside, to the crowd's growing horror, was revealed a headless and legless body.[2]

Hearing the news, Hearst devoted almost the entire front page to the grisly murder, including a $1,000 reward for clues leading to the killer. Shortly afterward, a *Journal* reporter, taking a drink at a local tavern, overheard two men mention that one of the masseurs at the Russian and Turkish Baths at 113 West 42nd Street had gone missing. On a hunch, the reporter visited the baths and got the name of the "rubber," William Guldensuppe, along with Guldensuppe's address. Once the sketches of the corpse were published, the reporter found seven men who identified the corpse as the missing masseur. Hearst happily presented the $1,000 to his own reporter.[3]

Having identified the body, the *Journal* now wished to find the killer. For this purpose, Hearst ordered his artists to create a color reproduction of the red oilcloth, had it divided into twelve pieces, and gave the pieces to a dozen men with orders to canvas the merchants. This proved to be a good strategy. On the East Side, a reporter spoke to a married couple, the Rigers, who remembered selling identical oilcloth to a midwife, Augusta Nack, who lived in a Bronx tenement hall at 339 Fifth Avenue.

According to Frederick Palmer—Hearst's agent who initially negotiated the deal to acquire the *Journal*—with the game afoot Hearst sprang into action. Leading nearly the entire *Journal* staff on bicycles and hacks to the Fifth Avenue tenement, Hearst and the newspapermen began occupying the empty flats and hallways. Guards were posted to keep out competing reporters. Every day the *Journal* was able to report on a startling new revelation.

After a few days, with the help of the *Journal*, the police got the whole story.

Nack and her lover, Martin Thorn, a barber, had murdered Nack's former lover, William Guldensuppe. The motivation was petty theft and hatred. Thorn shot Guldensuppe in the back of the neck, decapitated him in a bathtub, and encased his head in plaster of paris. They dropped the head in the Long Island slip of the Greenpoint Ferry, the legs near the Brooklyn Navy Yard, and the torso in the East River.[4]

On June 30, the *Journal* boomed "Murder Mystery Solved By the Journal." The following day the *Journal* published letters of gratitude from several members of the New York City Police Department. Although the *New York Times* expressed aversion to the *Journal*'s "noisy police work," declaring that "the grossness and needless explicitness of this kind of news reporting must have a demoralizing influence upon the younger generation," the *Fourth Estate* joined the police in congratulating the *Journal*. "The marvelous energy that characterized the rise of the Journal continues," remarked the weekly newspaper.[5]

After the pair were convicted, Nack was sentenced to fifteen years in prison. Things went harder for Thorn. Sentenced to die, he would be electrocuted in Sing Sing on August 1, 1898.[6]

"You may like or dislike William Randolph Hearst," remarked Charley Michelson, "but he was the nearest thing to a genius as an editor and publisher that I encountered during my half a lifetime in the field of journalism. . . . In those days he was a tall, horse-faced fellow with a pair of pale bluish gray eyes. The only animals I know of that have that particular ocular coloring are the coyote and the shark."[7]

The *Journal*'s role in solving the Guldensuppe case was just one such sensation Hearst pulled off during the first half of 1897. Along with hiring Richard Harding Davis, Frederic Remington, and Stephen Crane as war correspondents, Hearst dazzled readers with Mark Twain's coverage of Queen Victoria's Diamond Jubilee, John Muir's firsthand accounts of the Klondike gold rush, and ex-senator John J. Ingalls's report on the Corbett-Fitzsimmons fight in Carson City, Nevada. Plus, there was love in Hearst's life.[8]

In either 1896 or 1897 Hearst met a fourteen-year-old dancer from Brooklyn, Millicent Willson, who along with her older sister, Anita, performed in the risqué musical comedy *The Girl from Paris* at the Herald Square Theater. There Milly and Anita played "bicycle girls" in the chorus, daring to show off their long legs. Hearst and his private secretary, George Pancoast, caught the vaudeville show several times. Unsurprisingly, James L. Ford's January 17, 1897, review of *The Girl from Paris* in the *Journal* was extremely enthusiastic.[9]

The Willson sisters next moved to the Casino Theater to perform in the even racier musical comedy *The Telephone Girl*. The *Democrat and Chronicle* chastised the play for its "exceptional vileness," commenting that though it had been adapted from a French play, in New York City it had been "Tenderloinized." Employing scandalous language and showing more leg than ever, Millicent played "Toots." It's a cinch Hearst caught the show. After *The Telephone Girl* closed, Millicent never again performed on Broadway.[10]

Although the gossip columnists recognized that reporting on the proprietor of the *Journal*'s newest dalliance was off limits, Phoebe's niece Anne Apperson Flint, speaking decades later, recalled the "outrage" their relationship caused, with Hearst being thirty-four years old and Millicent less than half his age. Anne Flint also recollected that her famous cousin had given Millicent "a hansom cab with a white horse . . . which she drove around in. This was well known. . . . We would all dodge when we'd see them because we didn't want to face them."[11]

Similarly, Millicent's mother, Hannah, was taken aback.

"Who *is* he?" Hannah asked Millicent. "Some young fellow from out West somewhere, isn't he?"

Hannah insisted that Anita accompany them. On one of their first dates, Hearst gave the sisters a tour of the third floor of the Tribune Building.

"Well, he took us down to the *Journal*—the *New York Journal*—we'd hardly heard of it," Millicent mentioned years later to her friend, the Hearst reporter Adela Rogers St. Johns, "and he showed us over it, *all over it.* I hadn't the foggiest notion what we were doing, walking miles on rough boards in thin, high-heeled evening slippers, and thought my feet would kill me. Of course this wasn't our idea of a good time. We wanted to go to Sherry's or Bustanoby's. More than that, Anita kept whispering to me, 'We're going to get thrown out of here, Milly[;] the way he behaves you'd think he *owned* it."

Millicent could scarcely have dreamed that about six years later she and Hearst would be married and that five children would follow.

As the Willson sisters became more of a fixture in Hearst's life, conjecture arose as to which of the young ladies the millionaire was courting. Naturally, some speculated that it could even be both. If Hearst caught any raised eyebrows, he didn't let that bother him much.

"He didn't care," Anne Apperson Flint commented. Ultimately the papers grew bolder.

In August 1897, the weekly newspaper *The Journalist* let it be known that "Billy Hearst is down the coast with a cottage, young friends and a yacht, sighing for the unattainable . . . fully occupied with what he believes to be Pleasure—with a capital P."[12]

Upton Sinclair commented about Hearst's devil-may-care attitude:

> Mr. Hearst turned traitor to his class. . . . It seems to have pleased him to defy *all* their conventions. I was told, for example, that when he first came to New York, he made himself a scandal in the "Tenderloin." I was perplexed. . . . But one young society man who had known Hearst well gave me the reason—and he spoke with real gravity: "It wasn't what he did—we all do it; but it was the way he did it. He didn't take the trouble to hide what he did."[13]

Meanwhile, events in Cuba intensified. Decades later, Josep Conangla reflected that during the summer of 1897 "the campaigning carried out on behalf of an exalted Spanish patriotism was increasingly inflamed. And as if the criminal reconcentration was not enough to plunge thousands of families condemned in this way to a slow and certain annihilation in conditions of misery, helplessness, and the most horrendous tribulations, Weyler's pre-Hitlerian ferocity ordered other punishments that were no less harsh."[14]

For one, Weyler ordered his military columns to destroy all plots of land and fruit-bearing trees that had the remotest possibility of being used by García and his Cuban army. For another, Weyler ordered special investigators in Havana and other strategic towns to ferret out men and women with Cuban sympathies, whom he called *infidencias,* and to punish them accordingly. Between establishing reconcentration camps, adopting a scorched-earth policy, and creating an investigative force that hearkened back to the Spanish Inquisition, Weyler was certainly a dangerous enemy. But he didn't scare the *New York Journal.*[15]

Taking a break from the social whirlwind he'd created, on one sweltering day in August, 1897 Hearst lolled in his editor chair in the Tribune Building, feeling uncharacteristically idle, when an employee came in and handed the Chief a telegram:

> Havana.
>
> Evangelina Cisneros, pretty girl of seventeen years, related to President of Cuban Republic, is to be imprisoned for twenty years on African coast, for having taken part in uprising Cuban political prisoners on Isle of Pines.[16]

According to Creelman, Hearst read it over a second time and whistled softly. Slapping his knee and laughing, Hearst called out "Sam!"

From next door Sam Chamberlain appeared.

"We've got Spain now!" Hearst exclaimed, showing Chamberlain the slip of paper. Soon Hearst was barking orders:

> Telegraph to our correspondent in Havana to wire every detail of this case. Get up a petition to the Queen Regent of Spain for this girl's pardon. Enlist the women of America. Have them sign the petition. Wake up our correspondents all over the country. Have distinguished women sign first. Cable the petitions and the names to the Queen Regent. Notify our minister in Madrid. We can make a national issue of this case. It will do more to open the eyes of the country than a thousand editorials or political speeches. The Spanish minister can attack our correspondents, but we'll see if he can face the women of America when they take up the fight. That girl must be saved if we have to take her out of prison by force or send a steamer to meet the vessel that carries her away—but that would be piracy, wouldn't it?[17]

In short order, Hearst's newspapermen visited some of the most noteworthy women in America and asked them to champion Evangelina's cause. Cables of Evangelina's plight also flashed to Cuba, France, England, and Spain. Hearst telegraphed several personally, including the president's wife, Ida Saxton McKinley.

"Will you not add your name to that of distinguished American women like Mrs. Julia Ward Howe . . . cabling petitions to Queen Regent of Spain for release of Evangelina Cisneros eighteen years old . . . threatened with twenty years imprisonment? She is almost a child," Hearst cabled, "sick, defenseless, and in prison. A word may save her. Answer at our expense. William Hearst."[18]

Thousands of responses poured in, including one from Clara Barton and another from President William McKinley's mother, Nancy Allison McKinley. Pope Leo XIII also asked for Evangelina's release. One letter from Jefferson Davis's widow, Varina Howell Davis, printed in the August 21, 1897, *New York Journal*, was particularly stirring.

> To Her Majesty, Maria Cristina, *Queen Regent of Spain:*—
>
> *Dear Madam:* In common with many of my countrywomen I have been much moved by the accounts of the arrest and trial of Senorita Evangelina Cisneros. . . . To you I appeal to extend your powerful protection over this poor captive girl—a child almost in years—to save her from a fate worse than death. . . . Do not, dear Madam, refuse this boon to us, and we will always pray for the prosperity of the young King, your son.[19]

Hearst also had his illustrators working double time. "We pictured all the terrible things we could think of," Michelson remarked, "with the possibility of her execution as an undertone to all our sympathetic concern. Looking back, it seems to me that we pictured the brutal Captain-General as giving more attention to persecuting the heroine than to coping with a revolution."[20]

In Washington, the assistant secretary of the navy was certainly paying attention. Beginning on August 2, 1897, Roosevelt became the acting secretary when his boss, John D. Long, began vacationing in Massachusetts. During the next twenty-two days Roosevelt displayed his customary manic energy, touring the Naval Militia, expediting a delayed order for diagonal-armor provisions, cutting through red tape to fill more appointments and build more cruisers and battleships, and firing Navy Department employees who tested with subpar marks in their semiannual fitness tests. In his letters, Roosevelt strived to keep Long in the dark.

"I shan't send you anything unless it is really important," Roosevelt prevaricated. "You must be tired, and you ought to have an entire rest." Roosevelt also professed that there was "not the slightest earthly reason" for Long to return before October.[21]

Roosevelt may have pulled the wool over Long's eyes, but the *New York Sun* saw the situation more clearly. On August 23 the *Sun* commented, "The liveliest spot in Washington at present is in the Navy Department. The decks are cleared for action. Acting Secretary Roosevelt, in the absence of Governor Long, has the whole Navy bordering on a war footing. It remains only to sand down the decks and pipe to quarters for action."[22]

In the first weeks of September, Queen Regent Maria Cristina, perhaps with Varina Howell Davis's letter acting as the tipping point, wrote to Weyler concerning Evangelina Cisneros. The queen regent commanded Weyler to transfer the young woman to a convent while the law determined her culpability. In what would prove a drastic mistake for his career, Weyler refused the queen.[23]

Characteristically, Hearst responded with action. From his Washington Bureau, Hearst summoned Karl Decker for the job of springing Evangelina from her Havana prison, the Casa de Recogidas. Michelson expressed disgust, wanting the assignment himself. But Decker was certainly the right man for the job, described by Hearst as "our most brilliant and daring young reporter." Born in Harpers Ferry, Virginia—the son of a colonel in the Confederacy—Decker was two hundred pounds, six feet tall, and handsome with an eagle's wing mustache and a jutting chin. Not only had he the look of the dashing hero, but he also had the brains to play the part.[24]

On August 24, Decker arrived in New York City and was asked if he could rescue Evangelina.

"You shall be entirely free to use your own discretion as to time and method," the managing editor of the *Journal* told him. "And, furthermore, I can assure you of Mr. Hearst's ample appreciations of your efforts if you succeed."[25]

Four days later on Saturday, August 28, Decker arrived in Havana and got right to work. That day he visited Evangelina in Casa de Recogidas.

"I found her far more beautiful even than she had been pictured," Decker recounted.

Through the grating of her cell and with the aid of a Spanish-speaking American acting as translator, Decker and Evangelina plotted her escape. In particular, Decker made notes about the "hideous squalor" of the prison. The following Friday, September 3, Weyler may have caught wind of Decker's presence, for he commanded that Evangelina be held incommunicado afterward, making Decker's attempt to spring her all the more difficult. But Decker didn't give up. When not plotting with a small band of companions, he drank cognac at the Inglaterra Hotel and commiserated with homesick Americans.

"No one suspected my mission save the men selected to help me and who I never saw except in the early morning hours, in the little half-furnished room I rented, in the lower part of Havana, as a rendezvous . . . out of the sight of spies," Decker recollected.[26]

With the prison located in the lowest part of Havana, Decker knew that even if he managed to free Evangelina from Casa de Recogidas it would be difficult getting her to a ship. At the same time, Havana's mazelike streets might be a blessing. "The streets of Havana are crooked, labyrinthic, and exceedingly narrow," the naturalist John Muir observed in 1868. Nearly thirty years later there had been no improvement. Decker considered the alleys surrounding the prison especially byzantine, in which they might shake their pursuers. He felt that he could have pulled off the escape—if Evangelina hadn't been placed incommunicado—by visiting her and knocking out a guard. As it was, Decker thought that his best bet was dynamiting part of the prison. To ask her opinion of this plan, a note was smuggled to Evangelina.[27]

Evangelina replied in Spanish:

> My plan is the following: To escape to the roof with the aid of a rope, descending by the front of the house at a given hour and signal. For this I require acid to destroy the bars of the windows and opium or morphine so as to set to sleep my companions. The best way to use it is in sweets, and thus I can also set to sleep the vigilants.
>
> Three of you come and stand at the corners. A lighted cigar will be the signal of alarm for which I may have to delay, and a white handkerchief will be the agreed signal by which I can safely descend. I will only bring with me the necessary clothes tied around my waist.[28]

Evangelina also provided a hand-drawn map of the locations. Decker looked over the plan and liked it except for the acid, which could be messy. The *Journal* reporter felt that their odds were better if he handled the bars personally, cutting through them with a saw.

On October 5, Decker put their plan in motion. With him that night were two companions, whom Decker referred to as "Hernandon" and "Mallory" but admitted were aliases, one of whom was actually Carlos Carbonell, a forty-seven-year-old Cuban American banker. The trio placed a twelve-foot ladder against the side of the prison on O'Farrill Street. Decker and Malloy had reached the roof when the ladder began to sway. They hauled Hernandon up, but at the same time a piece of weak cornice on which the ladder had been resting gave way and clattered to the street.[29]

Acting quickly, Decker and the others hauled up the ladder. By the time an inquisitive old guard appeared below with a candle, Decker and the others had three .44s pointed at him from concealment. Seeing nothing of interest, the guard returned, and Decker and the others crept to the window Evangelina had indicated. There they found the senorita waiting patiently, wearing a dark gown. Decker began cutting through a bar in the window, finding it slow going. Eventually Evangelina, worried that she'd be discovered, decided it would be best if she return to sleep and Decker return the next night to finish sawing the bar. Decker agreed.[30]

Before returning with the ladder, Decker made arrangements with the *Olivette* for passage from Havana to Key West. This would prove merely misdirection. Then on the night of October 6, the trio returned to O'Farrill Street.

"The night was still, hot and oppressive," Decker reflected. "Early in the evening a bank of heavy clouds gave promise of rain, but we were disappointed in our hopes, for by 9 o'clock the sky had cleared and the great round, white moon rode through the heavens . . . unflecked by clouds."[31]

Despite the weather being against them, the trio once again placed the ladder to the prison wall, climbed up, and hauled up the ladder. This time "as quietly as cats," as Decker described it, they made short work of the bar.

"Is the opening large enough?" Decker whispered.

In response, Evangelina's head emerged, and she began wriggling through the opening. Decker grasped her about the waist and lifted her into the night air. Soon after they descended the ladder and boarded a carriage, with Hernandon driving. Through deserted streets they made their way to the home of Carlos Carbonell, which they had selected as a hiding spot until they could smuggle Evangelina out of Cuba.[32]

The next day, October 7, the guards realized that Evangelina—who had become a focal point of the Cuban cause and an international person of interest—had escaped. In short order the news that Evangelina was on the loose became known throughout Havana and was telegraphed to Washington and Madrid. Detectives began shadowing Decker, but they had nothing to go by, and he was careful not to be caught returning to the stash house.

Commented Decker, "On the day she left her hiding-place I succeeded in shaking off my shadows by using certain methods which would have been ridiculed by a Pinkerton, but which were successful with the Spanish spies."[33]

The "greatest fright" of the entire adventure, as Decker observed, was when Evangelina boldly walked to the wharf, disguised as a young *marinero,* or sailor, with a blue shirt, a flowing tie, and her hair tucked beneath a slouch hat. The wind blew off her hat. Decker gripped his gun while Evangelina coolly plucked the hat from the ground and set it on her head, with no one the wiser. Ultimately, Evangelina boarded the *Seneca.* Afterward Decker boarded the *Panama,* a forged visa in his pocket, but not before wiring the *New York Journal.*[34]

On October 8, the *Journal* ran a short article announcing that Evangelina Cisneros had escaped Casa de Recogidas. A bar to her window had been sawed. Prison guards were being questioned. No one had any idea where she was. The following day, the *Journal* printed that General Weyler had resigned and that Evangelina was on her way to the United States. In actuality Weyler had been fired, though it wasn't quite as clean as the Hearst papers suggested. In early August 1897, the Spanish government had finally determined that Weyler needed to go and would be replaced by Governor-General Ramón Blanco y Erenas, set to arrive in Havana on October 30. Since that time Weyler had bitterly waited for Blanco's arrival, his feelings made plain in his memoir *Mi Mando en Cuba.* Desperately, Weyler schemed to hold onto power. But with Evangelina disappearing right under his nose, all hopes of Weyler keeping his command were dashed.[35]

"Weyler's wrath is beyond all bounds," gloated the *Journal.*[36]

On October 10, the *Journal* printed on the front page the entire astonishing story of the escape under the headline "Evangelina Cisneros Rescued by the Journal." Beneath the headline was Karl Decker's story, going under his penname Charles Duval and dated October 7, Havana, and October 9, Key West:

> I have broken the bars of Recojidas and have set free the beautiful captive of monster Weyler, restoring her to her friends and relatives, and doing by strength, skill and strategy what could not be accomplished by petition and urgent request by the Pope.
>
> Weyler could blind the Queen to the real character of Evangelina, but he could not build a jail that would hold against *Journal* enterprise when properly set to work.[37]

Sensing that this was only the beginning of the spectacle, Hearst set to work. Sparing no expense, he garbed Evangelina like a *princesa,* set her up in a Waldorf suite, held a parade and a rally for her at Madison Square Garden, and threw a dinner for her at Delmonico's.[38]

Marveling at Hearst's enterprise and character, Frederick Palmer noted, "In the midst of the bizarre and pompeian reception which was given to the young woman at Delmonico's, the man who footed the bills came into the room where she stood among the palms, shyly shook hands with the heroine whom his wonder machine had created, and then excused himself and hastened away in his automobile."[39]

After the banquet, Hearst threw Evangelina a grand ball in the Waldorf's opulent Red Room and sent her in style to Washington, D.C., where she was introduced to President McKinley. At every step Hearst's reporters wrote articles on the Cuban woman who, with the *Journal*'s help, had defied "Butcher Weyler."[40]

The effect was extraordinary.

"William Randolph Hearst . . . was mixing war, patriotism, and romance with Eva Cisneros, reported by Hearst to be of superlative and languishing beauty," recollected Charles Post, a cartoonist at the *Journal*. "This reporting was fragrant with circulation results, while we commoner folk began to boil and seethe with ardor to kill a Spaniard."[41]

More than ever war with Spain seemed imminent. No dummy, Roosevelt could see the Spanish-American War unfolding in his mind and was worried that unless they acted quickly the US Navy would be at a disadvantage.

"I believe that Congress should at once give us six (6) new battleships," Roosevelt wrote to Long that fall, "two (2) to be built on the Pacific and four (4) on the Atlantic; six (6) large cruisers, of the size of the *Brooklyn,* but in armament more nearly approaching the Argentine vessel *San Martin;* and seventy-five (75) torpedo boats, twenty-five (25) for the Pacific and fifty (50) for the Atlantic. I believe that we should set about building all these craft now, and that each one should be, if possible, the most formidable of its kind afloat."[42]

Roosevelt also called for the construction of drydocks, the implementation of smokeless powder, and a reserve of projectiles—"about nine thousand in all"—for each ship.

Around the same time, the *Boston Globe* praised Roosevelt's industry and influence:

> Mr. Roosevelt has said that the surest way of shooting a grizzly bear is to get close up to him. Evidently he applies the same aggressive principle to naval warfare and wishes to see our blue jackets prepared for a hand-to-hand encounter with the enemy. . . . Of all the entertainments in the great theater of our national life it is a fair guess that the people of the United States have

> got more for their money out of his continuous performance during the past 15 years than out of any other feature of Uncle Sam's gigantic all-star company. . . . It would never do, however, to permit such a man to get into the presidency. He would produce national insomnia.[43]

In January 1898, Fighting Joe Wheeler also made a rousing speech in favor of war with Spain. He professed to be "astounded" that his Republican colleagues across the aisle seemed to be afraid of war. He chastised such pacificism as the very thing that "dragged down the empires of Assyria and Rome and Greece and Carthage." Concluding, Wheeler gravely intoned, "God forbid that the growing generation should prefer to be money changers than brave soldiers, fighting and if need be dying, in the front rank of battle."[44]

That same month events in Cuba came to a boil. On January 11, 1898, a great mob rioted in Havana, protesting against a Spanish government that had overseen the implosion of the Cuban economy and a war with no end in sight, which through bloodshed, starvation, and disease had killed more than 150,000 Cubans by conservative estimates and by some estimates was closer to 600,000. To maintain American interests, President McKinley ordered the 324-foot battleship USS *Maine* from Key West to Havana.

On the morning of January 25, 1898, the *Maine* dropped anchor in Havana Harbor. The visit was ostensibly a friendly one. When Captain Charles Sigsbee mentioned that he'd like to attend a bullfight scheduled for Sunday, January 30, General Julián González Parrado sent him tickets. Sigsbee couldn't help noticing hard stares from Spaniards in the crowd, the martial atmosphere made worse by the presence of twenty Spanish soldiers stationed just in front of the captain's box seats. Not wishing to fan animosity, Sigsbee and his party returned to the *Maine* with the bull still living. It proved a good thing for the *Journal* that Sigsbee kept close to the *Maine*.[45]

On February 1, Julian Hawthorne sailed from New York City aboard Hearst's personal yacht, *Buccaneer.* On February 7, Hawthorne arrived in Havana Harbor with the intention of visiting the *reconcentrado* camps and describing the conditions. The Spanish had other ideas. Purportedly believing that Karl Decker was aboard, the Spanish boarded the *Buccaneer* and searched the vessel for the *Journal*'s agent. Meanwhile, Captain Sigsbee was apprised of the situation and let it be known that if Decker were found aboard and imprisoned, he wanted the prisoner brought to him. Decker was not aboard, but the incident sparked further outrage.[46]

Animosity between Spain and the United States hit a new low two days later when a handwritten letter critical to President McKinley, penned by the Spanish ambassador in Washington, Enrique Dupuy de Lôme, was sent to a friend in Havana and was somehow leaked to the press.

"Besides the natural and inevitable coarseness with which he repeats that the press and public opinion of Spain have said of Weyler," Dupuy de Lôme wrote, "it shows once more that McKinley is weak and catering to the rabble and, besides, a low politician who desires to leave a door open to himself and to stand well with the jingos of his party."[47]

A translated version of the letter was published in American morning newspapers throughout the United States on February 9, 1898. The *New York Journal* printed it below the headline "The Worst Insult to the United States in Its History." By that afternoon every newspaper was printing the letter. Dupuy de Lôme immediately resigned, but the damage had been done.

That same day seventy-six-year-old Clara Barton disembarked in Havana. As the founder and president of the American National Red Cross, she'd been granted permission by the US and Spanish governments to administer aid to the *reconcentrados.* Barton found that the Hearst newspapers hadn't been exaggerating. The survivors of the *reconcentrado* camps were famished and skeletal, many beyond saving. Distended bellies, bones showing through skin, and hollowed eyes were a common sight. Still, Barton did as best she could to procure food for the starving Cubans from Havana and nearby towns, generating hostility from Spanish officials. After accepting Sigsbee's invitation to lunch aboard the *Maine,* Barton couldn't help juxtaposing the "strong ruddy and bright" faces of the American crew with the nightmarish oppression of the Cuban populace.[48]

On February 12, Julian Hawthorne's piece in the *Journal* on Havana's *reconcentrado* camp went several steps further.

> Not in this age, certainly, has a crime been perpetuated more revolting to the humanity than Weyler committed when he forced the women and children of the patriots in the Cuban army to come within the Spanish lines, and then deliberately starved them there. His ostensible purpose was to weaken the heart of the resistance by attacking its tenderest point, but his real aim was the literal extinction of the Cuban race, and he has so far succeeded that out of the million and a half inhabitants of this island when the war began, six hundred thousand at least, by far the most of them women and

> children, have been destroyed, either by direct murder or by the slower and more agonizing torture of famine and of disease caused by famine.[49]

Hawthorne tallied more than a hundred daily Cuban fatalities in Havana's *reconcentrado* camp alone. The illustrations of suffering women and children amplified the damning article.

Three nights later on February 15, 1898, Josep Conangla—having transferred from Aguacate to Havana—met with two companions at the Albisu Theater. There they decided to skip the Spanish opera that was playing, as they had already seen it, and instead catch a Creole comedy at the Alhambra Theater on Consulado Street.[50]

That same evening George Bronson Rea of the *New York Herald* was enjoying the evening at a café outside Havana's Central Park. Joining him was Harry Scovel of the *New York World*—who had been allowed back into Cuba a few months after being expelled—and Scovel's wife, Frances. The trio chatting amiably while masked and costumed merrymakers paraded by.[51]

Then at 9:40 p.m., the world seemed to explode.

Amid a great roar, the windows of the café shattered. Despite their shock, Rea and Scovel were reporters at their core. They quickly hailed a cab and ordered the driver to make for the harbor. It was as they feared. One look at the ocean and they could tell the source of the blast. The *Maine* had exploded.

"Great masses of twisted and bent iron plates and beams were thrown up in confusion amidships," Rea recollected. "The bow had disappeared; the foremast and smoke stacks had fallen; and to add to the horror and danger, the mass of wreckage amidships was on fire."[52]

Scovel observed that "the superstructure alone loomed up, partly colored by the red glare of flames glancing upon the black water. At first it appeared as if her bow was totally demolished. The mass of beams and braces was seen . . . blown forward by the awful rending."[53]

Similarly, Conangla had been chatting amiably with his companions and a lieutenant colonel at the Alhambra Theater when the sound of a "huge explosion" stunned everybody into confused silence. But the truth wasn't long in coming.[54]

"The *Maine* has exploded!!" someone shouted.

The theater quickly emptied of people. Later that evening Conangla recalled a captain exclaiming, "Now the war will end!"

"Unless another one breaks out," prophesized another officer in a low voice.

Clara Barton and her assistant had been working near the harbor when the "deafening roar" was heard. "The table shook from under our hands, the great glass door opening on to the veranda, facing the sea flew open; everything in the room was in motion or out of place. . . . And off to the right, out over the bay, the air was filled with a blaze of light."[55]

Naturally rushing for the San Ambosio Hospital, where more than thirty wounded men had been taken, Barton found a horrific scene. "They had been crushed by timbers, cut by iron, scorched by fire, and blown sometimes high in the air, sometimes driven down through the red hot furnace room and out into the water, senseless, to be picked up by some boat and gotten ashore. Their wounds were all over them—heads and faces terribly cut, internal wounds, arms, legs, feet and hands burned to the live flesh."

Captain Sigsbee, who had been aboard the *Maine* at the time of its explosion, got the worst view. Fighting through the Stygian darkness, he blundered into Marine Private William Anthony. The pair finally emerged just in front of the superstructure, and Sigsbee began barking orders to help the survivors.[56]

All told, fewer than 100 men survived the wreckage of the *Maine*, the explosion killing upwards of 250 men. The most accepted theory is that because of a flaw in the design of the battleship, a coal bunker near the munitions caught fire, causing the explosion. But the American newspapers had a different interpretation, with the proprietor of the *New York Journal* setting the tone.[57]

According to his own 1940 account, Hearst had just returned from a late night at the newspaper when his butler, George Thompson, stopped him at the door.

"There's a telephone from the office," Thompson said. "They say it's important news."[58]

Calling up the office, Hearst asked, "Hello, what is the important news?"

"The battleship *Maine* has been blown up in Havana Harbor."

"Good Heavens, what have you done with the story?"

"We have put it on the first page, of course."

"Have you put anything else on the front page?

"Only the other big news."

"There is not any other big news. Please spread the story all over the page. This means war."

Theodore Roosevelt. Courtesy of Huntington Research Library, San Marino.

Bust of Joseph Wheeler. Sculpture by Margaret Whetstone. Courtesy of the Alabama Department of Archives and History. Photograph by Zachary Tonkins.

William Randolph Hearst. Courtesy of California History Society, San Francisco.

Richard Harding Davis. Courtesy of Huntington Research Library, San Marino.

Stephen Crane. Courtesy of Wikimedia Commons.

Theodore Roosevelt and Richard Harding Davis. Courtesy of Wikimedia Commons.

— PART III —

THE GAME

A low rumbling sound was heard; a subterraneous hum;
and then all held their breaths.
Herman Melville, Moby-Dick

—12—

REMEMBER THE *MAINE*

On the morning of February 16, 1898, less than twenty-four hours after over 250 American sailors died aboard the *Maine,* Fighting Joe Wheeler telegrammed President William McKinley: "To the Honorable President: In case of any trouble with Spain, remember that my tender services is on file at the war department. Joseph Wheeler."[1]

Wheeler's daughter, Annie, tried to talk her father out of it.

"Father," Annie implored, "you surely had fighting enough to do from sixty-one to sixty-five; let the young men go to war this time."[2]

"Daughter," Wheeler replied, "if a fish had been out of water for thirty-three years, and suddenly came in sight of a great pond, he'd wiggle a little, at any rate."

Wheeler and his family weren't alone in believing that war with Spain was imminent. Despite the strong possibility that the explosion aboard the *Maine* was an accident, all one had to do was look at the *San Francisco Examiner* or the *New York Journal* to see the way the wind was blowing.

"THE BATTLESHIP MAINE BLOWN UP IN HAVANA HARBOR," the *Examiner* declared.[3]

The *Journal* was equally belligerent: "CRISIS IS AT HAND. 253 KNOWN TO BE LOST. CABINET IN SESSION; GROWING BELIEF IN SPANISH TREACHERY."[4]

That same day Theodore Roosevelt wrote to fellow Harvard man Harrison Diblee. "Being a Jingo . . . I will say, to relieve my feelings, that I would give anything if President McKinley would order the fleet to Havana tomorrow. This Cuban business ought to stop. The *Maine* was sunk by an act of dirty treachery on the part of the Spaniards *I* believe; though we shall never find out definitely, and officially it will go down as an accident."[5]

The next day's edition of the *Journal* published Roosevelt's sentiment, and though characteristically citing no hard evidence, it removed all doubt as to the destruction of the *Maine:* "DESTRUCTION OF WAR SHIP MAINE WAS THE WORK OF AN ENEMY. Assistant Secretary Roosevelt Convinced the Explosion of the War Ship Was Not an Accident. The Journal Offers 50,000 Reward for the Conviction of the Criminals Who Sent 258 American Sailors to Their Death. Naval Officers Unanimous That the Ship Was Destroyed on Purpose."[6]

Putting him at odds with his top subordinate, Secretary of the Navy John D. Long disagreed with Roosevelt's assessment. On February 17, 1898, Long wrote in his journal:

> There is an intense difference of opinion as to the cause of the blowing up of the Maine. In this, as in everything else, the opinion of the individual is determined by his original bias. If he is a conservative, he is sure that it was an accident; if he is a jingo, he is equally sure that it was by design. The former is sure that no design could have been carried out without discovery; the latter is equally sure that no accident could have happened in view of the precautions which were taken. My own judgment is, so far as any information has been received, that it was the result of an accident, such as every ship of war, with the tremendously high and powerful explosives which we now have on board, is liable to encounter.[7]

McKinley sided with the conservatives. As he mentioned to a friend, "I don't propose to be swept off my feet by the catastrophe. My duty is plain. We must learn the truth and endeavor, if possible, to fix the responsibility. . . . The Administration will go on preparing for war, but still hoping to avert it."[8]

Despite conservatives claiming that the destruction of the *Maine* must have been accidental, chants of "Remember the *Maine!* To hell with Spain!" were heard throughout the country. Hearst, taking his carnivalesque journalism to the next level, proposed raising a regiment of baseball sluggers, football players, and heavyweight boxers to rid Cuba of the Spanish. "Buffalo Bill" Cody thought he could do one better: with thirty thousand Indian warriors he could expel the Spaniards in sixty days. Jesse James's brother Frank, who had traded outlawry for working as the doorkeeper at St. Louis's Standard Theater, suggested that he avenge the *Maine* by leading a company of cowboys.[9]

On February 18 on the floor of the Senate, William E. Mason of Illinois—claiming that he wished for the United States to put an end to "human slavery and inhuman warfare" in Cuba—opened up a copy of the February 12 edition of the *New York Journal* and read aloud Hawthorne's two-column article on Havana's *reconcentrado* camp. Hawthorne's damning descriptions that Mason was a Republican, usually allied with the conservatives, spoke volumes.[10]

As discussions of war with Spain grew daily, from the lowliest saloons and townhalls to Capitol Hill and the White House, so too did Wheeler's role in the coming conflict. Dozens of newspapermen, particularly in the Deep South, praised Wheeler and advocated for him to receive command.

As the *Henderson Gold Leaf* commented, "the fact that General Joseph Wheeler . . . has tendered his services to President McKinley in the event of war between the United States and Spain, gives evidence that the men who wore the gray are willing to fight for the old flag as though there had never been any war between the States."[11]

The *Savanna News* echoed these sentiments, declaring that if "Joe Wheeler should be called upon, and could get a command as followed him in the last days of the Confederacy, the country would have in its service a 'critter company' which could live on less and do more fighting and fight in more ways than any other force which could be put in the field."[12]

Alabama's *Scottsboro Citizen* was almost jubilant at the thought of the South once again following Wheeler into war. "When Congress adjourns and Gen. Wheeler returns . . . you will hear a noise something akin to the old 'rebel yell.' The boys in the trenches are for that dashing Cavalier, that 'wizard of the saddle,' the great tribune of the people, Gen. Joe Wheeler." The *Scottsboro Citizen* also predicted that under Wheeler's generalship, the American flag would fly above Havana's Morro Castle within only sixty days of war.[13]

Meanwhile, the assistant secretary of the navy had some predictions of his own. On Friday, February 25, 1898, Theodore Roosevelt sent the following cablegram to Admiral George Dewey:

> Dewey, Hong Kong:
>
> Order the squadron, except the Monocacy, to Hong Kong. Keep full of coal. In the event of a declaration of war with Spain, your duty will

> be to see that the Spanish squadron does not leave the Asiatic coast, and then offensive operations in Philippine Islands. Keep Olympia until further orders.
>
> Roosevelt[14]

In his own autobiography, Dewey remarked that Roosevelt's cablegram was the "first real step" in active naval preparations for the coming war.[15]

As much as Roosevelt wished to devote all of February 25 to war preparations, he could not, for Edith had been sick with fever for weeks. "Edith had more fever yesterday," Roosevelt wrote Bamie that same day from their Dupont home at 1810 N Street, "and though she went down again last night she seems so weak that I have concluded to get Dr. [William] Osler, the great Baltimore expert, in consultation. I have not felt the loss of the Maine nearly as much as I would if I had not had so much worry over in my own home."[16]

Even still, Roosevelt spent that momentous February 25 doing all he could to put the United States on war footing. This included ordering guns from the Navy Yard shipped to active vessels, authorizing the limitless enlistment of seamen, and writing a letter to General Charles Foster Tillinghast Jr. of the National Guard that in the event of war "pray remember, that in some shape I want to go."[17]

When on the following day, February 26, 1898, Secretary of the Navy John D. Long returned to his office and discovered the paper trail of Roosevelt's actions, he hit the roof.

"The very devil seemed to possess him yesterday afternoon. . . . [H]e has gone at things like a bull in a china shop," Long complained in his diary.[18]

On March 4—the eleventh anniversary of young W. R. Hearst taking over the *Examiner*—the *Journal* published a long article by Roosevelt's journalist friend, Alfred Henry Lewis, on conditions in Havana. "A riot is in order at any moment in that feverish city," Lewis reported. "With a city full of Spaniards, whose strongest impulse is hatred of Americans, weak and shallow as the Spaniard is, the half hundred Americans would not last as long as a drink of whiskey on the Bowery."[19]

As the drumbeat for war increased in tempo, in no small part due to Wheeler, Roosevelt, and Hearst, praise for Wheeler spread north. The *Washington Times* congratulated Fighting Joe for offering his sword to the government.

Wheeler's position proved popular throughout the country. Although McKinley seemed at first reluctant, the cynics held that he was too much of a politician to thwart the will of the people. McKinley hadn't declared war yet, but the word from his cabinet was that he was preparing to do so. When on March 8 McKinley asked for a $50 million appropriations bill "for the defense of the nation's honor," the bill passed Congress without a dissenting vote. Wheeler himself rose, delivering a fiery two-minute speech wherein he declared that "twenty million people south of the Potomac" supported the appropriations bill.[20]

"And to the those who cry, 'Peace! Peace!' let me say that the best way to preserve peace is to be thoroughly prepared for war," Wheeler stated, recalling the tactics of Roman general Publius Flavius Vegetius Renatus and Prussian general Carl von Clausewitz. "Certainly that is the only way to preserve peace and at the same time maintain the honor of our people."

Wheeler also said, "For a century American mothers have taught their sons that an ounce of glory earned in battle was worth more than a million pounds of gold!" Before taking his seat, Wheeler shocked the Capitol building by giving vent to the old rebel yell. For his remarks and zeal, he received a standing ovation by members of Congress. Of Wheeler's victorious shout, the Washington, D.C., *Evening Star* commented that among the old Confederates in Congress, the feeling was now "completely American."[21]

Two days later on March 10, it was announced that the US cruiser *Montgomery* had launched for Cuban waters.

With the belief that war with Spain was imminent and that Wheeler might just be called to lead it, letters began pouring into the Wheeler household from old soldiers who wished to join his staff.

A traveling salesman in Chicago wrote to Wheeler: "Yourself, General Forrest, and Morgan gave us cavalrymen lots of trouble years ago. I missed two shots which I meant for you. It would give me a great deal of pleasure to enlist under your leadership. I have been a commercial traveler for nearly 30 years. I am ready at any time to kick my sample case in the gutter and to shoulder to shoulder with the friends of the South to defend and honor the flag."[22]

From a nephew of Colonel John Bonham, who had died defending the Alamo, came a letter: "My father commanded the Third Alabama in some of the hardest fights during the Civil War. I herewith make an application for a commission on your staff."

In a typed letter, Thomas Clark Jr. of the Empire State Rubber Company volunteered as well. "I am filled with the desire to follow in the footsteps of so distinguished a member of the family as yourself. I feel I could not make a better start or be under better guidance than that of fighting 'Joe. Wheeler.'"[23]

Even Professor David F. Boyd of Louisiana State University, who had been both a Confederate and a good friend of General William Tecumseh Sherman, wanted in on the action. To Wheeler, Boyd wrote, "Though I am now 63 years old I have not been sick a day in nearly 40 years. I feel as strong and active as ever I was and believe I could do good military duty."[24]

That tens of thousands of Americans were about to see military duty seemed almost a certainty, but Hearst was taking no chances. On March 14 he published further damning illustrations of skeletal Cubans in the *reconcentrado* camps. Women and children were shown wearing only rags, with distended bellies and emaciated skin over prominent rib cages. Any reader who doubted that the Spanish blew up the *Maine* couldn't deny that the Spanish Empire's brutal subjugation of Cuba was barbarism, shades of Andersonville and a precursor to the Nazi concentration camps, on an industrial level.

That same day Hearst published Julian Hawthorne's article, "The Spectacle of Death," imploring McKinley to take action:

> I say it is significant that this load of human misery should be lying at our doors. For we cannot evade our share of responsibility for its existence. President McKinley has a difficult problem to solve, no doubt; he has to consider many things, and it is hard for a man of his calibre and temperament to be sure enough that he is right to go ahead. But the pictures of the starving wretches printed to-day in this paper ought to haunt his dreams the rest of his life; for he might have saved them and he did not. Let his look upon these ghastly faces and awful limbs and reflect.[25]

On March 17, 1898, one month and two days after the destruction of the *Maine,* Senator Redfield Proctor of Vermont, having returned from a tour of the *reconcentrado* camps, gave a powerful speech on the floor of the Capitol building denouncing the atrocities he had witnessed. That same day the *Journal* published a Davenport illustration of a Wall Street stock broker standing on a Cuban skeleton. This captured a growing sentiment that righteous war with Spain was being prevented by millionaire politicians who didn't want to see their commercial interests disrupted.[26]

Fighting Joe Wheeler thought he could turn the commercial aspect of the conflict to the advantage of the jingoes. On March 18 he introduced a joint resolution in the House. He asked that a joint committee, consisting of five members of the House and five members of the Senate, draft a document declaring to Spain that "American interests in Cuba must be protected, and atrocities now being perpetrated in that island must cease." Wheeler's request was quickly resolved.[27]

The following day, March 19, the *New York Journal* quoted Roosevelt in a front-page interview as saying that "it is cheering to find a newspaper of the great influence and circulation of the *Journal* tell the facts as they exist and ignore the suggestions of various kinds that emanate from sources that cannot be described as patriotic or loyal to the flag of this country." The *Journal* had made up the quote, of course, which Roosevelt explained in the March 21 edition of the *New York Post:* "The alleged interview with me in today's New York *Journal* is an invention from beginning to end," Roosevelt declared. "It is difficult to explain the kind of infamy that resorts to such methods."[28]

But as critical as Roosevelt could be of Hearst's *Journal,* no one could doubt that during that particularly tumultuous spring the two men were playing on the same team. Considering Senator Mark Hanna's powerful influence on McKinley, Roosevelt must have enjoyed it when Hearst reprinted Davenport's cartoon of the Ohio senator covered with dollar signs alongside a front-page article titled "Hanna vs. Honor."[29]

Five days later Roosevelt also minced words with Hanna. On Saturday, March 26, Roosevelt served as the special guest of honor at the Gridiron Dinner in Washington, a precursor to the White House Correspondents Dinner sans the White House, where politicians and newspaper wits dined on a sixteen-course banquet while poking fun at each other. With the war on everyone's mind, the menu displayed a warship sporting the Gridiron flag making for "To-Morrow Castle," a play on Havana's Morro Castle, and Roosevelt was playfully elevated to the position of vice admiral of the Gridiron Navy. But Roosevelt, seated at the head of the table across from Senator Hanna, wasn't feeling entirely playful. How could he be? That morning's copy of the *New York Journal* contained an exclusive interview with Clara Barton from the *reconcentrado* camps describing them as rife with "hunger, starvation, and death."[30]

"We will have this war for the freedom of Cuba, Senator Hanna," Roosevelt insisted, "in spite of the timidity of the commercial interests."[31]

"It was a very dramatic moment," recorded Washington journalist Arthur Wallace Dunn, "and there was no one present at the dinner who did not thoroughly understand that war was inevitable."[32]

Two days later on March 28, 1898, the *Maine* report was made public. The investigative court determined that the explosion had been caused by the battleship's forward magazines having exploded due to an external device. This removed blame from the US Navy for any "fault or negligence" and without explicitly saying so cast the preponderance of doubt on the Spanish. That investigations conducted years later concluded that the explosion of the *Maine* was likely caused by poor design had no bearing on the political and martial reality of 1898.[33]

Naturally, the opinion of Spanish naval engineers differed. They determined that the explosion of the *Maine* was due to a magazine powder igniting aboard the *Maine.* Rumors also spread across Havana that the Americans had deliberately destroyed their own battleship for the Machiavellian purpose of blaming Spain for the tragedy, to be followed by a declaration of war.[34]

The same day the *Maine* report was publicized, Stephen Crane—who dodged his American creditors by moving with Cora to England, where he wrote the western classics "The Bride Comes to Yellow Sky" and "The Blue Hotel" and mixed with Jessie and Joseph Conrad—shipped out of Liverpool aboard the *Germanic.* Also aboard the White Star Line ocean liner was a letter Cora had written to Harry Scovel.

> Dear Harry:
>
> Stephen is coming on the ship that carries this letter to America, as correspondent in the U.S. Spain row. I suppose you will see him as doubtless Key West will be the headquarters for newspaper men. We have thought it best for me to remain in England. I am writing to you to ask you and your good wife—if ye be in the same town, to look after him a little. He is rather seedy and I am anxious for him, for he does not care to look out for himself.[35]

As for Richard Harding Davis, the veteran reporter had been in Paris, a mere hour away from entraining to Belgrade and a trip to Serbia and Bulgaria, when he'd heard about the *Maine.* Davis immediately canceled the trip. Like Hearst, he knew this meant war.

"If I do miss it," Davis wrote to his brother Charles, "I shall be wild."[36]

In London and New York City, Davis found employment: the *Times of London, Scribner's,* the *New York Herald* and their affiliated syndicate of fourteen newspapers. In those two cities Davis also outfitted himself for the excursion: a raking cap, a canvas shooting jacket, a revolver and cartridge belt, a leather flask, and top boots. A photograph of Davis landed in the *Critic,* provoking derision and amusement.

The *Memphis Commercial Appeal* declared that Davis was "as impressive as a golf hero and as haughty as Emperor Bill." The *Springfield Republican* quipped, "If he were cut up into small pieces, he would furnish the insurgents with arms and equipments for a whole winter." The *Boston Herald,* part of the syndicate which Davis was now associated, was somewhat gentler in their description: "Davis . . . is the picture of an intrepid war correspondent who is in for a long siege."[37]

In early April, Davis left New York City for Florida.

On April 1 Albert J. Hopkins, a Republican congressman from Illinois, presided over a caucus of about fifty other Republican members of the House and demanded their support for war with Cuba. When the caucus failed, Wheeler made the most of it, delivering a derisive speech on the House floor.

"Early this morning," Wheeler chastised, "the people hastened to this hall. They came to hear the rights of the people proclaimed in tones of thunder; they came to be told that the sufferings of the patriots of Cuba had at last reached the ears and hearts of the great Republican party; they came to see patriotism triumph."[38]

Instead, the patriotic Americans in the galleries had looked on with horror and disgust at the Republicans who had failed to answer the call.

"Mr. Speaker," Wheeler concluded, "I know of no more certain way to bring on war than the action of the Republican party this morning. Already this surrender . . . has been cabled to Madrid and has no doubt encouraged the Spaniards to assume a more defiant attitude."[39]

Immediately afterward Wheeler boarded a train, that day reaching New York City. There he met at the Waldorf Astoria hotel with several famous veterans of the American Civil War: Joshua L. Chamberlain, James Longstreet, Daniel E. Sickles, Alexander McCook, Granville Dodge, O. O. Howard, and Lew Wallace. Their purpose was to raise an army of at least one million volunteers for the coming conflict. Back in the White House, however, McKinley was still hoping for peace. On April 4, taking seriously the rumors of concessions from Madrid, the president delayed a war messaged he'd planned to send to Congress. Outraged, war hawks in Congress—now the vast majority—marched to the White House, obligating McKinley to lock certain documents in the safe.[40]

To newspapermen, Roosevelt commented that Henry Adams seemed correct in his assessment that McKinley was "a jellyfish."[41]

Once in a while McKinley would grouse to his assistant attending surgeon, Leonard Wood, about Wood's new friend, the assistant secretary of the navy.

"Well, have you and Theodore declared war yet?" McKinley asked.[42]

"No, Mr. President, we have not, but we think you should take steps in that direction, sir."

As for Fighting Joe Wheeler, even the northern newspapers were singing his praises. On April 6 a wit for the *New York Sun* wrote a five-stanza poem praising Wheeler's patriotism, the fourth stanza the most telling:

I'm ready for the Spanish
If they should come ashore,
And with ten thousand horsemen
I'd like to lead once more,
This time a troop of Yankees,
A rebel at the fore.[43]

With mounting pressure from the yellow journalists and with Congress almost completely caught up in the war craze, McKinley issued a call for 125,000 volunteers to join the standing 28,000 regular army. Secretary of War Russell A. Alger set about looking for a colonel to lead the three regiments McKinley had ordered "to be composed exclusively of frontiersmen possessing special qualifications as horsemen and marksmen." This was a role Roosevelt seemed born to play, and Alger offered the command to him. Roosevelt felt certain he could "learn to command the regiment in a month" but begged off all the same. He felt that a month might make all the difference. Yet, he would happily serve as lieutenant colonel if Leonard Wood served as colonel. The arrangement suited both Wood and Alger, and in a flash Roosevelt began preparations for arming and equipping a volunteer cavalry corps.[44]

Poultney Bigelow, a thirty-two-year-old reporter and a Yalensian, recalled in his 1925 autobiography that "Roosevelt made up by enthusiasm what he lacked in experience; and he raved like a maniac about the Washington bureaux until he secured all that he asked for."[45]

In late April, McKinley finally had his ducks lined up. On April 25, 1898, the president formally forwarded to Congress a declaration of war against Spain:

> I now recommend the adoption of a joint resolution declaring that a state of war exists between the United States of America and the Kingdom of Spain, that the definition of the international status of the United States as

> a belligerent power may be made known and the assertion of all its rights in the conduct of a public war may be assured.
>
> Be it enacted by the Senate and House of Representatives of the United States of America in Congress assembled, First. That war be, and the same is hereby, declared to exist, and that war has existed since the 21st day of April, A. D. 1898, including said day, between the United States of America and the Kingdom of Spain.[46]

"War was demanded and war was soon declared," Hearst reflected.[47]

On the afternoon of April 26, William C. Oates met with McKinley at the White House just before a cabinet meeting. Oates, the former governor of Alabama, had fought as a colonel in the 15th Alabama at the Battle of Gettysburg, where he led a number of ferocious charges against the Union line at Little Round Top, ultimately repulsed by Joshua Chamberlain's 20th Maine. Rather than offer Oates an army position, McKinley broached the subject of Wheeler once more going to war, this time as a major general of volunteers. Oates thought this was a dandy choice and that Wheeler was a brave man, "one of the bravest that the Civil War developed," Oates added.[48]

Shortly afterward the president wrote to Wheeler that he would like him to call on him at the White House at 8:30 that evening.

"I was prompt in replying," Wheeler recalled.[49]

Ushered into the room, Wheeler was greeted by McKinley and five men who constituted the president's inner circle. Along with Attorney General John W. Griggs and Secretary of War Russell A. Alger, McKinley had with him three friends from Ohio: Major Russell Hastings, Major Webb Hayes, and former congressman Albert C. Thompson. After the pleasantries McKinley said, "General, I have sent for you to ask you if you want to go, and if you feel able to go."[50]

One account, which seems out of step considering Wheeler's zeal for once more leading troops, described Wheeler initially declining McKinley's request, giving his advanced age as a reason. McKinley confided that for the excursion an ex-Confederate was required and stated, "There must be a symbol that the old days are gone. You are needed."[51]

Although McKinley probably had this in mind when he asked Wheeler to serve his country, Wheeler's version told it differently. Immediately after McKinley offered him a place in the war, Wheeler replied, "Yes, Mr. President. Although I am sixty-one years old I feel as strong and capable as when I was forty, and I desire very much to have another opportunity to serve my country."[52]

"I have got to appoint fifteen major-generals; and it would have given you great pleasure to have heard the pleasant things said about you while we were discussing the matter yesterday." McKinley responded.

They conversed for a short while before McKinley led Wheeler into a separate room so they could speak privately. By the time the conversation was over, Wheeler knew he'd be going to war once more, assured that he would receive a commission as major general of volunteers. Wasting no time, Wheeler entrained for the depot named in his honor, Wheeler Station, just north of his home on Pond Spring, to await instructions. There letters of congratulations poured in.[53]

"Fighting *Joe* Wheeler Now Major *General* U.S. Volunteers!" began one, before paraphrasing *Twelfth Night*: "The whirligig of time brings strange metamorphoses!"[54]

That same day the papers announced that McKinley had appointed Assistant Secretary of the Navy Theodore Roosevelt to the rank of lieutenant colonel, serving under Colonel Leonard Wood. They would both be subordinate to Fighting Joe Wheeler.[55]

Five days later on the other side of the globe, Admiral George Dewey and his Asiatic Squadron made their move. In one of the most momentous and wildly lopsided naval battles in history, from aboard the *Olympia* Dewey led his squadron into Manila Bay, the waters outside the capital of the Philippines. Caught completely unprepared, having rested their hopes on the belief that Manila Bay was unassailable, the Spanish lost their entire fleet, composed of one transport ship, five gunboats, and seven cruisers. All told the Spaniards suffered 77 dead and 271 wounded to American gunfire. The Americans, on the other hand, lost no ships and counted among their ranks only 9 wounded and 1 fatality, and that one a fluke. Francis B. Randall, the chief engineer aboard the *McCullough,* had died of a heart attack.

The next day, May 2, Hearst had printed on the front page of the *Journal* "How do you like the *Journal*'s war?" as well as the *Journal*'s swollen circulation: 1,468,759.[56] He also published a supposed eyewitness account of the Battle of Manila Bay that Charley Michelson and Ned Hamilton had actually written from their desks in New York. "It was a shameless bit of fakery," Michelson explained, "but all the newspapers were doing it."[57]

That same day Wheeler received notice from the War Department that his appointment had been finalized. On May 4 the Senate formally approved Wheeler's appointment.

Two days later the *Journal* commented, "This war has been called a war brought on by the *New York Journal* and the press which it leads. This is merely another way of saying that the war is the war of the American people, for it is only as a newspaper gives voice to the American spirit that it can be influential with the American masses. The *Journal* is powerful with the masses because it believes in them."[58]

With the country's belief in Wheeler high, on May 9 he received his orders:

> War Department, Adjutant-General's Office,
> Washington, D.C., May 9, 1898, 6:18 p.m.
> Major-General Joseph Wheeler,
> Washington:
>
> Under instructions from the Secretary of War, the Major-General Commanding Army directs, as necessary for public service, that you proceed to Camp George H. Thomas, Chickamauga, Ga., and report in person to Major-General John R. Brooke for assignment to duty. Prompt action imperative.
>
> H. C. Corbin,
> Adjutant-General[59]

Wheeler and Joe Jr.—the son having graduated from West Point in 1895—immediately packed their trunks and left on the first train to Georgia. Early on the morning of May 11, Wheeler reported to General Brooke, who had fought for the Union at Antietam, Chancellorsville, and Gettysburg.

"I was very much pleased with General Brooke; he is a large, handsome man, and impressed me very favorably," Wheeler noted. Wheeler must have been doubly pleased when news came that the cruiser USS *Marblehead* had that same day cut the cables off Cienfuegos, impeding Spanish communication.[60]

The following day Wheeler received orders that he was to take command of the cavalry leaving for Florida and in Tampa meet General Nelson Miles. Wheeler and his son rushed to the depot and caught the 2:07 train. They reached Tampa the next day, and Wheeler met with General William R. Shafter, who had been placed in charge of the Volunteers and the Fifth Army Corps. Shafter, who had won the Medal of Honor during the Battle of Fair Oaks while serving as a 1st lieutenant in the 7th Michigan Volunteer Infantry Regiment and been nicknamed "Pecos Bill" during the Indian Wars, impressed Wheeler.

"I readily saw that he possessed administrative ability," Wheeler wrote, "and that he was fitted for important command."

Wheeler's opinion of Shafter wasn't universally held. With short legs, a bulbous head, and a pipsqueak voice and weighing in at about three hundred pounds, "Pecos Bill" didn't fit the image of a commanding general. "Shafter . . . couldn't walk two miles in an hour," an aide divulged, "just beastly obese."[61]

As for Tampa, Wheeler didn't think much of it as a jumping-off place. For one, the mercury rose to 110 degrees. For another, the whole place was a chaotic hub filled with mosquitoes, gnats, and thousands of poorly provisioned soldiers, most of whom had never seen a war, crowding campsites, piling in from Tampa's one-track depot, and hanging about the Tampa Bay Hotel. Five stories tall and made of red brick topped by silver minarets, the Tampa Bay Hotel was the type of establishment W. R. Hearst would have enjoyed. Nine miles from the ocean, spreading out over six acres, and boasting nearly five hundred rooms, the hotel contained an indoor swimming pool, a casino, a golf course, and imported European treasures, including statuary, tapestries, Turkish rugs, and exotic furniture wrought of ebony and gold, the treasure trove costing over a million dollars. Wheeler and his son made for the enormous hotel, where a gaggle of staff officers, newspapermen, sightseers, politicians, hucksters, pickpockets, prostitutes, and idlers conversed and caroused. The military men sat on rocking chairs drinking iced tea and speculating on the particulars of the war.[62]

"This was the rocking-chair period of the war," remarked Richard Harding Davis in *The Cuban and Porto Rican Campaigns.* "It was an army of occupation, but it occupied the piazza of a big hotel."[63]

At the Tampa Bay Hotel, Wheeler found that he wasn't treated as any sort of general or congressman, either unrecognizable or inconsequential among the hubbub. He was eventually given a small room on the sunny side of the hotel, and when he entered the dining room he was shuffled off to a corner far away from the flower-bedecked table reserved for military men and generals. A would-be war correspondent grew to pity the old stranger, giving him "a goblet of iced tea out of his own pitcher and . . . half an omelet."[64]

Later the journalist spied the man and a younger duplicate, who could only have been Wheeler's son, sleeping in a small tent when an orderly approached.

"I have—I bring dispatches and a bundle for the commanding general," stammered the orderly.

Wheeler pulled from the bundle a blue military uniform. Dressing, he stepped out of the tent a new man: Major General Joseph Wheeler, US Volunteers, commanding the cavalry. Wheeler's eyes flashed as he caught sight of a troop of cavalry, the guidon signifying them as Troop A, 3rd Cavalry.

"And how does it feel, General, to wear the blue again?" an officer inquired.

"It is only when I look at Joe," Wheeler replied, indicating his son, "and see his shoulder straps, that I realize that thirty[-]seven years and four months have passed since I followed that guidon. I feel as though I had been away on a three-week furlough, and had but just come back to my own colors."

With Wheeler once more in command, the veterans of the Union and the Confederacy could expect great things from their sixty-one-year-old champion, so long as Fighting Joe remembered which war he was fighting.

13
BADGE OF COURAGE

This time, Stephen Crane would make it to Cuba or die trying.

At 11:53 p.m. on April 21, 1898, the *Germanic* slipped into New York Harbor, docking at Pier 45. The following day, Crane—having failed the physical exam for the US Navy—collected his passport and signed with Pulitzer's *New York World* for three thousand dollars to report on the war with Spain. Finally, Crane was netting "Richard Harding Davis rates" for journalism. But to his English friend Jimmy Hare, a thirty-one-year-old photographer, Crane confided the military pass he got from the *World* would give him the opportunity to write a book on the war.[1]

Knowing better than to linger in New York City, on April 24 Crane stopped in Washington to see Lily Brandon Munroe. With the *New York Journal* that morning printing his article about English torpedo boats—"The Little Stilettos of the Modern Navy Which Stab in the Dark"—Crane was feeling especially bold. Meeting at the Library of Congress, he asked Lily once more to run away with him. Lily, whom Crane had told about his love affair with Cora shortly after he survived the sinking of the *Commodore,* refused. Crane continued on to Key West. The young author stayed at the Key West Hotel but found it crowded. Guests who could not find a room paid five dollars a day for a cot placed in the hallway.[2]

"The Key West Hotel was a bedlam of a place," recalled Ralph Paine, now working for the *New York World* and the *Philadelphia Press.* Abandoning the crowded hotel, Crane and Paine snuck off nights to a local gambling house, the Eagle Bird. Paine noticed that while Crane was at the roulette wheel about to take another spin, the young author smiled tiredly and drawled the lines:

Oh, five white mice of chance,
Shirts of wool and corduroy pants,
Gold and wine, women and sin,
All or you, if you let me come in—
Into the house of chance.[3]

These were the same lines the *New York World* had printed two weeks earlier from Crane's article on gambling.[4]

Charley Michelson was also a keen observer of Crane's vices.

"He liked small gambling—dice or poker—but never seemed to get much of a thrill out of it; his luck was usually bad," Michelson recollected.[5]

While in Key West, Crane reunited with the top man on the *World*'s staff, Harry Scovel, who took young Crane under his wing. Both men knew that before the invasion of Cuba began, the biggest stories were with the US Navy. This meant getting aboard USS *New York,* serving as the headquarters of Admiral William T. Sampson and the flagship of the Atlantic Squadron, sent to protect American transport ships, blockade the Cuban coast, and intercept the Spanish fleet helmed by Admiral Pascual Cervera y Topete. Despite an order forbidding the press aboard the *New York*, Crane needed to be on that ship.

Naturally, Richard Harding Davis was well ahead of him.

"Roosevelt telegraphed me the longest and strongest letter on the subject a man could write instructing the Admiral to take me on as I was writing history," Davis wrote to his mother on April 24 from aboard the *New York Herald*'s yacht *Smith.*[6]

Later that day Davis transferred to the gunboat USS *Dolphin,* which had served as the presidential yacht under Chester A. Arthur. That night the *Dolphin* chased a Spanish vessel believed to be the *Panama* for three hours, firing three shells at the ship before losing it in the darkness. The following day, April 25, Davis and Rufus Zogbaum, a frequent illustrator for *Harper's Weekly,* boarded the *New York.* As much as Davis must have been awed by the *New York*—a 384-foot armored cruiser boasting twelve 4-inch guns and six eight-inch guns—Davis saved special admiration for Sampson.

"Admiral Sampson is a fine man; he impressed me very much," Davis related to his family on April 26. "He was very much bothered at the order forbidding correspondents on the ship, but I talked like a father to him, and he finally gave in."[7]

With Davis having opened the floodgates, other members of the press soon wheedled their way aboard the *New York.* Stephen Bonsal, Davis observed, was already on deck but as an interpreter rather than a correspondent. That Bonsal happened to be working for *McClure's* was no one's business but his. Fortunately for the *New York World* correspondents, Harry Scovel was well acquainted with the admiral. Davis described his fellow Pennsylvanian as having "done so much secret service work for the admiral, running in at night and taking soundings, and by day making photographs of the coast, also carrying messages to the insurgents." At Scovel's behest, on April 29 Ralph Paine and Stephen Crane were brought aboard as well.[8]

Crane—who grew up on the swashbuckling sea tales of James Fenimore Cooper—liked Sampson, calling him "the most interesting personality in the war" and that "just plain, pure, unsauced accomplishment" characterized the admiral. But initially Crane thought that Sampson was bored by the conflict in Cuba. This may have been Crane projecting, for watching the *New York* oversee the idling Key West fleet wasn't the excitement he yearned for. Later, however, Crane determined that "hidden in [Sampson's] indifferent, even apathetic, manner, there was the alert, sure, fine mind of the best sea captain that America has produced" since David Farragut and Isaac Hull.

Unfortunately for the young author, when Paine left the *New York* Crane found those shoes hard to fill. Paine was charismatic and polished, while Crane could be a fish out of water amid certain social situations, occasions where Davis thrived.

On April 30, Sampson confided to Davis in his cabin, "I have received three different orders from the Secretary, one of them telling me I could have such correspondents on board as were agreeable to me. He now tells me that they must all go. You can do as you wish. You are perfectly welcome to remain until the conflict of orders is cleared up."[9]

Davis could tell that Sampson was angry at the orders and wanted him to stay. The captain of the *New York,* French Ensor Chadwick, was in the cabin at the time. Chadwick suggested, "Perhaps Mr. Davis had better remain another twenty-four hours."

"Ships are going to Key West daily," Sampson added.

While Stephen Crane and the other correspondents were shuffled off on press boats, Davis elected to stay aboard the *New York.* Shortly afterward, the flagship began bombarding Matanzas. Davis was overjoyed by his good fortune at having the exclusive story, writing as much to his folks later that day.

"Bonsal missed the bombardment and so too did Stephen Crane. All the press boats were away except The Herald's. I had to write the story in fifteen minutes, so it was no good except that we had it exclusively. . . . I think my position here very strong and the admiral is very much my friend as are also his staff. Crane on the other hand took the place of Paine who was exceedingly popular with every one and it has made it hard for Crane to get into things—I am having a really royal time, it is so beautiful by both night and day and there is always color and movement and the most rigid discipline with the most hearty good feeling."

Having missed the big excitement, Crane made do with what little he'd seen and heard aboard the *New York*. In "Sampson Inspects Harbor at Mariel," published in the *World* on May 1, Crane recalled that on daybreak of April 29 the *New York* rendezvoused with the *Wilmington, Mangrove, Indiana, Iowa, Detroit,* and *Algonquin* off the coast of Havana. At midafternoon they reached the Bay of Mariel, thirty-five miles west of Havana, with Crane noting that the "lifeless and desolate . . . town . . . seemed like a cemetery around the large church."[10]

The *New York* had continued thirteen miles down the coast and was off the harbor of Cabanas when the boatswain in "a voice like the watery snuffle of a swimming horse cried out, 'Man the port battery! Man the port battery!'"[11]

In an instant a troop of dismounted Spanish cavalry, situated in the crumbling hacienda of a tobacco plantation, opened fire at the *New York* with muskets. The *New York* came about, with Captain Chadwick personally aiming the after-starboard 4-inch gun at the Spanish.

"The captain's shell dropped in the middle of their formation," Crane noted, "and they wildly scattered."

Ever the student of the American Civil War, Crane observed that the gunner's mate Lentile "grumbled bitterly" that two of the 8-inch guns, nicknamed "General Lee" and "Stonewall Jackson," were not called into action. Crane concluded the piece, stating "the flagship has returned to her station. The torpedo-boats are evidently keeping Havana rather nervous to-night, for the searchlights have been frantically flashing on the horizon."

Mixing with more reporters, Crane met Frank Norris of *McClure's,* who in 1897 had lampooned Crane's most famous works in San Francisco's weekly magazine *The Wave* under the fanciful title "The Green Stone of Unrest." Crane was in good company, for Norris had also needled Ambrose Bierce, Bret Harte, Sir Anthony Hope, and Rudyard Kipling.[12]

On May 8, Crane, Scovel, and Norris sailed out of Key West aboard the *Three Friends,* observing the American warships blockading the Cuban coast. Proving the truth of Davis's assessment that Crane struggled socially, Norris soon took a dislike to Crane.

"Crane . . . was wearing a pair of duck trousers grimed and fouled with all manner of pitch and grease and oil. His shirt was guiltless of collar or scarf," Norris recollected, "and was unbuttoned at the throat. His hair hung in ragged fringes over his eyes. . . . Between his heels he held a bottle of beer against the rolling of the boat, and when he drank was royally independent of a glass."[13]

Years later Norris's wife, Jeannette Black, dished to Norris's biographer Franklin Walker that "Crane . . . drank too much and made a fool of himself."[14]

Despite liking Crane, Charley Michelson agreed with Norris concerning Crane's appearance. "Crane . . . was the dirtiest man in the army," Michelson observed.[15]

Although Scovel and Norris shuffled off, Crane was soon joined aboard the *Three Friends* by Paine and two correspondents for the *New York Herald,* Ernest W. McCready and Harry Brown. On the evening of May 14, 1898, they reached the northwest of Haiti, heading for the French cable station at Môle-Saint-Nicolas.

Paine, in his biography, recalled that the correspondents had a rip-roaring time drinking with the Haitian soldiers, crescendoing with a dance on the beach while singing "There'll Be a Hot Time in the Old Town To-Night." Although it seems over the top—Crane even declaring it "a purple night with spangled trimmings"—McCready corroborated the story, recalling that Crane, typically unshaven and unkempt, "went native," considered swimming the deadly shark-infested harbor to steal a cache of rum hidden in a ship, and "successfully invited a seduction."[16]

Throughout May the newspapers continued to predict that the invasion of Cuba was imminent. But with the army mired in Tampa, Crane and the floating correspondents had little to report on. The terms "opera bouffe" and "opéra comique" were frequently in use to describe the interminable buildup to war. At one point off the coast of Cardenas, a sailor aboard the gunboat *Machias* called out plaintively, "Have you onions, potatoes or eggs?" Upon learning that the crew had been stationed there for three weeks, Crane and the others "patriotically" donated their last spuds. The biggest story Crane had to report, which the *World* did on May 9, was overhearing the commander of the *Porter* shout through a megaphone that on May 7 two torpedo boats had tried to run the American blockade of Havana and were chased back by the *Wilmington* and the *Iowa.* It wasn't exactly the scintillating news *World* readers hungered for.[17]

On May 15 Crane filed another report from Puerto Plata, San Domingo, present-day Dominican Republic. Mixing with the five thousand or so inhabitants, Crane spoke with one merchant of African heritage who had some choice words about the Spanish Empire: "The history of Spain is the history of cruelty."[18]

Five nights later while aboard the *Three Friends* off the coast of Key West, Crane had another run-in with the *Machias*. This time the gunboat, not seeing the *World*'s dispatch boat in the dark, shouldered the side of the *Three Friends* as she passed.

"We wanted to demand the return of our potatoes," Crane complained in a report printed on May 29. "But, after all, this one thing is certain. If we had been a Spanish gunboat there would not have been enough left of us to patch a tooth."[19]

For four days while idling on the *Three Friends*, Crane's mind drifted to the plight of his friend and rival, Richard Harding Davis. By the end of May every Cuba-bound war correspondent knew that Davis had been offered a captaincy in the war. In Frederic Remington's room in Tampa, Davis discussed it with the artist and Fitzhugh Lee, with both of them talking Davis into refusing and to continue on as a war correspondent. Lee had even composed Davis's telegram and sent it to William McKinley.

"On reflection I am greatly troubled that I declined the captaincy," Davis wrote to his brother Charles on May 14 from Tampa. "It is unfortunate that I had not time to consider it. We shall not have another war and I can always be a war correspondent in other countries but never again have a chance to serve in my own."[20]

The majority of war correspondents appeared to feel the same way as Davis now did and weren't shy in speaking their minds, but Crane seemed to think it was a tempest in a teapot. "It is now the fashion of all hotel porches at Tampa and Key West to run Davis down," Crane wrote in a June 2 letter, "because he has declined a captaincy in the army in order to keep his contract with his paper. The teaparty has to have a topic."[21]

Still, the wags continued their mockery. The Davis of eight years ago, they snickered—who had made headlines his first day in New York by single-handedly arresting a grifter—would have been more bold. The Davis of today was apparently all talk and no action. Stung, the star reporter felt the comments acutely. As the American war machine reawakened in Tampa, so too did Davis's desire to prove himself.

On June 8, Hearst gave the war correspondents something else to chuckle at. The *New York Journal* published an article about Colonel Reflipe W. Thenuz, purported to be an Australian artillery officer serving the Spanish who had died in combat. Not to be outdone, on June 9 Pulitzer's *World* also reported on the death, tacking it onto a lengthy dispatch from Paine concerning the coming battle and adding details of the dispatch: "On board the *World* dispatch boat *Three Friends*, off Santiago de Cuba, via Port Antonio, Jamaica."[22]

Having successfully lured the *World* into their trap, the *Journal* exposed the whole thing as a hoax. "Reflipe W" was an anagram for "We pilfer," hence the *World* had admitted—having been caught red-handed—that "We Pilfer the News." This had been the brainchild of Arthur Brisbane, Davis's old boss at the *Evening Sun*, who had traded that paper for the *Journal*. With devilish delight, the *Journal* roundly mocked the *World*, printing a cartoon of Colonel Thenuz with the caption "Specially taken for the *World*, by the *World*'s special photographer." The *Journal* also suggested that a monument be erected in honor of Colonel Thenuz, memorialized the fallen colonel with a poem, and supposedly collected Confederate script, Chinese money, and repudiated bonds for the Thenuz Memorial Fund.[23]

The next day, all the laughter stopped.

On June 10, 1898, the top brass finally pulled the trigger on the Cuban invasion. That day the *Marblehead*, *Dolphin*, and *Vixen* bombarded the beaches and enemy trenches of Guantanamo Bay seeking to intimidate General Felix Pareja, who was rumored to be just inland with an army of 5,000 Spaniards. The *Yankee*, *Adria*, and *St. Louis* soon joined the other American ships. Commander Bowman McCalla and Admiral Sampson determined that the marines would land at Fisherman's Point, part of the outer bay, and establish a camp along the cliffs. In short order, 650 US Marines of the First Marine Battalion, commanded by Lieutenant Colonel Robert Huntington, thundered into Fisherman's Point, the Americans' first foray into taking enemy territory in Cuba.

Crane, Paine, and McCready watched while the marines began establishing a coaling station. This was integral for the American strategy, which did not include the blockade becoming Swiss cheese every time part of the fleet began making the ninety-mile voyage to Key West to recoal. That evening Paine and McCready took the *Three Friends* to Port Antonio, Jamaica to cable their stories to New York and Philadelphia. Crane, however, went to shore, mixing with the soldiers. Despite Pulitzer's wishes, Crane felt he was in Cuba for other reasons.[24]

"Stephen Crane stayed ashore with the marines because he foresaw much personal enjoyment," Paine explained. "A hawser could not have dragged him away from the show. . . . It was his business, as he viewed it, to gather impressions and write them as the spirit moved." If Paine suspected that Crane's decision to remain with the marines was based on the desire to distance himself from the *Three Friends* and the *World* until the "Colonel Thenuz" flap died down, Paine kept it to himself.[25]

That night under a sliver of a moon, Crane kept awake while the marines dug trenches and laid out on a hilltop Camp McCalla, named after Captain McCalla of the *Marblehead*. Having easily taken Guantanamo Bay—almost too easily—some of the soldiers stripped naked and dove into the bay. In this manner they found themselves helpless when Spaniards began shooting from the chaparral. With no time to don their clothing, the naked soldiers grabbed their rifles and returned fire. It was tense battle, the air filled with bullets from the Spaniards' rapid-firing smokeless Mausers and the Americans' rapid-firing Model 1895 Lee Navy rifles. Crane determined that the marines were up against "practicos, or guides, who knew every shrub and tree on the ground." The firing continued for hours but at a distance.[26]

The next day, June 11, 1898, fighting at Camp McCalla intensified, with the Spanish attacking from the chaparral at daybreak. Along with returning fire, the *Marblehead*—commanding the bay—fired its big guns at the Spanish position. Under heavy fire, the Spanish retreated back into the brush. But they hadn't given up.

At about 1:00 in the early hours of June 12, Crane was nearby while Acting Assistant Surgeon John Blair Gibbs bandaged the hand of a wounded private. From six hundred to seven hundred yards away, a Spanish soldier squeezed the trigger of his rifle, sending a ball whistling into Gibbs's chest. The next thirty minutes were pure agony for the fatally shot surgeon.

"I was a child who, in a fit of ignorance, had jumped in the vat of war," Crane reflected. "He was dying hard. Hard. It took him a long time to die. . . . There was only the bitter strife for air which pulsed out into the night in a clear penetrating whistle, with intervals of terrible silence in which I held my own breath in the common unconscious aspiration to help. I thought the man would never die."[27]

A half hour after being shot Gibbs was a corpse, but Crane didn't linger over much. He spent most of the dark hours embedded in a trench with four marines tasked to signal the *Marblehead* at night with a lantern. Crane described the actions of himself and the marines in an article titled "Marines Signalling under Fire at Guantanamo":

> It was my good fortune—at that time I considered it my bad fortune, indeed—to be with them on two of the nights when a wild storm of fighting was pealing about the hill; and, of all the actions of the war, none were so hard on the nerves, none strained courage so near the panic point, as those swift nights in Camp McCalla. With a thousand rifles rattling; with

> the field-guns booming in your ears; with the diabolic Colt automatics clacking; with the roar of the *Marblehead* coming from the bay, and, last, with Mauser bullets sneering always in the air a few inches over one's head, and with this enduring from dusk to dawn, it is extremely doubtful if any one who was there will be able to forget it easily.[28]

A quick study, Crane also witnessed the particulars of the marines' actions. "The signal squad had an old cracker-box placed on top of the trench. . . . Signalling in this way is done by letting one lantern remain stationary—on top of the cracker-box, in this case—and moving the wig-wagging code. . . . How, in the name of wonders, those four men at Camp McCalla were not riddled from head to foot and sent home as repositories of Spanish ammunition than as marines is beyond all comprehension."[29]

For fear that a marine would be shot to death and fall on him, Crane would roll away whenever one of the marines rose atop the cracker-box to signal the cruiser with the lantern.[30]

This article in particular caught Davis's attention.

"His story of the marine at Guantanamo, who stood on the crest of the hill to 'wigwam' to the war-ships, and so exposed himself to the fire of the entire Spanish forces[,] . . . illustrates that in his devotion to duty, and also in his readiness at the exciting moments of life, Crane is quite as much of a soldier as the man whose courage he described," Davis praised.[31]

One reason Crane's Guantanamo Bay piece was so well received was because he composed it four months after the battle, having the ability to choose his words carefully. It would inevitably be published in *McClure's Magazine* in February 1899 and again in Crane's 1900 book on the conflict, *Wounds in the Rain*. But Pulitzer wasn't in the habit of waiting on literary correspondents. To compete with Hearst, Pulitzer needed hard-hitting stories now.

Knowing the boss's mind, McCready attempted to cajole Crane back to the *Three Friends* so they could write up the story.

"What the hell's the rush?" Crane shot back.[32]

Ultimately the promise of cigarettes, food, and drink won the battle. Once aboard, Crane composed the article while McCready dictated. It quickly became apparent that McCready didn't like Crane's word choices, probably thinking the whole thing too colorful and flowery. Uncompromisingly, "Mac" crossed out lines and inserted others. McCready knew that the boss wanted terse, factual reporting, not Crane's mad compositions. Crane was soon up in arms.

"Read it aloud, Mac, as far as it goes," Crane demanded. "I believe you are murdering my stuff."

"I dropped a few adjectives here and there, Steve," McCready responded. "This has to be news, sent at cable rates. You can save your flubdub and shoot it to New York by mail. What I want is the straight story of the fight."

McCready got his way. The dispatch, titled "In the First Land Fight Four of Our Men Are Killed," was a straight-to-the-point account, and appeared the next day, June 12, in the *New York World.* Because Crane and McCready considered it jointly written, it contained no byline.

Meanwhile, the battle for Camp McCalla—which had developed into a sort of siege—was still ongoing. By the evening of June 12, the Spanish were within fifty yards from the camp. The Americans suffered several casualties before driving off the attackers. Blood trails were discovered, indicating that Spanish soldiers had been wounded or killed.[33]

The next day the marines were reinforced by around sixty Cuban revolutionaries under the command of Lieutenant Enrique Tomás, all of whom had been equipped by Commander McCalla with rifles and white duck uniforms from the *Marblehead.* Tomás ordered his men to burn the chaparral around the camp, denying the Spanish cover. But this wasn't enough. Laborde, a Cuban guerrilla colonel, proposed an aggressive plan. The key to a full Spanish retreat from Camp McCalla lay in destroying the Cuzco Well, atop Cuzco Hill, from where the Spanish drew water and a force of about five hundred Spanish were mustered.

Huntington liked the plan.

At 8 a.m. on June 14, after reveille sounded, the plan came to life. Lieutenant Louis J. Magill struck south with about forty men, seeking to secretly flank the Spanish atop Cuzco Hill. The *Dolphin* would support from the waters of Guantanamo Bay, firing upon the Spanish with her six-pound guns and Hotchkiss revolving cannons. Meanwhile, Captain George Frank Elliott would command the main force, composed of Company C, Company D, and about fifty Cuban scouts under the leadership of Cuban lieutenant colonel Enrique Tomás. All that and one plucky reporter with a nose for trouble.

Crane certainly hoped he found trouble before it found him. After ascending a chalky cliff with the marines of Company C, he marched with them through a narrow path surrounded by a claustrophobic tangle of brush, everyone scanning for the Spanish.

"No word was spoken; one could only hear the dull trample of the men, mingling with the near and far droning of insects raising their tiny voices under the blazing sky," Crane recalled in "The Red Badge of Courage Was His Wig-Wam." "From time to time in an hour's march we passed pickets of Cubans, poised with their rifles, scanning the woods with unchanging stares. They did not turn their heads as we passed them. They seemed like stone men."[34]

Soon they reached a steep ridge festooned with chapparal and cactus and overlooking the sea, where the *Dolphin* could be seen. The ridge also boasted a stone house, recently abandoned by the Spanish garrison. There the Cuban scouts called a halt. Once the scouts determined the that Spanish were over the next ridge, Colonel Enrique Tomás, with a machete in one hand and a revolver in the other, signaled them to advance.

"The main body was moving over a lower part of this ridge when the firing broke out," Crane observed. The "pop!" and "Prut—prut—pr-r-r-rut—pr-rut! Pop—pop—poppetty—pop!" of the Mausers and Lees filled the air, along with the screams of the wounded and the dying. But Captain Elliott and 2nd Lieutenant Philip M. Bannon kept their heads.

"To the tune of this furious shooting Captain Elliott and Lieut. Bannon's platoon of C Company scrambled madly up the hill, tearing themselves on the cactus and fighting their way through the mesquite," Crane wrote. For three minutes the brown-clad Americans and white-clad Cubans raced across the ridge toward the Spanish line.

"The whole thing was an infernal din," Crane recounted. He watched as a Cuban guerrilla toppled, shot just below the heart. Crane captured the weariness of a Company D marine shot in the ankle as two comrades attended to him, the panting of the marines "drunk from the heat and the fumes of the powder," a glimpse of a dirty white jacket and a dodging head through the underbrush, the crash of the Lees and Mausers, the roar of the *Dolphin*'s guns, and the rain of deadly brass shells.

"This terrible exchange of fire lasted a year, or probably it was twenty minutes," ruminated Crane. Time and place certainly seemed out of joint for the young writer, for when Captain Elliott required someone to deliver messages to his commanders, Crane stepped up. Along with risking gunfire to run messages, Crane hauled supplies, dragged artillery up the ridge, and helped fire the guns.

Then disaster seemed to befall the Americans. As the shells of the *Dolphin* pulverized the thicket, sending up stones, soil, and bushes, Crane and others saw that 2nd Lieutenant Magill and his men were right in the line of fire.

"Lieutenant Magill and his men had crowned a hill which covered entirely the flank of the fighting companies, but when the *Dolphin* opened fire, it happened that Magill was in the line of the shots," Crane later reported. "It became necessary to stop the *Dolphin* at once."[35]

When Captain Elliott called for a signalman, Sergeant John H. Quick rose at once. Tying a large blue polka-dot neckerchief to a long, crooked stick, Quick dashed to a ridge, signaling the *Dolphin* to alter its line of fire. All the while Quick's back was exposed to Spanish gunfire. Crane marveled that there must have been at least twenty rifles concentrated on him.

"As I looked at Sergeant Quick wig-wagging there against the sky, I would not have given a tin tobacco tag for his life," Crane wrote. "Escape for him seemed impossible. It seemed absurd to hope that he would not be hit; I only hoped that he would be hit just a little, little, in the arm, the shoulder, or the leg."[36]

Miraculously, luck was with Quick. The brave sergeant signaled that the *Dolphin* was unscathed; the *Dolphin* shifted its fire, pouring heavy fire into the Spanish. In a flash, Magill and his band of forty opened up with a barrage of gunfire. Routed, the Spanish turned and ran.

"There they go! See 'em! See 'em!" someone shouted. The marines let loose, and so too did the Cubans.

"*Fuego! fuego! fuego! fuego! fuego!*" howled Colonel Tomás, frenziedly slashing the air with his machete. Twenty Cubans chased the disappearing Spanish. Meanwhile, Lieutenant Lewis Lucas led a squad, burning the commander's house and destroying the Spanish well. Eventually as dusk deepened, a count was made on the Spanish dead: fifty-eight. Crane also reflected on his joy to see the sergeant of the guard, who brought with him hardtack, beans, and coffee and whose presence signaled rest, sleep, and peace.

With Cuzco Well destroyed and the Spanish routed, Guantanamo Bay now belonged to the Americans and the revolutionaries. No further attacks on Camp McCalla would be forthcoming. Yet, as much as the architects and heroes of the battle had reason to cheer—Huntington, Laborde, Tomás, Elliott, and Quick—Stephen Crane may have been equally happy. For one, he hadn't been shot to death. For another, having finally been on the front lines during a momentous battle, he reckoned that he could write something particularly worthwhile. Finally, he'd gained the respect of Captain Elliott, who in his official report remarked that Crane "was of material aid during the action."[37]

Years later, Davis paid respect as well. To Ames Williams, a great-nephew of Confederate general James Longstreet, Davis called Crane's dispatch on the battle—printed by Pulitzer on July 1—"one of the finest examples of descriptive writing of the war. Incidentally, Crane was no idle spectator during this engagement, but lent a hand to the Marines for which he was officially commended to the Secretary of the Navy by the commanding officer of the Marine detachment, Captain G. F. Elliott."[38]

Three days after the momentous battle, Crane, Scovel, and British correspondent Alexander Kenealy established *New York World* headquarters near Santiago. To better spy on the Spanish fleet, Crane and Scovel swam two small Jamaican ponies from the *Triton* to Cuban soil. Mounted, the two men then traversed a nearly impassable two-thousand-foot mountain overlooking the Spanish fleet within Santiago Harbor. On June 20, they reported their observations to Admiral Sampson.[39]

Just then Guantanamo Bay and Santiago Harbor wasn't so much on Sampson's mind. What was on his mind was a little strip of beach called Daquiri, twenty-five miles east, for it was there that the First Volunteer US Cavalry, and its typhoon-like lieutenant colonel were preparing to make landfall.

14

ROUGH RIDERS

Theodore Roosevelt took the scenic route to Cuba.

At 7:30 a.m. on May 15, 1898, Roosevelt reached San Antonio, Texas. A big sign pointed the way to Camp Wood: "This way to Camp of Roosevelt's Rough Riders." Two miles later Roosevelt found the training ground, where drill had commenced for the 1st United States Volunteer Cavalry.

Such a regiment had never existed. Initially it was to have the strength of nearly 750 soldiers. Roughly, 80 were to come from Oklahoma Territory, 170 from Arizona Territory, 170 from Indian Territory, and 340 from New Mexico Territory. Recruitment in Texas and volunteers from the East ultimately put the number at 1,000. Along with the westerners, Roosevelt attracted collegiates and New York policemen, a perfect hodgepodge of the lieutenant colonel's different walks of life.[1]

Among the prominent Harvard men were Dudley Dean, the former quarterback and racquetball player; Bob Wrenn, a champion tennis player; and Woodbury Kane (Woody Kane, as Roosevelt called him), a yachtsman and a close friend to Roosevelt in college. Yale volunteers included football players Jack Greenway, Horace Devereaux, and Roscoe Channing as well as the notable polo star Joe Stevens. Twenty-four-year-old Hamilton Fish, whose grandfather had served as President Ulysses S. Grant's secretary of state, represented Columbia University, where Fish had captained the rowing crew. Roosevelt's friend Cecil Spring Rice, who had rowed crew at Balliol College in Oxford, England, was also a volunteer.[2]

Several New York City policemen decided to once again team up with their old commissioner. These included patrolman Hal Haywood of the Madison Street Station, who had come to Gotham from Walla Walla, Washington, and Phil Sweet, of the East 22nd Street Station, an early supporter of Roosevelt's crackdown on the saloons. Both became sergeants in K Troop, proudly wearing their police badges.[3]

As for the westerners, they proved a wild bunch.

Allyn K. Capron, whom Roosevelt considered "the best soldier in the regiment," hailed from Indian Territory. A skilled horseman, Capron quickly became the captain of L Troop. Ed Culver, of Cherokee descent, came from Indian Territory as well. Among the notables from New Mexico Territory were Maximiliano "Max" Luna, the former sheriff of Valencia County; Charles L. Ballard, who had worn the star of a deputy sheriff in Chaves County and Roswell, helping to bring down Black Jack Christian's High Five Gang; and William H. H. Llewelyn, who had served as an Indian agent on the Mescalero Apache Reservation and, as Roosevelt phrased it, "had been shot four times in pitched fights with red marauders and white outlaws."[4]

From Yavapai County in Arizona Territory came Henry Bardshar, a giant of a man who worked the gold mines outside Prescott, along with Alexander Brodie, whom Roosevelt called "a grizzled old frontier soldier," and Emilio Cassi, who had been born in Monte Carlo, had served as a soldier of fortune in Egypt and with the Chasseurs d'Afrique in southern China, and now hungered for "Cuba Libre." Also signing up was William "Buckey" O'Neill, Yavapai County's former sheriff who was famous for his exploits against the Apache. Described by Roosevelt in *The Rough Riders* as "a wild, reckless fellow, soft spoken, and of dauntless courage and boundless ambition," it was no surprise that O'Neill became the captain of A Troop, outranking Cassi, who would serve as Troop A's second trumpeter.

The deadliest gunslinger of the bunch was probably Benjamin Franklin Daniels, who had served as assistant marshal in Dodge City, where he'd lost half an ear—"bitten off," he told Roosevelt—before shooting a man in Dodge and becoming a gambler in Cripple Creek, Colorado. Daniels donned the uniform of a private in D Troop, initially joined by twenty-seven-year-old Billy McGinty, a broncobuster out of Oklahoma Territory before McGinty transferred to the undermanned K Troop. Roosevelt's Scottish hunting friend and ranch partner Bob Ferguson also volunteered, taking the role of one of 2nd lieutenant in K Troop.[5]

American Indians—Creeks, Chickasaws, Choctaws, Cherokees, and Pawnees—volunteered as well. The Chickasaw chief Benjamin Colbert was the most famous of the American Indian Rough Riders, Roosevelt having heard of him even before their meeting. But it was the Pawnee William Pollock to whom the lieutenant colonel took a shine, calling Pollock one of the "gamest fighters and best soldiers in the regiment."[6]

Although Roosevelt appreciated all of his soldiers, he felt that there was something special about the westerners, who totaled about three-fourths of the regiment, many of whom insisted on carrying their own guns and wearing their sombreros and Stetsons rather than army-issued felt hats.[7]

"In all the world there could be no better material for soldiers than that afforded by these grim hunters of the mountains, these rough riders of the plains," Roosevelt remarked. "They were accustomed to handling wild and savage horses; they were accustomed to following the chase with the rifle. . . . They were used, for all their lawless freedom, to the rough discipline of the round-up and the mining company. Some of them came from small frontier towns; but most were from the wilderness, having left their lonely hunters' cabins and shifting cow-camps to seek new and more stirring adventures beyond the sea."[8]

Like the westerners Roosevelt so admired, Colonel Leonard Wood also felt the call. "Wood . . . was by nature a soldier of the highest type, and, like most natural soldiers, he was, of course, born with a keen longing for adventure," Roosevelt reflected. Roosevelt and Wood got along swell, for they were cut from the same cloth. Born in New Hampshire in 1860, Wood was a Harvard man who graduated from Harvard Medical College and was a man of action, serving in Arizona Territory fighting Apache under General Nelson Miles and in California, where he was promoted to captain. Wood gained the respect of the regiment through his organizational skills, though he made no attempt to befriend anyone. "Old Poker Face" was Wood's nickname, and with good reason.

"He would," remarked Corporal David L. Hughes of B Troop, "go to the end of the earth for one of his men but he was not showy about it."[9]

Having busied himself training the regiment, Wood happily turned drilling the regiment over to Roosevelt upon his arrival.

"This was a piece of great good fortune for me," Roosevelt noted in his autobiography, "and I drilled the men industriously, mounted and unmounted. I had plenty to learn, and the men and the officers even more; but we went at our work with the heartiest good will."[10]

To drill the regiment, Roosevelt called upon the three years' experience he'd gained in the New York National Guard and what he'd learned in the 1896 booklet *Drill Regulations for Cavalry, United States Army*.[11]

A typical day amid the grassy park of Camp Wood formally began at 5:30 a.m. with the sound of reveille. One thousand soldiers answered the roll call, the men sizing up each other, their commanding officers, and the cottonwood, pecan, and sycamore trees and meandering San Antonio River that bordered their camp. At 6:10 stable call was sounded, initiating tending the horses and breakfasting themselves. Between 8:30 and 9:30 the soldiers watered the horses in the river and saddled up for drill. Roosevelt supervised while Wood pored over logistics in the shade of the tent.[12]

"Our lines were somewhat irregular," Roosevelt admitted, describing the early days of the regiment.[13]

At 1:30 the regiment was usually given a break from hard drilling, and the men would engage in bronco busting before lunch, a great deal more bronco busting than anticipated. As quickly became apparent, most of the mounts, purchased seven miles north at Fort Sam Houston, with the Alamo equidistant to both, hadn't been broken in.[14]

"Some of the damn horses bucked like hell," recollected Private Arthur Tuttle of Buckey O'Neill's A Troop.[15]

In K Troop, Billy McGinty put his bronco-busting skills to good use. While demonstrating to the "hunters, polo players, and rich men's sons," as the McGinty described them, how best to rope, throw, and shoe a horse with their feet sticking up into the air, Roosevelt looked on in amazement.

"That is bully!" Roosevelt remarked to K Troop's 2nd lieutenant, Horace Devereaux.[16]

Skirmish practice followed. When McGinty was reprimanded for being unable to keep step, the trooper responded that "he was pretty sure he could keep step on horseback."[17]

At 3:30, with the regiment caked in grime composed of dust and sweat, the men were allowed two spigots of water with which to wash. Most took their soap down to the San Antonio River instead. At 5:00 the troops lined up for dress parade, bedecked in boots, canvas leggings, duck brown trousers and jackets, blue flannel shirts, and signature Rough Rider neckerchiefs. Those not partial to their own hat wore the army-issued gray slouch. After supper, night school commenced for the officers. Roll call sounded at 8:30, and finally taps concluded at 9:00. But while others slept, Roosevelt lit his table lamp and composed letters.[18]

"*Dear Mr. President,*" began one such letter. "This is just a line to tell you that we are in fine shape. Wood is a dandy Colonel, and I really think that the rank and file of this regiment are better than you would find in any other regiment anywhere. . . . We are ready now to leave at any moment, and we earnestly hope that we will be put into Cuba with the very first troops; the sooner the better."[19]

On May 19, Roosevelt wrote Lodge that they were "working like beavers . . . getting the regiment into shape. . . . It would do your heart good to see some of the riding. The Eastern men are getting along very well. You would be amused to see three Knickerbocker club men cooking and washing dishes for one of the New Mexico companies. . . . The dust, heat and mosquitoes prevent existence being at all sybaritic. I am heartily enjoying it nevertheless."[20]

As for his own mounts—Little Texas and Rain-in-the-Face—Roosevelt got them from a Texan, John Moore, with whom he had once hunted javelinas on the banks of the Nueces River. Although McGinty described Little Texas as "a fine bay horse," Roosevelt was initially undecided on the animals. "I have a couple of scrawny horses," Roosevelt confided to Lodge, "which they say are tough. I hope so, as otherwise I shall probably have to eat them and continue my career on foot."[21]

Edward Marshall, Hearst's seasoned Sunday editor, recorded in his 1899 history *The Story of the Rough Riders* that Sunday, May 22, may have been the regiment's most impressive day in San Antonio. Early that morning for an hour and a half the Articles of War were read to each uniformed soldier. After breakfasting, religious services were held, led by the Episcopalian reverend A. Brown from Prescott, and "twenty Western terrors melodiously acted as the choir," giving a rousing rendition of "How Firm a Foundation" and "Onward, Christian Soldiers." The only instrument to accompany them was the silver trumpet of Emilio Cassi.[22]

Marshall, who hadn't yet joined the Rough Riders, missed the regiment's tales that grew saltier at night. Some of the more red-blooded westerners began slipping through holes in the camp fence and into San Antonio, desiring whiskey and women. They found plenty of both. Early on, an Arizonan was arrested and fined $100 for brandishing a butcher knife, chasing everyone off the street, and afterward upsetting a buggy containing two women as he tried to escape six policemen. Private William Owens of B Troop took on the moniker "Smoke-em-up-Bill" after shooting out the lights of a San Antonio automobile. At another time Sergeant Hamilton Fish forced a number of soldiers away from assaulting the fairground's beer stand. But no one could stop the rapscallions on one memorable Friday night. According to the *San Antonio Light*, while watching a concert at a San Antonio park, a group of Rough Riders pulled their pistols and fired them into the air, and while the crowd screamed and made tracks, the boys gathered up the barrels of beer and smuggled them back to camp.

Roosevelt reflected that on a night where some of the rougher characters decided "to paint San Antonio red," one man was captured and placed in jail and never rejoined the regiment. The other scamps were disciplined "in a way that prevented a repetition of the occurrence," as Roosevelt phrased it in the *Rough Riders.* To Lodge, Roosevelt dished that the knaves were placed in the guardhouse. But Roosevelt could also get unbuttoned. One day he treated the entire regiment, sans Wood, to beer in San Antonio and afterward sheepishly apologized to Wood for the infraction. Legend had it that on another occasion while recruiting soldiers in San Antonio's famous Menger Hotel—built in 1859 and still standing—the lieutenant colonel shot the wall near the mirror. True or not, the bullet holes can still be seen.[23]

As for the ladies, reports that town girls were known to slip the soldiers a kiss were greatly understated.[24]

On May 23, Roosevelt ordered the men to teach the mounts to withstand the bark of gunfire, the Rough Riders firing their pistols in the air from horseback. The majority of the mustangs went wild, the men cursing as they fought for control. Sergeant William Greenwood of O'Neill's A Troop suffered a mild casualty when Fred Bugbee's pistol discharged in the confusion, the muzzle flash burning Greenwood's foot.[25]

"Horses totally unfit for service," complained Greenwood.[26]

Still, Roosevelt was pleased. "You would enjoy seeing the mounted drill," Roosevelt wrote Lodge on May 25, "for the way the men have got their wild half-broken horses into order is something marvellous."

While Roosevelt spent his days at drill, his evenings recruiting, and his nights writing, Wood covered more of the administrative duties. Although both Roosevelt and Wood chafed that the Ordnance Bureau slowed down the process by sending what was absolutely needed by freight instead of express, through Wood's efforts the men were equipped with Model 1896 .30-caliber Krag-Jorgensen carbines and .45-caliber Colt revolvers. Despite many soldiers preferring their own pistols and Winchesters, a good many took to the six-shot Krag carbine, praising Roosevelt and Wood for their procurement. Along with the rifles, revolvers, and ammunition, every day saw the arrival of more horses, saddles, blankets, tents, and volunteers. Roosevelt also felt that the uniforms suited them.[27]

"In their slouch hats, blue flannel shirts, brown trousers, leggings and boots they looked exactly as a body of cowboy cavalry should look," Roosevelt determined.[28]

Out of uniform, they were quite the menagerie.

Corporal Wilber French of C Troop wrote that they were "garbed in the various habiliments and fashions of the time. . . . The millionaires in Fifth Avenue duds. . . . The cowboys in chaps, high-heeled boots and spurs. The miners and down-and-outers in soiled and ragged blue denim overalls and jumpers."[29]

Eventually, on May 28 the order to rendezvous with the army in Tampa arrived as well. After reading the telegram, Wood calmly handed it to Roosevelt. Roosevelt read its import, threw his hat in the air, and let loose a whoop of exhilaration. The boys lingering nearby cheered too, guessing the letters contents. But that was nothing compared to the ruckus they made when Colonel Wood officially announced that marching orders had come at last. The regiment began an exuberant cheer lasting several minutes and punctuated by dancing and hats thrown skyward.[30]

"No wilder hurrah was heard . . . than that which went up in San Antonio when marching orders were received," Marshall remarked. "Lieutenant-Colonel Roosevelt . . . and Colonel Wood embraced like schoolboys."[31]

Small wonder Roosevelt was overjoyed. In twelve years' time he'd balanced being a rancher, a deputy sheriff, a politician, a civil service commissioner, a family man, a writer, a police commissioner, and assistant secretary of the navy. But now as a lieutenant colonel in San Antonio, Theodore Roosevelt—who daydreamed back in Dakota Territory of raising a cowboy regiment of "harum-scarum roughriders" and leading them to war—was fitting himself to just that role with hopes of one last transformation, one that could conceivably launch him into the oval office—war hero—so long as he didn't get shot and killed along the way.[32]

On the eve of their departure, Roosevelt reflected that he felt glad to have raised the regiment in the city where the Alamo stood as a testimony to the bravery of David Crockett, James Bowie, and their band of frontier heroes. But Roosevelt was more excited than sorry to go. Considering that the tents had been infested with centipedes, chiggers, and mosquitoes, the troops felt very much the same. It took the rest of the day to break camp, the soldiers scrambling to ship their excess baggage to western cow towns and eastern chateaus. Woody Kane, who had become a 1st lieutenant in K Troop, sheepishly admitted that among the gear he and his dandy companions left behind were swallowtail coats and full dress suits.[33]

"Just why these gentlemen took dress suits to war with them," Marshall pondered, "I do not know."[34]

On May 29, reveille rang out at three o'clock. The men breakfasted quickly and awkwardly, the utensils already having been packed. Roosevelt recalled that soon after "we marched out of our hot, windy, dusty camp to take the cars for

Tampa. . . . The journey by rail from San Antonio to Tampa took just four days, and I doubt if anybody who was on the trip will soon forget it."[35]

Food proved hard to come by on the train cars. Their first dinner consisted of a thin slice of canned beef sandwiched between hardtack crackers. But when they stopped, crowds of southerners came to cheer them, bringing them watermelon, sandwiches, fried chicken, and pails of fresh milk. Along with seeing to the best of his ability that the horses were watered and fed, technically the responsibility of the railroads but a task at which they were frightfully lax, Roosevelt himself fetched coffee for the men. At longer stops the troops were allowed liberty under noncommissioned officers, but several took advantage and hit the sauce. They were punished with "necessary severity," Roosevelt described, as an example to the others.[36]

Notably, Roosevelt saw Allyn Capron as an example to the men and began to rely more on him for his "extraordinary energy" and "executive capacity." Roosevelt also marveled that they were traveling through the heart of the old Confederacy—where the grizzled veterans had raised their sons on the stories of Nathan Bedford Forrest, John Tyler Morgan, and Thomas "Stonewall" Jackson—yet everywhere the Stars and Stripes waved. Mingling with the Rough Riders at the depots, old Confederates would laugh, half amazed, that they had never dreamed back in the dark days of the war that they would proudly send their sons to serve under that flag and to die under it if they must.

After an outbreak of measles hit the train—the first man to be taken off was Private Charles Nicholson of K Troop—many began fearing that they would die long before they reached Cuba. But eventually after four arduous days they reached Ybor City, a suburb of Tampa, with everyone alive. Unfortunately, the port city proved to be "a perfect welter of confusion," as Roosevelt dubbed it. "Tampa lay in the pine-covered sand-flats at the end of a one-track railroad, and everything connected with both military and railroad matters was in an almost inextricable tangle."

Not a soul was there to tell them where to camp, and no one issued them food rations for twenty-four hours. Roosevelt and the other well-to-do officers were forced to purchase from their own pockets food for the troops. Eventually Wood walked into Tampa proper to determine where they were supposed to bivouac, and in his absence a white-bearded man wearing a blue uniform with the stars of a major general rode up on horseback. This was General Joseph "Fighting Joe" Wheeler.

Wheeler ordered Major Alexander O. Brodie to have the troops detrain and camp there for the night.[37]

Little sleep was had as the Rough Riders engaged in offloading their baggage throughout the small hours. Having just survived four days on a train and now beset by flies, tarantulas, and ever more centipedes, one trooper grumbled that "war is hell." Clearly, most Rough Riders would have preferred combat to the drudgery of trains and travel. In the morning they were obliged to seize wagons to carry their spare baggage more than seven miles to camp, on a point that the 6th Cavalry had formerly drilled, behind the Tampa Bay Hotel.[38]

"Once on the ground, we speedily got order out of confusion," Roosevelt recalled. "Under Wood's eye the tents were put up in long streets, the picket-line of each troop stretching down its side of each street. . . . The camp was strictly policed, and drill promptly begun."[39]

While the men drilled, Roosevelt took in the hubbub occurring around the hotel. Naturally he visited with Richard Harding Davis, who kept a good room in the hotel and had been there since May.

At any moment, Davis recalled in an article to *Scribner's*, one could run into "General O. O. Howard, and Ira Sankey, who bustled about in the heat, preaching and singing to the soldiers; Miss Clara Barton, of her own unofficial Red Cross Army [and] General Fitzhugh Lee, looking like a genial Santa Claus, with a glad smile and glad greeting for everyone."[40]

Davis was especially taken with General Joe Wheeler, whom he described as "the best type of the courteous Southern gentleman . . . on whom politics had left no mark, who was courteous because he could not help being so, who stood up when a second lieutenant was introduced to him, and who ran as lightly as a boy to help a woman move a chair, or to assist her to step from a carriage."[41]

Of the seventeen thousand military men Davis had to choose from, the veteran reporter saved Roosevelt for his finale, painting him as a man "with energy and brains and enthusiasm enough to inspire a whole regiment."[42]

Along with Roosevelt, Davis knew Woody Kane, Joe Stevens, and a few of the "gentlemen" Rough Riders, having met on the East Coast. Davis happily let them use the first-rate facilities in his hotel room, and before long word was out that Davis's room was a good place to wash up and escape the flies.

"They use my bathroom continuously," Davis wrote to his brother, "and I never open the door without finding a heap of dirty canvas on the floor and a cheery voice splashing around in the tub and calling out, 'It's all right don't mind me. I'm one of Teddy's 'Brownies.'"

One June 2 Edith Roosevelt arrived at the Tampa Bay Hotel as well, reuniting with her husband under the hotel rotunda. Colonel Wood gave Roosevelt special dispensation to spend the night with his wife. Dinner was followed by a bath and then the bedroom. At 4 a.m., despite his exhaustion, Roosevelt crept out of the room to join the Rough Riders for reveille.

Suffering through Tampa's humidity, Edith wrote to her sister later that morning that "I am writing in my thinnest nightgown in a comfortable room with a bath room adjoining."

Roosevelt likely could have spent more time with Edith had he pressed Wood, but that would have set him further apart from the men, something he couldn't have been keen on. Having already offended the regular army officers by inviting Bob Ferguson and another New York clubman to dinner, Roosevelt needed to step carefully to avoid alienating any others. In a letter to his children he mentioned Edith only once: "Mother stays at a big hotel about a mile from the camp."[43]

The men were somewhat bored when on Sunday, June 5, Chaplain Henry Brown delivered the service. Only half paying attention, Corporal Wilbur French and a band of Arizonans were lounging in a palmetto grove when French happened to glance backward and caught sight of General Wheeler. For the first time French sized him up. Despite Wheeler's slight stature, the corporal thought well of their commanding general:

> He had a remarkably shaped head, and wonderfully expressive eyes. . . . I have known another man with the same shaped head, same eyes and features. Eyes that seemed to be looking a thousand years into the future. That man was Colonel Alex O. Brodie. Joe Wheeler and Alex Brodie were in a class by themselves. Two men out of millions. . . . Others may be more spectacularly, but it is the Wheelers and the Brodies that have made and will continue to make us a great nation.[44]

The following morning with Roosevelt occupied with the regiment, it fell to Davis to escort Edith and a party of foreign diplomats to observe some formal cavalry exercises. As impressive as the two thousand riders were at full gallop—the Rough Riders distinct among the cavalry for brandishing Cuban machetes rather than regulation sabers—Davis realized that with warfare changing, this was a fleeting moment.

"There will be few such chances again," Davis later wrote, "to see a brigade of cavalry advancing through a forest of palms in a line two miles long."[45]

That same morning the *New York Herald* came out with Davis's response to a scurrilous article by Poultney Bigelow published in the *London Times.* In those pages Bigelow criticized the US army in Tampa, stating that there was not a single regiment that ready to take the field. In particular, Bigelow considered Wheeler too antiquated to understand modern cavalry. To counter Bigelow's criticism of the army as a whole, Davis spoke to General Nelson Miles, who deemed every regiment in Tampa perfectly ready. "There is no army corps anywhere in the world that is better supplied with men and officers of courage, fortitude and intelligence," Miles declared.[46]

As for Wheeler, Davis commented that Bigelow was criticizing "the most gallant cavalry leader of the Confederate army, the author of a book on cavalry tactics and a gentleman who has studied and followed the changes in tactics that have occurred from year to year ever since the civil war."

Davis concluded that Bigelow's article was "the sort of treason that should be pointed out quickly." As Davis's "Defense of the Army" article was reprinted in newspapers across the country, censure for Bigelow grew. Davis expressed little sympathy. Criticizing the army at a pivotal moment during the war, certainly a seasoned war correspondent such as Davis couldn't possibly fall into that trap. Or so everyone believed at the time.

Meanwhile, Roosevelt grew irate for a reason unrelated to the press. Later that morning he learned that there was not enough room on their transport ship for all the Rough Riders. Three hundred men would have to be left behind.[47]

"There had been the wildest excitement and heart-burning among the men when it was found that some troops were to be left behind and some were to be chosen to go to Cuba," Marshall recalled.[48]

Just as bad, only the officers' horses would be shipped with them. In a flash Roosevelt's Rough Riders became "Wood's Weary Walkers," as their comrades playfully mocked them. On the evening of June 7, General Shafter was dining at the Tampa Bay Hotel when he received a telegraph from the White House commanding the army to immediately set sail. Wood and Roosevelt ordered the Rough Riders to pack up camp and make for the railroad to transport them to the port. By midnight they reached the station, eventually compelling a coal train to take them eight miles south. Confusion at the harbor was high; ten thousand soldiers jostled for position, all attempting by hook or crook to board a transport for Cuba, for the word was that those soldiers who didn't board a transport would miss the war.[49]

"I was determined that we should not be among the men left off," Roosevelt recounted.[50]

Despite the *Yucatan* having been assigned to the New York 71st Volunteer Regiment and the US Army's 2nd Regulars, Wood and Roosevelt saw the transport as salvation so long as they could bully and bluster their way aboard. To that end Wood, boarded a motorboat and made for the *Yucatan* to negotiate with its captain.

Meanwhile, Roosevelt boldly marched the Rough Riders past the New York volunteers and commanded that his men to hold the gangway. This was neatly done, particularly because Lieutenant Colonel Roosevelt outranked the commander of the New Yorkers. But as for the army regulars, that was a different story. When their commanding officer, a higher-ranking lieutenant colonel, demanded that the Rough Riders cede them the gangway, Roosevelt employed Elizabethan diplomacy.

"I played for time," Roosevelt reflected in his autobiography. "I sent respectful requests through his officers to the commander of the regulars, entered into parleys, and made protestations, until the transport got near enough so that by yelling at the top of my voice I was able to get into a—highly constructive—communication with Wood."[51]

Roosevelt couldn't actually hear a damn word Wood was saying, but the fact that they appeared to be in communication suited Roosevelt's purposes. Roosevelt informed the regulars that his superior officer—"to my great regret, etc. etc."—had commanded them not to yield to the regulars and to instead board the *Yucatan*.[52]

As soon as the transport ship came around "we put our men aboard on the double," Roosevelt recalled while the 71st Regiment marched off in a cloud of acrimony and coal dust from the *Yucatan*'s bunkers.[53]

While his men filed aboard the *Yucatan,* Roosevelt's roaming eyes noticed a pair of photographers standing beside a great tripod on which a camera sat.

"What are you men up to?" Roosevelt inquired.

"We are the Vitagraph Company, Colonel Roosevelt, and we are going to Cuba to take moving pictures of the war."[54]

His eye on the prize, Roosevelt said to them, "I can't take a regiment, but I might be able to handle two more." Soon enough the photographers were escorted up the gangplank.[55]

On Roosevelt's symbiotic relationship with the press, Poultney Bigelow commented, "He became a popular idol, and almost legendary in deeds of prowess when barely mature in years, and no Barnum ever fed the press more industriously with items calculated to keep the world interested in his every move."

Once aboard the *Yucatan,* the military adage "hurry up and wait" never seemed more apropos. The following day they still hadn't left the harbor, amid rumors that the Spanish fleet was on the move. In fact, the opposite was true. Cervera's fleet had been spotted in Santiago Harbor, prompting Admiral Sampson to telegram Secretary of Navy Long the following message:

> MOLE, HAYTI, June 7, 1898
>
> Secretary of Navy, Washington:
>
> Bombarded forts at Santiago 7:30 A.M. to 10 A.M. to-day, June 6th. Have silenced works quickly, without injury of any kind, though stationary within 2,00 yards. If 10,000 men were here, city and fleet would be ours within forty-eight hours. Every consideration demands immediate army movement. If delayed, city will be defended more strongly by guns taken from fleet.
>
> SAMPSON.[56]

A man of action, Roosevelt was driven to distraction by the wait and appalled at the inefficiency.

Major General Wheeler, aboard the *Rio Grande,* was more sanguine. "Dear Caroline . . . having spent the night reaching this place, we hope to sail tomorrow," Wheeler wrote on June 8 before giving implicit instructions on how to handle the press and press releases in his absence.

> I want you to have some of the supplements so that you can refer to them easily, and when persons ask for facts regarding me they can be sent to them. I received your telegram saying that you had a copy of the Sunday Editor of the "Herald." I think you ought to have ten thousand more copies struck off[;] . . . you had better tell the National Publishing Company that you will want some more copies or the supplement of the "Citizen" but that you will bring them about half a column of new matter to put in. Then you and Julia had better fix up a supplement of the best articles that have appeared for me. . . . I think you should put in an article from the "Birmingham Age Herald" which I saw copied in the Scottsboro Citizen about two weeks ago. . . . You could leave out any matter that was no particularly valuable and only put in that part of each article which was complimentary and beneficial in a political sense. You know how you could arrange that. . . .
>
> With all my love
>
> Your dearest father
> J Wheeler[57]

Meanwhile, Roosevelt was falling to pieces. After two more days passed, the impatient lieutenant colonel poured his frustrations out to Lodge in a June 10 letter, describing "the troops jammed together under the tropical sun," that belowdecks was "suggestive of the Black Hole of Calcutta," and that men were sickening and horses were dying.

Two days later, Roosevelt wrote Lodge again urging him to tell "the President, and if necessary the Secretary of War, just what is going on here and damage that is being done."[58]

Lodge was smart enough not to bother McKinley with Roosevelt's complaints. Caroline Wheeler, on the other hand, sprang into action after reading her father's letter. On June 13 she wrote her "Dear papa" from Washington that she had procured fifty sacks of documents for him, spoken to the superintendent of public documents about securing forty-two sets of the president's speech, and visited the Interior Department about shipping the sacks.

"Please take care of yourself," Caroline urged.[59]

That same day, June 13, the *Yucatan, Alleghany, Miami,* and *Rio Grande*—on which sailed Wheeler's cavalry—finally began making waves for Cuba along with the rest of the American armada, forty-eight ships in all.[60]

"Teddy Roosevelt organized his picturesque 'Rough Riders,'" William Randolph Hearst reflected decades later. "Then everybody sailed away as if on a crusade."[61]

The next evening Roosevelt stood on the bridge of the ship watching the red sun sink into the sea and listening to the band playing the "Star Spangled Banner' and "The Girl I Left Behind Me."[62]

Joseph Wheeler also marveled at the beauty of the Gulf of Mexico. Now aboard the *Alleghany,* he wrote in his journal. "*Wednesday, June 15.*—The sky in the evening is perfectly beautiful, the stars very bright, and appear much more numerous than in more northern latitudes."[63]

Richard Harding Davis, aboard Shafter's flagship the *Seguranca,* wasn't enjoying himself half as much. Having left behind a will at the Tampa Bay Hotel, he soon had cause to long for the hotel dinner table as well. "No words can tell the discomforts and beastliness and boredom of the troop ship," Davis wrote home. "The food is impossible and it is so overcrowded that never for an instant are you alone."[64]

On June 16 Wheeler recorded that they began paralleling the Cuban coast, sailing easterly and bearing south. Occasionally they saw a strange sail that usually turned out to be a dispatch boat or a freight vessel. Wheeler reflected that if they were pirates it was too great a risk to tangle with the American fleet.[65]

But there was one pirate Wheeler hadn't accounted for. With W. R. Hearst having successfully petitioned Secretary of War Alger for permission to sail to Cuba as part of the press corps, on June, 18, 1898, the *New York Times* reported the following:

> The British steam *Sylvia,* Quebec Steamship Line, which arrived from Barbadoes a few days ago with a load of asphalt, will leave . . . Long Island City, to-day bound for Cuba. The steamer has been chartered by William R. Hearst, proprietor of the *New York Journal,* who proposes to publish the first paper printed in English in Cuba. He will personally superintend its production.
>
> Besides editors and skilled workmen the vessel takes a complete printing outfit, including stereotyping apparatus and an army hand-press.
>
> he party expects to reach Santiago by Wednesday, and will effect a landing at the safest point in the vicinity.[66]

Sparing no expense, Hearst provisioned the *Sylvia*—the yacht now a refitted steamer leased from the Baltimore Fruit Company—with weapons, rations, medical supplies, and transformed belowdecks into a state-of-the-art darkroom. Along with a retinue of stewards, cooks, and illustrators, Hearst took along his star war correspondent, James Creelman; his right-hand man, George Pancoast; his cameraman, John C. Hemment; his motion picture cameraman, Billy Bitzer (complete with the prototype of an early motion picture camera requiring batteries weighing two thousand pounds); his old Harvard friend turned ranch hand Jack Follansbee; and naturally two chorus girls, Anita and Milly Willson.[67]

"Goodbye dear mother," Hearst wrote Phoebe. "Take care of yourself. You are much more likely to get sick than I am to get injured and your life and health [are] just as dear to me as mine is to you. Your loving son, etc."[68]

On June 19, Wheeler noted that the sea became rough but at 3 p.m. calmed as they caught sight of Cape Maisa.

"The shore seems to be lined with high hills or mountains, say from one thousand to fifteen hundred feet," Wheeler observed. "We see clouds of smoke; very possibly Spaniards preparing to retreat to Santiago. We are now about one hundred and twenty miles from that place."[69]

By dawn on June 20, they had closed that distance to thirty miles from Santiago and gazed upon the jungles and mountains of Cuba.[70]

One American already in Cuba was Richard Harding Davis.

Having landed on June 20, Davis stuck with the top brass. Davis and three other correspondents accompanied a band of twenty led by Admiral Sampson and General Shafter. Their destination was Aserraderos, eighteen miles west of Santiago. With steeds few and far between, Shafter and Davis were the only ones mounted, Shafter because of his girth and Davis because of an attack of sciatica. At that mountain rendezvous, Cuban general Calixto García discussed strategy with his American counterparts. Cuban revolutionaries, noting that humongous Shafter and handsome Davis were the only riders, might have surmised that the two yanquis were equals. The American soldiers could have corrected them. In nearly everyone's mind, Davis was clearly Shafter's superior.[71]

Like Shafter, W. R. Hearst also required a horse. Docking the *Sylvia* in Kingston, Jamaica, Hearst and Follansbee meandered a few miles out of Kingston to purchase polo ponies at a racetrack while Hemment gathered a shipment of ice for his darkroom. Next, the whole party enjoyed a lavish meal at the Crystal Springs Hotel before loading the horses and making for Cuba. After ten hours of fighting rough seas, they spied the US squadron blockading the mouth of Santiago Harbor. Slipping through the American blockade, they located the flagship the *New York* in front of Santiago's Morro Castle. At twilight Hearst, Creelman, and Hemment voyaged out in a launch and clambered up the rope ladder, meeting with Admiral Sampson.

"We have men ashore," Sampson told Hearst, "and have located the position of Cervera's entire fleet. Everyone of his vessels is lying safe from our guns behind that high hill there with such a narrow entrance with thick fields of mines that the navy can do nothing but stay here and prevent any egress." Sampson also explained that the army needed to take the city while his fleet was bottled up Cervera.[72]

The army was on its way.

On the morning of June 22, the *Yucatan* neared the small village of Daquiri in southeast Cuba, twenty-five miles east of Santiago and thirty-five miles west of Guantanamo Bay.

"There was plenty of excitement to the landing," Roosevelt recalled. "In the first place, the smaller war-vessels shelled Daiquiri, so as to dislodge any Spaniards who might be lurking in the neighborhood, and also shelled other places along the coast, to keep the enemy puzzled as to our intentions."[73]

Davis was back with the fleet at this point, hoping to cover the landing. But he grew outraged to learn that Shafter had forbade reporters from docking until all the soldiers, animals, and provisions had been taken to shore. Striding up to the promenade deck where Shafter and Adjutant General E. J. McClernand were attempting to oversee the chaotic landing, Davis addressed Shafter.

"General, I see the order for disembarkation directs that none but fighting men be allowed in the boats of the first landing party," Davis said. "This will keep back reporters."[74]Shafter, who personally believed no reporter should be allowed to follow the army, told Davis that the policy was to protect reporters from any Spanish hiding in the hills. Davis argued that he and his colleagues in the *Seguranca* were no mere newspaper reporters and instead were historians. At this Shafter lost his cool.

"I do not care a damn what you are," Shafter snapped. "I'll treat all of you alike."

Davis stormed off, but neither he nor Shafter would forget the exchange.

Meanwhile, the men abord the *Yucatan* realized that the Spanish, before scattering, had stripped the dock of planks, making it a mere skeleton. Worse, the *Yucatan* was attempting to land at high tide. From another transport the mules and horses were unceremoniously thrown overboard on the assumption that they would swim to shore. One of Roosevelt's horses, Rain-in-the-Face, drowned. The other, Little Texas, survived. A boat carrying rifles and African American infantrymen capsized, spilling rifles and "buffalo soldiers," as they were called, into the sea. As the buffalo soldiers swam for shore, Corporal Charles Knoblauck of E Troop, a champion swimmer at the New York Athletic Club, dove from the skeletal dock into the surf, managing to rescue most of the rifles. When two infantrymen didn't surface, Buckey O'Neill plunged into the water to save them. O'Neill couldn't rescue them but did manage to save himself. It wasn't until late afternoon that every living man, horse, and mule of the remaining Rough Riders were ashore.[75]

Now that they were on Cuban soil at last, their fears of drowning were over. Sure, their chances of dying of disease or being shot to death had multiplied exponentially, but that was a risk they were all willing to take. And besides, with Theodore Roosevelt on their side, what could possibly go wrong?

—15—
YANKEES ON THE RUN

Once ashore at Daquiri, Fighting Joe Wheeler spotted the red and yellow of the Spanish flag flying atop a nearby blockhouse. The red was fine, but Wheeler thought that the yellow ought to be replaced with white and blue and directed Colonel Wood to see to it. In short order, the Spanish flag was hoisted down and the American flag run up. With the stars and stripes flying in the breeze, soldiers from the fleet gave a great cheer, punctuated by shrill steam whistles from the fleet.

While more soldiers landed, Roosevelt found his horse, Little Texas. Roosevelt had no saddle for the horse, but fortunately Edward Marshall had the solution. Shafter had at first promised the *New York Journal* reporter that the Hearst team would be allowed to bring their horses. Shafter afterward refused to allow any of the *Journal* horses aboard the transport, leaving the war correspondents with a surplus of saddles.

"I had one myself," Marshall reflected, "old and worn and perfectly comfortable. . . . In Colonel Roosevelt's distress I came to his rescue and loaned him that saddle."[1]

Roosevelt also observed the countryside, describing it as "a mass of rugged and precipitous hills, covered for the most part by dense jungle." He estimated that five hundred Spanish soldiers, who had fled that morning at the sight of the fleet, could have prevented the American disembarkation. In their place a hundred Cuban revolutionaries appeared, come to greet the Americans. Roosevelt described them as "a crew of as utter tatterdemalions as human eyes ever looked on, armed with every kind of rifle in all stages of dilapidation."[2]

Wheeler had more pressing business. After securing horses for the thousand-pound Sims-Dudley dynamite gun and leaving it in the care of Sergeant Hallet A. Borrowe of I Troop in the Rough Riders, Wheeler mounted his own horse and set off. It was as though Cuba were Georgia.[3]

"I rode forward some three and a half miles to examine the country," Wheeler recalled, "and when I returned it was late at night."[4]

In Wheeler's absence, with almost half the American forces having landed, a sprawling camp had arisen. Roosevelt and the Rough Riders camped in a dusty brush-covered valley between two hills bordering the Daquiri River. It proved to be a home to lizards, hairy tarantulas, and huge land crabs, with a murky pool ringed by palm trees on one side and the jungle on the other. From the palm trees Roosevelt and other enterprising men, with the help of the Cuban insurgents, furnished thatched shelter. With pride, Roosevelt reflected that the only impedimenta he had with him was a raincoat and a toothbrush.[5]

Camping that night, Wheeler took stock. As the major general of cavalry, he commanded two brigades. The 1st Brigade was composed of the 3rd Regular Cavalry (420 men), the 6th Regular Cavalry (437 men), and the 9th Regular Cavalry (410 men, mostly buffalo soldiers). Leading the 1st Brigade was fifty-year-old Brigadier General Samuel S. Sumner, who had fought for the Union at Fair Oaks and Antietam. Sumner kept a staff of 2 men. The 2nd Brigade consisted of the 1st Regular Cavalry (540 men), the 10th Regular Cavalry (465 men, mostly buffalo soldiers whose intrepid first lieutenant, John "Black Jack" Pershing, would become the senior commander to American forces on the Western Front during World War I), and the 1st US Volunteer Cavalry (550 men), otherwise known as the Rough Riders. Leading the 2nd Brigade was forty-eight-year-old Brigadier General Samuel Young, who had joined the 12th Pennsylvania Infantry at the outbreak of the American Civil War and by the Siege of Petersburg was a full-fledged colonel. Young kept a staff of 5 men. Wheeler himself kept a staff of 11 men, including Joe Jr., who was eager to prove himself. Of these 2,822 cavalrymen who had sailed from Tampa, almost 1,000 had landed, chief among them Fighting Joe.[6]

Naturally, Richard Harding Davis attached himself to the 1st US Volunteer Cavalry.

"You get more news with the other regiments," Davis wrote Charles, "but the officers, even the Generals, are such narrow minded slipshod men that we only visit them to pick up information."[7]

The next morning Roosevelt joined the soldiers at the beach, attempting to help bring provisions to shore. The small amount they were able to transport did them little good, for having left their mule train in Tampa, they quickly realized they were going to have a serious supply problem. While Roosevelt worried on logistics, fifty-five-year-old Brigadier General Henry Lawton—who had fought against Wheeler at Stones River and Chickamauga—sent out reconnoitering parties and established outposts. Lawton soon learned that Cuban forces under Brigadier General Demetrio Castillo Duany, a thirty-one-year-old Cuban revolutionary who had been born in Santiago but studied in France and the United States, had forced the Spanish to abandon the port of Juraguacito, better known as Siboney, seven miles to the west. Because Siboney's port offered more shelter than Daquiri, Shafter called for Wheeler to scout the area and throw out pickets.

"General Wheeler, a regular game-cock, was as anxious as Lawton to get first blood," Roosevelt recounted, "and he was bent upon putting the cavalry division to the front as quickly as possible. . . . General Wheeler made a reconnoissance [*sic*] in person."

"I rode rapidly to this place," Wheeler recalled, having ordered four squadrons of dismounted cavalry to follow with three Hotchkiss guns. This small army was made up of one squadron each from the 1st Regulars and the 3rd Regulars and two squadrons from the Rough Riders.[8]

Wheeler quickly determined that the Spanish had secured a strong position about three miles beyond Siboney and that General Castillo, with a band of about one hundred Cubans, had attacked their flank. This action resulted in nine wounded Cubans.

"I saw one dead Spaniard," Wheeler noted, "but do not know what other casualties they suffered."

Wheeler hastened back to Siboney, where at 8 p.m. the four squadrons arrived with the Hotchkiss guns, having marched single file through a hilly jungle trail, known as the Camino Real. The rest of Wheeler's 964-man army—the third that had disembarked—soon followed, their uniforms soaked with perspiration. The beach was also a hubbub of activity, with some transports having arrived from Daiquiri and drenched soldiers coming through the surf to the camp.[9]

Wheeler knew better than to leave his superiors totally in the dark. In his pocket-sized McDonald's stylograph rapid order copying book—designed so that pen marks were legible on the following page—Wheeler scribbled to Adjutant General H. C. Corbin that he'd learned that "Genl Linares was here yesterday and left in the rain." Wheeler didn't know it, but General Arsenio Linares had tasked General Antero Rubin to stop the Americans dead in their tracks.[10]

In Siboney, Wheeler also conferred with General Castillo, the two poring over a rough map. Learning the features of the country, Wheeler determined that he would attack the Spanish force, which Cuban scouts estimated to be about two thousand strong, early the next morning, June 24, the first step in hopefully driving the Spanish from the hills above Santiago, where they could conceivably position their own artillery and demand the surrender of the city and Cervera's fleet. Meeting that night with General Young and Colonel Wood, Wheeler discussed his plan of attack.[11]

"He had the power to do this," Roosevelt commented, "as when General Shafter was afloat he had command ashore." Roosevelt also took in the camp, describing the gathering thunderclouds and frenzied cookfires. "The men cooked their coffee and pork, some frying the hard-tack with the pork. The officers, of course, fared just as the men did. Hardly had we finished eating when the rain came, a regular tropic downpour. We sat about, sheltering ourselves as best we could, for the hour or two it lasted."[12]

When the sky cleared, Roosevelt sauntered over to L Troop, where he caught sight of Captain Allyn Capron and Sergeant Hamilton Fish talking near a campfire. "Their frames seemed of steel," Roosevelt recounted, "to withstand all fatigue; they were flushed with health; in their eyes shone high resolve and fiery desire . . . filled with eager longing to show their mettle."[13]

Near midnight when Wood explained Wheeler's battle plan to Capron, whose twenty-seventh birthday was scant minutes away, Capron took it stoically. "Well," Capron said, "tomorrow at this time the long sleep will be on many of us."[14]

Capron was more right than he knew.

Wheeler slept that night in the former home of the Spanish *comandante* if he slept at all, for pervading the hot night air was "a pandemonium of noise," as Davis described it.

> It was one of the most weird and remarkable scenes of the war. . . . An army was being landed on an enemy's coast at the dead of night, but with the same cheers and shrieks and laughter that rise from the bathers at Coney Island on a hot Sunday. . . . The men still to be landed from the "prison hulks," as they called the transports, were singing in chorus, the men already on shore were dancing naked around the camp-fires on the beach, or shouting with delight as they plunged into the first bath that had offered in seven

> days, and those in the launches as they were pitched head-first at the soil of Cuba, signalized their arrival by howls of triumph. On either side rose black overhanging ridges, in the lowland between were white tents and burning fires, and from the ocean came the blazing, dazzling eyes of the search-lights shaming the quiet moonlight.[15]

No sleep was had by Wood or Roosevelt. "Wood looked worn and haggard, and his voice was cracked and hoarse," Marshall recalled. "Roosevelt was as lively as a chipmunk, and seemed to be in half a dozen places at once."[16]

Meanwhile, three miles north General Rubin's Spanish troops busied themselves by chopping down trees to improve the defenses on the ridge above Las Guasimas.[17]

Reveille sounded at 3:15 on the morning of June 24. At 5:00 the army was on the move, Wheeler ordering Colonel Wood to march the Rough Riders up the left-hand westerly road. At the same time, he ordered the 1st and 10th Cavalry to march with General Castillo and two hundred Cubans up the main Santiago Road, to the east, with the Hotchkiss guns, and Wheeler believed that a team of horses carrying the dynamite gun was expected at any moment. The distance between the two roads was at times between seven hundred and eight hundred yards, eventually merging into a wagon trail at an apex called Las Guasimas, named for the abundant hognut trees. Unfortunately, neither the dynamite gun nor General Castillo and his two hundred Cubans arrived. But someone else, to Roosevelt's irritation, showed up instead.

"As we landed from a despatch boat we saw the last troop of the mounted infantry wending slowly over the top of a huge hill," Stephen Crane recalled in a *New York World* article. "Three of us promptly posted after them upon hearing the statement that they had gone out with the avowed intention of finding the Spanish and mixing it up with them."[18]

Crane began by mixing with Ernest McCready, Edward Marshall, and Burr McIntosh, a *Journal* correspondent and photographer who had sportingly raced tarantulas on his first night in Cuba and had been badly bitten as a result. Still persona non grata with Roosevelt, Crane trailed behind the Rough Riders while Davis rode alongside the lieutenant colonel.

At 6:00 Roosevelt and the Rough Riders started up the steep trail that overlooked Siboney. Kennett Harris of the *Chicago Record* noted "Capron's tall figure striding over the boulders in the steep ascent." Aside from their rifles, pistols, and machetes, each man carried a blanket roll, a full cartridge belt, a canteen of water, hard tack, green coffee beans, canned tomatoes, and canned beef. Along with the chirp of birds filling the air, some men of B Troop began singing "There'll Be a Hot Time in the Old Town Tonight."[19]

Davis, bedecked in a blue jacket, a white shirt, and a felt hat with a white puggaree, was dismissive of an imminent battle. "I doubted that there were any Spaniards nearer than Santiago," Davis reflected.[20]

To the east of the Rough Riders, Brigadier General Young reached an open glade a little before 7:30. He was soon joined by Captain A. L. Mills and two troopers, having returned from the ruins of an old building, sporting a sundial on one wall, 150 yards away. Mills reported that at that building they had spied a few hundred yards to the north the Spanish breastworks in the shape of an obtuse triangle, with the salient jutting toward the American forces. This was much closer than where General Castillo had told Wheeler to expect the enemy. Young responded by deploying the 1st Regular Cavalry to hold both sides of the road, keeping the 10th in reserve. At this point Fighting Joe Wheeler arrived. Young pointed out to Wheeler the straw hats of the Spanish jutting from beyond the distant breastworks.[21]

Meanwhile, Stephen Crane was "frightened almost into convulsions," as he later admitted, following the Rough Riders as "they wound along this narrow winding path, babbling joyously, arguing, recounting, laughing; making more noise than a train going through a tunnel."[22]

Soon a loud order came down the line: "There's a Spanish outpost just ahead and the men must stop talking."

"Stop talkin, can't ye,—it," a sergeant bawled.

"Ah, say, can't ye stop talkin'?" another howled.

For once Crane kept his trap shut, convinced that by talking "Teddie's Terrors" were making targets of themselves and about to blunder into a heap of trouble. He wasn't entirely wrong. At the front Wood came across a fresh corpse, though whether it was Spanish or Cuban he could not tell.

With a Spanish outpost now in sight, Wood sent word for silence and to "load chambers and magazines." The rattle of breech bolts and the snap of magazine covers were soon heard, but the enormity of the coming battle still didn't seem to register.[23]

"The men were totally unconcerned," Roosevelt remembered, "and I do not think they realized that any fighting was at hand; at any rate, I could hear the group nearest me discussing in low murmurs, not the Spaniards, but the conduct of a certain cow-puncher in quitting work on a ranch and starting a saloon in some New Mexican town."[24]

Marshall also overheard a sweltering B Troop private ask, "By God! How would you like a glass of cold beer?

At the front, Wood began deploying the regiment. Troops G, K, and A were ordered to form a skirmish line under Roosevelt, not far from Captain Allyn Capron's L Troop; in particular, Wood expected Buckey O'Neill's A Troop to link up with the Regulars where the trails merged. Major Alex Brodie was ordered to extend the line to the left with D, E, and F Troops. Captain James McClintock's B Troop would remain in reserve behind L Troop.[25]

With the thickness of the jungle preventing anyone from seeing the Spanish, Roosevelt, Captain William Llewelyn, 1st Lieutenant Woody Kane, 1st Lieutenant Jack Greenway, and some troopers made it to a point jutting over a ravine. From there they could see some of the Spanish entrenchments, which from that distance seemed abandoned. Though Roosevelt didn't know it, this was all part of the Spanish plan. Marshall later got it from a Spanish prisoner aboard the *Olivette* that General Rubin's pickets and sharpshooters, hiding in the jungle, knew precisely where the Rough Riders were but had been instructed not to fire until the Americans marched blithely into a cul-de-sac, at which point the Spanish were ready to shoot them down.[26]

Still largely oblivious to the danger, Roosevelt returned from the point over the ravine and was talking to Marshall about a dinner they had shared in New York City with Marshall's boss at the *Journal,* W. R. Hearst. A former employee of the *Journal* was nearby, Richard Harding Davis. Still suffering from sciatica, Davis rode a government mule. Roosevelt's eyes were on the barbed-wire fence, which had been cut between two posts.

"My God!" Roosevelt exclaimed, "This wire has been cut today."[27]

"What makes you think so?" Marshall asked.

"The end is bright," Roosevelt replied, "and there has been enough dew, even since sunrise[,] to put a light rust on it, had it not been lately cut."

Just then Major Henry Lamotte appeared, riding a mule and making a racket. Roosevelt urged the man to be quiet. But it was too late for that. All at once the Spanish soldiers, with their rapid-firing Mausers trained on the Rough Riders, opened fire.

On the other side of the ridge, Fighting Joe was in a mood to make some fresh corpses. While time itself seemed to take deep breaths, Wheeler and Young examined the enemy position and deployed lines. Eventually Wheeler directed Young to open fire with the Hotchkiss gun across a ravine northwest of the Spanish breastworks. As the one-pound shell shot forth with an explosive whine toward the straw-hatted Spaniards, Captain William D. Beach, chief engineer of the 1st Cavalry, jotted down the time in his notebook: 8:15. But his hand jerked back as rifle fire poured forth from the breastworks. Around Wheeler, several enlisted men and officers crumpled to the ground.[28]

"The enemy replied, and the firing immediately became general," Wheeler reflected in his official report to Shafter, still aboard the *Seguranca*. "Colonel Wood had deployed his regiment, his right nearly reaching the left of the Regulars."[29]

As the bullets from the smokeless Spanish Mausers ripped into his men and the mules carrying the machine guns bolted for the rear, Roosevelt could tell he was in a fix.[30]

"We could hear the faint reports of the Hotchkiss guns and the reply of two Spanish guns, and the Mauser bullets were singing through the trees over our heads," Roosevelt recalled, "making a noise like the humming of telephone wires; but exactly where they came from we could not tell."[31]

Worst of all, Roosevelt knew that Capron and his men were off somewhere to the right, from where the gunfire was pouring. Some thought the firing might have been coming from Capron, accidentally firing at them in confusion, but Roosevelt correctly figured it to be the Spanish; he just didn't know where they were. In desperation, he ordered a volley fired into the jungle. When no cries of wounded filled the air, he realized he'd guessed wrong. In the meantime, his men continued to take fire.

"Everyone went down in a lump without cries," Marshall observed, but the chug "of bullets striking flesh is nearly always audible."[32]

One of the first men struck was Sergeant Hamilton Fish. The slug slammed into his left side, tore out his right side, and buried itself into the chest of Private Ed Culver.

"That bullet hit both of us," Fish gasped before falling dead. Culver could only stare blankly at Fish's corpse before crawling away from the front. Phil Sweet, the former New York policeman, looked on in horror from twenty-five feet away.

"In the space of three minutes," Davis remarked, "nine men were lying on their backs helpless. . . . One man near me was shot through the head."

Fortunately, the tide was about to turn, for the luck of R. H. D. was with them.

"It was Richard Harding Davis who gave us our first opportunity to shoot back with effect," Roosevelt recollected. "He was behaving precisely like my officers, being on the extreme front of the line, and taking every opportunity to study with his glasses the ground where we thought the Spaniards were."[33]

"There they are, Colonel; look over there; I can see their hats near that glade," Davis exclaimed, pointing across the valley to the right.

Soon Roosevelt saw them as well, called for his best sharpshooters, and ordered the men into a firing line.

"Then the woods became aglow with fighting," Crane reported. "Our people advanced, deployed, reinforced, fought, fell—in the bushes, in the tall grass, under the lone palms—before a foe not even half seen. . . . They were under a cruel fire."[34]

Thomas Jefferson Isbell, a private of Cherokee descent in L Troop, fired into the jungle and killed a Spaniard, after which a furious volley erupted. Isbell escaped being wounded for two minutes until a Mauser bullet caught him in the neck, but he stuck to the firing line. Even when six more bullets took him—one in the left thumb, another in his left hand, one that passed clean through near his hip, a graze to the head, and two more to the neck—he continued to fire. Roosevelt recorded that when blood loss grew too great Isbell was ultimately sent to the rear, though many of his companions hadn't been so fortunate.[35]

With the fighting heating up, Roosevelt left Little Texas behind, dashing about on foot while directing fire. This soon began to have an effect, with the Rough Riders advancing and the Spanish retreating before making another stand. "The advances were made in quick, desperate rushes—sometimes the ground gained was no more than a man covers in sliding for a base," Davis remarked.[36]

Not to be outdone, Crane also described the advance. "The Rough Riders advanced steadily and confidently under the Mauser bullets," Crane wrote. "They spread across some open ground—tall grass and palms—and there they began to fall, smothering and threshing down in the grass, marking man-shaped places among those luxuriant blades."[37]

Crane himself was conspicuous for his disregard for personal safety. Langdon Smith, a reporter for the *Journal,* watched as Crane calmly rolled a cigarette while Spanish bullets cut the leaves all around him and men fell only a few feet from him.[38]

During particularly ferocious Spanish volleys, Roosevelt and his men sought cover from whatever was handy: a mound, a bush, a tree trunk. During one such volley, Roosevelt was behind a palm tree when a Mauser bullet bored through a palm frond, sending dust and splinters flying into his left eye and ear. Sometimes Roosevelt didn't even bother taking cover.[39]

In his official report to headquarters, Brigadier General Samuel Young noted, "Both Col. Wood and Lieut. Col. Roosevelt disdained to take advantage of shelter or cover from enemie's fire, while any of their men were exposed to it—an error of judgement but happily on the heroic side."[40]

When Harry Haefner of G Troop was shot through the hips, Roosevelt helped drag him behind a tree. Haefner asked for a canteen and a rifle, which Roosevelt gave him. The mortally wounded soldier poured hot lead at the Spanish until they retreated, and Roosevelt and the others left Haefner to die alone while pressing the attack.

"No man was allowed to drop out to help the wounded," Roosevelt reflected. "It was hard to leave them there in the jungle, where they might not be found again until the vultures and the land-crabs came, but war is a grim game and there was no choice."[41]

Soon Roosevelt lost touch with his wing, commanded by Major Micah Jenkins and Captain Buckey O'Neill. To find them, Roosevelt sent Jack Greenway; Marcus Russell of Troy, New York; and George Roland, whom Roosevelt described as "a New Mexican cow-puncher." The trio descended into the valley. Russell died there in a fierce firefight. When Greenway and Roland returned, they informed Roosevelt of Russell's death and the whereabouts of Jenkins and O'Neill and continued firing on the line. Shortly afterward, Roosevelt noticed Roland bleeding from his side. Roland dismissed it. Roosevelt figured that the cowpuncher had broken a rib and ordered him to the field hospital in the rear. Roland grumbled but left. After fifteen minutes he returned, saying he could not find the hospital. Roosevelt doubted him but let him stay, and Roland returned to his position on the line.[42]

Having helped Roosevelt spot the Spanish, Davis decided to join G Troop as it moved up the trail. With them he witnessed "the grewsome pictures of war."[43]

"The rocks on either side were spattered with blood and the rank grass matted with it," Davis observed. "Blanket rolls, haversacks, carbines, and canteens had been abandoned all along its length. . . . Except for the clatter of the land-crabs, those hideous orchid-coloured monsters that haunt the place of the dead, and the whistling of the bullets in the trees, the place was as silent as the grave."

From out of the brush a hospital steward appeared and called to Davis, "Lieutenant Thomas is badly wounded in here, and we can't move him. We want to carry him out of the sun some place, where there is shade and breeze." This was 1st Lieutenant John R. Thomas Jr. of L Troop, whose family had fought in the Revolutionary War, the War of 1812, the Mexican-American War, and the Civil War. Davis noticed that Thomas had been shot in the leg. Together, Davis and the hospital steward caught hold of the corners of his blanket and lifted the injured man.

"You're taking me to the front, aren't you?" Thomas howled in pain. "You said you would. They've killed my captain—do you understand? They've killed Captain Capron. The—Mexicans! They've killed my captain."[44]

If that were so, it was more than a grievous loss. Not only did Roosevelt consider Captain Allyn Capron "simply invaluable," but if Capron had died John Thomas would have command of L Troop. Thomas's demands to be taken to the front would then be not a request out of gallantry or pride; L Troop needed a leader.

"For God's sake, take me to the front," Thomas pleaded. "Do you hear? I order you; damn you, I order—We must give them hell; do you hear? We must give them hell. They killed Capron. They've killed my captain."

Fifty yards later Davis found Capron in the hands of the surgeons. But it was as Thomas said. Capron was dead, his face white as a ghost and a black wound in his chest. Davis passed more bodies as he struggled to help L Troop; one boy had taken a bullet between his eyes, and the body of a sergeant was strewn along the trail. Ultimately, Davis borrowed a carbine from a wounded soldier and joined with L Troop, where he saw 2nd Lieutenant Richard Cushing Day had taken command. With Day as he walked up and down the line was an Irish sergeant, John Byrne, who seemed to be taking some maniacal pleasure in the battle, as evidenced by his comments and observations. Davis quickly determined that L Troop needed a little assistance. As a noncombatant and a self-appointed historian, Davis wasn't supposed to take sides. But Davis was tired of playing by the rules. And just because he wasn't wearing a uniform didn't mean he couldn't shoot a gun. Marching to the front line with the carbine in hand, Davis targeted the Spanish and opened fire.[45]

"Richard Harding Davis was over to my right with L Troop," recounted Marshall, "and pumping wildly at the Spaniards with a carbine."[46]

Marshall had the same idea, firing at the Spanish with smokeless revolver cartridges he'd been given in Tampa. But luck wasn't with Marshall. A bullet took him in the body near the spine. Davis rushed to his side.[47]

"Edward Marshall, of the New York *Journal,* who was on the firing-line to the left . . . was shot through the body near the spine," Davis later observed," and when I saw him, he was suffering the most terrible agonies, and passing through a succession of convulsions."[48]

Crane, hearing a soldier mention that a correspondent had been "all shot to hell," sought out the reporter, finding Marshall where the surgeon had left him.[49]

"Hello, Crane!" Marshall greeted.

"Hello, Marshall! In hard luck, old man?"

"Yes, I'm done for."

"Nonsense. You're all right, old boy. What can I do for you?"

"Well, you might file my despatches," Marshall replied. "I don't mean file 'em ahead of your own, old man—but just file 'em if you find it handy."

Considering that Crane worked for Pulitzer and that Marshall worked for Hearst, this was a big ask. But Crane didn't give a damn. He promised he would file Marshall's copy back at Siboney, come hell or high water.

Also shot was Major Alex Brodie. Roosevelt and the Arizonan had been on the front lines when a bullet shattered Brodie's arm and whirled him around. At first Brodie refused to go to the rear, but the pain became so great that he eventually relented. It was at that point that Colonel Wood directed Roosevelt to take charge of the left wing and push it forward. Roosevelt did as commanded.[50]

"A perfect hail of bullets was sweeping over us as we advanced," Roosevelt recalled. "Once I got a glimpse of some Spaniards, apparently retreating, far in the front, and to our right, and we fired a couple of rounds after them."[51]

Along with lamenting that he should have left his sword with Little Texas, for it continuously got between his legs as he tore through the jungle, Roosevelt noted that the combination of the smokeless powder from the Spanish Mausers and the thick vegetation made spotting the enemy very tough. Eventually he became convinced they were being fired upon by Spanish soldiers in some large buildings with red-tiled roofs, part of a ruined ranch five hundred yards off. Taking a rifle from a wounded soldier, Roosevelt fired several shots at the building. Hearing cheering to the right, Roosevelt figured that Wood had ordered a charge and so sprang up and ordered his men to charge the buildings.

"They came forward with a will," Roosevelt recounted. "There was a moment's heavy firing from the Spaniards, which all went over our heads, and then it ceased entirely. When we arrived at the buildings, panting and out of breath, they contained nothing but heaps of empty cartridge-shells and two dead Spaniards, shot through the head."[52]

Having taken the ranch, Roosevelt still couldn't see much through the jungle, and at the extreme left he was worried about being flanked. At that moment a man came up and repeated a rumor conjured up by the fog of war that Colonel Leonard Wood was dead. Believing the information to be true, Roosevelt quickly set about taking command of the regiment. In a flurry of activity, he sent men to fill canteens with water, ordered men to take cover in an abandoned sunken road, and directed several wounded men and a dozen suffering from exhaustion into the ranch buildings. Then he set out for the main body.[53]

Meanwhile, the fog of war had descended over Fighting Joe and his staff as well. From their imperfect vantage point, they couldn't be sure if they were winning or losing the battle. Despite wanting the glory of victory for himself, Wheeler worried that there would be no victory if he couldn't get more men to the field. It may have been a relief when Major M. J. Beach suggested to Wheeler, "We have nine big regiments of infantry only a few miles back on the road. Let me send to General Lawton for one of them and close this action up."[54]

"All right," Wheeler agreed.

As Beach began preparing the message, he asked, "Shall I say 'request' or 'direct'?"

After a moment, Wheeler said, "Direct."

Wheeler needn't have worried. Overjoyed, Roosevelt discovered Wood alive and well, who informed him that the Spanish were retreating. Through the tall grass and jungle, the American soldiers could make out a body of three hundred panic-stricken Spaniards running like jackrabbits. On the orders of Captain Robert Huston of D Troop, his soldiers opened fire, and half a dozen Spaniards dropped. Wood ran over and boomed, "Don't shoot at retreating men!" But his voice was lost in the din of battle, and the men continued to fire. Ultimately, the colonel called for Emilio Cassi. Recognizing the call of cease-fire on Cassi's trumpet, the men finally stopped.

Wheeler felt the excitement as well. From atop his horse, he witnessed the Spanish retreat from the summit. Victory was now at hand. Standing up in his stirrups he shouted in joy. "We've got the damned Yankees on the run!"[55]

Realizing that Fighting Joe in the heat of battle had forgotten which war he was fighting, his surrounding officers burst out laughing. One of his officers reflected that though this was "an embarrassing moment for the General," Wheeler joined in the laughter as well. And why not? Against all odds, having been imprisoned for treason thirty-three years ago, Joseph Wheeler had donned an American uniform and won what newspapers would soon call the Battle of Las Guasimas. The whole affair had taken about an hour and a half. The credit would go to Wheeler, Young, Sumner, Wood, Roosevelt, and all of Wheeler's nearly thousand-man army.

When Brigadier General Adna R. Chaffee arrived at the head of a column of infantry, Roosevelt described him as "rather glum" to see the fighting over. Chaffee wasn't the only one piqued. Shafter, still dawdling aboard the *Seguranca,* sent an aide with a message. "General Shafter express[ed] his pleasure at the good news of the fight, . . . but he instructed me very positively not to move forward so as to become engaged with the enemy, as he did not wish any further engagement to take place until we could advance with the entire force," Wheeler recalled.[56]

Wheeler may have breathed a sigh of relief. In his letter to Shafter—a copy of which remained in his stylograph copying book—Wheeler wrote, "General Shafter . . . The enemy retreated . . . but our men were too fatigued to pursue."[57]

Wheeler also had the hard task of determining the number of wounded and dead. All told, sixteen Americans had perished: Allyn Capron, Jesse Stark, Otto Krupp, Alexander Slemere, Emel Bjork, Gustave Kolbe, Marcus Russell, Peter Dix, Jack Berlin, William White, Edward Leggett, Hamilton Fish, George Dougherty, William Irvine, Harry Haefner, and Tildon Dawson. Fifty-two men were wounded.

As for the Spanish, Wheeler could only guess, but he believed that the number of Spanish casualties "far exceeded the losses which our troops sustained." In his after-action report to Shafter, Wheeler remarked, "We are finding dead and wounded men in the high grass thickets, but I hope that 22 killed and 70 or 80 wounded will even the loss." Wheeler's estimate proved low. Thirty-nine Spanish corpses were soon located, and Wheeler later learned from the Spanish generals that Rubin's casualties totaled about 200.[58]

Just as important, they'd pushed the Spanish back and had momentum on their side. "From the generals to the privates all were eager to march against Santiago," Roosevelt recalled.[59]

But two critical points still stood in the way: the fortified village of El Caney and the Spanish breastworks atop the San Juan Heights.

16

SAN JUAN HILL

Immediately after the battle, Roosevelt met with Generals Joseph "Fighting Joe" Wheeler, Henry Lawton, and Adna R. Chaffee and Colonel Leonard Wood, the top brass, resting on a bank. Roosevelt was relieved to hear his superiors express appreciation for his conduct during the battle. But the good cheer wasn't exultant, for the bodies needed to be collected. In short order the fallen were located, and that afternoon Wheeler's ragtag army marched two and a half miles toward Santiago before setting up camp on the summit of the trail. The next morning, June 25, 1898, Roosevelt watched as Chaplain Henry Brown gave the Episcopalian service for their fallen comrades and the men sang "Rock of Ages" while vultures wheeled eerily overhead.[1]

Shortly afterward, the American army marched another two miles toward the Spanish lines to the westward slope on the Las Guasimas ridge. Roosevelt recalled camping in "a marshy open spot close to a beautiful stream." Conspicuously absent among the reporters was Stephen Crane, who had kept his word, traveling back to Siboney to file Marshall's report for the *New York Journal* and his own short column for the *New York World*. Although Crane described the battle as "a gallant blunder" and Roosevelt and the Rough Riders as having been "ambushed," in Washington they celebrated the Battle of Las Guasimas as a victory and didn't care about the details. To the people, Roosevelt was the dashing hero. Talk of promoting him to brigadier general became commonplace, and a coalition of independent Republicans in New York announced their intention of nominating him for governor that September.[2]

But first Roosevelt had to win the war.

That day Roosevelt wrote to his sister Corinne:

> Yesterday we struck the Spaniards and had a brisk fight. . . . We lost a dozen men killed or mortally wounded, and sixty severely or slightly wounded. Brodie was wounded; poor Capron and Ham. Fish were killed. Will you send a this note to Fish's father? . . . The last charge I led on the left using a rifle I took from a wounded man; and I kept three of the empty cartridges we got from a dead Spaniard at this point, for the children. . . . Richard Harding Davis was with me in the fight and behaved capitally. The Spaniards shot well; but they did not stand when we rushed. It was a good fight. I am in good health.[3]

Roosevelt may have been in good health, but the same could not be said for the commander of the Fifth Corps. General William R. Shafter was not only suffering from the heat and an attack of gout but somehow had also contracted a scalp condition that required near-constant scratching by his aides. Little sympathy was given to "Pecos Bill," with the common soldiers blaming him for the "maddening" mismanagement of the unloading in Siboney, which kept food, supplies, and reinforcements from them.[4]

Part of the trouble was that rather than repairing the pier at Daiquiri, Shafter had ordered a pier constructed at Siboney but so close to shore that it was of little use. Supplies were thus laboriously placed on tugboats and lighters before being ferried to shore. Adding to the quagmire was lack of authority. The transport ship captains, who had leased their services to the US government but weren't strictly military, didn't see a reason to bend to Shafter's will. Whenever gunfire erupted from the shore, they would scurry farther out to sea, with their precious cargo aboard, causing further delays.

"Had there been a strong man in command of the expedition," Davis wrote, "he would have ordered them into place," and "stern and bow anchors would have kept them there."[5]

The average soldier was less polite. In earshot of Roosevelt's acquaintance, Black Jack Pershing, one officer referred to Shafter as "a fat old slob." Pershing came to Shafter's defense, saying that once Shafter won the campaign "these things will be forgotten." Roosevelt, for one, didn't forget or forgive.[6]

"There was nothing like enough transportation with the army," Roosevelt groused, "whether in the way of wagons or mule-trains; exactly as there had been no sufficient number of landing-boats with the transports. . . . [B]ut none of us had much, and the shelter-tents proved only a partial protection against the terrific downpours of rain."[7]

Naturally, the weather made everything worse.

The torrential downpours flooded the camp every afternoon. As for food, along with their own hardtack and pork they feasted on chickens found staked out near the Spanish trenches. Beans found in the saddlebags of dead Spanish mules were left uneaten, for believing they might be poisoned, orders came down not to touch them. Cuban insurgents traded sugarcane, plantains, and mangos for American hardtack and canned beef. Enterprising privates learned how to fry mangos and, when the tobacco ran out, smoke dried grass, roots, and manure. Roosevelt himself organized a couple of expeditions to the coast, taking along officers' horses, stray mules, and a number of the hardiest adventurers. They returned with beans, canned tomatoes, and—because of "a silly regulation," as Roosevelt put it—canned vegetables that he had to personally purchase for the men.[8]

William Randolph Hearst also helped with provisions. Having landed at Siboney shortly after the Battle of Las Guasimas, he and the other *Journal* men set up headquarters—"a cozy little Cuban dwelling"—next to the Red Cross. Working alongside Clara Barton as a nurse was Wheeler's twenty-nine-year-old daughter, Annie. Noticing that the Red Cross nurses were in desperate need, Hearst donated a shipment of ice. Afterward, his entourage led the Chief to a Cuban shanty, painted blue and white, with red tiles on the roof and tropical plants growing outside. This was the headquarters of the Cuban leader, General Calixto García.

García, dressed in a white suit and wearing a wide-brimmed Panama hat, was known for his temper but appeared in good spirits with Hearst. Sweating, García took off the hat. This revealed the dramatic scar on his forehead, a reminder of his attempt to take his own life to avoid capture just as the Ten Years' War came to a close.

To Hearst, García was especially grateful, having recognized the effect that Hearst's *Journal* had on the war. In thanks, he presented Hearst with a Cuban flag riddled with bullet holes made by Spanish Mausers.

"*Cuba Libre!*" García shouted.[9]

Hearst, who could be shy outside his own social circles, felt the gravity of the moment.

"*Cuba Libre!*" Hearst echoed, rising to the occasion.

In a letter to Phoebe, Hearst mentioned the meeting with pride along with doing his best to quell her fears.

> Dear Mother:
>
> I am at the front and absolutely safe, so don't worry. Since poor Marshall was shot the General has made strict rules limiting newspapermen to certain localities that are well within the lines so that there is no opportunity for any of us to get hurt even if we wanted to.
>
> The landing of troops, guns and horses is most interesting and [the] march to the front very impressive. I have interviewed Admiral Sampson, General Shafter and General Garcia. The last named gave me his headquarters flag which has seen much service and is riddled by bullets. He said the Journal had been the most potent influence in bringing the United States to the help of Cuba and that they would always remember the Journal as a friend when friends had been very few. Now he said that they had many friends but ranked the Journal above all others.
>
> I have been greatly interested in everything and of some service to the hospital ship providing them with ice and delicacies which they lacked. I think the standing of the paper will profit by me being there. Other proprietors are safely at home—and I will be soon. I hope you are well and not at all alarmed about me for honestly there is no occasion.[10]

As for Wheeler, there was occasion to be alarmed. On June 29 he began to feel sick, as he admitted in a subsequent letter to his children. Despite the illness, he continued to be active. Reconnoitering about five miles northwest of Siboney, Wheeler selected campsites based on defensibility and proximity to water and ordered men to repair the Camino Real.[11]

"[W]e got it in very fair condition," Wheeler was pleased to note.[12]

From a hilltop called El Pozo, Wheeler could see the fortified Spanish village of El Caney atop the hills to his right. To the west, only about a mile and a half away, were the entrenched San Juan Heights. These included a hill on top of which a giant kettle would soon give it its name—Kettle Hill—and the blockhouse a third of a mile to the west atop San Juan Hill. Beyond the heights Wheeler could see portions of Santiago, the capture of which could mean victory and the end of the war.[13]

Hearst agreed with this assessment. Having crested a ridge overlooking Santiago Harbor, he considered the military position. On June 30, the *Journal* printed the following story under Hearst's byline:

> It is satisfactory to be an American and to be here on the soil of Cuba, at the very threshold of what may prove to be the decisive battle of the war. The fight for possession of the City of Santiago and the capture of Cervera's fleet seem to be only a few hours away, and from the top of the rough, green ridge where I write this, we can see dimly on the sea the monstrous forms of Sampson's fleet lying a semi-circle in front of the entrance of Santiago harbor. . . . Now that I am here on the spot . . . I am satisfied that McKinley is right in deciding to attack Santiago rather than Havana.[14]

Eventually Shafter himself landed, and on the morning of June 30, 1898, six days after the Battle of Las Guasimas, he rode into camp on a mule. By Shafter's own testimony, he was "nauseated and very dizzy," suffering from the heat, gout, and the mysterious illness that inflamed his scalp.[15]

Having taken Shafter's measure during their interview, Hearst described him as a "bold, lion-headed hero[,] . . . a sort of human fortress in blue coat."

Hearst was being kind. Commenting on Shafter's poor mule, one Rough Rider quipped, "He looks like he could carry the mule he was riding better than the mule could carry him."[16]

Despite his discomfort, Shafter was still the man in charge. After making it up El Pozo to personally get the lay of the land, he convened a war council. Surrounded by his aides and top subordinates, Shafter sat in shirtsleeves and suspenders, his great gouty foot wrapped in burlap. Wheeler was all for action. He told Shafter that El Caney was defended by only five hundred Spaniards.[17]

"I described the defences to General Shafter," Wheeler recollected, "and urged that I be permitted to attack the place with a large force of artillery; my argument being that the fire from a number of guns upon the forces at El Caney would soon make their position untenable."[18]

Wheeler argued that as the Spanish fled El Caney for Santiago, a division of infantry or dismounted cavalry could, lying in wait, catch them in the open. Possibly noticing how sick Wheeler seemed, Shafter admitted that the plan was feasible but decided that General Lawton should lead the attack on El Caney, which would commence the next morning, July 1, at dawn. Figuring it would take Lawton only a half hour to take El Caney, Shafter would then have Lawton join Wheeler's cavalry and the infantry division under Brigadier General J. F. Kent—a

Philadelphian who had served at Spotsylvania and Petersburg—in their attack of San Juan Heights. Considering that eight thousand Spanish soldiers were rumored to be on their way to Santiago to join the twelve thousand in and around the city, everyone knew that the moment was now.[19]

The war council was scarcely over when a staff officer rode to Rough Rider headquarters with startling news. Not only was the entire Fifth Corps—sixteen thousand troops—to march to El Pozo later that day, but Generals Wheeler and Young had been struck with fever. This meant a shift in command.

"Brigadier-General Sam Sumner, an excellent officer, who had the second cavalry brigade, took command of the cavalry division, and Wood took command of our brigade, while, to my intense delight," Roosevelt wrote in his autobiography, "I got my regiment."[20]

Around noon, the Rough Riders struck camp, waiting for orders to march. At 3:30, a violent rainstorm struck, making them wish they still had their tents. At 4 p.m. the march began, the logistics of the 16,000-man army moving at once a typical Shafterian nightmare. The Camino Real narrowed into a claustrophobic ditch, sucking at their boots as they clambered through it.

"Once or twice we had to wade streams," Roosevelt recalled. "Darkness came on, but we still continued to march. It was about eight o'clock when we turned to the left and climbed El Poso hill, on whose summit there was a ruined ranch and sugar factory, now, of course, deserted. Here I found General Wood, who was arranging for the camping of the brigade."[21]

Fortunately, the rain had stopped. Historians such as Davis (though he was now considered a Rough Rider in all but name for his actions at Las Guasimas) could see the peculiar tableau in all its strange glory. Frederic Remington was atop the hill drawing sketches of artillery pieces. John Jacob Astor IV, one of the richest men in America, was a member of Shafter's staff. Shafter himself awoke during the night, finding himself unable to rise because the gout was so bad. The commanding general would direct the next day's battle through messengers while lying on his cot.[22]

Wheeler, in a typed letter sent home and dated June 30, 1898, wrote, "Dear children, I have not heard a word from the United States for the last 16 days. . . . We are now closing up on Santiago and hope for good results. With all my love, Your affectionate Father, Joe Wheeler."[23]

Colonel Roosevelt and General Wood slept that night on a pile of saddle blankets while still in their raincoats. Sleeping nearby was Captain A. L. Mills, who had been the first to point out the Spanish to General Young during the Battle of

Las Guasimas, and Brigade Quartermaster William "Willie" E. Shipp, a North Carolinian and the first southerner who had graduated from West Point since the American Civil War. Roosevelt admired both Mills and Shipp for their "quiet, soldierly" manner. Roosevelt and Wood slept soundly except for waking once to make their rounds and checking in on the sentries, a task that must have reminded Roosevelt of his midnight patrols in New York City when he'd been police commissioner. Before dawn they were up and eating breakfast. They barely spoke, both knowing that today, July 1, 1898, would mean fighting.[24]

As the sun rose, orders came that artillery under Captain Allyn Capron—the father of the fallen Rough Rider captain—was to make a diversion while Lawton's infantry division attacked and captured El Caney. Roosevelt noticed that Wheeler, though sick and unable to retain command of the cavalry, stuck to the front "with his usual indomitable pluck and entire indifference to his own personal comfort."[25]

At about 6 o'clock Roosevelt heard the boom of Capron's cannons from El Caney, and clouds of white smoke gathered above the ridgeline. Roosevelt and Wood sat pensively for the next couple of minutes, Wood remarking that he wished their brigade could be moved elsewhere, for they were in line with the Spanish battery. Almost immediately after Wood stated this a great whistling filled the air, followed by the sound of something exploding over their heads: shrapnel from the Spanish batteries. Roosevelt and the others sprang to their feet, charging toward the horses. A second shot burst above them.

"From the second shell one of the shrapnel bullets dropped on my wrist," Roosevelt recalled, "hardly breaking the skin, but raising a bump about as big as a hickory-nut."[26]

Four other Rough Riders were hit by that shell, including Mason Mitchell of K Troop, who lost a leg. Two more shells exploded around them, one in the midst of a group of Cubans, many of whom fell wounded or dead, the rest scattering. Wood's horse was shot through the lungs.[27]

"Isn't it awful?" exclaimed a nearby reporter, grabbing Richard Harding Davis by the arm.[28]

"Very disturbing, very disturbing," Davis replied.

Roosevelt acted quickly. Hustling the Rough Riders into the dense jungle, he formed them into a fighting column.[29]

Meanwhile, at about 6:30 a.m. Private Charles Johnson Post—who had quit the *Journal* after the destruction of the *Maine* to join the 71st New York Regiment—heard the sound of Capron's battery while marching down Santiago Road. Since word had reached Capron that his son had been killed a week earlier at Las Guasimas, Post had noticed that Capron often drank himself to sleep at night, muttering "I'll get 'em, Allyn, I'll get 'em, goddamn 'em." Now Capron had his chance.[30]

"For the first time it dawned on us that there might be fighting ahead," Post recalled.

Beside the road, Post spied something strange. From beneath the shade of a jaunty, felt-brimmed straw hat with a scarlet band, someone was watching them through blue-gray eyes. He was tall and handsome, wore black civilian clothes, and sat a horse. Suddenly, one of the New Yorkers recognized the man.

"Hey, Willie!" the soldier called. Then everyone recognized him.

"Hey, Willie!" the men chorused.

Poker-faced, William Randolph Hearst looked on impassively.

"If he thought we were jeering he was wrong," Post explained. "We were just glad to see someone from home."

James Creelman of the *Journal* galloped up.

"Hello, Jimmy!" the men cried. Creelman smiled and waved.

"Boys, you're going into battle," Creelman announced. "Good luck!"

Hearst, having realized they weren't jeering but rather cheering him, slightly lightened.

"Good luck!" Hearst called. "Boys, good luck be with you."

The Rough Riders certainly needed some good luck. They'd been given only vague orders of marching to the right and connecting with Lawton after his infantry seized El Caney, but it soon became obvious that taking El Caney was a harder nut to crack than previously surmised. Nevertheless, Wood formed up the 2nd Brigade with the Rough Riders in the van, giving Roosevelt orders to follow the 1st Brigade up the Camino Real toward San Juan Heights. Roosevelt marched them in columns of four to the San Juan River. The spot where the Camino Real met the San Juan River soon took up a different name: the Bloody Ford.[31]

Because no one had made a proper reconnaissance, the exact Spanish position and strength were unknown. Shafter had sent up a captured Spanish balloon, but Roosevelt figured it was "worse than useless."[32]

"I was now ordered to cross the ford, march half a mile or so to the right, and then halt and await further orders; and I promptly hurried my men across, for the fire was getting hot, and the captive balloon, to the horror of everybody, was coming down to the ford," Roosevelt recounted. "Of course, it was a special target for the enemy's fire. I got my men across before it reached the ford. There it partly collapsed and remained, causing severe loss of life, as it indicated the exact position where the Tenth and the First Cavalry, and the infantry, were crossing."[33]

As luck had it, 1st Lieutenant Pershing of the 10th Cavalry was standing in the San Juan River, the water up to his waist, shepherding his men across when the balloon began drawing Spanish fire. Despite the terrific Mauser fire and exploding shells, Pershing led his squadrons to the other side.[34]

"Pershing . . . was as cool as a bowl of cracked ice," Captain George Ayres remembered.[35]

While bringing his squadrons across, Pershing caught sight of Fighting Joe Wheeler and his staff mounted on their horses in the middle of the river. The moment Pershing saluted a shell landed between them, splashing both men with water. Drenched, Wheeler returned the salute, wheeled his horse, and made for dry ground.[36]

West of the San Juan River, Roosevelt personally led one column of the Rough Riders through the heat and tall grass of the jungle. To their left was the 1st Brigade, trading bullets with the Spaniards on the hills. Eventually they came to a sunken lane with a wire fence on both sides. Here Roosevelt halted his men and sent back for orders. Facing San Juan Heights, Roosevelt was champing at the bit to charge. For one, the army was becoming an organizational mess, with the Rough Riders (the 1st Cavalry) and the 3rd, 6th, 9th, and 10th Calvaries all starting to overlap at places. To the left, Kent's infantry was also coming up, sure to add to the confusion.

As the Rough Riders waited for orders from Shafter, the minutes stretched interminably. Roosevelt with the help of Captain A. L. Mills, whom he relied on as an aide, got the men sheltered as best he could. Some lay under the lip of the sunken lane. Others crouched below the bank of the San Juan River, while more took Wheeler's example and lay down in the tall grass.[37]

"The heat was intense, and many of the men were already showing signs of exhaustion. . . . The fight was now on in good earnest, and the Spaniards on the hills were engaged in heavy volley firing," Roosevelt reflected. "The Mauser bullets drove in sheets through the trees and the tall jungle grass, making a peculiar whirring or rustling sound."[38]

One Mauser bullet caught Horace Devereaux, the Yalensian football player, as he crouched down in the river. Another ripped into the stomach of Ernest "Eddy" Haskell, a West Point cadet who had joined the Rough Riders while on vacation. Despite being in great pain, Haskell didn't want his injury to weaken morale.

"All right, Colonel, I'm going to get well," Haskell said, shaking Roosevelt's hand. "Don't bother about me, and don't let any man come away with me."[39]

Roosevelt figured that Haskell was a dead man, but Haskell and Devereaux both lived. Others were not so lucky. After Roosevelt gave an order to one of his men, the soldier rose, saluted, and then fell across Roosevelt's knees with a bullet in his brain.[40]

Billy McGinty, who was deployed with K Troop in a glade of high grass just beyond the river, recollected, "The fire from the enemy had intensified, and as we took cover, I could hear the bullets whizzing through the grass as if they were mowing it down in front of us, but when I looked up I didn't find any grass missing, but some of the boys were."[41]

The most dramatic casualty occurred after almost an hour of waiting. Smoking a cigarette as he walked the line was Captain Buckey O'Neill. The men of A Troop begged him to get down, but O'Neill would have none of it. When a sergeant said "Captain, a bullet is sure to hit you," O'Neill blew out a cloud of smoke, laughed, and said, "Sergeant, the Spanish bullet isn't made that will kill me." Moments later while discussing the direction of Spanish fire with some of the officers, a bullet smashed into O'Neill's mouth and tore through the back of his head. The captain was dead before he hit the ground.[42]

Davis, naturally, laid their deaths at the gouty feet of Brigadier General Shafter:

> This was endured for an hour, an hour of such hell of fire and heat, that the heat itself, had there been no bullets, would have been remembered for its cruelty. Men gasped on their backs, like fishes in the bottom of a boat, their heads burning inside and out, their limbs too heavy to move. They had been rushed here and rushed there wet with sweat and wet with fording streams, under a sun that would have made moving a fan an effort, and they lay prostrate, gasping at the hot air, with faces aflame, and their tongues sticking out, and their eyes rolling. All through this the volleys from the rifle-pits sputtered and rattled, and the bullets sang continuously like the wind through the riggings in a gale, shrapnel whined and broke, and still no order came from General Shafter.[43]

During this time, having given up on Shafter, Roosevelt sent messenger after messenger to Wood and Sumner asking for permission to attack. Around the time O'Neill was killed, Roosevelt had all but determined that he better march to the sound of the guns. Just then Lieutenant Colonel Joseph H. Dorst of Shafter's staff rode up through a hail of bullets, followed shortly by Shipp with the same message from Wood. It was Dorst who first relayed the command Roosevelt hungered for: "to move forward and support the regulars in the assault on the hills in front."[44]

"The instant I received the order I sprang on my horse and then my 'crowded hour' began," Roosevelt reflected, using the phrase made famous by Sir Walter

Scott: "One crowded hour of glorious life is worth an age without a name." In a letter to Lodge several days after the battle, Roosevelt again recollected the words, writing "then came the order to advance, and with it my 'crowded hour.'"[45]

Roosevelt started at the rear of the regiment. Because of the withering heat and to better see the men he was organizing for the advance, he was mounted on Little Texas. With the assistance of Captain A. L. Mills and Captain Loyd McCormick, Roosevelt rode up and down the line barking orders at captains and lieutenants. One soldier taking cover behind a small bush failed to jump up when Roosevelt ordered him, instead looking at the colonel with hesitation.

"Are you afraid to stand up when I am on horseback?" Roosevelt jeered.[46]

Just then a bullet, of which Roosevelt felt he must have been the target, struck the poor man through the body, killing him. Creating a moving target, Roosevelt urged Little Texas forward, rallying the men to the front and soon finding himself at the head of the regiment. Heavy fire poured down on them while Roosevelt and the Rough Riders advanced up Kettle Hill at the front of the advance with the 1st and 9th Cavalries. Trailing them were the 3rd and 6th Cavalries as well as the 10th Cavalry, whose Captain Ayres charged in advance of his buffalo soldiers, waving his hat and shouting.[47]

Soon Roosevelt came upon a captain, commanding the rear platoons, who had ordered his men to fire but not charge the Spanish. Roosevelt told them they must take them in a rush, but the stubborn captain said he could not do so without orders. When Roosevelt asked where the colonel was and the captain responded that he wasn't in sight, Roosevelt said, "Then I am the ranking officer here and I give the order to charge." Still the captain hesitated.[48]

"Then let my men through, sir," Roosevelt blustered. This the captain allowed. When Roosevelt reached the left wing of the Ninth, he waved his hat and gave the order to charge up the right hill. At that moment, portions of the Rough Riders and the 3rd, 9th, and 10th Cavalries "slipped the leash," as Roosevelt remembered, with *Julius Caesar* on his mind.[49]

"Roosevelt," Davis marveled, "mounted high on horseback, and charging the rifle-pits at a gallop and quite alone, made you feel that you would like to cheer."[50]

While Mills ordered three troops to rush forward, Roosevelt galloped back to help 2nd Lieutenant David M. Goodrich get D Troop across the road to attack the hill from that side. At last it was time to lead the charge.

"Wheeling around, I then again galloped toward the hill, passing the shouting, cheering, firing men, and went up the lane, splashing through a small stream;

when I got abreast of the ranch buildings on the top of Kettle Hill, I turned and went up the slope," Roosevelt recollected.[51]

Back at El Pozo, a member of the press corps watching from the hill cried out, "By God! There go our boys up the hill!"[52]

Stephen Crane, standing nearby, listened to the foreign military attachés discuss the charge.

"It is very gallant, but very foolish," said one.[53]

"They can't take it, you know," agreed another.

"Never in the world," said a third. "It is slaughter. Absolute slaughter."

Crane noted that the Japanese military man simply shrugged his shoulders.

Davis agreed with the wisdom of the crowd. Describing Roosevelt's blue polka-dot handkerchief floating about behind him "like a guidon," Davis was almost certain Roosevelt was racing to his doom.

"No one who saw Roosevelt take that ride expected him to finish it alive," Davis later wrote.[54]

Roosevelt certainly made a hell of a target, the only man making the charge on horseback. Drawing enemy fire, one bullet nicked his elbow. More grazed Little Texas. When a bullet whipped centimeters in front of Roosevelt, smashing the pince-nez glasses from his face, he fished another pair from his pocket. The only Rough Rider who could keep pace with Roosevelt was Henry Bardshar, the enormous gold miner from Prescott who had taken over A Troop moments after Buckey O'Neill had fallen and since had become Roosevelt's orderly. Pausing to aim, Bardshar fired on the Spanish running from the ranch buildings atop Kettle Hill. Trailing him were Dudley Dean and a number of Arizonans.[55]

"Roosevelt was a hundred feet ahead of his troops," wrote the *New York Journal*, "yelling like a Sioux, while his own men and the colored cavalry cheered him as he charged up the hill. There was no stopping as men's neighbors fell, but on they went, faster and faster."[56]

About forty yards from the summit, Roosevelt came across a wire fence. Hopping off Little Texas, he ran up the hill with Bardshar, who emptied his magazine at two Spaniards, felling both. Almost immediately afterward Kettle Hill swarmed with Rough Riders along with soldiers from the Ninth and Tenth, all of which would later take credit for being the first to take the hill. In particular, Roosevelt recalled seeing Captain Frederick "Fritz" Muller of E Troop, Captain Max Luna of F Troop, and Captain William Llewelyn of G Troop lead men up the hill. In the buildings one Spaniard was captured, and another was shot while trying to hide. A few others were shot as they ran. American casualties included Lieutenant Richard Cushing Day, shot in the arm. Day lived, though things went worse for Willie Shipp, shot down leading a charge.

From the top of Kettle Hill, Roosevelt could see the Spaniards atop San Juan Hill to the left. They could also see him. The Spanish opened up with their Mausers and one or two pieces of artillery, the shells exploding directly over their heads. Roosevelt could also see Kent's infantry, led by General Hamilton Hawkins, a veteran of Gettysburg, charging to their left up San Juan Hill.

"Obviously the proper thing to do was to help them," Roosevelt recounted, "and I got the men together and started them volley-firing against the Spaniards in the San Juan block-house and in the trenches around it."[57]

For five or ten minutes the Rough Riders advanced toward San Juan Hill, keeping up a brisk fire. As they neared the crest of the hill, Roosevelt stopped them so they would not blunder into Hawkins's men, who were preparing for the final rush. Once ready to charge the next line of trenches, Roosevelt jumped the wire fence and ran a hundred yards before realizing that only five men had followed him. Bullets ripped the grass around them. Clay Green of E Troop fell mortally wounded. Near the crest Captain A. L. Mills was shot through the head, the bullet permanently blinding one eye and temporarily blinding the other. Winslow Clark of Harvard was shot in the leg and through the body. Clark asked Roosevelt to leave his canteen, which Roosevelt did before charging back, hopping over the wire fence and rejoining his regiment that had failed to follow him.[58]

In an instant Roosevelt realized in the confusion of battle that they must not have heard his order to charge. Even as he taunted them "bitterly" and called them "cowards," he had to keep from smiling when they cried out, "We didn't hear you, we didn't see you go, Colonel; lead on now, we'll sure follow you."[59]

This time as Roosevelt led the charge, every man followed him, even soldiers from various other regiments. Jack Greenway and David Goodrich soon outpaced him, but Roosevelt and Bardshar stuck together.

"Holy Godfrey, what fun!" Roosevelt shouted to Bardshar.[60]

Not everyone was enjoying themselves. Phil Sweet recalled as Roosevelt shouted "Come on boys! There they go; damn them!" that it seemed as if the "gates of hell had opened." All around him men fell wounded. Sweet fell too but got back up, unhurt. His friend and fellow New York City policeman, Hal Haywood, fared worse. A Mauser bullet punched through Haywood's abdomen.[61]

Atop San Juan Hill, the Rough Riders found most of the Spaniards in the trenches dead, their light blue and white uniforms splattered with blood and their brains leaking out of bullet holes in their heads. Only a handful were alive though still dangerous. As Roosevelt and Bardshar continued to run toward the blockhouse at the summit, two Spaniards leapt from the trenches and fired at the Americans. Both bullets missed. But Roosevelt knew they wouldn't miss forever. In Roosevelt's hand was a Colt .45 revolver that his brother-in-law William S. Cowles (his sister Anna's husband in the navy) had salvaged from the wreck of the *Maine*. Roosevelt squeezed the trigger twice. The first shot missed. The second killed one of the Spaniards. Roosevelt later determined that he'd "shot the man in the left breast as he turned."[62]

It was a moment of personal triumph for Roosevelt, who had hunted grizzlies and outlaws but never killed a man. "All men who feel any power of joy in battle," Roosevelt later reflected, "know what it is like when the wolf rises in the heart."[63]

Catching sight of his old hunting pal, Sergeant Bob Ferguson, Roosevelt confided that he had just "doubled up a Spanish officer like a jackrabbit."[64]

Ferguson admitted to being a bit in awe of Roosevelt. In a letter to Edith Roosevelt written on July 5 about her husband having killed a man, Ferguson wrote, "No hunting trip so far has ever equaled it in Theodore's eyes. . . . I really believe firmly now they can't kill him."[65]

Roosevelt was also impressed by Ferguson, whom he praised for "gallantry on the field of action." For this Ferguson was promoted to 2nd lieutenant. Roosevelt also praised Captain Llewelyn in his memoirs. Although the story later circulated was probably apocryphal—that Llewelyn had mislaid his pistol and instead charged up San Juan Hill with an axe—Roosevelt recalled that Llewelyn led a series of charges despite being sick and exhausted.[66]

Shortly after shooting a Spanish soldier and seizing the blockhouse, Roosevelt's "crowded hour" came to a close as the surviving Spaniards fled San Juan Hill. The Americans, with an army of 6,000, had engaged a force of about 4,500 Spanish soldiers and won the day. Roosevelt counted 1,071 casualties. Concerning individual heroism, Roosevelt observed that George Roland, the cowpuncher who had refused to leave the field at Las Guasimas, had "again distinguished himself by his fearlessness." Roosevelt also commended Dudley Dean, Woody Kane, Jack Greenway, David Goodrich, William Pollock, and Richard Cushing Day for leading charges and always being near the enemy.

As for the press corps, one man in particular stood out.

—17—

THE DARKEST DAY OF THE WAR

Things weren't looking so good for the Spanish, but Richard Harding Davis was on a roll. Embedding himself with the artillery on the afternoon of July 1, 1898, he followed Roosevelt and the Rough Riders as they pivoted from Kettle Hill to San Juan Hill. Naturally, Davis was the first reporter to crest the rise. Commanding the whole field, he saw the Spanish positioning themselves closer to the city of Santiago—maybe five hundred or a thousand yards away—with the American artillerymen preparing to fire and Roosevelt charging around like Galahad.[1]

When the artillerymen fired, the black smoke attracted the Spanish Mausers, and Davis found it prudent to take Santiago Road. That too was under fire. Fortunately, after hoofing it about seventy-five yards through the din of battle, he came across General Leonard Wood and a number of Rough Riders digging a trench, for though the Spanish trenches had been all captured, more were needed.

Just then Stephen Crane appeared with a stranger, Jimmy Hare, who'd been photographing the battle for *Collier's Weekly.* Davis and Hare hopped into the trench and crouched down, but Crane—wearing a long India rubber raincoat and smoking a pipe—didn't seem to mind the bullets whistling passed him. The bohemian author walked to the crest and looked out toward the Spanish rifles, plain as day.

General Wood, who like every sane man in the trench was crouched low, called for Crane to get down. Crane walked farther away. "You're drawing the fire on these men," Wood thundered. But Crane kept on walking.[2]

"He appeared as cool as though he were looking down from a box at the opera," Davis recounted.

"You're not impressing any one by doing that, Crane," Davis called.

Hating to look like a poseur, Crane dropped to his knees.

"I knew that would fetch you," Davis said.

"Oh, was that it?" Crane said with a grin.

Crane was soon on his feet again. Davis, determined to save Crane's life, leapt up as well. As he pulled Crane down, a bullet knocked off Davis's hat, and another struck his binocular case, leaving a dent.[3]

Crane had an opportunity to repay Davis when the Philadelphian fell stricken with another attack of sciatica. Crane and Hare each put a shoulder under Davis's arms, hauling him down the road toward Crane's bivouac near El Pozo, where Crane promised coffee and a blanket. As bullets flashed by them, Davis protested that the three of them were too conspicuous. He could make it to camp on his own after dark. But his companions refused to leave him. Davis then sat down in the road and declared that he wouldn't budge until they left him. Crane, who possessed an extraordinarily underdeveloped sense of mortality, pointed out the grandeur of the sun setting behind the palm trees. Recognizing that he was fighting a losing battle, Davis acquiesced and allowed the two men to help him to camp.

Leaving Davis to recover his strength, Hare asked Crane, "Who's this pal of yours we just brought down the hill?"[4]

"Beg pardon, Jimmy," Crane replied. "I thought you knew him. That's Richard Harding Davis."

Hare had heard of Davis, of course. But most of the stories over the last few months had been unfavorable. Davis had turned down a captaincy at the outset of the war. He had fired a gun at Las Guasimas, forfeiting his noncombatant status. But, having met the man, Hare was impressed. Davis had been in the thick of it while his critics were at the rear. Even in white-faced agony, Davis had tried to turn down their help for fear they would be shot on his account. This was the Davis of legends.

Thirty-six-year-old John Fox Jr., working at that time as a war correspondent for *Harper's Weekly,* was also impressed by Davis, particularly with how he dealt with adversity. "I saw him writhing on the ground with sciatica during that campaign, like a snake," Fox recalled, "but pulling his twisted figure straight and his tortured face into a smile if soldiers or a stranger passed."[5]

But there was little time for sentimentality. Wood, Roosevelt, and Hawkins may have won the Battle of San Juan Hill, but the war was far from over. While eleven thousand American soldiers held the heights, Roosevelt put the number of Spanish soldiers amassed in the valley and the low hills below at nine thousand, with more holding the city of Santiago and Santiago Harbor. For the rest of the afternoon, many Rough Riders lay in the grass spread over the crest of the ridge and in the trenches, trading bullets with the Spanish second line. The dynamite gun was also brought up and placed to the right of the firing line in a spot that the men began calling "Fort Roosevelt." The dynamite gun didn't actually fire dynamite; it fired ten-pound shells filled with an explosive nitrocellulose-based gelatin. Roosevelt's assessment of it was mixed.[6]

"The dynamite gun . . . was more effective than the regular artillery because it was fired with smokeless powder, and as it was used like a mortar from behind the hill, it did not betray its presence, and those firing it suffered no loss," Roosevelt observed. "Every few shots it got out of order. . . . The shots from the dynamite gun made a terrific explosion, but they did not seem to go accurately."[7]

Still, Roosevelt was pleased to see the dynamite gun strike part of a Spanish trench. Another shot targeted Spanish guns beneath a mango tree. "Up in the air went the mango tree and part of the crew and their gun," McGinty recalled. When it struck a Spanish building, a swarm of Spanish cavalry and infantry poured from it, and in the minute it took the Spanish soldiers to find cover, the Rough Riders' Colt automatics "played with good effect."[8]

But so too did the Spanish Mausers and artillery.[9]

"Some of the Spanish sharp-shooters were in trees in our front," Roosevelt recalled, "where we could not possibly place them from the trenches; and these were able to reach little hollows and depressions where the men were entirely safe from the Spanish artillery and from their trench-fire. Moreover, in one hollow, which we thought safe, the Spaniards succeeded in dropping a shell, a fragment of which went through the head of one of my men."[10]

To hunt the Spanish snipers, Roosevelt sent Trooper Goodwin (who might have been James, John, or Richard Goodwin, all of whom had enlisted) and William B. Proffitt, described by Roosevelt as "an excellent shot and a thoroughly good soldier" and the son of a Confederate officer. Together, Goodwin and Proffitt notched eleven kills between them. Davis, when he recovered from his latest bout of sciatica, took it upon himself to help.[11]

"Dick stalked out in the open with his field-glasses [and] searched for the supposed sharpshooters in the trees," Fox remembered. Neither Davis, Goodwin, nor Proffitt were injured. Things went worse for other American soldiers, as Spanish bullets continued to find American targets.[12]

Joseph "Fighting Joe" Wheeler had resumed command at this point, on the afternoon of July 1, making Wood a colonel once more and Roosevelt a lieutenant colonel. Meanwhile, the battle for El Caney was still raging. Hearst, who rode eight miles that day with Cuban colonel Honore Laine acting as an escort, witnessed the bulk of the battle.

"We found Captain Capron blazing away with four guns," Hearst wrote, "where he should have had a dozen. . . . He was aiming to reduce the large stone fort which stood on the hill above the town and commanded it. . . . [D]ozens of shells had struck the fort, but it was not yet reduced. . . . Our men were popping away continuously, as a string of firecrackers pops, and the Spaniards were firing in volleys whenever our men came in sight in the open spaces."[13]

For hours, the Spaniards fired upon Lawton's advancing 12th Infantry and 25th Infantry from slits in the stone fort, while cannons banged and shells screamed. Eventually, around 5 p.m. the infantrymen reached a group of trees at the base of the hill on which the fort stood. In a great rush, the infantrymen poured from the trees and captured the fort. The first soldier into the blockhouse was T. C. Butler, a Black private in Company H of the 25th Infantry.[14]

"Then you should have heard the yell that went up from the knoll on which our battery stood," Hearst recalled. "Gunners, drivers, Cubans and correspondents swung their hats and gave a mighty cheer. Immediately our batteries stopped firing for fear we would hurt our own men."[15]

James Creelman, embodying the spirit of a Hearst newspaperman, refused to wait on the sidelines.

"I ran into the fort and found there a Spanish officer and four men alive. Seven lay dead in one room. The whole floor ran with blood," Creelman described. "The walls were splashed with blood. Three poor wretches put their hands together in supplication. One had a white handkerchief tied on a stick which he lifted and moved towards me. It was a perfect hogpen of butchery. . . . I took the guns from all and threw them outside the fort."[16]

After calling for some soldiers to take the Spaniards prisoner, Creelman dashed outside and personally captured the Spanish flag. Showing it to some of the American troops, they gave a cheer. Creelman could have been more circumspect. Just as he turned to speak to Harry Haskell, the captain of Company F in the 12th Infantry, a Spanish soldier in the trenches beyond the fort fired. The Mauser bullet struck the celebrity correspondent in his left arm and back, whirling him around. Creelman staggered inside the fort, finding a hammock. Major John A. Logan Jr. and five of his men soon hustled Creelman out of a hole in the fort and down the hill, where he lay with the wounded, the Spanish colors thrown over him.

While bullets sang over their heads and surgeons worked on the wounded men, Creelman felt someone put his hand to his fevered brow. "Opening my eyes, I saw Mr. Hearst, the proprietor of the *New York Journal,* a straw hat with a bright ribbon on his head, a revolver at his belt, and a pencil and note-book in his hand. The man who had provoked the war had come to see the result with his own eyes and, finding one of his correspondents prostrate, was doing the work himself."[17]

Finding Creelman unable to write the story himself, Hearst wrote down Creelman's account of the battle. Creelman later noted that Hearst appeared unmoved by the volleys of Mauser bullets that periodically interrupted Creelman's report.

In his autobiography, Creelman recalled Hearst saying "I'm sorry you're hurt, but," his face radiant with enthusiasm, "wasn't it a splendid fight? We must beat every paper in the world."[18]

Creelman also related that Hearst, having gotten the story and making him as comfortable as possible, dashed off to the seacoast to have the story printed. Sure enough, a few days later both Hearst's and Creelman's rendition would be in papers throughout the United States.[19]

Back on San Juan Heights, Wheeler took inventory of the evening's casualties. At 10:25 p.m. Wheeler scribbled a letter to Shafter informing the general that five men under his command had been killed and fourteen others had been wounded.[20]

That night the sound of trench warfare died down, but few of the Rough Riders slept, working with picks and shovels to expand the captured trenches. This was tough work for the half-starved and exhausted soldiers, but little food could be had. The organizational morass below had yet to be solved, resulting in no food being brought up from the American ships. Looking for solutions, Oscar Wager of A Troop braved Spanish gunfire to return with water from the San Juan River. Enterprising soldiers ground coffee beans with stones and the butts of their pistols, and Richard Stanton of B Troop delivered coffee to some of the men digging trenches. Peas and rice abandoned by the Spanish were also rationed. Roosevelt was given the luxury of hot soup.[21]

"George King," Roosevelt wrote in *The Rough Riders,* "spent a leisure hour in the rear making soup out of some rice and other stuff he found in a Spanish house; he brought some of it to General Wood, Jack Greenway, and myself, and nothing could have tasted more delicious."[22]

Commenting on the lack of food, Fighting Joe Wheeler praised the soldiers. Not only had they worked through the night with little sleep and empty bellies, but they had also fought a battle earlier that day.

"These details, and the depletion of the ranks from absolute exhaustion," Wheeler wrote in *The Santiago Campaign,* "so reduced this force that it is doubtful if there were more than three thousand on the ridge by midnight; but still they worked, and by daylight had constructed breastworks sufficiently strong to enable them successfully to repulse an attack. All this were done under fire from the enemy, who were but a few hundred yards off."[23]

After Bardshar found a Spanish blanket, Roosevelt, Goodrich, and the giant climbed underneath and fell asleep, exhausted. They awoke around 3 a.m. to the sound of a Spanish attack. At the sound of gunfire everyone jumped to their feet, grabbed their rifles, and ran for the trench at the top of San Juan Hill. The sputtering shots ultimately quieted, and Roosevelt—who had made the cover of a small tree his headquarters—drifted off to sleep again. They were awakened at dawn by another attack. Shrapnel burst above the tree, wounding Stanley Hollister of Harvard and killing Theodore Miller of Yale.

That morning, July 2, firing increased between the two entrenched armies. Wheeler, headquartered southwest of the San Juan blockhouse, kept active. Realizing that the blockhouse was undermanned, Wheeler respectfully wrote to General Lawton to send a platoon of infantry to shore up defenses. At 10:15 Wheeler also sent a letter to an artilleryman on El Pozo Hill: "In shelling the city from your present position please bear in mind that . . . to the left of the blockhouse is a hill-side about 400 yards nearer than the blockhouse is."[24]

Looking over the enhanced breastworks, Wheeler felt pleased with their accomplishments. But there was also a sense of panic and desperation in the air. After all, there had been no forward movement since they captured San Juan Hill, on whose slopes they had lost over a thousand soldiers. And the death toll kept climbing.[25]

Roosevelt observed that Captain Llewelyn, sick from fever and exhaustion, was in such a bad state that he had to be taken to an improvised hospital set up behind San Juan Hill. Joining Llewelyn was Cassi, shot in the hand. Cassi and Llewelyn lived, but patrolman Haywood didn't make it, dying from the bullet wound in his stomach.[26]

Billy McGinty was spared becoming a casualty by blind luck. Overhearing Roosevelt and Kane discussing getting some coffee, hardtack, and tomatoes to the boys in the forward trenches, McGinty volunteered.

"Wait, I'll go with you," Roosevelt told him.[27]

"No, Colonel Roosevelt, if anyone goes with him, I will go," Kane interjected. "The whole regiment is depending on you, but no one is depending on either of us."

McGinty persuaded his superiors that there was "no sense risking two men." Hunched over and with the case on his back, McGinty got caught in cross fire. A bullet that might have caught him in the spine instead made a casualty of the tomatoes, splashing tomato juice across his face and back.

By July 3, morale had considerably worsened for the Americans. All told, 134 American casualties were reported over July 2 and 3, overwhelming the medical staff. Along with doctors having a dearth of surgical tools, the wounded lacked pillows, hammocks, cots, clothing, and rubber blankets. Because the hospital was peppered with gunfire, the medical staff had little sleep, further sapping their strength.[28]

Davis was especially active during this time. Gouverneur Morris IV—who would become a popular writer at Hearst's *Cosmopolitan*—reflected on Davis that "R. H. D. hunted men in Cuba. He hunted for wounded men who were out in front of the trenches and still under fire, and found some and brought them in. The Rough Riders didn't make him an honorary member just because he was charming and a faithful friend, but largely because they were a lot of daredevils and he was another."[29]

The weather also plagued the soldiers and erstwhile correspondents. Hot sun was followed by afternoon torrential rain, followed by more sun. Everyone was sweating and cramped from crouching in one place for two days, all of their clothing stinking with steam, sweat, rain, and dew.

"My clothes smell so that I can't use them for a pillow," Davis wrote to his mother.[30]

Commented Marshall, "No one was ever, for a moment, comfortable except by accident. The rations were scanty and bad. . . . Tobacco was not to be had for any price, although there was plenty of it out on some of the transports."[31]

Communication between General Shafter and Admiral Sampson was equally bleak. Sampson had bottled up Admiral Cervera in Santiago Harbor, but—as Sampson reminded Shafter—until Shafter took the city and dealt with the mines, Sampson could not help him. On July 3, Shafter wrote a despondent telegram to Washington explaining that the army might have to retreat five miles to the high ground between the San Juan River and Siboney. In short, this would give the Spanish back San Juan Hill, a piece of Cuban land that had claimed 1,609 casualties, over 10 percent of the American soldiers engaged.

Upon reading the telegram in Washington, Secretary of War Alger declared this "the darkest day of the war."[32]

Hearing talk of retreat, Roosevelt dug in his heels. To Wheeler, Roosevelt said, "Well, General, I really don't know whether we would obey an order to fall back. We can take that city by a rush, and if we have to move out of here at all I should be inclined to make the rush in the right direction."[33]

Wheeler paused a moment, for he'd seen mad rushes aplenty during the American Civil War. As for Roosevelt's desire to not retreat, Wheeler "expressed his hearty agreement," as Roosevelt phrased it. Wheeler recalled that "appeals of the strongest character were made for the army to withdraw for fear an attack would drive them in a rout from their position. I discountenanced this in every way possible."

To the men who championed retreat, Fighting Joe reminded them that they had beaten back the Spanish at Las Guasimas, and overtaken them at San Juan Hill. "These facts will convince the Spaniards that we will continue our attack upon their next line; and with that expectation it is unreasonable and not to be expected that they will return and attack us in the strong position we now hold," Wheeler argued. Wheeler ordered members of his staff to reassure the troops. Roosevelt attempted to buck up the men, but a letter scribbled to Lodge betrayed his inner despair.[34]

> Outside Santiago, July 3, 1898
>
> Dear Cabot:
>
> Tell the President for Heaven's sake to send us every regiment and above all every battery possible. We have won so far at a heavy cost, but the Spaniards fight very hard and charging these intrenchments against modern rifles is terrible. We are within measurable distance of a terrible military disaster; we *must* have help—thousands of men, batteries, & *food,* & ammunition. The other volunteers are at a hideous disadvantage owing to their not having smokeless powder. Our General is poor; he is too unwieldy to get to the front. I commanded my regiment, I think I may say with honor. We lost a quarter of our men. For three days I have been at the extreme front of the firing line;

how I have escaped I know not; I have not blanket or coat; & have not taken off my shoes even; I sleep in the drenching rain, & drink putrid water.

Best love to Nannie.[35]

Davis, for one, wasn't buying any good cheer that Wheeler and Roosevelt publicly expressed. Considering the state of the men, Davis observed, "They were hanging to the crest of the San Juan hills by their teeth and finger-nails, and it seemed as though at any moment their hold would relax and they would fall."[36]

On that same dark day, Davis toured the rifle pits and interviewed the commanders. From his observations and conversations he wrote a long dispatch to the *New York Herald.* Davis pulled few punches.

"Little reply was made to the constant fire from Santiago last night," Davis wrote. "The Spaniards opened upon the entire line with shrapnel and Mausers. . . . Another such victory as July 1 and our troops must retreat. Judging from the quality and quantity of the rations left behind them in the trenches, the Spaniards are bountifully supplied with food. Their fire is constant and heavy, showing no lack of ammunition. . . . It is not a question of weeks but hours. This may sound hysterical, yet it is written with the most serious and earnest intention. . . . We are in the face of possible disaster."[37]

Davis wasn't shy about placing blame.

"General Wheeler," Davis continued, "who refused to remain in bed with his fever, is here beside me asleep on a rubber blanket, bullets passing over him. . . . If he is ill he should be relieved; if not, the presence of some man with absolute authority is necessary at the front. I am quoting what brigade commanders demand. The commanding General's orders are disobeyed without a moment's hesitation. I have heard them countermanded in my presence by colonels. This is written with the sole purpose that the press of the country will force instant action at Washington to relieve the situation."[38]

Considering the newfound friendship between Davis and Crane, it's very likely that Crane did not read a draft of Davis's July 3 dispatch to the *New York Herald.* Had Crane read it he might have cautioned Davis that such a report would be fine, almost expected, from that son of a bitch Stephen Crane, who courted disasters as fervently as he courted women, be they prostitutes, married, or, in the case of Cora, both. But Davis wasn't a bohemian writer dying of tuberculosis. Davis was going to have to live in this world, and by stating that Fighting Joe Wheeler needed to be relieved from duty because of either illness or incompetence and that mere colonels felt free to ignore Shafter's orders, the whole thing sounded a wee bit like treason. Along with flying in the face of military protocol, Davis's article would further demoralize the American army while bolstering the morale of the Spanish, potentially resulting in severe American setbacks.

In other words, Richard Harding Davis, who had lived the life of the most grandiose star reporter at the height of New York City's Gilded Age and had always been so careful to protect his sterling image, was now in real danger of seeing his name made mud. He had made the greatest journalistic rookie error since he asked where he could find a boiled shirt in the ruins of Johnstown but this time with far greater consequences. There wasn't a chance that Shafter would suddenly be recalled and that Roosevelt—as Davis certainly hoped—would be miraculously promoted over everyone else to become commanding general. The likelier outcome was that if Davis's sleep-deprived article heartened the Spanish and changed the course of the war, Roosevelt wouldn't be able to protect him. Friendship or no, Roosevelt might not even want to.

Crouched down in the trenches carved into San Juan Ridge, with bullets whistling overhead, Davis had time to reflect on what a great risk he had taken by writing and sending off the incendiary dispatch. The only thing that could possibly save him was if the war somehow ended in the next twenty-four hours before the article was published.

But what were the odds of that?

18

CITIZEN HEARST

On the morning of July 3, 1898—while up on San Juan Heights the soldiers in the Fifth Corps continued to die from Spanish sharpshooters, and talk of retreat was floated by Brigadier General Shafter—William Randolph Hearst was in Kingston, Jamaica, filing his firsthand account of the battles of El Caney. Hearst knew that the next day's papers would disseminate the story throughout the United States.

"Tonight, as I write this, the ambulance trains are bringing wounded soldiers from the battle around the little inland village of El Caney," Hearst's article began. Capron's artillery bombardment, the advance of Lawton's infantry, and the bloodbath witnessed by Creelman made for scintillating reading. Along with the content, the reading public realized that Hearst personally covering the war was something extraordinary.[1]

"Bravo, Hearst!" the New Orleans's *Semi-Weekly Times-Democrat* had cheered in response to his June 30 article in the *New York Journal.* Considering that Hearst was now covering battles while they were happening, even the rival newspapers were going to have to sit up straight.[2]

That Hearst, unlike Pulitzer and all the other newspaper editors, had become a war correspondent put him in a league of his own. Sure, there were some who thought that Hearst should be tried as a war criminal, but he didn't let that bother him much.

"It was a strange war, when we think of what war is today," Hearst reminisced. "It was a war of adventure. A knight errant war."[3]

Meanwhile, something unexpected was going on in Santiago Harbor: signs of movement from Cervera's fleet.

This seemed almost unthinkable. Admiral Sampson had been so certain that Cervera would lay at anchor that, aboard the *New York,* he steamed for Siboney to confer with his counterparts on land. No fool, Sampson left blocking Santiago Harbor to the American squadron, consisting of the battleships *Texas, Oregon, Iowa,* and *Indiana* as well as the armored cruiser *Brooklyn* and several smaller vessels. Sampson reckoned this was more than a match for the Spanish. Every American sailor knew that Cervera attempting to sail the Spanish fleet through the American blockade—or, worse, engage it—was tantamount to suicide. But aboard the *Brooklyn,* Quartermaster Neils Anderson thought he saw through his binoculars black smoke billowing through the fog.[4]

"That smoke looks as if it was moving toward the entrance, sir," Anderson told the ship's navigator, Lieutenant Albon C. Hodgson. Taking the binoculars from Anderson, the lieutenant studied the entrance to the harbor for a moment. Then Hodgson turned on his heel.[5]

"Afterbridge, there! Report to the commodore! The enemy's ships are coming out!"

In moments the entire American squadron was notified and ready amid a clangor of gongs, bugles, and the boom of one of the *Iowa*'s six-pounders. As unbelievable as it seemed, the Spanish fleet was leaving the harbor.

First out was the Spanish flagship *Infanta Maria Teresa,* looking majestic. Its hull had been painted black and polished until it shined, contrasting sharply with the white superstructure. Newly gilded figureheads stood out on the bow. The awnings were brightly colored, and great silk battle flags fluttered proudly in the breeze. On Admiral Cervera y Topete's orders, who was aboard the ship, one flag was emblazoned with the signal "Viva Espana."[6]

With Sampson on his way to Siboney, that left Commodore Winfield Scott Schley—a veteran of the siege of Port Hudson, Louisiana—in command of the fleet. Standing on a wooden platform next to the conning tower aboard the *Brooklyn,* Schley called to Hodgson, "Can you see the flagship?"[7]

"No, sir," Hodgson replied. "The *New York* is out of sight."

Schley smiled with satisfaction. With Sampson out of the picture, this would make him the central figure to what would become the final climactic sea battle in the Spanish-American War, so long as he won the battle.

"Commodore," Hodgson shouted, "they are coming right at us!"

"Go right for them!" Schley answered.

Trailing the *Infanta Maria Teresa* one by one at ten-minute intervals were Spain's equally flamboyant battleships *Viscaya, Cristóbal Colón,* and *Almirante Oquendo* as well as the destroyers *Plutón* and *Furor.* At 10:05 the *Infanta Maria Teresa* and the *Brooklyn* were within six hundred yards of each other. But it was Captain "Fire-eating" Bob Evans of the *Iowa* who got the first strike against Cervera's flagship.

"The *Maria Teresa* passed me at a distance of about twenty-six hundred yards," Evans recalled, "and, as she crossed my bows, our forward twelve-inch guns were fired and I was confident that I saw both shells strike the Spanish ship."[8]

Cervera, surviving, later confirmed the hits. "One of the first projectiles burst an auxiliary steam pipe on board the *Maria Teresa,*" the admiral recalled. "A great deal of steam escaped, which made us lose the speed on which we had counted. About the same time another shell burst one of the fire mains."

Incredibly, the *Infanta Maria Teresa* continued to steam west, hugging the coast. The rest of the Spanish fleet was close behind, neck and neck with the *Iowa, Texas,* and *Brooklyn*, and the rest of the American blockade far behind. With the Spanish ships having left the harbor at full steam, Cervera had the advantage.

From the rocking deck of the *Iowa,* Captain Evans watched with dread as the *Vizcaya* and the *Cristóbal Colón* pulled ahead of his ship. He ordered a broadside to port, then had the great forward turret swing starboard for another shot. But it was the *Cristóbal Colón* that got off the most telling strike. "As she passed she struck me twice—two as beautiful shots as I ever saw made by any ship," Evans recalled. "The fist shell . . . struck on the starboard side a little forward of the bridge, about four feet above the water line, passed through the cellulose belt, and exploded on the berth deck, demolishing the dispensary, breaking almost every medicine bottle in it, and doing great damage."[9]

The second shot blasted a gaping hole into the *Iowa* at the waterline. Miraculously, no one was injured. While the *Iowa* lost speed, the *Almirante Oquendo* closed to about 1,500 yards. That's when the *Brooklyn,* among other American ships, fired its guns at the *Almirante Oquendo.*

"At this time she was under the concentrated fire of several of our ships," Evans recollected, "and the effect was most striking. . . . As I looked at her I could see the shot holes come in her sides and our shells explode inside her, but she pluckily held on her course and fairly smothered us with a shower of shells and machine-gun shots."

Hearst heard the sound of the guns and knew just what they meant.

"We in our newspaper ship heard heavy firing afar off and promptly put to sea to find what it was all about," Hearst recalled. "The Spanish fleet was steaming out of Santiago Harbor and filing westward along the coast of Cuba in one long line. The American fleet was paralleling the Spanish ships, pouring deadly fire into them and crowding them toward the shore."[10]

Aboard the *Almirante Oquendo,* Lieutenant Calandria was notified that a fire had engulfed part of the after torpedo rooms. After personally witnessing the flames issuing from the hatchway, Calandria sped to the bridge and informed the captain that the torpedoes were in danger of exploding. The captain ordered the torpedoes jettisoned.

The Spanish flagship was also afire.

"I realized that that ship was doomed," Cervera recalled, "and cast about for a place where I could run her aground without losing many lives."[11]

Cervera steered to a small beach, running aground just as the engine stopped. There Cervera gave the painful order to lower the flag.

As Captain Evans recalled,

> The Spanish flagship headed for the shore, in flames, fore and aft, and soon took the ground about seven miles west of the entrance of Santiago Harbour, and a few minutes later the Oquendo followed her, the flames bursting out through the shot holes in her sides and leaping up from the deck. . . . It was a magnificent, sad sight to see these beautiful ships in their death agonies, but we were doing the work we had been educated for, and we cheered and yelled until our throats were sore.[12]

The rest of the Spanish fleet lasted only a little longer. The *Brooklyn* and the *Texas* did for the *Vizcaya,* which, with its deck in flames, hauled down its flag while making for shore.

"Don't cheer, boys!" Captain J. W. Philip of the *Texas* ordered. "Those poor devils are dying!"[13]

The *Furor* and the *Plutón* were engaged by the *Gloucester,* which had served as J. P. Morgan's yacht *Corsair* before being converted to a military vessel. Commanding the *Gloucester* was the great-great-grandson of Benjamin Franklin, Lieutenant Commander Richard Wainwright, who had served as the executive officer aboard the *Maine.* With both Spanish destroyers struck repeatedly by the *Gloucester*'s six-pound guns, the *Furor* sank, while the *Plutón* grounded on the beach west of Cabanas Bay. Afterward, Wainwright secured Admiral Cervera from the wreck of the *Infanta Maria Teresa.*[14]

"I congratulate you, sir," said Wainwright to Cervera, "on having made as gallant a fight as was ever seen on the sea."[15]

Gallant but doomed. Outgunned and with only a small quantity of coal, Cervera had known that even if his fleet managed to survive engagement with the superior American battleships, there was almost no chance of reaching a safe port. But General Blanco, safe in Havana, had ignored Cervera's protests. To preserve Spanish honor, Blanco desired the fleet to go down fighting rather than be captured in Santiago Harbor.

Racing ahead, the *Cristóbal Colón* might have made it well into the Caribbean Sea had it not been for the *Oregon.* At 12:20 the battleship overtook the Spanish ship, firing at the Spaniards from its heavy bow guns. Outmatched, Captain Paredes decided to run the ship aground rather than sacrifice all the lives aboard and made for the beach at the mouth of the Tarquino River.

At 1:15 p.m. the Battle of Santiago was over.[16]

By the time Hearst and the *Sylvia* reached the battle, all of the Spanish ships were afire, sunk, or grounded, with the Spanish-American War all but won. One hundred fifty-one Spaniards had been wounded, 323 had been killed, and about 1,800 had surrendered. In contrast, the only American fatality was George Ellis, chief yeoman of the *Brooklyn,* who had been behind the forward turret when he was decapitated by a shell.[17]

Up on San Juan Hill, the top brass knew what the destruction of Cervera's fleet signified and ordered the flag of truce hoisted up. Fighting Joe Wheeler made certain that his men obeyed the order. To thirty-seven-year-old Matthew F. Steele—the aide a West Pointer from Huntsville—Wheeler instructed two messages to be sent: one to General Sumner and the other to Colonel Leonard Wood: "The Maj. General directs that the flag of truce will remain out till 10:00 A.M. tomorrow and further that you will not fire unless fired upon until further orders."[18]

The flag of truce still flew early the next morning, July 4, when Hearst and his bold crew determined to more closely inspected the ruins of Spain's navy. Coming alongside the wrecked and beached *Almirante Oquendo,* they witnessed the terrible destruction of war.

"Dead Spaniards were floating all about in the water, stripped to the waist, as they had stood to a man their guns," Hearst noted. "We steered nervously among the bodies, feeling much pity, and some satisfaction, too, that the Maine had been again so well remembered."[19]

Jumping into a launch, they also boarded the *Viscaya,* now a gutted shell. Hearst looked with interest at a molten heap of warped silver money a Spanish soldier must have stowed. Hearst and the others collected souvenirs, dropped into their launch, and were heading back to the *Sylvia* when the revenue cutter *Dixie* spotted them.

"What were you doing on the ship?" an officer demanded.[20]

"Just looking about, sir, at the results of the battle," Hearst replied.

"Can't you mind your own business?"

"Not very well, sir, and be good newspapermen."

Later that day, Hearst and the others spotted some Spanish sailors on the shore. They weren't holding weapons. Instead, they were waving a white handkerchief or a white shirt. Evidently they had survived the sea battle and were looking to surrender. Hearst and his crew were only too happy to oblige.

"I jumped overboard, swam ashore, and told them we were going to take them aboard our boat to the admiral," Hearst recounted in the *Journal.*[21]

Decades later Hearst reflected, "The poor Spanish sailormen—battered and bruised, half clothed, half drowned, half starved—were only too happy to be taken prisoner. They helped us launch the boat back through the surf, and after several trips we got them all aboard our steamer. There were twenty-nine of them. We gave them food and drink and clothes."[22]

Ultimately, Hearst delivered the prisoners to the *Harvard.* Knowing that few people back home would believe without proof that William Randolph Hearst, the great yellow journalist, had taken twenty-nine Spanish prisoners, Hearst demanded a receipt. It read "Received of W. R. Hearst twenty-nine Spanish prisoners."[23]

Atop San Juan Heights, the mood was as jubilant as it was among the American navy. With Shafter's spine stiffened by the naval victory, he decided to stay the course. General José Toral y Velázquez, inside Santiago, soon sent word that he was willing to discuss terms of surrender. Days passed without an agreement.[24]

In the meantime, the *New York Herald* published Davis's damning article on July 7, causing a great sensation. Word was that the article was quickly cabled from New York to Paris, from Paris to Madrid, and from Madrid to Santiago. Spanish authorities hoped that learning how divided and despondent the Americans were would encourage General Toral to persevere. But Toral knew that the sea battle outside Santiago had been the last throw of the dice. Instead of heartening the Spanish, Davis's article caused a smattering of somewhat deserved censure of the war correspondent in newspapers and magazines, some of which had helped make his name. The *Evening Sun* declared him "the head of the marshmallow school of fiction," and *Harper's Weekly* stated that Davis "betrays" the army by criticizing it in "the face of the enemy." But because of the victory on July 3 (and possibly the luck of R. H. D.), no one was calling for Davis's head.[25]

Naturally, that Hearst—a private citizen—had personally captured Spanish sailors also made ink around the country. On July 7, 1898, the same day that the *Herald* published Davis's controversial article, the *New York Times* commended Hearst's verve, though with a splash of derision.

"We observe that the proprietor of our esteemed and enterprising yellow contemporary *The Journal* has carried his characteristic enterprise into Cuban waters," remarked the *Times* reporter. "He has there, with his own hand, so to speak, captured some twenty survivors of the *Maria Teresa* huddled on the beach, and turned them over to the proper authorities. This is the most genuine as well as the most legitimate increase of circulation, so to speak, which he has of late achieved, and is a subject for honest pride, beyond the fear of rivalry."[26]

Similarly, the *San Francisco Call* commented on July 6 that "it is fair to say that Hearst is sending extraordinary stuff from Cuba" but threaded this praise with complaints that "he paints himself yellow."[27]

But most readers only cared about the extraordinary. When on July 8 the *Call* went on to declare that "W. R. Hearst deserves to be placed in irons and sent under armed escort to the nearest prison," the *Salt Lake Herald* clapped back: "What's the matter? Has the Examiner been gathering in some more scoops?"[28]

As for the actual war, negotiations with the Spanish dragged on. But Hearst remained active, furnishing the Cuban newspaper he'd promised. This was to a large degree due to the ingenuity of George Pancoast, who established the newspaper office in a wood-paneled cabin, filled with correspondents working on hand presses fastened to planks suspended on barrels. With the whole place reeking of cigars, on July 10 they ran off a four-page newspaper. The English-language version was called the *Examiner-Journal*, while the Spanish version was called *El Journal de Nueva York*. Hearst playfully referred to it as the "*Siboney American*." The two versions were circulated among Americans and Cubans (and probably even curious Spaniards), and the contents featured not just reports of the war but also sports stories, entertainment articles, and the latest from Europe. The front page boasted illustrations of President William McKinley and Vice President Garrett Hobart with a message from McKinley's private secretary, J. Addison Porter:

> The President takes great pleasure in commending the enterprise of Mr. Hearst in publishing an American newspaper under the stars and stripes on Cuban soil. He regards it as a unique exemplification of modern journalism, and has no doubt that the Army and Navy in Santiago will receive the publication with the utmost cordiality. The President extends the thanks of the country to the soldiers and sailors for their gallant conduct. The eyes of the world are upon them, and they are furnishing an inspiration that will last forever.[29]

Three days later General Miles arrived in Cuba, and headway was finally made at the negotiating table. With Toral, Wheeler, Shafter, and Miles all in consultation, Toral agreed to end hostilities if acceptable terms could be fashioned. Wheeler—who by this time had been joined by Annie, anxious that he receive the best care—was appointed to head a three-man commission to negotiate the terms.[30]

"I was up till nearly one o'clock last night in the open air negotiating with the Spaniards," Wheeler wrote to his children on July 15. "I hope we will be through this job soon so as to go to Porto Rico."[31]

On the morning of July 16 after reading a draft of the terms, Toral finally surrendered.

At nine o'clock the following morning, July 17, two hundred members from both armies attended the surrender ceremony, held in a grove of trees. Toral signed the document Wheeler had drawn up, and the two generals shook hands and lit cigars. A military procession through Santiago followed, with Shafter and Wheeler each heading a column. At noon the American flag was hoisted atop a flagpole outside the governor's mansion, signifying that the United States had officially taken possession of the city. This was temporary, for the United States would recognize Cuba as an independent nation (although Uncle Sam decided to keep Guantanamo Bay). Before the year was through, Spain would also cede Puerto Rico, Guam, and the Philippines. With Alaska already established and Hawaii annexed in August 1898, there was no doubt that the world was now watching the inexorable expansion of the American empire.[32]

One man less thrilled with the surrender ceremony was Calixto García. Because Shafter did not trust the Cuban soldiers to behave, he barred them from Santiago. It was a move that proved diplomatically disastrous, still felt today in US-Cuban relations. Although García was allowed to join the ceremony, he was accidentally turned away by an American soldier who later reported that he did not recognize the Cuban general. Shortly afterward, García resigned.[33]

On the other hand, Roosevelt—who would almost certainly be running for governor of New York that November—was ecstatic over his victory. Hearst was less so. On July 19 two days after the war ended and three days after Milly's sixteenth birthday, Hearst cabled Phoebe. "Don't worry. Everything is over here now, and we are coming home."[34]

Having collected Marshall and Creelman, Hearst sailed back to the United States. In Charleston, South Carolina, Hearst chartered a steamer. Charley Michelson joined him there. The Chief wanted Michelson to keep tabs on Schley in case there was one last sea battle. There wasn't one, but Michelson didn't mind.[35]

"I was with the Hearst organization, with some intervals, for thirty years," Michelson later reflected. "During that time we put over some queer exploits, but never in all that period did Mr. Hearst admit an unworthy purpose. All was done in the public interest, even though the net result appeared to be increased circulation, advertising, or prestige."[36]

Hearst could have used some of Michelson's kind words just then. Returning to New York City, the young millionaire shut himself inside the Astor House and composed a melancholy letter to Phoebe:

> I guess I'm a failure. I made the mistake of my life in not raising the cowboy regiment I had in mind before Roosevelt raised his. I really believe I brought on the war but I failed to score in the war. I had my chance and failed to grab it, and I suppose I must sit on the fence now and watch the procession go by. It's my own fault. I was thirty-five years of age, and of sound mind—comparatively—and could do as I liked. I failed and I'm a failure and I deserve to be for being as slow and stupid as I was. Outside of the grief it would give you I had better be in a Santiago trench than where I am. . . . Goodnight, Mama dear. Take care of yourself. Don't let me lose you. I wish you were here tonight. I feel about eight years old—and very blue.[37]

Hearst often pulled his mother's leg in his letters, but rather than being playful he seemed quasi facetious, for there is a strong element of truth in his Astor House letter. Hearst recognized Roosevelt as the coming man. As the hero of the war, Roosevelt had amassed immense political capital, enough that many of his enemies—even within his own party—became worried that he might seize the White House. Knowing that he wasn't yet in Roosevelt's league, Hearst decided to capitalize on the *New York Journal*'s indisputable role as the leading newspaper of the Spanish-American War.

For one, Hearst rehired Stephen Crane.

Suffering from delirium and high fever and what he called "a languorous indifference to everything in the world," Crane had left Siboney, Cuba, aboard the *City of Washington* on July 8, 1898. Eventually a doctor diagnosed him with yellow fever. Later Crane was diagnosed with malaria. For five days he bore the agony of the waves, the twin illnesses, and the horrors of what he'd seen in the war. Although he mostly tried to keep a brave face during the battles, in the article "War Memories" Crane described what he'd seen as "overwhelming, crushing, monstrous," but acknowledged that he couldn't do it justice.[38]

The transport docked in Old Point Comfort, Virginia, on July 13. In late July, Crane traveled to New York to collect expenses from the *New York World*'s financial manager, John Norris. Instead of giving Crane money, Norris fired him.

"I have just kissed your little friend Stephen Crane good-bye," Norris told Don Carlos Seitz, the *World*'s business manager. "He came here asking for another advance. Don't you think you have had enough of Mr. Pulitzer's money without earning it?"[39]

Crane had filed two dozen dispatches while in Cuba, so the problem wasn't with his work that came back to bite him. He had filed Marshall's copy for the *Journal,* and the *World*'s manager of Cuban staff, Henry N. Cary, described him Crane as "a drunken, irresponsible and amusing little cuss."[40]

Of course, all of these were positive characteristics at the *Journal.* With an ally in Charley Michelson, Crane was rehired by the *Journal.* But his health took a turn for the worse. That same week Crane traveled three hundred miles north and checked into the Adirondack Cottage Sanitorium. There, Dr. Edward Trudeau examined his lungs. That Crane was suffering from pulmonary tuberculosis and probably had been since a child soon became common knowledge.[41]

Michelson met with Crane days after he left the sanitorium and noticed that he was "shambling, with hair too long, usually lacking a shave, dressed like any of the deck hands, hollow-cheeked, sallow, destitute of small talk, critical if not fastidious, marked with ill health—the very antithesis of the conquering male."[42]

But Crane wouldn't let his poor health keep him down. In early August 1898, he once again teamed up with Richard Harding Davis, this time in Puerto Rico, with Crane working for the *New York Journal* and Davis for the *New York Tribune.* The pair were now old friends, having proven themselves to be the premier war correspondents of their era.[43]

As for the premier editor in chief of the era, Hearst had another trick up his sleeve.

With Sampson, Schley, and the victorious fleet set to return to New York on Saturday, August 20, 1898, the *Journal* argued that New York businessmen and politicians declare a holiday. When Macy's and New York City mayor Robert Van Wyck agreed, the others fell in line. Even Thomas Edison shut down his laboratory in Orange, New Jersey. That day, between 750,000 and a million cheering people crowded Grant's Tomb, Staten Island, and Battery Park. A *Journal* balloon floated over Grant's Tomb, dusting the crowd with colorful confetti. When the fleet came into sight, it wasn't the *New York* or the *Brooklyn* that led the line of ships but rather Hearst's yacht *Anita*, with the *Journal* banners proudly waving.[44]

Despite his notoriety, Hearst made no secret of his ultimate goal: to call the White House home.

"Will is simply marvelous," Hearst's friend Orrin Peck wrote to Phoebe from Munich. "It is only a question of time when you will be doing the honors in the White House as the mother of the President—now mark my words and keep the dust off of 'our Emeralds' for the occasion."[45]

For a brief time Hearst considered running against Roosevelt for governor of New York, Hearst with the Democrats and Roosevelt with the Republicans. Phoebe promised Hearst the funds, but he ultimately decided not to runt. Instead, he directed Arthur Brisbane to have the *Journal* do its best to undercut Roosevelt in the press.

"There is no humiliation to which Mr. Roosevelt will not submit that he may get the nomination for Governor," the *Journal* editorialized on September 22. "The Roosevelt that was, was a humbug. The Theodore Roosevelt that is, is a prideless office-seeker."[46]

Despite the New York Democrats and the *Journal* working in concert, Roosevelt narrowly won the governorship on November 8, 1898. Six weeks later on December 22, Roosevelt attended a celebratory dinner at the 93rd Annual Festival of the New England Society in the City of New York, held at the Waldorf Astoria. Along with Governor-elect Roosevelt, notables included Brigadier General Shafter, Admiral Sampson, former vice president Levi P. Morton, Collis Huntington, J. P. Morgan, and Major General Wheeler, who had easily won reelection in November. At the head of the room were the coats of arms of the New England states. Dinner included mignons of lamb, grouse with gooseberry jelly, and old-fashioned Boston baked beans. A little ditty called "Comrades in Arms" by John Jerome Rooney for Major General Joseph Wheeler was printed for all to see:

> Says Stonewall Jackson to "Little Phil": "Phil, have you heard the news?
> Why our Joe Wheeler—'Fighting Joe'—has gone and joined the Blues."

"Come, Stonewall, put your hand in mine: Joe's sworn old Samuel's oath;
We're never North or South again,—he kissed the book for both!"[47]

First to speak, naturally, was Roosevelt, greeted by cheers. "The Puritan came from a stock which carried the Bible in one hand, and in the other the sword," Roosevelt began. "I think we of the present generation have awakened to a livelier sense of what we owe to these men."[48]

When Wheeler—resplendent in full dress uniform—was asked to rise, he paid tribute to Roosevelt and discussed the Cuban campaign. Wheeler also mentioned that as for expansion, "this country could not back down from the task imposed upon it by Providence."[49]

In other words, Fighting Joe backed annexation of Cuba's tropical territories. This stance would soon land him in hot water with his own Democratic colleagues, who largely began positioning themselves as antiexpansionist. Wheeler's martial resolve would lead him to serve in the Philippines, but the independent streak he displayed at Las Guasimas would not be tolerated by his immediate superior, Major General Arthur McArthur, who quickly relegated Wheeler to rear duty. Wheeler would ultimately resign from Congress and the army to live quietly with Annie on Pond Spring and later New York, an American legend but yesterday's man.[50]

Roosevelt wasn't about to live quietly. Like Hearst, Roosevelt had his eye on the White House. Richard Harding Davis helped Roosevelt's ambitions by painting Roosevelt as the dashing hero in *The Cuban and Porto Rican Campaigns,* published by Charles Scribner's Sons in late 1898. Roosevelt wasn't shy about returning the favor. Years later in a book of reflections on Davis, Roosevelt spoke highly of his old friend, whose actions had been heroic at Las Guasimas and who had earned the respect of the common soldiers throughout the Spanish-American War.[51]

Commented Roosevelt, "Davis . . . was indomitably cheerful under hardships and difficulties entirely indifferent to his own personal safety and comfort. He so won the esteem and regard of the regiment. . . . We gave him the same medal worn by our own members."[52]

Although Roosevelt didn't like it, Davis celebrated Crane in *Harper's New Monthly Magazine* in May 1899.

"Crane is quite as much of a soldier as the man whose courage he described. . . . It never occurs to Crane that to sit at the man's feet as he did close enough to watch his lips move and to be able to make mental notes for a later tribute to the marine's scorn of fear, was equally deserving of praise," Davis remarked.[53]

Considering the war correspondents in Cuba, Davis allowed that Crane was on a different level. "Mr. Crane easily led all the rest. Of his power to make the public see what he sees it would be impertinent to speak."[54]

Although Crane would be best remembered for his fiction—*The Red Badge of Courage*, *Maggie*, and "The Bride Comes to Yellow Sky"—for his nonfiction his description of the sinking of the *Commodore* and his Spanish-American War writing were undeniably powerful, helping to cement his place as one of the greatest American writers.

As for Hearst's ambitions, by May 1899 he had a new scheme. That month Phoebe, depressed and outraged that Hearst had asked her for money to buy another newspaper, wrote from Europe to Orrin Peck.

"Will is insisting upon buying a paper in Chicago. Says he will come over to see me if I do not go home very soon. It is impossible for me to throw away more money in any way for the simple reason that he has already absorbed almost all. . . . It is *madness*. I never know when or how we will break out into some *additional* expensive scheme."[55]

"I cannot understand Will's demand," Orrin replied in a letter. "As you say, it is madness. He doubtless wishes to control the press of the U.S. That's alright but the main thing is to get the present established *Journal* under control. It's like dashing along a mad road with runaway horses and trying to harness in another."[56]

Later that year Hearst finally got his runaway horses under control, able to tell Phoebe with a straight face that the *Journal* was actually making money. As for the Chicago paper, Hearst bided his time. But Phoebe knew that her son would not sit on his hands forever. Like his father, Hearst was all action.

"Journalism is a quick game," Hearst reflected. "It needs prompt decision, and prompt and vigorous response."[57]

Heeding his own advice, Hearst quickly determined what to do with the receipt he'd been handed for delivering to the *Harvard* twenty-nine Spanish prisoners on that Fourth of July.

"Those were the wonderful days and happy achievements of youth," Hearst mused. "No grandiose performance of later years. Life was not 'one damn thing after another' then. It was one wonderful adventure after another. The competition of journalism was a glad sport; and yet back of it all was a sense of responsibility—a genuine desire to use the powers and opportunities of the press to serve and save. There was delight in work, happiness in service, joy in life—for we were young."[58]

Hearst had the receipt framed.[59]

EPILOGUE

Retrospective

The great paradox of the Spanish-American War was that in a time of hyperbole, truth was stranger than fiction.

All of it seemed extremely improbable. A Harvard man became a Dakota cowboy, expressed a desire to lead a cowboy regiment into a battle, and then made it happen. An old Confederate cavalryman was appointed by the president of the United States to the position of major general in a war against the Spanish Empire. A hedonistic writer suffering from tuberculosis swam to shore after the gun-running ship he was aboard sank. The most famous celebrity writer in America became a soldier in the regiment he was supposed to be covering. A millionaire newspaper editor poured an extraordinary amount of his considerable energy into bringing about a war with Spain and sailed to Cuba on a yacht to personally cover it.

That it happened is unquestionable. But questions still remain.

Chief among them is how much direct effect William Randolph Hearst had on bringing on the war. Essays, articles, and books have been written on the probably apocryphal "You furnish the pictures, and I'll furnish the war" telegram. But it's Hearst's hands-on direction of the *New York Journal* that most clearly demonstrates how he influenced public perception.

Hearst had been at the helm of the *Journal* for less than six months before sending Murat Halstead to Cuba. When Hearst published Halstead's findings in March 1896, including Halstead's call for war with Spain and annexation of Cuba, jingoistic Americans such as Theodore Roosevelt and Joseph Wheeler took that plan into consideration. In April, Wheeler went so far as to call for war on the House floor, and days later—after the *Journal* published Fred Lawrence's shameless yellow journalism piece about a female Cuban cavalry unit killed by Spanish bullets and machetes—Senator John Tyler Morgan followed Wheeler's lead.

Soon all the big New York newspapers had their best war correspondents in Cuba. Some stories, such as the articles in the *Sun* and the *Journal* that the Spanish had been feeding Cuban prisoners to sharks, were shameless examples of yellow journalism. Others were more hard-hitting, including James Creelman's accounts of General Don Valeriano Weyler, who presided over the *reconcentrado* camps and inspired hatred from his fellow Spaniards, such as Josep Conangla, who secretly prayed for an independent Cuba. But ultimately it was Hearst's idea to send a reporter to free Evangelina Cisneros from a Havana prison that made the biggest difference.

Embodying the epitome of the heroic adventurer, Karl Decker pulled off one of the greatest prison breaks in history, successfully sawing through the bars in Cisneros's window on the night of October 6, 1897, and helping her flee the city aboard a ship. The story became a media sensation, resulting in all hopes of General Weyler holding onto power being dashed.

John L. Offner looked at the broad picture of the media's influence in his 1992 history *An Unwanted War*, particularly in the role Hearst played. "Sensational journalism had only a marginal impact," Offner concluded. "Hearst played on American prejudices; he did not create them. . . . Hearst published the de Lôme letter, but he did not make it up. Hearst charged that the Spaniards had sunk the *Maine*, yet he did not write the naval report that propelled the nation towards war. . . . Had there been no sensational press, only responsible editors, the American public nevertheless would have learned about the terrible conditions in Cuba, [and] would have wanted Spain to leave."[1]

Possibly. But despite the naval report indicating that the *Maine* had been blown up in Havana Harbor, only the jingoes blamed this on Spain. The conservatives needed more of a reason to support the war effort. To that end, Hearst's focus on the *reconcentrado* camps provided a stronger casus belli. He sent Julian Hawthorne to examine Havana's *reconcentrado* camp, reported on Clara Barton's findings there as well, and made sure his illustrators didn't fail to move the American public with pictures of the emaciated prisoners.

As a result, many conservatives determined that war was not only inevitable but was also the right course of action. Hearst and the *Journal* didn't do it single-handedly. Senator Redfield Proctor, Clara Barton, and droves of reporters and politicians played a part. But of all the American editors covering the conflict, Hearst displayed the most nerve and certainly did more than any other editor to ignite the war.

Why did Hearst do all this? Was it all for good copy?

William Randolph Hearst has always been a polarizing figure. Even people who knew him well could scarcely agree on what made him tick. As noted earlier, Irwin Stump—who kept the books for Senator George Hearst and had seen W. R. grow from a Harvard scoundrel to an inventive newspaper editor—maintained that W. R. "kept a real sympathy for the submerged man and woman, a real feeling of his own mission to plead their cause." Creelman, on the other hand, believed that Hearst saw his world as "an enchanted playground in which giants and dragons were slain simply for the fun of the thing."[2]

In the case of Cuba, both men were right. By sending Karl Decker to rescue Evangelina Cisneros, Hearst had helped take down the dragon Weyler for the fun of it and because it was the right thing to do. It is hard to imagine that Hearst, walking around his New York office and determining the best layout for the countless illustrations of starved Cuban women and children, wasn't moved, wasn't outraged. He wanted to help if he could and—like the megalomaniacal narcissist he was—felt that there was nothing he couldn't do.

The effect that Richard Harding Davis played on the Spanish-American War wasn't as dramatic as Hearst's. How could it be? Davis didn't own two newspapers with which to spread his opinion, nor was he the inheritor of a mining empire with a fortune in copper, silver, and gold to draw upon. But Davis was both popular and famous and as a one-man show had a great deal of pull.

So, it was Davis's most enduring novel, *Soldiers of Fortune*—published opportunely in 1897—that succeeded in romanticizing war and creating a fantasy of beneficial American military intervention in Latin America. In this respect, Davis helped create a psychic blueprint for the Spanish-American War.

Was this deliberate on Davis's part? It definitely wasn't pure calculation, for Davis was more instinctual than Machiavellian. But it wasn't dumb luck either. A quick study, Davis always knew which way the wind blew and worked tirelessly to hammer out exactly the type of story the reading public yearned for, whether they knew it or not. In fact, luck didn't play as much of a role as Davis contended, despite again and again shrugging off his good fortune in letters to his family as "the luck of R. H. D." This was Davis being both charmingly modest and airily dismissive of his most distinctive characteristics so that they wouldn't become common knowledge. The truth was that although happening to be in the right place at the right time factored into Davis's spectacular rise, the shrewd Philadelphian relied on charm, guile, and hard work to become the most celebrated reporter during the pivotal 1890s.

Part of Davis's appeal was that he represented the American man as he himself would like to be: a debonair action hero both down to earth and larger than life. In Davis we can see the hunger for adventure that epitomized the 1890s. Forever on the move, chasing stories from Russia, Greece, Brazil, and Cuba, Davis always did what he felt was right and was rewarded by a reading public who loved him for it. Motivated by financial security, fin de siècle luxuries, the adoration of his fans, and a desire to outshine his competitors, Davis had published dozens of short stories and seven books prior to the Spanish-American War and would write twenty books afterward. None of his works would stand the test of time, but when Davis was alive and in the center of things—with his magazine cover good looks, quintessentially Victorian manner, and unfeigned noblesse oblige—people enjoyed reading Richard Harding Davis stories simply because Davis had written them.

"In 1889 Mr. Davis was just a reporter on the Evening Sun," Thomas Beer reflected over a quarter century later. "In October of 1890 he was already R. H. D., and battle raged among the virgins of a famous school for girls in the Hudson valley over a signed photograph of the new god stolen by one young female from a brother."[3]

Davis's best work, of course, was his nonfiction during the course of the Spanish-American War. Davis used all of his charm to secure the best locales—aboard the *New York* with Sampson, alongside Roosevelt at Las Guasimas and San Juan Hill—and couldn't stop himself from playing the hero, forfeiting his role as a noncombatant by shooting at the Spanish soldiers during a desperate attack on the Rough Riders. Whether he was standing up to bullies in college, con men in New York City, or Spanish soldiers in Cuba, Davis's heart was always on display. In Cuba this aspect increased his already legendary status, infusing his writing with his own personal flair. Undoubtedly, the only war correspondent in Cuba in his league was his nemesis and friend, Stephen Crane.

In many ways, Crane served as the mirror image of Davis. Where Davis was concerned with Victorian ideals and could be somewhat priggish and high-minded as a result, Crane blazed a more hedonistic path. Time and again Crane demonstrated his desire to sleep with any woman with a pretty smile, regardless of promises elsewhere. But outside of bars and boudoirs, he lacked Davis's refined social skills. Although Crane could play on his youth to attract mentors and fans—Hamlin Garland for one and, at least initially, Theodore Roosevelt for another—Crane proved a fish out of water among powerful men, whereas Davis moved among politicians, military officers, and titans of industry as easily as if they were old friends at the local clubhouse.

But Crane had something Davis lacked.

Crane's greatest western short stories—"The Bride Comes to Yellow Sky" and "The Blue Hotel"—were instant classics. *Maggie* grew in popularity over the years as well, and *The Red Badge of Courage* and "The Veteran" continued to hold appeal. Like Davis's best works, Crane's captured the American spirit during the 1890s and encouraged that spirit imperceptibly toward war. Contrary to some modern scholars who call *The Red Badge of Courage* an antiwar novel, Crane's American Civil War masterpiece was a tale of cowardice in battle followed by redemption through bravery in battle. It was not a story that stopped young men from joining the army in 1898; instead, *The Red Badge of Courage* glamorized the cathartic emotion of victory on a battlefield. The message of the "The Veteran" was even more apropos to American intervention in Cuba. When Henry Fleming rushed into the burning barn to save a pair of colts, he was acting heroically and admirably despite the danger.

That metaphor is a perfect one for Stephen Crane as a man. Throughout his life he constantly rushed into burning barns to do what was right, no matter the danger or the cost. Defending Dora Clark in New York City, joining the filibusterers aboard the *Commodore,* acting to save Davis's life on San Juan Ridge, and filing Edward Marshall's copy for the *Journal* are just a few examples. But Crane wasn't quite the adventurous hero that Davis was. Although Crane rushed into his share of burning barns, in several cases he had a hand in setting that fire himself.

Yet, for all his faults, there is something great about Crane. Few American writers ever burned so bright so quickly and, for someone who at times seemed so reviled, was ever so beloved. Ernest Hemingway famously opined, "The good writers are Henry James, Stephen Crane, and Mark Twain. That's not the order they're good in. There is no order for good writers."[4]

Fighting Joe Wheeler's role in the conflict was more multifaceted. As a soldier, Wheeler was a solid pick to lead the American cavalry in Cuba. A West Point graduate, he had fought in dozens of battles and skirmishes in the Civil War—Shiloh, the siege of Corinth, Stones River, Chickamauga, Perryville, Ringgold Gap, Brown's Mill, Aiken, and Benton, to name a handful—and acquitted himself well.

Like the Cuban leaders Calixto García and Máximo Gómez Baez, Wheeler had years of warfare experience to draw upon. This fact grew in significance when juxtaposed with the youth and inexperience of some of his key subordinates, Leonard Wood and Roosevelt in particular.

Wheeler's role as a Confederate during the Civil War—fighting against the country he had sworn to protect—could have counted against him had he not adopted the role of a reconciler during the spring of 1895. In his speeches at Memphis and Shiloh, Wheeler pivoted away from the familiar Lost Cause bellyache, instead praising the soldiers in the Union and the Confederacy during the great conflict. That this met with universal approval helped him shape the narrative that he was the right man to lead troops against the Spanish in Cuba.

President William McKinley thought so too. Whether or not McKinley actually admitted to Wheeler that he needed a symbol to reunite the North and the South and that Wheeler would be that symbol is unlikely. Wheeler later denied it, and McKinley was generally considered too circumspect to say the quiet part out loud. But as it happened, Wheeler was the symbol the country needed. With James Longstreet out of favor in the South and with Robert E. Lee and Thomas "Stonewall" Jackson long dead, Wheeler was the best-known Confederate officer still on the green side of the grass. Furthermore, Wheeler had been an early advocate for American intervention in Cuba. For these reasons, he was appointed major general of volunteers.

As McKinley anticipated, Wheeler's role as a symbol made a difference. The barrels of ink devoted to Wheeler's appointment, particularly from southern newspapers, spoke to the pride old Dixie had in their former champion now leading American soldiers. This helped cement good relations between old northerners and southerners. With Wheeler at the fore, the top brass knew that the one enemy American troops had to worry about in Cuba—excluding the fever—were the Spanish and that the chances of old hostilities breaking out between the sons of Billy Yank and Johnny Reb were greatly reduced.

Wheeler once again demonstrated himself as an effective battlefield commander. At the Battle of Las Guasimas and during the turmoil atop San Juan Ridge—where he managed through great adversity to keep his command together—he secured personal military glory. Returning home, Wheeler continued to call for American expansion. This was despite his own party aligning itself against the rising tide. But Wheeler knew that nothing could stop the sea change of American imperialism, and he chose to be an active participant.

Signifying his complete transformation from when he fought against the United States, Wheeler became incensed to learn in the fall of 1899 while serving in Manila that American anti-imperialists were celebrating the victories of the Philippine Revolutionary Army over American forces. This smacked of treason, and that wasn't something Fighting Joe took lightly. In an unofficial report to McKinley, Wheeler stated that he was "fearful to think of American soldiers being killed by ignorant half savages who are encouraged to do so by expressions of American citizens."[5]

Out of favor with his own Democratic colleagues for championing expansionism, Wheeler resigned from Congress on April 20, 1900. Judge William Richardson, Wheeler's old nemesis, handily won Wheeler's seat. That fall on September 10, 1900—his sixty-fourth birthday—Wheeler resigned from military service as well. Shortly afterward, he and Annie moved to New York. During the election of 1900, which pitted William McKinley and Theodore Roosevelt against William Jennings Bryan and Adlai Stevenson, Wheeler largely stayed silent.

After the Republican blowout, Wheeler admitted, "I felt it and knew that Mr. McKinley would be overwhelmingly elected. I could have told our people six months ago, but what was the use?"[6]

Alabama newspapermen pounced. Although the *Selma Times* praised Wheeler's "grand military career in defense of the Lost Cause," it expressed scorching criticisms for the new Wheeler. Wheeler had grown close with McKinley. No longer a party man, Wheeler leaned Republican. What the newspapermen missed was that he had moved beyond North-South divisions. Instead, Fighting Joe was hoping to see the American flag spread across the globe, and he had found it just to lead the United States into the American century.[7]

As for the man whose motivations and energy were both singular and all over the map, Theodore Roosevelt used his success in Cuba to power his vaulting ambition. The publication of *The Rough Riders* and its wild success exemplified two of the most fascinating aspects of Roosevelt's rapid rise: his mastery in influencing the media to shape his personal narrative and the realization of his desire to lead scions of the Wild West into battle.

As Doris Kearns Goodwin deftly expressed in her history *Theodore Roosevelt, William Howard Taft, and the Golden Age of Journalism*, Roosevelt was a master manipulator of the press. It was no coincidence that he took his camera along with him while hunting outlaws in the Dakotas; he cultivated friendships with media stars such as Richard Harding Davis, Jacob Riis, and, for a brief time, Stephen

Crane; and invited along cameramen as he boarded a transport ship to war-torn Cuba. Roosevelt knew the power of the press and sought to create a symbiotic relationship with members of the media. In this he was largely successful.

One example is how Roosevelt charmed Michigander Ray Baker, the prominent journalist. Immediately after the war, Roosevelt allowed Baker to visit him in Oyster Bay and journey with him to Camp Wikoff in Montauk, New York, where the Rough Riders were quarantined. For *McClure's*, Baker wrote, "I talked with a number of officers and troopers in Mr. Roosevelt's regiment, and I found their admiration of their colonel to be boundless. 'Why, he knows every man in the regiment by name,' said one. 'He spent $5,000 of his own money at Santiago to give us better food and medicine.'" Recognizing how the game was played, Roosevelt was not shy about writing Baker a thank-you letter expressing delight in the article.[8]

"Roosevelt . . . is a master of the art of feeling the public pulse," Upton Sinclair noted in the *Industrial Republic.* The political activist also explained that "Roosevelt is a complete anomaly in our political life; he was probably the last Republican in the country who would have been selected to rule us. He made himself governor by a shrewd device called 'the Rough Riders.'"[9]

Published in 1899 by Charles Scribner's Sons, Roosevelt's *The Rough Riders* immediately became his most popular book and an excellent example of self-promotion. The book also captured one of the most extraordinary aspects of the war, that a regiment composed primarily of westerners, a smattering of eastern collegiates, and a few New York City policemen came together under Lieutenant Colonel Roosevelt, a man who had experience as all three.

Readers were delighted by Roosevelt's rendition of the war, as were reviewers. "Roosevelt's account of the Rough Riders is the one to stand in history," declared New Jersey's *Bridgerton Pioneer.* The *Chicago Times-Herald*'s humorist Finley Peter Dunne was more playful. Dunne's alter ego Martin Dooly reviewed it with pizazz: "Tis Th' Biography iv a Hero be Wan who Knows. Tis Th' Darin' Exploits iv a Brave Man be an Actual Eye Witness," Dooley commented. "If I was him, I'd call th' book, 'Alone in Cubia.'"[10]

The line caused a sensation, and no one laughed louder than Theodore Roosevelt. Roosevelt recalled that after being elected governor of New York he met a quick-witted young lady at a reception. "Oh, Governor," she said, "I've read everything you ever wrote." "Really! What book did you like the best?" "Why that one, you know, *Alone in Cuba.*"[11]

That Roosevelt loved to retell this anecdote was partially due to the criticism being unfair. Many of the Rough Riders he described in his book—and he described dozens—became immortal as a result.

"My men were children of the dragon's blood," Roosevelt wrote in the book's final page. The affection he held for them was easy to see. The affection that the country held for them was just as strong, for the story of the Rough Riders captured a rich segment of American history—the American West, a regional and cultural phenomenon that had occurred nowhere else on Earth—and breathed life into it just as the fire was beginning to die down.[12]

According to the Census Bureau, the frontier had officially closed in 1890. Historian Frederick Jackson Turner's 1893 essay "The Significance of the Frontier in American History" followed suit, claiming that "the free lands are gone, the continent is crossed, and all this push and energy is turning into channels of agitation."[13]

That may have been so, but in *The Rough Riders* readers could experience the Wild West once again, this time going to war. It was better than a dime novel, was more exciting than the front page of the *New York Journal*, and starred Theodore Roosevelt, Fighting Joe Wheeler, Richard Harding Davis, and an amalgamation of western heroes and dangerous men. It seemed too good to be true.

To Roosevelt's consternation, more than a few people thought so. Despite *The Rough Riders* helping elevate Roosevelt to the governorship, it did not net him the military honor he coveted. "Gen. Wheeler say he intends to recommend me for the medal of honor; naturally I should like to have it," Roosevelt had written Lodge, but to no avail. Roosevelt would just have to console himself with the presidency.[14]

After Vice President Garrett Hobart died of heart disease at age fifty-five on November 21, 1899, McKinley selected Theodore Roosevelt to run with him as vice president on the Republican ticket. This was both to bolster McKinley's reelection campaign and to shoehorn Roosevelt into a largely ceremonial position where he could do little damage. At first it seemed to have worked like magic. With the charismatic Rough Rider beside him, McKinley was handily reelected, once again defeating William Jennings Bryan, this time with a crushing electoral college victory of 292 to 155. But the party elders were in for a rude shock when on September 6, 1901, while touring the Pan-American Exposition in Buffalo, New York, McKinley was shot twice—once in the chest and once in the abdomen—by the anarchist Leon Czolgosz. On September 14, 1901, President McKinley died, and Theodore Roosevelt, all of forty-two years old, was elevated to chief executive.

Republican boss Mark Hanna was furious. "I told William McKinley it was a mistake to nominate that wild man at Philadelphia. . . . I asked him if he realized what would happen if he should die. Now look, that damned cowboy is President of the United States."[15]

As president, Roosevelt channeled his manic energy toward regulating big business at home and expanding American influence abroad. This was the dawn of America as an empire, demonstrating that the United States had become a powerful player on the world stage. With Roosevelt using his "big stick" approach, the United States gained control of the Panama Canal by deploying the US Navy to support Panama's independence from Colombia. Roosevelt also continued to maintain a military presence in Cuba and Puerto Rico and introduced the Roosevelt Corollary to the Monroe Doctrine, in essence declaring that the whole Caribbean was subject to police actions by the US Navy. In December 1907, Roosevelt capped his glory by having the so-called Great White Fleet, consisting of sixteen battleships, begin a fourteen-month mission to circumnavigate the globe.

Of course, Roosevelt could not control everything. He watched with horror as William Randolph Hearst became ever more influential by establishing the *Chicago American* to go along with the *San Francisco Examiner* and the *New York Journal*. These newspapers would be the foundation from which Hearst would build the greatest media empire of the early twentieth century. Caught up in his own dislike of Hearst, Roosevelt likely missed the fact that as the American empire grew in power, the growth of powerful media branches was unavoidable.

"Hearst has edited a large number of the very worst type of sensational, scandal-mongering newspapers," Roosevelt wrote to a friend in October 1906. "They have been edited with great ability and with entire unscrupulousness."[16]

Along with being unable to curb the freedom of the yellow press, Roosevelt failed to obtain the Medal of Honor, despite continuous lobbying. However, on January 16, 2001, President Bill Clinton corrected that, posthumously awarding Theodore Roosevelt the Medal of Honor in the Roosevelt Room, giving the medal to Roosevelt's great-grandson, Tweed Roosevelt.

"TR was a larger-than-life figure who gave our Nation a larger-than-life vision of our place in the world," Clinton told the audience. "Part of that vision was formed on San Juan Hill. His Rough Riders were made up of all kinds of Americans from all walks of life. They were considered unpolished and undisciplined, but they were true citizen soldiers."[17]

Roosevelt couldn't have agreed more.

POSTSCRIPT

Stephen Crane

Having caught yellow fever and malaria in Cuba and continuing to smoke, Stephen Crane's tuberculosis worsened. In the spring of 1900, Crane and Cora journeyed to a fabled sanitorium in Badenweiler, Germany, outside the Black Forest. Crane's lungs hemorrhaged shortly after arriving, and he died on June 5, 1900, at only twenty-eight years old. When the world heard of his death, praise filled newspaper obituaries, the best coming from Richard Harding Davis. Crane's *The Red Badge of Courage* remains a well-read American classic.

Joseph Wheeler

Joseph "Fighting Joe" Wheeler was honored while still alive. Invitations to Washington receptions, including at the White House, arrived at his home in Alabama and Washington, D.C. He was celebrated across the country as the only former Confederate general to see action as a US major general. When Wheeler died in 1906, eulogies poured in from everywhere, including the cowboy in the White House, Theodore Roosevelt. In 1925, Berthod Nebel's bronze statue of Wheeler was unveiled in the US Capitol. Although the Confederate uniform is provocative, Wheeler's statue continues to stand in the National Statuary Hall.

Richard Harding Davis

For his actions in Cuba, Richard Harding Davis also received praise from Roosevelt. After the war Davis married, divorced, and married again, and he and second his wife had a daughter, Hope. As the greatest living war correspondent of his generation, Davis covered World War I before his luck ran out, dying in 1916 at age fifty-one of a heart attack. Despite Davis being a prolific author, none of his books stand the test of time. Davis is best known for his correspondence during the Spanish-American War, his friendship with Roosevelt and Crane, and living a wildly adventurous life.

Theodore Roosevelt

Using the governorship of New York as a stepping stone, Roosevelt secured the vice presidency, and—following William McKinley death from an assassin's bullet on September 14, 1901—the presidency itself. Roosevelt proved to be the great winner of the Spanish-American War and the right man to lead the American empire into the twentieth century. In 1904 he ran for a full term as president and was elected. After declining to run for a second term in 1908, Roosevelt sought the presidency again in 1912. Refused the nomination by the Republican Party, he joined the Progressive Party, later nicknamed the Bull Moose Party, and ran against his old secretary of war and the incumbent president, William Howard Taft. Roosevelt defeated Taft but lost to the Democratic challenger, Woodrow Wilson. Attempting to reinvent himself, in December 1913 Roosevelt embarked on an adventure in Brazil mapping the Rio da Dúvida, later named the Roosevelt River. The misadventure ruined his health. Roosevelt died relatively young, at sixty years old, in 1919. Vice President Thomas R. Marshall commented that "death had to take Roosevelt sleeping, for if he had been awake, there would have been a fight."[1]

William Randolph Hearst

William Randolph Hearst, the first American media tycoon, lived to be eighty-eight years old. From newspapers he expanded into magazines, radio, and motion pictures. He and Milly married and had five boys. The family lived in a luxurious mansion that Hearst had built in San Simeon's Santa Lucia Mountains overlooking the Pacific Ocean. When Hearst fell for a chorus girl, Marion Davies, Milly refused to divorce him, and Hearst simply carried on with both a wife and a girlfriend. He remained jealous of Roosevelt's success in the Spanish-American War but helped Roosevelt's fifth cousin, Franklin Delano Roosevelt, be elected as president in 1932. Although known for yellow journalism, Hearst expressed pride in the reporting of the Spanish-American War he oversaw. Hearst died in 1951. The Hearst corporation still flourished and today is known as Hearst Communications. The estate in San Simeon, which Hearst named La Cuesta Encantada (The Enchanted Hill), is now known as Hearst Castle and is a California State Park open to the public. Above all, energizing the American war machine in the 1890s may be Hearst's most significant and controversial achievement.

ACKNOWLEDGMENTS

A great deal of research and hard work went into bringing this book to life.

Special thanks to the University of Washington, Seattle, for making accessible the *New York Journal*; to California Polytechnic State University in San Luis Obispo for printing copies of the *San Francisco Examiner*; to Ken Barr at the Alabama Department of Archives and History in Montgomery, who let me peruse the Joseph Wheeler Papers; to the Bancroft Library at the University of California, Berkeley, where I looked over the Hearst Papers; to the Huntington Research Library, which provided a steady treasure trove of rare and valuable material; and to Dr. Edward Kohn and Dr. Michael Cullinane for their expertise and support.

Friends and family helped along the way. Jarik Hille generously drove us from Portland to Seattle. Mary-Jane Bernstein, Brex-Anna Stragnell, and Ben Stragnell encouraged the project with their enthusiasm. Ron Bernstein, Gregory Urbach, and Chris Stewart looked over several drafts. Lita Fice listened to each chapter on our long drives, providing valuable feedback.

The team at the University of Oklahoma Press, while always top-notch, raised the bar with their hard work. My heartfelt gratitude to Andrew Berzanskis, editorial director; Joe Schiller, acquisitions editor; Steven Baker, managing editor; Brendan Thomas, editorial assistant; Anna María Rodríguez, production coordinator; Katie Baker, marketing director and publicity manager; Amy Hernandez, marketing assistant; Tony Roberts, cover designer; and Yvonne Ramsey, whose careful copyediting and research helped polish the book.

Considering the biographies and sketches of each giant, in particular I enjoy W. A. Swanberg's captivating *Citizen Hearst,* which first opened my eyes to William Randolph Hearst's outrageous life story. Arthur Lebow's benchmark history *The Reporter Who Would Be King: A Biography of Richard Harding Davis* is highly engaging. John P. Dyer's *From Shiloh to San Juan: The Life of "Fighting Joe" Wheeler* demonstrates an endearing homespun quality. Charles Michelson's poignant observations of Stephen Crane, published as the "Introduction" in volume 11 of *The Works of Stephen Crane,* help illuminate the bohemian author.

As for Theodore Roosevelt, David McCullough's *Mornings on Horseback* shines particularly bright, unique in its focus and take. The depth and breadth of Edmund Morris's *The Rise of Roosevelt* is matched only by the almost Shakespearean conflict between the two central figures in Doris Keans Goodwin's *The Bully Pulpit: Theodore Roosevelt, William Howard Taft, and the Golden Age of Journalism.* And, of course, there's Candice Millard's thrill ride of a book, *River of Doubt: Theodore Roosevelt's Darkest Journey.*

Finally, I would like to pay my respects to the bold giants themselves—Stephen Crane, Richard Harding Davis, William Randolph Hearst, Theodore Roosevelt, and Joseph Wheeler—who wrote down their experiences and whose experiences were worth writing down.

NOTES

Prologue

1. Evan Thomas, *The War Lovers: Roosevelt, Lodge, Hearst, and the Rush to Empire, 1898* (New York: Back Bay Books, 2010), 302.
2. Thomas, *War Lovers*, 302.
3. Thomas, 302.
4. Crane, quoted in Dale L. Walker, *Rough Rider: Buckey O'Neill of Arizona* (Lincoln: University of Nebraska Press, 1975), 162.
5. Thomas, *War Lovers*, 303–4.
6. Walker, *Rough Rider*, 304.

Chapter 1. Deputy Sheriff Roosevelt

1. William Wingate Sewall, *Bill Sewall's Story of T.R.* (New York: Harper & Brothers, 1919), 58–59.
2. Theodore Roosevelt, *Ranch Life and the Hunting-Trail* (New York: Century Co., 1888), 114.
3. Sewall, *Bill Sewall's Story of T.R.*, 60.
4. Roosevelt, *Ranch Life*, 114.
5. Edmund Morris, *The Rise of Theodore Roosevelt* (New York: Random House, 1979), 318; and Roosevelt, *Ranch Life*, 115.
6. Roosevelt, *Ranch Life*, 115.
7. Sewall, *Bill Sewall's Story of T.R.*, 61.
8. Sewall, 61.
9. Roosevelt, *Ranch Life*, 115, 116.

10. Morris, *Rise of Theodore Roosevelt*, 319; and Roosevelt, *Ranch Life*, 115, 116.
11. Sewall, *Bill Sewall's Story of T.R.*, 62–63.
12. Roosevelt, *Ranch Life*, 116.
13. Roosevelt, *Ranch Life*, 116; and Morris, *Rise of Theodore Roosevelt*, 323.
14. Morris, *Rise of Theodore Roosevelt*, 294.
15. Sewall, *Bill Sewall's Story of T.R.*, 62–63.
16. Roosevelt, *Ranch Life*, 118.
17. Morris, *Rise of Theodore Roosevelt*, 181–82.
18. Morris, 181–82.
19. Morris, 185.
20. Morris, 188–89.
21. Morris, 190.
22. The quotations and the following account draw from Morris, 198, 209–11.
23. Michael R. Canfield, *Theodore Roosevelt in the Field* (Chicago: University of Chicago Press, 2015), 146.
24. Morris, *Rise of Theodore Roosevelt*, 213, 229–30.
25. Morris, 269.
26. Morris, 250.
27. The quotations and the following account draw from Morris, 246–47.
28. Morris, 257–59.
29. Morris, 269–70.
30. Morris, 273–74.
31. Morris, 275–76.
32. Morris, 295–96.
33. Sewall, *Bill Sewall's Story of T.R.*, 45–46.
34. Morris, *Rise of Theodore Roosevelt*, 291, 298–99.
35. Morris, 301–2.
36. Morris, 303.
37. Morris, 303.
38. Morris, 303–4, 307.
39. Morris, 313.
40. Roosevelt, *Ranch Life*, 120; and "ROOSEVELT AND THE BOAT THIEVES" sign, Theodore Roosevelt National Park, viewed June 19, 2015. The sign "ROOSEVELT AND THE BOAT THIEVES," in what is now Theodore Roosevelt National Park reads: "In the spring of 1886 thieves stole Theodore Roosevelt's boat from his Elkhorn Ranch, 25 miles south of here. Roosevelt pursued the thieves past this point and captured them at the mouth of Cherry Creek about 24 miles downstream. He then marched the thieves overland to Dickinson where they were tried and convicted."
41. Roosevelt, *Ranch Life*, 120.
42. Sewall, *Bill Sewall's Story of T.R.*, 64; and Roosevelt, *Ranch Life*, 120.
43. Sewall, *Bill Sewall's Story of T.R.*, 64.
44. Roosevelt, *Ranch Life*, 120.
45. Morris, *Rise of Theodore Roosevelt*, 322–25, 335.

46. *Herington Tribune* (Kansas), August 12, 1886.
47. Morris, *Rise of Theodore Roosevelt*, 336.

Chapter 2. Hearst's First Newspaper War

1. Kenneth Whyte, *The Uncrowned King: The Sensational Rise of William Randolph Hearst* (New York: Counterpoint, 2009), 19–20; Ben Procter, *William Randolph Hearst: The Early Years, 1863–1910* (Oxford: Oxford University Press, 1998), 32; and W. A. Swanberg, *Citizen Hearst: A Biography of William Randolph Hearst* (New York: Colliers, 1961), 26–27.
2. The following 1885 letter from Hearst to his father outlining his plan for sensationalizing the *Examiner* can be found among the George and Phoebe Apperson Hearst Papers in the Bancroft Library, University of California, Berkeley, and is drawn from Matthew Bernstein, *George Hearst: Silver King of the Gilded Age* (Norman: University of Oklahoma Press, 2021), 158–59:

> Dear Father: I have just finished and dispatched a letter to the Editor of the *Examiner* in which I recommended Eugene Lent to his favorable notice, and commented on the illustrations, if you may call them such, which have lately disfigured the paper.
>
> I really believe that the *Examiner* has furnished what is thus far the crowning absurdity in illustrated Journalism, in illustrating an article on the chicken show by means of the identical Democratic roosters used during the late campaign.
>
> In my letter to the editor, however, I did not refer to this for fear of offending him, but I did tell him that in my opinion the cuts that have recently appeared in the paper bore an unquestionable resemblance to the Cuticura Soap advertisements, and I am really inclined to believe that our editor has illustrated many articles from his stock on hand of cuts representing gentlemen before and after using that efficacious remedy.
>
> In case my remarks should have no effect, and he should continue in his career of desolation, let me beg of you to remonstrate with him and thus prevent him from giving the finishing stroke to our miserable little sheet.
>
> I have begun to have a strange fondness for our little paper—a tenderness like unto that which a mother feels for a puny or deformed offspring, and I should hate to see it die now after it had battled so long and so nobly for existence; in fact, to tell the truth, I am possessed of the weakness which at some time or other of their lives pervades most men; I am convinced that I could run a newspaper successfully.
>
> Now if you should make over to me the *Examiner*—with enough money to carry out my schemes—I'll tell you what I would do!
>
> In the first place I would change the general appearance of the paper and make seven wide columns where we now have nine narrow ones,

then I would have the type spaced more, and these two changes would give the pages a much cleaner and neater appearance.

Secondly, it would be well to make the paper as far as possible original, to clip only when absolutely necessary and to imitate only some such leading journal as the *New York World* which is undoubtedly the best paper of that class to which the *Examiner* belongs—that class which appeals to the people and which depends for its success upon enterprise, energy and a certain startling originality and not upon the wisdom of its political opinions or the lofty style of its editorials. And to accomplish this we must have—as the *World* has—active, intelligent and energetic young men; we must have men who come out west in the hopeful buoyancy of youth for the purposes of making their fortunes and not a worthless scum that has been carried there by the eddies of repeated failures.

Thirdly, we must advertise the paper from Oregon to New Mexico and must also increase our number of advertisements if we have to lower our rates to do it, thus we can put on the first page that our circulation is such and our advertisements so and so and constantly increasing.

And now having spoken of the three great essential points let us turn to details.

The illustrations are a detail, though a very important one. Illustrations embellish a page, illustrations attract the eye and stimulate the imagination of the masses and materially aid the comprehension of an unaccustomed reader and thus are of particular importance to that class of people which the *Examiner* claims to address. Such illustrations, however, as have heretofore appeared in the paper nauseate rather than stimulate the imagination and certainly do anything but embellish a page.

Another detail of questionable importance is that we actually or apparently establish some connection between ourselves and the *New York World*, and obtain a certain prestige in bearing some relation to that paper. We might contract to have important private telegrams forwarded or something of that sort, but understand that the principal advantage we are to derive is from the attention that such a connection would excite and from the advertisement we could make of it. Whether the *World* would consent to such an arrangement for any reasonable sum is very doubtful, for its net profit is over one thousand dollars a day and no doubt it would consider the *Examiner* is beneath its notice. Just think, over one thousand dollars a day and four years ago it belonged to Jay Gould and was losing money rapidly.

And now to close with a suggestion of great consequence, namely, that all these changes be made not by degrees but at once so that the improvement will be very marked and noticeable and will attract universal attention and comment.

> There is little to be said about my studies. . . . Congress is as stupid as it is possible to conceive of. . . .
>
> Well, good-by. I have given up all hope of having you write to me. . . . By the way, I heard you had bought 2,000 acres of land the other day and I hope some of it was the land adjoining our ranch that I begged you to buy in my last letter.
>
> Your affectionate son,
> W. R. Hearst

3. David Nasaw, *The Chief: The Life of William Randolph Hearst* (New York: Mariner Books, 2001), 27.
4. *San Francisco Examiner*, March 10, 1887; Sam Moskowitz, *The History of the Movement: From 1854 to 1890* (West Kingston, RI: Donald M. Grant, 1980), 225; and *San Francisco Examiner*, March 4, 1887.
5. Swanberg, *Citizen Hearst*, 41; and Nasaw, *The Chief*, 69.
6. *New York Times*, May 2, 1907; Swanberg, *Citizen Hearst*, 60; and Nasaw, *The Chief*, 68.
7. *San Francisco Examiner*, March 19, 1887.
8. Ambrose Bierce, *A Sole Survivor: Bits of Autobiography*, edited by S. T. Josshi and David E. Schultz (Knoxville: University of Tennessee Press, 1998), 201.
9. *San Francisco Examiner*, April 5, 1887.
10. *San Francisco Examiner*, April 3, 1887.
11. *Santa Cruz Sentinel*, June 7, 1887.
12. *Oakland Tribune* (California), April 18, 1887.
13. Charles Michelson, *The Ghost Talks* (New York: Putnam, 1944), 77.
14. Nasaw, *The Chief*, 70.
15. Nasaw, 71.
16. Nasaw, 70.
17. Nasaw, 71.
18. *San Francisco Examiner*, June 21, 1887.
19. *San Francisco Examiner*, June 6, 1887.
20. Whyte, *Uncrowned*, 32.
21. *Santa Cruz Sentinel*, June 7, 1887.
22. *San Francisco Examiner*, September 16, 1887.
23. Swanberg, *Citizen Hearst*, 48–52.
24. Nasaw, *The Chief*, 81.
25. Swanberg, *Citizen Hearst*, 48–52.
26. Nasaw, *The Chief*, 68.
27. Nasaw, 82–84.
28. *Oakland Tribune* (California), February 25, 1888.
29. Swanberg, *Citizen Hearst*, 52–53.
30. *Critic* (Washington, DC), December 10, 1888.
31. Swanberg, *Citizen Hearst*, 54; and *Delaware County Daily Times* (Pennsylvania), August 22, 1940.

Chapter 3. The Unexpected Rise of Richard Harding Davis

1. Gerald Langford, *The Richard Harding Davis Years: A Biography of a Mother and Her Son* (New York: Holt, Rinehart and Winston, 1961), 94.
2. Arthur Lubow, *The Reporter Who Would Be King: A Biography of Richard Harding Davis* (New York: Charles Scribner's Sons, 1992), 36–37.
3. David G. McCullough, *The Johnstown Flood* (London: Hutchinson & Co., 1968), 207; and Lubow, *Reporter Who Would Be King*, 37.
4. McCullough, *Johnstown Flood*, 207.
5. McCullough, 136. See also Langford, *Richard Harding Davis Years*, 89.
6. *Topeka Daily Capital*, November 15, 1895.
7. Lubow, *Reporter Who Would Be King*, 29.
8. Lubow, 38.
9. Lubow, 38.
10. Langford, *Richard Harding Davis Years*, 94.
11. Langford, 94, 89.
12. McCullough, *Johnstown Flood*, 208; and Lubow, *Reporter Who Would Be King*, 39.
13. Richard Harding Davis, *Adventures and Letters of Richard Harding Davis*, edited by Charles Belmont Davis (New York: Cosimo, 2005), 97; Lubow, *Reporter Who Would Be King*, 19–20, 21, 27; and Langford, *Richard Harding Davis Years*, 76.
14. Davis, *Adventures and Letters*, 34.
15. Lubow, *Reporter Who Would Be King*, 68.
16. Lubow, 43.
17. Langford, *Richard Harding Davis Years*, 96; Lubow, *Reporter Who Would Be King*, 8; and James M. Hutchisson, *Poe* (Jackson: University Press of Mississippi, 2005), 58–59.
18. Ron Powers, *Mark Twain: A Life* (New York: Free Press, 2005), 176.
19. Davis, *Adventures and Letters*, 34; and Lubow, *Reporter Who Would Be King*, 7.
20. Davis, *Adventures and Letters*, 34.
21. *Philadelphia Times*, October 20, 1889.
22. John D. Stevens, *Sensationalism and the New York Press* (New York: Columbia University, 1991), 67.
23. Davis, *Adventures and Letters*, 33; Lubow, *Reporter Who Would Be King*, 46–47; and Langford, *Richard Harding Davis Years*, 96. This rendition of how Davis came to be hired by the *Sun* was related by Davis's brother, Charles. Brisbane's version of the events differed dramatically. Instead, Brisbane related that Davis stopped by the offices of the *Sun* on his way to the *World* and that Brisbane hired him there, not on a park bench in City Hall Park. Brisbane's account is almost certainly the correct version. For Davis's brother's account to be accurate, Davis would have had to walk from the *World* to City Hall Park, bypassing the Sun Building, where Davis already had a connection. What is likelier is that Charles was simply repeating a sensationalized version Davis had told him. This flair for the dramatic would serve Davis well in New York City.
24. Lubow, *Reporter Who Would Be King*, 47; and Langford, *Richard Harding Davis Years*, 102.

25. Lubow, *Reporter Who Would Be King*, 45.
26. Frank M. O'Brien, *The Story of the Sun* (New York: George H. Doran Company, 1918), 219; Lubow, *Reporter Who Would Be King*, 45; and *San Francisco Examiner*, September 1, 1886.
27. Samuel V. Kennedy III, *Samuel Hopkins Adams and the Business of Writing* (Syracuse, NY: Syracuse University Press, 1999), 22; and Lubow, *Reporter Who Would Be King*, 45.
28. Scott Compton Osborn and Robert L. Phillips Jr., *Richard Harding Davis* (Boston: Twayne Publishers, 1978), 37.
29. Lubow, *Reporter Who Would Be King*, 46–47.

Chapter 4. Some Kind of Predatory Insect

1. Paul Sorrentino, *Stephen Crane: A Life of Fire* (Cambridge, MA: Belknap Press of Harvard University, 2014), 66–68.
2. Sorrentino, *Stephen Crane*, 68.
3. Sorrentino, 69.
4. R. W. Stallman, *Stephen Crane: A Biography* (New York: George Braziller, 1968), 33; Sorrentino, *Stephen Crane*, 76; Michael Robertson, *Stephen Crane, Journalism, and the Making of Modern American Literature* (New York: Columbia University Press, 1997), 55, 67; and James B. Colvert, *Stephen Crane* (New York: Harcourt Brace Jovanovich, 1984), 23.
5. Sorrentino, *Stephen Crane*, 69–70.
6. Sorrentino, 70–73.
7. Sorrentino, 73–74.
8. Harold Bloom, *Stephen Crane: Bloom's Modern Critical Views* (New York: Bloom's Literary Criticism, 2009), 8.
9. Sorrentino, *Stephen Crane*, 71, 75–77.
10. Sorrentino, 77.
11. Stephen Crane, *The New York City Sketches of Stephen Crane and Related Pieces*, edited by R. W. Stallman and E. R. Hagemann (New York: New York University Press, 1966) xiv; and Stallman, *Stephen Crane*, 31.
12. Crane, *New York City Sketches*, xiv–xv; and *New York Tribune*, June 1, 1891.
13. Stallman, *Stephen Crane*, 31–32.
14. Sorrentino, *Stephen Crane*, 88.
15. Stephen Crane, *Stephen Crane: Letters*, edited by R. W. Stallman and Lillian Gilkes (New York: New York University Press, 1960), 299.
16. Sorrentino, *Stephen Crane*, 79.
17. Sorrentino, 88–90.

Chapter 5. Fighting Joe

1. *Atlanta Constitution*, April 28, 1891.
2. *Seattle Post-Intelligencer*, March 29, 1891.
3. Matthew Bernstein, *George Hearst: Silver King of the Gilded Age* (Norman: University of Oklahoma Press, 2021), 208.

4. *Buffalo Morning Express*, December 28, 1891.
5. *Inter Ocean* (Chicago), December 8, 1891; and *Buffalo Morning Express*, December 28, 1891. Had Wheeler been appointed as chair of the Committee of Military Affairs in 1891, he wanted on his team Congressman Charles Belknap of Michigan, whom Wheeler had captured during the war and nearly shot as a spy. Approaching Belknap, Wheeler said to him, "General, I have been assured that I will be given the chairmanship of the Committee of Military Affairs. When you and I first met I came near taking your head. Now I am anxious to have the aid of the intelligence in that head upon this committee."
6. *Buffalo Morning Express*, December 28, 1891.
7. *Kansas City Star*, January 16, 1892; *Atchinson Daily Patriot* (Kansas), January 16, 1892; and *Iola Farmer's Friend* (Kansas), January 30, 1892.
8. *Atlanta Constitution*, January 17, 1892.
9. John Witherspoon DuBose, *General Joseph Wheeler and the Army of the Tennessee* (New York: Neale Publishing Company, 1912), 52.
10. *Weekly Times-Democrat* (Greenville, Mississippi), February 19, 1892.
11. Theodore Roosevelt, *The Selected Letters of Theodore Roosevelt*, edited by H. W. Brands (Lanham, MD: Roman & Littlefield, 2001), 82.
12. *Sheffield Weekly Enterprise* (Alabama), August 13, 1892; *Limestone Democrat* (Athens, Alabama), July 23, 1892; and *Choctaw Advocate* (Butler, Alabama), June 8, 1892.
13. *Florence Herald* (Alabama), August 11, 1892.
14. Paul Sorrentino, *Stephen Crane: A Life of Fire* (Cambridge, MA: Belknap Press of Harvard University Press, 2014), 99.
15. *New York Tribune*, August 21, 1892.
16. *New York Tribune*, August 24, 1892.
17. James B. Colvert, *Stephen Crane* (New York: Harcourt Brace Jovanovich, 1984), 37.
18. Linda H. Davis, *Badge of Courage: The Life of Stephen Crane* (Boston: Houghton Mifflin, 1998), 50.
19. Sorrentino, *Stephen Crane*, 99.
20. R. W. Stallman, *Stephen Crane: A Biography* (New York: George Braziller, 1968), 56.
21. Paul Auster, *Burning Boy: The Life and Work of Stephen Crane* (New York: Henry Holt and Company, 2021), 84.
22. *Florence Herald* (Alabama), November 3, 1892.
23. *Birmingham News*, November 6, 1892.
24. *San Francisco Examiner*, November 9, 1892.
25. Sorrentino, *Stephen Crane*, 101.
26. Sorrentino, 104.
27. *Weekly Advertiser* (Montgomery, Alabama), March 3, 1893.
28. Richard Harding Davis, *Adventures and Letters*, edited by Charles Belmont Davis (New York: Cosimo, 2005), 84.
29. *Moulton Advertiser* (Alabama), January 19, 1893; *Montgomery Advertiser*, May 9, 1893; *Scottsboro Citizen* (Alabama), August 30, 1894; and Edward G. Longacre, *A Soldier*

to the Last: Maj. Gen. Joseph Wheeler in Blue and Gray* (Washington, DC: Potomac Books, 2007), 209.

30. George Hillyer to Joseph Wheeler, February 6, 1894, Joseph Wheeler Papers, Alabama Department of Archives and History.
31. *New Decatur Adviser* (Alabama), April 2, 1914; Andrew Nelson Lytle, *Bedford Forrest and His Critter Company* (Nashville: J. S. Sanders & Company, 1984), 93; and *Independence Daily Reporter* (Kansas), August 25, 1896.
32. *Montgomery Advertiser*, August 26, 1894; and *Montgomery Advertiser*, August 28, 1894.
33. *Scottsboro Citizen* (Alabama), August 30, 1894.
34. *Alabama Enquirer* (Hartselle), October 25, 1892.
35. *Evening Star* (Washington, DC), December, 6, 1894.
36. Kenneth Whyte, *The Uncrowned King: The Sensational Rise of William Randolph Hearst* (New York: Counterpoint, 2009), 255; and *San Francisco Examiner*, September 20, 1895.
37. *Greenleaf Sentinel* (Kansas), January 4, 1895.

    With interest in the Civil War on the rise, the month after excerpts of Crane's *The Red Badge of Courage* appeared in newspapers, Governor William C. Oates of Alabama appointed Joseph Wheeler chair of a commission to determine the whereabouts of Alabama troops in Chattanooga and Chickamauga.
38. *Commercial Appeal* (Memphis), April 14, 1895.

Chapter 6. Police Commissioner Roosevelt

1. Edmund Morris, *The Rise of Theodore Roosevelt* (New York: Random House, 1979), 205.
2. Doris Kearns Goodwin, *The Bully Pulpit: Theodore Roosevelt, William Howard Taft, and the Golden Age of Journalism* (New York: Simon & Schuster, 2013), 204.
3. Goodwin, *Bully Pulpit*, 204.
4. *New York World*, May 17, 1895.
5. Thomas F. Byrnes, *Professional Criminals of America* (New York: Cassell & Company, 1886), 11; and *New York Times*, May 8, 1910.
6. William Bryk. "Inspector Thomas F. Byrnes, Inventor of the Third Degree," *New York Press*, September 4, 2001; and *New York Times*, May 8, 1910.
7. Morris, *Rise of Theodore Roosevelt*, 499.
8. Bryk, "Inspector Thomas F. Byrnes."
9. Goodwin, *Bully Pulpit*, 207.
10. Paul Sorrentino, *Stephen Crane: A Life of Fire* (Cambridge, MA: Belknap Press of Harvard University Press, 2014), 195; and David Freeland, *Automats, Taxi Dances, and Vaudeville: Excavating Manhattan's Lost Places of Leisure* (New York: New York University Press, 2009), 80.
11. Morris, *Rise of Theodore Roosevelt*, 507.
12. Morris, 506.

13. *San Francisco Examiner*, May 25, 1895.
14. Morris, *Rise of Theodore Roosevelt*, 507.
15. *San Francisco Examiner*, May 26, 1895.
16. Tom Buk-Swienty, *The Other Half: The Life of Jacob Riis and the World of Immigrant America* (New York: Norton, 2008), 250.
17. Buk-Swienty, *The Other Half*, 250–51; and Morris, *Rise of Theodore Roosevelt*, 508–509.
18. Buk-Swienty, *The Other Half*, 250–51; Goodwin, *Bully Pulpit*, 206; and Morris, *Rise of Theodore Roosevelt*, 509.
19. Morris, *Rise of Theodore Roosevelt*, 507, 509; Goodwin, *Bully Pulpit*, 208; and Buk-Swienty, *The Other Half*, 251.
20. *Salt Lake Herald*, July 28, 1895.
21. Arthur Lubow, *The Reporter Who Would Be King: A Biography of Richard Harding Davis* (New York: Scribner, 1992), 68.
22. Richard Harding Davis, *Adventures and Letters of Richard Harding Davis*, edited by Charles Belmont Davis (New York: Cosimo, 2005), 46.
23. Peggy Samuels and Harold Samuels, *Teddy Roosevelt at San Juan: The Making of a President* (College Station: Texas A&M University Press, 1997), 92
24. The following account on Davis's manner of speaking is drawn from John Fox Jr., Augustus Thomas, Theodore Roosevelt, and Gouverneur Morris, *R. H. D.: Appreciations of Richard Harding Davis* (New York: Scribner, 1917), 41.

    Although some thought that Davis's peculiar manner of speaking was a mix of Philadelphian crossed with an affected London accent, the St. Louis playwright Augustus Thomas disagreed. At his first meeting with Davis at the Lambs Club in a brownstone at 34 West 26th Street in the spring of 1889, Thomas noted that Davis did not pronounce his surname as a midwesterner might but instead as a Londoner would. "To spell his pronunciation Dyvis is to burlesque it slightly, but that is near as it can be given phonetically. Several other words containing a long *a* were sounded by him in the same way. . . . I am told that other men educated in certain Philadelphia schools have a similar diction, but at that time many of Mr. Davis's acquaintances thought the manner was an affectation. I mention the peculiarity, which after years convinced me was as native to him as the color of his eyes."
25. Goodwin, *Bully Pulpit*, 228.
26. Morris, *Rise of Theodore Roosevelt*, 509–10.
27. Morris, 510–11.
28. Lubow, *Reporter Who Would Be King*, 167.
29. *Indianapolis Journal*, June 10, 1895.
30. Lubow, *Reporter Who Would Be King*, 126.
31. Theodore Roosevelt, *The Selected Letters of Theodore Roosevelt*, edited by H. W. Brands (Lanham, MD: Rowman & Littlefield, 2001), 104.
32. Morris, *Rise of Theodore Roosevelt*, 511–12, 687; Goodwin, *The Bully Pulpit*, 208; Evan Thomas, *The War Lovers: Roosevelt, Lodge, Hearst, and the Rush to Empire, 1898* (New York: Back Bay Books, 2010), 59; Louis Auchincloss, *Theodore Roosevelt: The 26th President, 1901–1909*, The American Presidents (New York: Henry Holt, 2001),

32; Peggy Samuels and Harold Samuels. *Teddy Roosevelt at San Juan: The Making of a President* (College Station: Texas A&M University Press, 1997), 39; and Theodore Roosevelt, *The Rough Riders* (New York: Fall River, 2014), 28.

33. Janet B. Pascal, *Jacob Riis: Reporter and Reformer* (New York: Oxford University Press, 2005), 129; and Morris, *Rise of Theodore Roosevelt*, 503.
34. Morris, *Rise of Theodore Roosevelt*, 512–13.
35. Morris, 513.
36. Morris, 111–12.
37. Morris, 488.
38. Morris, 513.
39. Morris, 513, 518.
40. Roosevelt, *Selected Letters*, 104.
41. Morris, *Rise of Theodore Roosevelt*, 519.
42. Morris, 519–20.
43. Goodwin, *Bully Pulpit*, 211.
44. Morris, *Rise of Theodore Roosevelt*, 525.
45. Morris, 523.
46. Morris, 526.
47. Goodwin, *Bully Pulpit*, 210.
48. David Nasaw, *The Chief: The Life of William Randolph Hearst* (New York: Mariner Books, 2001), 97–98.

Chapter 7. The Invasion

1. David Nasaw, *The Chief: The Life of William Randolph Hearst* (New York: Mariner Books, 2001), 99; and *Los Angeles Herald*, October 5, 1895.
2. Nasaw, *The Chief*, 99–100.
3. Kenneth Whyte, *The Uncrowned King: The Sensational Rise of William Randolph Hearst* (New York: Counterpoint, 2009), 82.
4. Nasaw, *The Chief*, 99.
5. Whyte, *Uncrowned King*, 144.
6. W. A. Swanberg, *Citizen Hearst: A Biography of William Randolph Hearst* (New York: Colliers, 1961), 81; William Randolph Hearst, *William Randolph Hearst: A Portrait in His Own Words*, edited by Edmond D. Coblentz (New York: Simon and Schuster, 1952), 46; and *San Francisco Examiner*, September 3, 1888.
7. Nasaw, *The Chief*, 68.
8. Whyte, *Uncrowned King*, 279.
9. Nasaw, *The Chief*, 96; and Whyte, *Uncrowned King*, 228.
10. Willis J. Abbot, *Watching the World Go By* (Boston: Little, Brown, 1933), 145.
11. Whyte, *Uncrowned King*, 228, 230, 234.
12. Whyte, 228; Nasaw, *The Chief*, 113; and Judith Choate and James Canora, *Dining at Delmonico's: The Story of America's Oldest Restaurant* (New York: Stewart, Tabori & Chang, 2008), 49, 126, 129.
13. *Saint Paul Globe* (Minnesota), October 27, 1895.

14. Whyte, *Uncrowned King*, 288; and *Standard Union* (Brooklyn), December 7, 1895.
15. *Democrat and Chronicle* (Rochester, New York), December 26, 1895; *Idaho Statesman* (Boise), April 11, 1896; and Nasaw, *The Chief*, 81–82.
16. *Idaho Statesman* (Boise), April 11, 1896; and Nasaw, *The Chief*, 82.
17. Whyte, *Uncrowned King*, 105–6.
18. Whyte, *Uncrowned King*, 106; and Nasaw, *The Chief*, 103–4.
19. Swanberg, *Citizen Hearst*, 81–82; and Ferdinand Lundberg, *Imperial Hearst: A Social Biography* (New York: Random House, 1936), 53.
20. Swanberg, *Citizen Hearst*, 82.
21. Dennis Drabelle, *The Great American Railroad War: How Ambrose Bierce and Frank Norris Took on the Notorious Central Pacific Railroad* (New York: St. Martin's, 2012), 134.
22. Drabelle, *The Great American Railroad War*, 135.
23. Drabelle, 135.
24. Robert L. Duffus, "The Tragedy of Hearst," *World's Work*, October 1922, 624.
25. Upton Sinclair, *The Industrial Republic: A Study of the America of Ten Years Hence* (New York: Doubleday, Page & Co., 1907), 200, 202.
26. Sinclair, *The Industrial Republic*, 202.
27. *Buffalo Courier*, January 22, 1896.
28. *Saint Paul Globe* (Minnesota), October 27, 1895.
29. *Richmond Climax* (Kentucky), May 27, 1896.
30. Swanberg, *Citizen Hearst*, 82; and Nasaw, *The Chief*, 104.
31. *Buffalo Evening News*, January 23, 1896.
32. Swanberg, *Citizen Hearst*, 83.
33. Whyte, *Uncrowned King*, 107–8.
34. *Democrat and Chronicle* (Rochester, New York), February 22, 1896.
35. *New York Times*, March 2, 1896.
36. *Idaho Statesman* (Boise), April 11, 1896.
37. *Idaho Statesman*, April 11, 1896.
38. *Santa Cruz Sentinel*, March 20, 1896.
39. Theodore Roosevelt, *The Selected Letters of Theodore Roosevelt*, edited by H. W. Brands (Lanham, MD: Roman & Littlefield, 2001), 116.
40. Theodore Roosevelt, *Theodore Roosevelt: An Autobiography* (New York: Da Capo, 1985), 213.
41. *Democrat and Chronicle* (Rochester, New York), March 14, 1896.
42. *Buffalo Morning Express*, March 18, 1896.
43. Swanberg, *Citizen Hearst*, 83.
44. Richard Harding Davis, *Adventures and Letters of Richard Harding Davis*, edited by Charles Belmont Davis (New York: Cosimo, 2005), 132; and Richard Harding Davis, *A Year from a Reporter's Note-Book* (New York: Harper & Brothers, 1898), 5.
45. *New York Tribune*, April 20, 1898.
46. Drabelle, *Great American Railroad War*, 178–79.
47. *San Francisco Call*, April 26, 1896; and *New York Tribune*, April 20, 1896.

48. Davis, *Adventures and Letters*, 139.
49. *New York Times*, May 24, 1896; *Pittsburgh Post*, May 27, 1896; and *Kansas City Journal*, May 29, 1896.
50. *Buffalo Enquirer*, June 10, 1896.
51. *Brooklyn Journal*, June 30, 1896; and Swanberg, *Citizen Hearst*, 84.
52. Swanberg, *Citizen Hearst*, 84–85.
53. Swanberg, *Citizen Hearst*, 84–85. See also Duffus, "The Tragedy of Hearst," 627.
54. Swanberg, *Citizen Hearst*, 86.
55. Whyte, *Uncrowned King*, 200, 201; R. W. Stallman, *Stephen Crane: A Biography* (New York: George Braziller, 1968), 201; and Paul Auster, *Burning Boy: The Life and Work of Stephen Crane* (New York: Henry Holt, 2021), 359–60.
56. Whyte, *Uncrowned King*, 200, 201; and Stallman, *Stephen Crane*, 201.
57. Ben Procter, *William Randolph Hearst: The Early Years, 1863–1910* (Oxford: Oxford University Press, 1998), 47; Whyte, *Uncrowned King*, 260; Stallman, *Stephen Crane*, 221; and George Bronson Rea, *Facts and Fakes about Cuba* (New York: G. Munroe's Sons, 1897), 147.

    In his 1897 history *Facts and Fakes in Cuba*, Charles Bronson Rea dished that it was Frederic Lawrence's inflammatory article on Spain's General Weyler in the *New York Journal* that caused Weyler to expel Lawrence from Cuba.
58. Paul Sorrentino, *Stephen Crane: A Life of Fire* (Cambridge, MA: Belknap Press of Harvard University Press, 2014), 205.
59. Stallman, *Stephen Crane*, 227–28.
60. Sorrentino, *Stephen Crane*, 206–7; and Linda H. Davis, *Badge of Courage: The Life of Stephen Crane* (Boston: Houghton Mifflin, 1998), 164–66.
61. Stallman, *Stephen Crane*, 232; and Sorrentino, *Stephen Crane*, 209.
62. Stallman, *Stephen Crane*, 221.
63. Stephen Crane, *Active Service* (New York: Frederick A. Stokes, 1899), 50–51.
64. Hearst, *William Randolph Hearst*, 258.
65. Sorrentino, *Stephen Crane*, 210.

Chapter 8. Silver and Gold

1. *Scottsboro Citizen* (Alabama), September 20, 1895.
2. *Courtland Enterprise* (Alabama), October 18, 1895.
3. Joseph Wheeler and Charles H. Grosvenor, "Our Duty in the Venezuelan Crisis," *North American Review* 161, no. 468 (November 1895): 628–33.
4. Joseph Wheeler and Charles H. Grosvenor, "Our Duty in the Venezuelan Crisis" *North American Review* 161, no. 468 (November 1895): 628–33.
5. Grover Cleveland, "Message Regarding Venezuelan-British Dispute," December 17, 1895, Presidential Speeches: Grover Cleveland Presidency, Miller Center, University of Virginia.
6. *San Francisco Examiner*, October 31, 1891; *New York Journal*, December 22, 1895; and Kenneth Whyte, *The Uncrowned King: The Sensational Rise of William Randolph Hearst* (New York: Counterpoint, 2009), 90.

7. Theodore Roosevelt, *The Selected Letters of Theodore Roosevelt*, edited by H. W. Brands (Lanham, MD: Roman & Littlefield, 2001), 112.
8. Theodore Roosevelt, *Letters and Speeches*, edited by Louis Auchincloss (New York: Penguin Putnam, 2004), 80, 81.
9. Evan Thomas, *The War Lovers: Roosevelt, Lodge, Hearst, and the Rush to Empire, 1898* (New York: Back Bay Books, 2010), 70–71; Roosevelt, *Selected Letters*, 72; *Los Angeles Herald*, June 9, 1887; Matthew Bernstein, *George Hearst: Silver King of the Gilded Age* (Norman: University of Oklahoma Press, 2021), 168; and Joseph Wheeler, *A Revised System of Cavalry Tactics: For the Use of the Cavalry and Mounted Infantry, C.S.A.* (Mobile, AL: S. H. Goetzel & Co., 1863), i.
10. Quoted *Stevenson Chronicle* (Alabama), July 20, 1896.
11. Edward G. Longacre, *A Soldier to the Last: Major General Joseph Wheeler in Blue and Gray* (Washington, DC: Potomac Books, 2007), 216.
12. George Bronson Rea, *Facts and Fakes about Cuba* (New York: G. Munroe's Sons, 1897), 162, 172.
13. Longacre, *Soldier to the Last*, 216; *New York Sun*, October 6, 1896; *Evening Journal*, October 6, 1896; John Lawrence Tone, *War and Genocide in Cuba, 1895–1898* (Chapel Hill: North Carolina Press, 2006), 8, 9; and Rea, *Facts and Fakes*, 180.

    In early October 1896, the *Sun* and the *Evening Journal* whipped up further outrage against Spain by printing fictitious articles brimming with selachian atrocities. Printed in the *Sun* on October 6, 1896, was this headline: "WEYLER—BUTCHER. *His Shocking Crimes Against Civilization.* Prisoners Fed to Sharks." The *Evening Journal* also ran the story: "CUBANS FED TO SHARKS. *Sixty-three Prisoners Disappear in Twenty-six Days, and Marked as Released.* Cries Heard at Night. They are Taken Outside the Harbor, and the Silent Ferryman Comes Back Alone."
14. Roosevelt, *Selected Letters*, 116–17.
15. Josep Conangla, *Memoir of My Youth in Cuba: A Soldier in the Spanish Army during the Separatist War, 1895–1898* (Tuscaloosa: University of Alabama Press, 2017), 54–55.
16. *The Scottsboro Citizen* (Alabama), April 23, 1896; *Moulton Advertiser* (Alabama), May 21, 1896; Louis W. Koenig, *Bryan: A Political Biography of William Jennings Bryan* (New York: Putnam, 1971), 274.
17. *Franklin Times* (North Carolina), September 18, 1896; and *New York Times*, January 28, 1896.
18. *Stevenson Chronicle* (Alabama), October 20, 1896.
19. *Franklin Times* (North Carolina), September 18, 1896.
20. *Franklin Times* (North Carolina), September 18, 1896.
21. *Evening Star* (Washington, DC), May 20, 1896; Ella Wheeler to Joseph Wheeler, July 4, 1889, Joseph Wheeler Papers, Alabama Department of Archives and History; and Ella Wheeler to Joseph Wheeler, June 11, 1896, Joseph Wheeler Papers.

    Tufts College Library in Massachusetts, the New England Historical Society, and the City Library Association in Boston were three of many libraries that accepted copies of the Wheeler-Jones family tree. Although the book was published in 1896,

Wheeler would produce a revised edition in 1902, including comparisons of the battles his ancestors fought to Spanish-American War battles.

22. *Stevenson Chronicle* (Alabama), October 20, 1896.
23. William T. Farley to Joseph Wheeler, August 9, 1896, Joseph Wheeler Papers.
24. *Birmingham News*, August 22, 1896.
25. *Chattanooga Daily Times*, September 2, 1896.
26. *Leighton News* (Alabama), September 28, 1896.
27. *Independence Daily Reporter* (Kansas), August 25, 1896.
28. *The Tennessean* (Nashville), October 3, 1896.
29. *The Tennessean* (Nashville), October 3, 1896; Christopher Maloney, "Oscar Hundley," Encyclopedia of Alabama, https://encyclopediaofalabama.org/article/oscar-hundley/; and *The Tennessean* (Nashville), October 3, 1896.
30. *Stevenson Chronicle* (Alabama), October 20, 1896.
31. David Nasaw, *The Chief: The Life of William Randolph Hearst* (New York: Mariner Books, 2001), 118.
32. Nasaw, *The Chief*, 118.
33. Nasaw, *The Chief*, 118.
34. Roosevelt, *Selected Letters*, 121–22.
35. William Randolph Hearst, *William Randolph Hearst: A Portrait in His Own Words*, edited by Edmond D. Coblentz (New York: Simon and Schuster, 1952), 36.
36. Roosevelt, *Selected Letters*, 124.
37. Joseph Wheeler circular, October 20, 1896, Joseph Wheeler Papers.
38. Edmund Morris, *Rise of Theodore Roosevelt* (New York: Random House, 1979), 530.
39. Nasaw, *The Chief*, 119.
40. Arthur Lubow, *The Reporter Who Would Be King: A Biography of Richard Harding Davis* (New York: Scribner, 1992), 136.
41. Nasaw, *The Chief*, 119; Robert L. Duffus, "The Tragedy of Hearst," *World's Work*, October 1922, 627; and Lubow, *Reporter Who Would Be King*, 136.
42. *Moulton Advertiser* (Alabama), January 6, 1898.
43. *Leighton News* (Alabama), December 31, 1897.

Chapter 9. Sunk

1. Paul Sorrentino, *Stephen Crane: A Life of Fire* (Cambridge, MA: Belknap Press of Harvard University Press, 2014), 213.
2. Charles Michelson. "Introduction," in Stephen Crane, *Midnight Sketches and Other Impressions* (New York: Knopf, 1926), iv.
3. Sorrentino, *Stephen Crane*, 213–14.
4. Stephen Crane, *Stephen Crane: Letters*, edited by R. W. Stallman and Lillian Gilkes (New York: New York University Press, 1960), 134.
5. "Houston Street: Jacksonville's Red Light District," *Metro Jacksonville*, January 22, 2008; Arthur Lubow, *The Reporter Who Would Be King: A Biography of Richard Harding Davis* (New York: Scribner, 1992), 126; and Sorrentino, *Stephen Crane*, 217.

6. Sorrentino, *Stephen Crane*, 218–19.
7. Sorrentino, 217–18.
8. Kenneth Whyte, *The Uncrowned King: The Sensational Rise of William Randolph Hearst* (New York: Counterpoint, 2009), 297.
9. Sorrentino, *Stephen Crane*, 219; and Stephen Crane, "Stephen Crane's Own Story," *New York Press*, January 7, 1897.
10. *Philadelphia Times*, October 8, 1896; *Philadelphia Inquirer*, October 11, 1896; Sorrentino, *Stephen Crane*, 220; and Ralph D. Paine, *Roads of Adventure* (Boston: Houghton Mifflin, 1922), 168.
11. Stephen Crane, "Stephen Crane's Own Story," *New York Press*, January 7, 1897; and Sorrentino, *Stephen Crane*, 220.
12. Crane, "Stephen Crane's Own Story."
13. Lars Schoultz, *That Infernal Little Cuban Republic: The United States and the Cuban Revolution* (Chapel Hill: University of North Carolina Press, 2009), 20.
14. Hugh Thomas, *Cuba or the Pursuit of Freedom* (New York: Harper and Row, 1971); and Robert Granville Caldwell, *The Lopez Expeditions to Cuba: 1848–1851* (Princeton, NJ: Princeton University Press, 1915), 45.
15. Tom Chaffin, *Fatal Glory: Narciso López and the First Clandestine U.S. War against Cuba* (Charlotteville: University Press of Virginia, 1996), 47–48; and Caldwell, *The Lopez Expeditions to Cuba*, 64.
16. *Daily News* (London), September 24, 1851; and Israel Smith Clare, *Library of Universal History* (New York: Union Book Company, 1906), 4,396.
17. *Richmond Enquirer* (Virginia), September 12, 1851.
18. Crane, "Stephen Crane's Own Story."
19. Sorrentino, *Stephen Crane*, 222.
20. Sorrentino, 223–34.
21. Crane, *Stephen Crane*, 136–37.
22. Sorrentino, *Stephen Crane*, 224.
23. Crane, *Stephen Crane*, 138.
24. Stephen Crane, "The Open Boat," *Scribner's Magazine*, June 1897.
25. Crane, 137.
26. Crane, 138.
27. Sorrentino, *Stephen Crane*, 224.

Chapter 10. Furnishing the Pictures

1. Arthur Lubow, *The Reporter Who Would Be King: A Biography of Richard Harding Davis* (New York: Scribner, 1992), 138.

   The following account of the difficulty of Hearst reporters traveling from Key West to Cuba is drawn from Charles Michelson, *The Ghost Talks* (New York: Putnam, 1944), 88.

   On the ill-fated voyage to Cuba with Davis and Remington aboard the *Vamoose*, Charley Michelson recalled, "Hearst kindly furnished us with his yacht Vamoose. . . .

It was a grand thing in the Hudson River, but I never could find a captain who would take us across the Gulf Stream to Cuba."

2. Lubow, *Reporter*, 138. Asked later about his scheme to throttle the Chinese cook and with Davis steal his makeshift raft, Remington explained that he didn't need the cook. "Why, Davis alone was worth a dozen sea-cooks."
3. Richard Harding Davis, *Adventures and Letters of Richard Harding Davis*, edited by Charles Belmont Davis (New York: Cosimo, 2005), 146–47.
4. Langford, *Davis*, 101.
5. Davis, *Adventures and Letters*, 146–47.
6. Kenneth Whyte, *The Uncrowned King: The Sensational Rise of William Randolph Hearst* (New York: Counterpoint, 2009), 294–96.

 In the following account from Ralph D. Paine, *Roads of Adventure* (Boston: Houghton Mifflin, 1922), 63, Paine recalled the meeting between himself and Hearst when he was first presented the sword:

> With dazzled eyes I beheld the costly weapon as it rested in a mahogany case. The scabbard was ornately adorned, the hilt plated with gold and sparkling with small diamonds. It had been made by a famous firm of Fifth Avenue jewelers. Here was a sword which looked like two thousand dollars. Displaying the blade, Mr. Hearst called attention to the engraved inscriptions, such as "To Maximo Gomez, Commander-in-Chief of the Army of the Cuban Republic," and "Viva Cuba Libre."
>
> "Very handsome," said I. "Old Gomez will be tickled to death, when he gets it."
>
> "That is the idea, when he gets it," observed the bland, debonair Mr. Hearst. "I have been trying to find somebody foolish enough to carry this elegant sword to Gomez. I am perfectly frank with you. These inscriptions would be devilish hard to explain to the Spanish army, if you happen to be caught, wouldn't they?"
>
> "And you want me to try to present this eighteen-karat sword to Gomez, with your compliments?"
>
> "If you don't mind," was the hopeful reply. "I swear I don't know what else to do with the confounded thing. Of course if you are nabbed at sea, you can probably chuck it overboard in time—"
>
> "And if I get surrounded on land, perhaps I can swallow it, Mr. Hearst. Never mind that. I am the damn fool you have been looking for. Tuck the glittering weapon in the mahogany case and I will lug it along right now."
>
> He shook hands with me and I passed out into the night, the long, polished box under one arm.

7. Lubow, *Reporter Who Would Be King*, 138; and Whyte, *Uncrowned King*, 296.
8. Lubow, *Reporter Who Would Be King*, 139.
9. Lubow, *Reporter Who Would Be King*, 139.

10. *San Francisco Examiner*, June 4, 1898.
11. Josep Conangla, *Memoir of My Youth in Cuba: A Soldier in the Spanish Army during the Separatist War, 1895–1898* (Tuscaloosa: University of Alabama Press, 2017), 71.
12. James Creelman, *On the Great Highway: The Wanderings and Adventures of a Special Correspondent* (Boston: Lothrop, 1901), 158–59; *New York Journal*, October 8, 1896; and Whyte, *Uncrowned King*, 263.
13. Lubow, *Reporter Who Would Be King*, 139.
14. Creelman, *On the Great Highway*, 178.
15. Creelman, *On the Great Highway*, 178.
16. Whyte, *Uncrowned King*, 301.
17. W. Joseph Campbell, *Yellow Journalism: Puncturing the Myths, Defining the Legacies* (Westport, CT: Praeger, 2001).
18. Whyte, *Uncrowned King*, 301.
19. W. A. Swanberg, *Citizen Hearst: A Biography of William Randolph Hearst* (New York: Colliers, 1961), 108; David Nasaw, *The Chief: The Life of William Randolph Hearst* (New York: Mariner Books, 2001), 127–28; and Whyte, *Uncrowned King*, 300–302.
20. Lubow, *Reporter Who Would Be King*, 140; and Laird W. Bergad, *Cuban Rural Society in the Nineteenth Century: The Social Economic History of Monoculture in Matanzas* (Princeton, NJ: Princeton University Press, 1990), 314, 318.
21. Lubow, *Reporter Who Would Be King*, 140.
22. Lubow, 140.

    The following account of Davis's feelings toward Remington and of Remington's history is drawn from Poultney Bigelow, *Seventy Summers*, Vol. 1 (London: Edward Arnold & Co., 1925), 302, 305–6; and Whyte, *Uncrowned King*, 290.

    Although initially Davis enjoyed Remington's company, that he would ultimately become aggravated by the artist was inevitable. At first glance, Remington seemed Davis's sort of fellow. Big, blond, and burly, Remington joined the Yale football team, dramatically dipping his jersey in blood from a New Haven slaughterhouse before lining up with his teammates against Harvard. After quitting the art school, Remington became a ranchman on the Rio Grande. There on the border of Texas and Mexico, his sheep "showed great capacity for absorbing disease and otherwise thinning his flock," as a fellow Yalensian, Poultney Bigelow, noted. Broke, Remington returned to New York City, merging his artistic talent with his wild experiences on the frontier. Along with sculpting and painting the American West, he enjoyed drawing "men with bark on," one of his favorite expressions. That Remington was a man's man who had bulled his way to the top of his field was something that Davis could very well appreciate.

    But as the weeks passed Davis began to realize he and the thirty-seven-year-old artist were as different as night and day. Davis quickly recognized Remington as a hard drinker, a braggart, and a chauvinist full of derisive and martial opinions. Ultimately, theirs proved to a mismatched partnership.
23. Davis, *Adventures and Letters*, 148–49.
24. Paul Sorrentino, *Stephen Crane: A Life of Fire* (Cambridge, MA: Belknap Press of Harvard University Press, 2014), 210–11; Harlan C. Herner, *The Arizona Rough Riders*

(Tucson: University of Arizona, 1965), 3; John Lawrence Tone, *War and Genocide in Cuba, 1895–1898* (Chapel Hill: University of North Carolina Press, 2006), 1, 16; and G. I. A. O'Toole, *The Spanish War: An American Epic, 1898* (New York: Norton, 1984), 35.

25. Sorrentino, *Stephen Crane*, 210–11; Tone, *War and Genocide*, 1, 17, 25, 26, 29; and Conangla, *Memoir of My Youth in Cuba*, 38.

Savage conditions in Cuba were worsened by Madrid's policy of grossly underpaying colonial officials, motivating Spaniards to implement a combination of taxation and graft to enrich themselves. Particularly in eastern Cuba, or the Oriente, a mountainous and rural region considered the Wild West of the island where outlawry became commonplace, guerrillas were loath to surrender to Spanish rule.

26. Davis, *Adventures and Letters*, 150–51.
27. Davis, 150–51.
28. Tone, *War and Genocide*, 9–10.
29. Lubow, *Reporter Who Would Be King*, 141.
30. Lubow, 137, 142.

The following account of George Bronson Rea and Harry Scovel is drawn from George Bronson Rea, *Facts and Fakes about Cuba* (New York: G. Munroe's Sons, 1897), 23, 201–2, 261–63; F. Lauriston Bullard, *Famous War Correspondents* (Boston: Little, Brown, 1914), 410, 411; Leslie Easton Clark, *George Bronson Rea, Propagandist: The Life and Times of a Mercenary Journalist* (Madison, NJ: Fairleigh Dickinson University Press, 2017), 2; and Joyce Milton, *The Yellow Kids: Foreign Correspondence in the Heyday of Yellow Journalism* (New York: HarperCollins, 1989), 143.

Although George Bronson Rea and Harry Scovel were two of the most successful war correspondents in Cuba before the United States joined the war, often traveling together, in some respects they were polar opposites.

A New Yorker struck with wanderlust, Rea had joined up with the US Navy before hiring on at a Cuban sugarcane plantation as an engineer and bookkeeper. When war broke out in 1895 and the Spanish burned the plantation, Rea found employment as James Gordon Bennett Jr.'s newest *New York Herald* war correspondent covering the Cuban War of Independence while traveling with Gómez. But Rea began to resent the behavior of Cuban *laborantes*, passive Cuban insurgents who fed American correspondents in Havana fictitious stories of Spanish atrocities. That and the fact that Bennett Jr. was said to be heavily invested in Spanish bonds may have influenced Rea to become one of the few American war correspondents in Cuba with a somewhat pro-Spanish slant. Eventually, Gómez accused Rea of being a spy. Pacified only slightly, when Gómez threatened to shoot Rea for his unflattering portrayals of him in the *Herald*, Rea temporarily returned to the United States.

Scovel, on the other hand, was fervently pro-Cuba, so much so in fact that Pulitzer Prize–winning historian Frederic Lauriston Bullard called him "the best known and most bitterly hated American in Cuba." Traveling to New York City, Scovel had gotten himself hired by the *World* as its newest war correspondent and soon proved his worth dispatching stories highlighting Cuban valor and Spanish oppression. Although

Scovel was expelled to the United States after being captured by the Spanish in 1897, he returned in 1898.

Along with Grover Flint, a correspondent for the *Journal* who spent four months in Cuba, Davis respected Rea and Scovel. Remarked Davis, "They are taking chances that no war correspondent ever took in any war in any part of the world. . . . The reckless bravery and the unselfishness of the correspondents in the field in Cuba today are without parallel. It is as dangerous to seek for Gomez as Stanley found it to seek for Livingstone. . . . [I]t is well that you should know that the names of these correspondents are Grover Flint, Sylvester Scovel and George Bronson Rae [*sic*]."

31. Rea, *Facts and Fakes*, 202.
32. Lubow, *Reporter Who Would Be King*, 142.

    The following account of Davis's time in Cuba while working for Hearst is drawn from Paine, *Roads of Adventure*, 61.

    Ralph D. Paine, also employed by Hearst's *Journal*, reflected on Davis in his 1923 autobiography. "Richard Harding Davis, probably the most brilliant war correspondent of his generation, was sent to Cuba by Mr. Hearst, but all his efforts to evade the elaborate espionage of the Spanish officials were thwarted. He saw what they permitted him to see."
33. Lubow, *Reporter Who Would Be King*, 142.
34. Ferdinant Lundberg, *Imperial Hearst: A Social Biography* (New York: Random House, 1936), 69; and Lubow, *Reporter Who Would Be King*, 142.
35. William Randolph Hearst, *William Randolph Hearst: A Portrait in His Own Words*, edited by Edmond D. Coblentz (New York: Simon and Schuster, 1952), 58.
36. *New York World*, February 17, 1897.
37. *New York World*, February 18, 1897; *New York World*, February 21, 1897; and *New York World*, March 12, 1897.
38. Lubow, *Reporter Who Would Be King*, 143–45.
39. R. W. Stallman, *Stephen Crane: A Biography* (New York: George Braziller, 1968), 197.
40. Davis, *Adventures and Letters*, 152.
41. Lubow, *Reporter Who Would Be King*, 123–25.
42. *Buffalo Morning Express*, May 30, 1897.
43. Davis, *Adventures and Letters*, 152–53. See also Lubow, *Reporter Who Would Be King*, 146.
44. Lubow, *Reporter Who Would Be King*, 146; and Stallman, *Stephen Crane*, 268.
45. Davis, *Adventures and Letters*, 152–53.
46. Davis, 155.
47. Davis, 155.
48. Stanley Wertheim and Paul Sorrentino, *The Crane Log: A Documentary Life of Stephen Crane, 1871–1900* (New York: G. K. Hall, 1994), 260.
49. Davis, *Adventures and Letters*, 157.
50. Lubow, *Reporter Who Would Be King*, 149; and Scott C. Osborn, "Stephen Crane and Cora Taylor: Some Corrections," *American Literature* 26, no. 53 (1954): 416–18.
51. Davis, *Adventures and Letters*, 159–60.

Chapter 11. Furnishing the War

1. *San Francisco Examiner*, April 7, 1897.
2. Thomas S. Duke, *Celebrated Criminal Cases of America* (San Francisco: James H. Barry Company, 1910), 641–43; Ferdinand Lundberg, *Imperial Hearst: A Social Biography* (New York: Random House, 1936), 60–61; and A. J. Liebling, "The Case of the Scattered Dutchman," *New Yorker*, September 24, 1955.
3. John D. Stevens, *Sensationalism and the New York Press* (New York: Columbia University, 1991), 92.
4. Duke, *Celebrated Criminal Cases of America*, 641–43; Lundberg, *Imperial Hearst*, 60–61; and Liebling, "The Case of the Scattered Dutchman."
5. *New York Journal*, June 30, 1897; *New York Journal*, July 1, 1897; and W. Joseph Campbell, *The Year That Defined American Journalism: 1897 and the Clash of Paradigms* (New York: Routledge, 2006), 84–85.
6. Duke, *Celebrated Criminal Cases of America*, 641–43; Lundberg, *Imperial Hearst*, 60–61; and Liebling, "The Case of the Scattered Dutchman."
7. Charles Michelson, *The Ghost Talks* (New York: Putnam, 1944), 81.
8. W. A. Swanberg, *Citizen Hearst: A Biography of William Randolph Hearst* (New York: Colliers, 1961), 107; and *San Francisco Examiner*, August 18, 1897.
9. David Nasaw, *The Chief: The Life of William Randolph Hearst* (New York: Mariner Books, 2001), 73, 113–14; and *Brooklyn Daily Eagle*, March 15, 1939.

   The following account of Hearst's friendship with Pancoast is drawn from *Harrisburg Evening News* (Pennsylvania), February 4, 1938, and Swanberg, *Citizen Hearst*, 54–55.

   On February 4, 1888, George E. Pancoast walked into an office in the Examiner Building. Pancoast was a practical joker with a puckish smile who had previously worked as a Boston printer and as a song-and-dance man at country road shows. He asked to see the foreman of the composing room.

   "I want a job," Pancoast said when the foreman arrived. Though born in New Hampshire, Pancoast spoke with a Boston accent.

   Dubiously, the foreman said, "Well, we have an opening, but I'm sick and tired of putting on 'boomers' [transient workers]. I'll tell you what I'll do, though—give me your word that if you'll make the grade you'll stay on the job at least six months."

   Pancoast stayed on the job for over fifty years. Initially, he caught Hearst's attention by playing a mild joke on Hearst's copy editor, Ike Allen. Moments later when Will asked Pancoast if he knew shorthand, Pancoast responded, "No, but I know longhand."

   "That's good enough for me," Hearst said, making Pancoast his personal secretary.

   Hearst quickly learned from Pancoast the joys of photography and the fine points of typesetting. Hearst also made a lifelong friend.
10. Nasaw, *The Chief*, 114; and *Democrat and Chronicle* (Rochester, New York), December 30, 1897.
11. Nasaw, *The Chief*, 115.

12. Nasaw, 115.
13. Upton Sinclair, *The Industrial Republic: A Study of the America of Ten Years Hence* (New York: Doubleday, Page & Co., 1907), 203.
14. Josep Conangla, *Memoir of My Youth in Cuba: A Soldier in the Spanish Army during the Separatist War, 1895–1898* (Tuscaloosa: University of Alabama Press, 2017), 106–7.
15. Conangla, *Memoir of My Youth in Cuba*, 107.
16. James Creelman, *On the Great Highway: The Wanderings and Adventures of a Special Correspondent* (Boston: Lothrop, 1901), 179–80.
17. James Creelman, *On the Great Highway: The Wanderings and Adventures of a Special Correspondent* (Boston: Lothrop, 1901), 179–80.
18. Nasaw, *The Chief*, 129.
19. *New York Journal*, August 21, 1897; *New York Journal*, August 26, 1897; and Nasaw, *The Chief*, 128–29.
20. Michelson, *Ghost Talks*, 88.
21. Edmund Morris, *The Rise of Theodore Roosevelt* (New York: Random House, 1979), 606–7.
22. *New York Sun*, August 23, 1897.
23. Kenneth Whyte, *The Uncrowned King: The Sensational Rise of William Randolph Hearst* (New York: Counterpoint, 2009), 323–24.
24. Whyte, *Uncrowned King*, 325; Michelson, *Ghost Talks*, 88; and William Randolph Hearst, *William Randolph Hearst: A Portrait in His Own Words*, edited by Edmond D. Coblentz (New York: Simon and Schuster, 1952), 58.
25. Evangelina Cisneros and Karl Decker, *The Story of Evangelina Cisneros* (New York: Continental Publishing, 1897), 62–65.
26. Cisneros and Decker, *The Story of Evangelina Cisneros*, 67–68.
27. Cisneros and Decker, *The Story of Evangelina Cisneros*, 73–74; and John Muir, *A Thousand-Mile Walk to the Gulf* (Boston: Houghton Mifflin, 1916), 155.
28. Cisneros and Decker, *The Story of Evangelina Cisneros*, 73–74.
29. W. Joseph Campbell, "Not a Hoax: New Evidence in the New York Journal's Rescue of Evangelina Cisneros," *American Journalism* 19, no. 4 (Fall 2002): 123.
30. Cisneros and Decker, *The Story of Evangelina Cisneros*, 74–83.
31. Cisneros and Decker, 84–101.
32. Campbell, "Not a Hoax," 123–24.
33. Cisneros and Decker, *The Story of Evangelina Cisneros*, 108.
34. Cisneros and Decker, 102–17.
35. Conangla, *Memoir of My Youth in Cuba*, 108; and William E. Leuchtenburg, "The Needless War with Spain," *American Heritage* 8, no. 2 (February 1957).
36. *New York Journal*, October 12, 1897, https://www.americanheritage.com/needless-war-spain.
37. Whyte, *Uncrowned King*, 325.
38. Nasaw, *The Chief*, 131.
39. Whyte, *Uncrowned King*, 332.

40. Nasaw, *The Chief*, 131; and Campbell, "Not a Hoax," 123–24.

Evangelina and the rescuer who put her up in his Havana house, Carlos Carbonell, married months after her escape. Together they had two daughters. Carlos died in 1916, Evangelina in 1970, both of them celebrated for their daring roles in the Cuban War of Independence.

41. Charles Johnson Post, *The Little War of Private Post: The Spanish-American War Seen Up Close* (Lincoln: University of Nebraska Press, 1999), 4–5.
42. Theodore Roosevelt, *Letters and Speeches*, edited by Louis Auchincloss (New York: Penguin Putnam, 2004), 121.
43. *Boston Globe*, September 19, 1897.
44. John P. Dyer, *From Shiloh to San Juan: The Life of Fightin' Joe Wheeler* (Baton Rouge: Louisiana State Press, 1941), 217.
45. G. I. A. O'Toole, *The Spanish War: An American Epic, 1898* (New York: Norton, 1984), 21, 25–26.
46. *New York Journal*, February 11, 1898; *New York Journal*, February 12, 1898; and Gary Scharnorst, *Julian Hawthorne: The Life of a Prodigal Son* (Urbana: University of Illinois Press, 2014), 155–56.
47. O'Toole, *The Spanish War*, 112.
48. O'Toole, 27.
49. *New York Journal*, February 12, 1898.
50. Conangla, *Memoir of My Youth in Cuba*, 112.
51. O'Toole, *The Spanish War*, 28.
52. O'Toole, 30–31.
53. O'Toole, 31.
54. Conangla, *Memoir of My Youth in Cuba*, 112–13.
55. O'Toole, *The Spanish War*, 29, 31.
56. O'Toole, 30.
57. Harlan C. Herner, *The Arizona Rough Riders* (Tucson: University of Arizona, 1965), 9.
58. Hearst, *William Randolph Hearst*, 59.

Chapter 12. Remember the *Maine*

1. *Indianapolis Journal*, February 17, 1898; and *Semi-Weekly Messenger* (Wilmington, NC), February 18, 1898.
2. John P. Dyer, *From Shiloh to San Juan: The Life of Fightin' Joe Wheeler* (Baton Rouge: Louisiana State Press, 1941), 219.
3. *San Francisco Examiner*, February 16, 1898.
4. *New York Journal*, February 16, 1898.
5. Evan Thomas, *The War Lovers: Roosevelt, Lodge, Hearst, and the Rush to Empire, 1898* (New York: Back Bay Books, 2010), 213.
6. *New York Journal*, February 17, 1898.
7. John D. Long, Journal entry, February 26, 1898, John Davis Long Papers, 1820–1943, Massachusetts Historical Society, Boston.

8. G. I. A. O'Toole, *The Spanish War: An American Epic, 1898* (New York: Norton, 1984), 125.
9. W. A. Swanberg, *Citizen Hearst: A Biography of William Randolph Hearst* (New York: Colliers, 1961), 143; Thomas, *War Lovers*, 223–24; *Courier-Louisville* (Kentucky), March 6, 1898; and *Inter Ocean* (Chicago), October 9, 1898.
10. Gary Scharnorst, *Julian Hawthorne: The Life of a Prodigal Son* (Chicago: University of Illinois Press, 2014), 156; and *San Francisco Examiner*, February 19, 1898.
11. *Henderson Gold Leaf* (North Carolina), February 24, 1898.
12. *Birmingham News*, February 24, 1898.
13. *Scottsboro Citizen*, March 3, 1898; and *Scottsboro Citizen*, March 10, 1898.
14. Theodore Roosevelt, *Theodore Roosevelt: An Autobiography* (New York: Da Capo, 1985), 218–19.
15. Roosevelt, *Theodore Roosevelt*, 218–19.
16. Thomas, *War Lovers*, 216; and Edmund Morris, *Rise of Theodore Roosevelt* (New York: Random House, 1979), 628.
17. Thomas, *War Lovers*, 217.
18. John D. Long, Journal entry, February 26, 1898, John Davis Long Papers, 1820–1943, Massachusetts Historical Society, Boston.
19. *New York Journal*, March 4, 1898; and Doris Kearns Goodwin, *The Bully Pulpit: Theodore Roosevelt, William Howard Taft, and the Golden Age of Journalism* (New York: Simon & Schuster, 2013), 482.
20. *New York Journal*, March 9, 1898.
21. *Washington Times*, March 6, 1898; *Gadsden-Times News* (Alabama), March 10, 1898; *Evening Star* (Washington, DC), March 14, 1898; *New York Journal*, March 9, 1898; and Edward G. Longacre, *A Soldier to the Last: Major General Joseph Wheeler in Blue and Gray* (Washington, DC: Potomac Books, 2007), 217.
22. Dyer, *From Shiloh to San Juan*, 219.
23. Thomas Clarke Jr. to Joseph Wheeler, April 25, 1898, Joseph Wheeler Papers, Alabama Department of Archives and History.
24. Dyer, *From Shiloh to San Juan*, 219.
25. *New York Journal*, March 14, 1898.
26. *New York Journal*, March 17, 1898; *New York Journal*, March 18, 1898; and John L. Offner, *An Unwanted War: The Diplomacy of the United States & Spain over Cuba, 1895–1898* (Chapel Hill: University of North Carolina Press, 1992), 130.
27. *International Gazette* (Black Rock, New York), March 19, 1898.
28. Thomas, *War Lovers*, 223.

The following account of Roosevelt's opinion of Hearst is drawn from Theodore Roosevelt, *Letters and Speeches*, edited by Louis Auchincloss (New York: Penguin Putnam, 2004), 503–4.

Years later in a letter to a friend, President Theodore Roosevelt reflected that there was some benefit to W. R. Hearst's actions. Calling him "a fearless man, and shrewd and farsighted," Roosevelt noted that "Hearst has often been of real use in attacking individuals of great wealth who have done what was wrong. In these matters he has often led the way." Yet, in that same letter Roosevelt launched a scathing rebuke:

> Hearst . . . preaches the gospel of envy, hatred and unrest. His actions so far go to show that he is entirely willing to sanction any mob violence if he thinks that for the moment votes are to be gained by so doing. He of course cares nothing whatever as to the results to the nation, in the long run . . . if for the moment he can gain any applause for so doing. He cares nothing for the nation, nor for any citizens in it. . . . I should think that Hearst would aspire to play the part of some of the least worthy creatures of the French Revolution. . . . [H]e is the most potent single influence for evil we have in our life.

29. Thomas, *War Lovers*, 223.
30. *New York Journal*, March 26, 1898; and Thomas, *War Lovers*, 222–23.
31. Thomas, *War Lovers*, 222–23.
32. Thomas, 223; and Arthur Wallace Dunn, *Gridiron Nights* (New York: Fredrick Stokes, 1915), 66, 71–72.
33. Morris, *Rise of Theodore Roosevelt*, 363.
34. Josep Conangla, *Memoir of My Youth in Cuba: A Soldier in the Spanish Army during the Separatist War, 1895–1898* (Tuscaloosa: University of Alabama Press, 2017), 114–15.
35. Linda H. Davis, *Badge of Courage: The Life of Stephen Crane* (Boston: Houghton Mifflin, 1998), 244–45.
36. Arthur Lubow, *The Reporter Who Would Be King: A Biography of Richard Harding Davis* (New York: Scribner, 1992), 154.
37. Lubow, *Reporter Who Would Be King*, 155–56.
38. Dyer, *From Shiloh to San Juan*, 217–18.
39. Dyer, *From Shiloh to San Juan*, 218.
40. *North Adams Transcript* (Massachusetts), April 1, 1898; Morris, *Rise of Theodore Roosevelt*, 638; and *Daily Star* (Fredericksburg, Virginia), April 9, 1898.
41. Margaret Leech, *In the Days of McKinley* (New York: Harper and Brothers, 1959), 169, 628.

    The following report of the president's reputation is drawn from the *Weekly Advertiser* (Montgomery, Alabama), April 1, 1898.

    Roosevelt and Henry Adams weren't alone in describing McKinley as a spineless creature of the deep. Montgomery's *Weekly Advertiser* commented, "The President is rapidly building the reputation for a jelly-fish backbone, and even his friends (except the Hanna combine) did not know what he will do."
42. Mark Lee Gardner, *Rough Riders: Theodore Roosevelt, His Cowboy Regiment, and the Immortal Charge up San Juan Hill* (New York: William Morrow, 2016), 15.
43. *New York Sun*, April 6, 1898.
44. Morris, *Rise of Theodore Roosevelt*, 642; and Roosevelt, *Rough Riders*, 23.
45. Poultney Bigelow, *Seventy Summers*, Vol. 1 (London: Edward Arnold & Co., 1925), 282.
46. Morris, *Rise of Theodore Roosevelt*, 642; and Roosevelt, *Rough Riders*, 23.
47. William Randolph Hearst, *William Randolph Hearst: A Portrait in His Own Words*, edited by Edmond D. Coblentz (New York: Simon and Schuster, 1952), 59.

The following account of the reaction to McKinley's declaration of war in Cuba is drawn from Conangla, *Memoir of My Youth in Cuba*, 120.

Josep Conangla noted that after McKinley's declaration of war was made public, General Blanco immediately declared martial law throughout Cuba. "I was convinced that most people were indifferent as they listened to the dramatic reading of martial law," Conangla recollected. "In the expressions of a good number of the attentive attendees, far from reflecting disgust or repulsion at the North American decision . . . they, like me, trusted that the war resolution of the United States against Spain would turn out to be favorable in the end to the triumph of the ultimate Cuban ideal of independence."

48. *Evening Times* (Washington, DC), April 26, 1898.
49. Joseph Wheeler, *The Santiago Campaign* (Port Washington, NY: Kennikat, 1971), 4.
50. Joseph Wheeler, *The Santiago Campaign* (Port Washington, NY: Kennikat, 1971), 4.
51. Longacre, *Soldier to the Last*, 218; and Charles Johnson Post, *The Little War of Private Post: The Spanish-American War Seen Up Close* (Lincoln: University of Nebraska Press, 1999), 214.
52. Wheeler, *Santiago Campaign*, 4.
53. Longacre, *Soldier to the Last*, 219; and Dyer, *From Shiloh to San Juan*, 220.
54. Joseph Wheeler Papers.
55. *Morning News* (Savannah, Georgia), April 26, 1898. General Miles recommended Leonard Wood receive the Medal of Honor for his conduct during the campaign that led to the capture of Geronimo. Wood's actions in Cuba may have factored into the decision to finally grant Wood the Medal of Honor in 1898.
56. *New York Journal*, May 2, 1898.
57. Charles Michelson, *The Ghost Talks* (New York: Putnam, 1944), 90; and Ben Procter, *William Randolph Hearst: The Early Years, 1863–1910* (Oxford: Oxford University Press, 1998), 47.

The following account of Hearst's talented reporters is drawn from the *San Francisco Call*, April 24, 1896; and Edward W. Morley, "On the Relative Motion of the Earth and the Luminiferous Ether," *American Journal of Science* 34, no. 203 (1887): 333–45.

Like Charley Michelson, Edward H. "Ned" Hamilton originally worked for the *Examiner* before transferring to the *Journal*. A talented investigative journalist, Hamilton was part of the "*Examiner* detective corps," described by the *San Francisco Call* as "a graceful and classic writer." As brilliant as Michelson and Hamilton were, they paled in comparison to Michelson's older brother Albert, who was the first person to measure the speed of light, subsequently becoming a physics professor and winning the Nobel Prize.

58. Wheeler, *Santiago Campaign*, 5–6; and *New York Journal*, May 6, 1898.
59. Wheeler, *Santiago Campaign*, 5–6.
60. Wheeler, *Santiago Campaign*, 5–6; and Harlan C. Herner, *The Arizona Rough Riders* (Tucson: University of Arizona, 1965), 72.
61. Lubow, *Reporter Who Would Be King*, 160; and *New York Times*, February 1, 1899.

Rather than William Shafter, many seemed to think the better choice to lead the army was Nelson Miles, the famed Indian fighter. But Miles and Secretary of War

Alger tended to clash. When Miles suggested to Alger that the army purchase cattle in Cuba from the locals, as was tradition, Alger disagreed, deciding that the army would make do with canned beef from a Chicago meatpacking corporation, a decision the army and Alger came to regret, as the quality of the meat was poor, creating a scandal after the war, with Miles dubbing it "embalmed beef." Miles was also married to Mary Hoyt Sherman, the niece of William Tecumseh Sherman and Alger's bitter political rival, John Sherman. So it was that Shafter rather than Miles was tasked with leading the Cuban campaign.

62. Dyer, *From Shiloh to San Juan*, 220–23; Lubow, *Reporter Who Would Be King*, 160; and Richard Harding Davis, "The Rocking Chair Period of the War," *Scribner's Magazine*, August 1898.
63. Richard Harding Davis, *The Cuban and Porto Rican Campaigns* (New York: Scribner, 1898), 50.
64. Dyer, *From Shiloh to San Juan*, 220–23.

Chapter 13. Badge of Courage

1. Paul Sorrentino, *Stephen Crane: A Life of Fire* (Cambridge, MA: Belknap Press of Harvard University Press, 2014), 274; Ralph D. Paine, *Roads of Adventure* (Boston: Houghton Mifflin, 1922), 170; Linda H. Davis, *Badge of Courage: The Life of Stephen Crane* (Boston: Houghton Mifflin, 1998), 246; and Stephen Crane, *The War Dispatches of Stephen Crane*, edited by R. W. Stallman and E. R. Hagemann (New York: New York University, 1964), 110.

   The following account is drawn from Ralph D. Paine, *Roads of Adventure* (Boston: Houghton Mifflin Company, 1922), 170.

   Ralph D. Paine and Ernest McCready stumbled upon Stephen Crane and Captain Edward Murphy shortly after Crane and Murphy survived the sinking of the *Commodore*. Paine, who had known Crane from their time as Asbury Park journalists, said of his old friend, "Stephen Crane had never been robust and there was not much flesh on his bones, at best. Sallow and haggard, he looked too fragile to have endured his battle for survival with the furious sea, but his zest for adventure was unshaken."
2. Sorrentino, *Stephen Crane*, 274, 277; Davis, *Badge of Courage*, 247; and *New York Journal*, April 24, 1898.
3. Paine, *Roads of Adventure*, 193; and Richard Harding Davis, *Adventures and Letters of Richard Harding Davis*, edited by Charles Belmont Davis (New York: Cosimo, 2005), 174.
4. Sorrentino, *Stephen Crane*, 277.
5. Charles Michelson, "Introduction," in Stephen Crane, *Midnight Sketches and Other Impressions* (New York: Knopf, 1926), iv.
6. Davis, *Adventures and Letters*, 172.
7. Davis, *Adventures and Letters*, 173, 174; and Crane, *War Dispatches*, 117.
8. Sorrentino, *Stephen Crane*, 274–78; and Crane, *War Dispatches*, 117.
9. Davis, *Adventures and Letters*, 177–78.
10. Davis, *Adventures and Letters*, 177–78.

11. *New York World*, May 1, 1898.
12. Sorrentino, *Stephen Crane*, 278; and Davis, *Badge of Courage*, 246.
13. Joseph R. McElrath and Jesse S. Crisler, *Frank Norris: A Life* (Chicago: University of Illinois Press, 2006), 223.
14. Sorrentino, *Stephen Crane*, 279.
15. *The Republic* (St. Louis), June 17, 1900.
16. Sorrentino, 280–81.
17. Sorrentino, 284; Davis, *Adventures and Letters*, 155; and McElrath and Crisler, *Frank Norris*, 226; and Crane, *War Dispatches*, 121, 135–36.
18. Crane, *War Dispatches*, 132.
19. Crane, 136.
20. Davis, *Adventures and Letters*, 121, 122.
21. Crane, *War Dispatches*, 181.
22. *New York World*, June 9, 1898.
23. Sorrentino, *Stephen Crane*, 286–87; and Kenneth Whyte, *The Uncrowned King: The Sensational Rise of William Randolph Hearst* (New York: Counterpoint, 2009), 442.
24. Paine, *Roads of Adventure*, 223–24.
25. Paine, 223–24.
26. Crane, *War Dispatches*, 150.
27. Crane, Stephen. "War Memories," *Anglo-Saxon Review*, December 1899.
28. Crane, *War Dispatches*, 148–51.

    Crane's "Marines Signalling [*sic*] under Fire at Guantanamo" appeared first in *McClure's Magazine* in February 1899 and then in 1899 in *Wounds in the Rain*.
29. Crane, *War Dispatches*, 151.
30. Crane, 151.
31. Richard Harding Davis, "Our War Correspondents in Cuba and Puerto Rico." *Harper's New Monthly Magazine*, May 1899, 938–48; and Crane, *War Dispatches*, 151.

    In Stephen Crane's Guantanamo article, which Davis considered some of his finest writing, Crane also reflected on the beauty of the sunrise, the excitement of morning coffee, and how long it took him to calm his nerves after the battle.
32. Sorrentino, *Stephen Crane*, 285.
33. Frank Keeler and Carolyn A. Tyson, eds., *The Journal of Frank Keeler, 1898*, Marine Corps Letter Series No. 1 (Washington, DC: Marine Corps Training and Education Command, 1967).
34. Crane, *War Dispatches*, 145; and Sorrentino, *Stephen Crane*, 288.
35. Crane, *War Dispatches*, 153.
36. Crane, *War Dispatches*, 144–45.

    For wigwaming the *Dolphin* at peril of his life, Sergeant John H. Quick would be awarded the Medal of Honor.
37. Crane, *War Dispatches*, 144–45.
38. Crane, 148.
39. Sorrentino, *Stephen Crane*, 289.

Chapter 14. Rough Riders

1. Theodore Roosevelt, *The Rough Riders* (New York: Fall River, 2014), 23–24; Evan Thomas, *The War Lovers: Roosevelt, Lodge, Hearst, and the Rush to Empire, 1898* (New York: Back Bay Books, 2010), 265, 266–67; and Harlan C. Herner, *The Arizona Rough Riders* (Tucson: University of Arizona, 1965), 53.

   Although unclear where the term "Roosevelt's Rough Riders" or simply "Rough Riders" originated, it has been bandied about that Roosevelt's remark that he was traveling west to join some "rough riding" men was the source. From the beginning newspapers in Texas and the East Coast used the term. Roosevelt initially fought against the name. So too did Wood. When it became apparent that the name would stick, both Roosevelt and Wood bent with the breeze. Characteristically unperturbed, Wood didn't let Roosevelt's popularity deter his command of the regiment.
2. Roosevelt, *Rough Riders*, 26–27; Edmund Morris, *The Rise of Theodore Roosevelt* (New York: Random House, 1979), 648; and Theodore Roosevelt, *The Selected Letters of Theodore Roosevelt*, edited by H. W. Brands (Lanham, MD: Roman & Littlefield, 2001), 184.
3. *New York World*, June 7, 1896; *Standard Union* (Brooklyn), May 13, 1899; and *New York Sun*, July 1, 1898.
4. Roosevelt, *Rough Riders*, 31; and *Santa Fe New Mexican*, December 20, 1895.
5. Roosevelt, *Rough Riders*, 23–24, 31–32, 37–38, 57; *Evening World-Herald* (Omaha, Nebraska), February 23, 1900; *Lansing State Journal*, March 20, 1920; Andrew Santella, *Roosevelt's Rough Riders* (Minnesota: Compass Point Books, 2005), 22; Roosevelt, *Selected Letters*, 184; and Billy McGinty, *Oklahoma Rough Rider: Billy McGinty's Own Story*, edited by Jim Fulbright and Albert Stenho (Norman: University of Oklahoma Press, 2008), 10.
6. Roosevelt, *Rough Riders*, 34–35.
7. Roosevelt, 31; and Herner, *Arizona Rough Riders*, 31.
8. Roosevelt, *Rough Riders*, 31.
9. Herner, *Arizona Rough Riders*, 50.
10. Theodore Roosevelt, *Theodore Roosevelt: An Autobiography* (New York: Da Capo, 1985), 233.
11. Roosevelt, *Theodore Roosevelt*, 234.
12. Roosevelt, *Rough Riders*, 37; Morris, *Rise of Theodore Roosevelt*, 649–50; and Herner, *Arizona Rough Riders*, 39.
13. Roosevelt, *Rough Riders*, 37.
14. Roosevelt, 37; and Herner, *Arizona Rough Riders*, 58.
15. Herner, *Arizona Rough Riders*, 58; Roosevelt, *Rough Riders*, Appendix A; *El Paso Herald*, May 10, 1898; and *Marshall Messenger*, July 1, 1898.

   Contrary to Appendix A of Roosevelt's account in *The Rough Riders* that Private Marshall Bird fractured his skull on August 8, 1898, in the line of duty, the Texas newspapers related that in May 1898 Bird was thrown while riding a horse bareback, fracturing his skull against a tree. Bird recovered but missed the war.

16. McGinty, *Oklahoma Rough Rider*, 12.
17. Roosevelt, *Rough Riders*, 37; and Morris, *Rise of Theodore Roosevelt*, 649–50.
18. Herner, *Arizona Rough Riders*, 56.
19. Morris, *Rise of Theodore Roosevelt*, 650–51.
20. Theodore Roosevelt, *Letters and Speeches*, edited by Louis Auchincloss (New York: Penguin Putnam, 2004), 147.
21. Roosevelt, *Letters and Speeches*, 147. See also Roosevelt, *Rough Riders*, 47; and McGinty, *Oklahoma Rough Rider*, 30.
22. Edward Marshall, *The Story of the Rough Riders* (New York: G. W. Dillingham, 1899), 44; *Evening World-Herald* (Omaha, Nebraska), February 23, 1900; and Herner, *Arizona Rough Riders*, 61.
23. Thomas, *War Lovers*, 267; Roosevelt, *Rough Riders*, 57; Herner, *Arizona Rough Riders*, 62; and Roosevelt, *Selected Letters*, 184.
24. Thomas, *War Lovers*, 267; Roosevelt, *Rough Riders*, 57; Herner, *Arizona Rough Riders*, 62–64; and *San Antonio Light*, May 22, 1898.
25. Herner, *Arizona Rough Riders*, 59–60.
26. Roosevelt, *Selected Letters*, 184.
27. Roosevelt, *Theodore Roosevelt*, 231–32; Roosevelt, *Rough Riders*, 61; and Herner, *Arizona Rough Riders*, 54–55.
28. Roosevelt, *Rough Riders*, 51.
29. Herner, *Arizona Rough Riders*, 55–56.
30. Roosevelt, *Theodore Roosevelt*, 231–32; Marshall, *Story of the Rough Riders*, 47; and Herner, *Arizona Rough Riders*, 65.
31. Marshall, *Story of the Rough Riders*, 47.
32. Morris, *Rise of Theodore Roosevelt*, 642.
33. Herner, *Arizona Rough Riders*, 66; and Marshall, *Story of the Rough Riders*, 48–49.
34. Marshall, *Story of the Rough Riders*, 49.
35. Roosevelt, *Rough Riders*, 62.
36. Marshall, *Story of the Rough Riders*, 52; Roosevelt, *Rough Riders*, 64; and Herner, *Arizona Rough Riders*, 69.
37. Herner, *Arizona Rough Riders*, 71.
38. Roosevelt, *Rough Riders*, 64–67; Herner, *Arizona Rough Riders*, 71; and Marshall, *Story of the Rough Riders*, 51, 53.
39. Roosevelt, *Rough Riders*, 67–68.
40. Richard Harding Davis, *The Cuban and Porto Rican Campaigns* (New York: Scribner, 1898), 55.
41. Davis, *Cuban and Porto Rican Campaigns*, 55–56.
42. Arthur Lubow, *The Reporter Who Would Be King: A Biography of Richard Harding Davis* (New York: Scribner, 1992), 168–69.

    The following account of Davis's demeanor in Tampa and the jealousy he inspired is drawn from Poultney Bigelow, *Seventy Summers*, Vol. 1 (London: Edward Arnold & Co., 1925), 286.

Poultney Bigelow caught Davis at a Tampa Bay Hotel dinner table, sitting at the head of the table with Frederic Remington, Rufus Zogbaum, and Stephen Bonsal around him. "Davis—the great Richard Harding Davis—extended a cautious finger of two by way of salutation," Bigelow wrote sarcastically in his autobiography. "*He* was acknowledged tacitly as *the* War Correspondent *par excellence.* No one else dressed the part. . . . Davis . . . brushed back his hair with some gelatinous polish, strapped on a pair of spurs, also his holster and field-glasses, and looked like one oppressed by the secrets of a Commander-in-Chief."

43. Roosevelt, *Selected Letters*, 185; and Thomas, *War Lovers*, 279–80.
44. Herner, *Arizona Rough Riders*, 75–76.
45. Morris, *Rise of Theodore Roosevelt*, 656–57.
46. *New York Herald*, June 6, 1898.
47. Thomas, *War Lovers*, 280.
48. Marshall, *Story of the Rough Riders*, 54.
49. *The Gazette* (Cedar Rapids, Iowa), November 26, 1898; and Roosevelt, *Theodore Roosevelt*, 237–38.
50. Roosevelt, *Theodore Roosevelt*, 238.
51. Roosevelt, 238.
52. Roosevelt, 239.
53. Thomas, *War Lovers*, 282; Roosevelt, *Theodore Roosevelt*, 238–39; and Morris, *Rise of Theodore Roosevelt*, 659.
54. Bigelow, *Seventy Summers*, 280.
55. Morris, *Rise of Theodore Roosevelt*, 659–60.
56. Joseph Wheeler, *The Santiago Campaign* (Port Washington, NY: Kennikat, 1971), 7.
57. Joseph Wheeler to family, June 8, 1898, Joseph Wheeler Papers, Alabama Department of Archives and History.
58. Roosevelt, *Selected Letters*, 186, 187.
59. Caroline Wheeler to Joseph Wheeler, June 13, 1898, Joseph Wheeler Papers.
60. Roosevelt, *Selected Letters*, 190.
61. William Randolph Hearst, *William Randolph Hearst: A Portrait in His Own Words*, edited by Edmond D. Coblentz (New York: Simon and Schuster, 1952), 59–60.
62. Roosevelt, *Selected Letters*, 190.
63. Wheeler, *Santiago Campaign*, 11.
64. Lubow, *Reporter Who Would Be King*, 171; and Marshall, *Story of the Rough Riders*, 76.
65. Wheeler, *Santiago Campaign*, 11–12.
66. *New York Times*, June 18, 1898.
67. David Nasaw, *The Chief: The Life of William Randolph Hearst* (New York: Mariner Books, 2001), 137.
68. Kenneth Whyte, *The Uncrowned King: The Sensational Rise of William Randolph Hearst* (New York: Counterpoint, 2009), 414–15.
69. Wheeler, *Santiago Campaign*, 11–12.

70. Wheeler, 11–12.
71. Lubow, *Reporter Who Would Be King*, 171.
72. Whyte, *Uncrowned King*, 415–416.
73. Roosevelt, *Rough Riders*, 83.
74. Lubow, *Reporter Who Would Be King*, 172.
75. Roosevelt, *Rough Riders*, 86; Marshall, *Story of the Rough Riders*, 65; and Evert Jansen Wendell, *New York Athletic Club of the City of New York: Constitutional By-Laws, Rules, and Alphabetical Lists of Members* (Cambridge, MA: Harvard College Library, 1918), 102.

Chapter 15. Yankees on the Run

1. Edward Marshall, *The Story of the Rough Riders* (New York: G. W. Dillingham Co., 1899), 78.
2. Theodore Roosevelt, *The Rough Riders* (New York: Fall River, 2014), 86.
3. Joseph Wheeler, *The Santiago Campaign* (Port Washington, NY: Kennikat, 1971), 17.
4. Wheeler, *Santiago Campaign*, 15–16.
5. Roosevelt, *Rough Riders*, 87; Marshall, *Story of the Rough Riders*, 71; and Billy McGinty, *Oklahoma Rough Rider: Billy McGinty's Own Story*, edited by Jim Fulbright and Albert Stenho (Norman: University of Oklahoma Press, 2008), 20.

    Billy McGinty related that in the town of Daquiri officers discovered bottles of rum, which they poured out into the sandy, gravelly streets. Some of the Rough Riders dipped tin cups into the grooves where the rum flowed and in this manner filled their canteens.
6. Wheeler, *Santiago Campaign*, 15.
7. Arthur Lubow, *The Reporter Who Would Be King: A Biography of Richard Harding Davis* (New York: Scribner, 1992), 172–73.
8. Wheeler, *Santiago Campaign*, 16, 18.
9. Wheeler, 16; Marshall, *Story of the Rough Riders*, 82–83; and Michael Blow, "One Learns Fast in a Fight." *MHQ: The Quarterly Journal of Military History* 7, no. 4 (Summer 1995): 20–29.
10. Stylograph, June 23, 1898, Joseph Wheeler Papers, Alabama Department of Archives and History.
11. Wheeler, *Santiago Campaign*, 16, 18; Roosevelt, *Rough Riders*, 92–93; Marshall, *Story of the Rough Riders*, 78–79; Richard Harding Davis, *Richard Harding Davis' War in Cuba & Spanish-American War: The Articles, Letters & Experiences of One of America's Finest War Correspondents* (Oakpast Ltd., 2021), 83; and Edward G. Longacre, *A Soldier to the Last: Major General Joseph Wheeler in Blue and Gray* (Washington, DC: Potomac Books, 2007), 224.
12. Roosevelt, *Rough Riders*, 90.
13. Marshall, *Story of the Rough Riders*, 88–89; and Edmund Morris, *The Rise of Theodore Roosevelt* (New York: Random House, 1979), 670.
14. Blow, "One Learns Fast in a Fight."
15. Davis, *Richard Harding Davis' War in Cuba*, 84.

16. Marshall, *Story of the Rough Riders*, 91.
17. Blow, "One Learns Fast in a Fight."
18. Paul Sorrentino, *Stephen Crane: A Life of Fire* (Cambridge, MA: Belknap Press of Harvard University Press, 2014), 289; and Marshall, *Story of the Rough Riders*, 76.
19. Harlan C. Herner, *The Arizona Rough Riders* (Tucson: University of Arizona, 1965), 104–6; and Blow, "One Learns Fast in a Fight."
20. Richard Harding Davis, *The Cuban and Porto Rican Campaigns* (New York: Scribner, 1898), 142.
21. Blow, "One Learns Fast in a Fight."
22. Stephen Crane, *The War Dispatches of Stephen Crane*, edited by R. W. Stallman and E. R. Hagemann (New York: New York University, 1964) 156; and Blow, "One Learns Fast in a Fight."
23. Herner, *Arizona Rough Riders*, 106.
24. Marshall, *Story of the Rough Riders*, 96.
25. Herner, *Arizona Rough Riders*, 106–7.
26. Roosevelt, *Rough Riders*, 100; and Marshall, *Story of the Rough Riders*, 93.
27. Marshall, *Story of the Rough Riders*, 99–100.
28. Wheeler, *Santiago Campaign*, 19; and Blow, "One Learns Fast in a Fight."
29. Wheeler, *Santiago Campaign*, 19.
30. Herner, *Arizona Rough Riders*, 107.
31. Roosevelt, *Rough Riders*, 100, 102.
32. Davis, *Richard Harding Davis' War in Cuba*, 88.
33. Roosevelt, *Rough Riders*, 102.
34. Crane, *War Dispatches*, 155–156.
35. Blow, "One Learns Fast in a Fight"; *New York Times*, August 25, 1898; Marshall, *Story of the Rough Riders*, 101; and Roosevelt, *Rough Riders*, 102.
36. Roosevelt, *Rough Riders*, 103; and Davis, *Richard Harding Davis' War in Cuba*, 89.
37. Crane, *War Dispatches*, 157.
38. Kenneth Whyte, *The Uncrowned King: The Sensational Rise of William Randolph Hearst* (New York: Counterpoint, 2009), 422.
39. Roosevelt, *Rough Riders*, 103, 105.
40. Letter from S. B. Young to E. J. McClernand, Joseph Wheeler Papers.
41. Roosevelt, *Rough Riders*, 106.
42. Roosevelt, 106; and Marshall, *Story of the Rough Riders*, 111.
43. Davis, *Cuban and Porto Rico Campaigns*, 153.
44. Davis, *Richard Harding Davis' War in Cuba*, 91.
45. Davis, 92–93.
46. Marshall, *Story of the Rough Riders*, 116.
47. Marshall, 116.
48. Davis, *Richard Harding Davis' War in Cuba*, 95.
49. Lubow, *Reporter Who Would Be King*, 177; and Whyte, *Uncrowned King*, 422.
50. Roosevelt, *Rough Riders*, 111.
51. Roosevelt, 112.

52. Roosevelt, 112.
53. Roosevelt, 112.
54. John P. Dyer, *From Shiloh to San Juan: The Life of Fightin' Joe Wheeler* (Baton Rouge: Louisiana State Press, 1941), 229–30.
55. Longacre, *Soldier to the Last*, 225.
56. Wheeler, *Santiago Campaign*, 40–41.
57. Stylograph, June 24, 1898, Joseph Wheeler Papers.
58. Longacre, *Soldier to the Last*, 226; Stylograph, June 24–25, 1898, Joseph Wheeler Papers; and Wheeler, *Santiago Campaign*, 40.
59. Roosevelt, *Rough Riders*, 126.

Chapter 16. San Juan Hill

1. Thedore Roosevelt, *The Rough Riders* (New York: Fall River, 2014), 123–24; and Edward Marshall, *The Story of the Rough Riders* (New York: G. W. Dillingham Co., 1899), 187.
2. Roosevelt, *Rough Riders*, 124. The following discourse on whether the Rough Riders had in fact been ambushed is drawn from Joseph Wheeler, *The Santiago Campaign* (Port Washington, NY: Kennikat, 1971), 33–34; Arthur Lubow, *The Reporter Who Would Be King: A Biography of Richard Harding Davis* (New York: Scribner, 1992), 177, 179–80; Theodore Roosevelt, *Theodore Roosevelt: An Autobiography* (New York: Da Capo, 1985), 241; Jack C. Lane, *Armed Progressive: General Leonard Wood* (Lincoln: University of Nebraska, 1978), 281; Edmund Morris, *The Rise of Theodore Roosevelt* (New York: Random House, 1979), 676–78; and Charles Johnson Post, *The Little War of Private Post: The Spanish-American War Seen Up Close* (Lincoln: University of Nebraska Press, 1999), 115.

In the days following the Battle of Las Guasimas, arguments over whether the Rough Riders had been ambushed took shape. In Colonel Leonard Wood's "Official Report" to Washington, which he composed on June 25, 1898, he didn't use the word "ambush" but did describe the Rough Riders encountering and being fired upon by a large force.

"At 7:10 our advanced point discovered what they believed to be signs of the immediate presence of the enemy," Wood wrote. "The command was halted and the troops deployed to the right and left, in open skirmish order, and the command ordered to advance carefully. The firing began almost immediately, and the extent of firing on each flank indicated that we had encountered a very heavy force. Two additional troops were deployed on the right and left, thus leaving only three (3) in reserve. . . . The firing on the immediate front was terrific."

The next morning, Roosevelt and the 1st US Volunteer Cavalry were still at camp when Crane's column in the *World* and Davis's report in the *New York Herald* appeared, both more cutting than Wood's report.

"Lieut. Col. Roosevelt's Rough Riders, who were ambushed yesterday, advanced at daylight without any particular plan of action as to how to strike the enemy," Crane began. Although Crane described the Rough Riders as displaying "much gallantry," he opined that the Rough Riders had "suffered a heavy loss, however, due to the remarkably wrong idea of how the Spanish bushwhack. It was simply a gallant blunder."

Davis made sure to paint the Rough Riders as the underdogs but otherwise wasn't much kinder, describing the battle as "an ambush with the advantages all on the side of the enemy." Suddenly the word "ambush" was everywhere.

Davis's personal correspondence was harsher.

"We were caught in a clear case of ambush," Davis wrote to his parents on June 25. "Every precaution had been taken but they knew the ground and our men did not. It was the hottest, nastiest fight I ever imagined. We never saw the enemy except glimpses." On June 26 he wrote Charles: "No one knew we were near Spaniards until both columns were on the place where the two trail meet."

Private Charles Johnson Post of the 71st New York Volunteer Regiment agreed with Davis. "The dismounted cavalry . . . only lacked a band at its head to give it a thoroughly festive and inconsequential air. It walked into an ambuscade at Las Guasimas," Post recollected.

Roosevelt, not wanting to look the fool, claimed that there had been no ambush whatsoever. In The *Rough Riders*, published in 1899, Roosevelt explained that the Rough Riders didn't immediately return fire because "the jungle covered everything" and the Spanish "were entirely invisible." In his 1913 autobiography Roosevelt demonstrably claimed, "There was no surprise; we struck the Spanish exactly where we had expected."

General Young, in his official report, didn't even allow that the Spanish had struck first: "The attack of both wings was simultaneous; and the junction of the two lines occurred near the apex of the angle on the ridge, which had been fortified with stone breastworks flanked by block-houses. The Spanish were driven from their position and fled precipitately toward Santiago."

Edward Marshall split the difference. In his 1899 account *The Story of the Rough Riders*, Marshall claimed the Rough Riders were not ambushed, "but the American troops met the Spaniards before they expected to."

3. Theodore Roosevelt, *Letters and Speeches*, edited by Louis Auchincloss (New York: Penguin Putnam, 2004), 150–51.
4. Morris, *Rise of Theodore Roosevelt*, 677; and Edward G. Longacre, *A Soldier to the Last: Major General Joseph Wheeler in Blue and Gray* (Washington, DC: Potomac Books, 2007), 226.
5. Richard Harding Davis, *The Cuban and Porto Rican Campaigns* (New York: Scribner, 1898), 181.
6. Tim McNeese, *Time in the Wilderness: The Formative Years of John "Black Jack" Pershing in the American West* (Lincoln: University of Nebraska Press, 2021), 207.
7. Roosevelt, *Rough Riders*, 124–25.
8. Roosevelt, 125–26; Post, *Little War*, 126; Morris, *Rise of Theodore Roosevelt*, 677–78; Billy McGinty, *Oklahoma Rough Rider: Billy McGinty's Own Story*, edited by Jim Fulbright and Albert Stenho (Norman: University of Oklahoma Press, 2008), 25; and Davis, *Cuban and Porto Rican Campaigns*, 176.
9. Evan Thomas, *The War Lovers: Roosevelt, Lodge, Hearst, and the Rush to Empire, 1898* (New York: Back Bay Books, 2010), 309–10.

10. WRH to PAH, undated, George and Phoebe Apperson Hearst Papers: Correspondence, 1864–1921, Bancroft Library, University of California.
11. Joseph Wheeler to children, July 15, 1898, Joseph Wheeler Papers, Alabama Department of Archives and History; and Wheeler, *Santiago Campaign*, 41.
12. Wheeler, *Santiago Campaign*, 41.
13. Morris, *Rise of Theodore Roosevelt*, 679; and Thomas, *War Lovers*, 325.
14. New York *Journal*, June 29, 1898.
15. *Semi-Weekly Times-Democrat* (New Orleans), July 1, 1898.
16. Lubow, *Reporter Who Would Be King*, 181.
17. Morris, *Rise of Theodore Roosevelt*, 680; and Wheeler, *Santiago Campaign*, 43.
18. Wheeler, *Santiago Campaign*, 41–42.
19. Morris, *Rise of Theodore Roosevelt*, 680; and Wheeler, *Santiago Campaign*, 43–44.
20. Roosevelt, *Theodore Roosevelt*, 245.
21. Roosevelt, *Rough Riders*, 129–30.
22. Thomas, *War Lovers*, 317.
23. Joseph Wheeler to children, June 30, 1898, Joseph Wheeler Papers.
24. Roosevelt, *Rough Riders*, 130–31.
25. Roosevelt, 131.
26. Roosevelt, 132–33.
27. Roosevelt, 133.
28. Thomas, *War Lovers*, 318.
29. Roosevelt, *Rough Riders*, 133.
30. G. I. A. O'Toole, *The Spanish War: An American Epic, 1898* (New York: Norton, 1984), 301; Kenneth Whyte, *The Uncrowned King: The Sensational Rise of William Randolph Hearst* (New York: Counterpoint, 2009), 418–19; and Post, *Little War*, 162–63, 245–46.
31. Roosevelt, *Rough Riders*, 136; and David F. Trask, *War with Spain in 1898* (Lincoln: University of Nebraska Press, 1996), 239.
32. Roosevelt, *Rough Riders*, 136.
33. Roosevelt, 136.
34. Kevin Hymel, "Black Jack in Cuba: General John J. Pershing's Experience in the Spanish-American War," *National Museum of the United States Army*, https://armyhistory.org/black-jack-in-cuba-general-john-j-pershings-experience-in-the-spanish-american-war/#:~:text=Pershing%20in%201902.,actions%20were%20quick%20to%20praise.
35. Herschel V. Cashin, *Under Fire with the Tenth U.S. Cavalry* (Niwot: University of Colorado Press, 1993), 226.
36. Hymel, "Black Jack."
37. Roosevelt, *Rough Riders*, 136–38; and Wheeler, *Santiago Campaign*, 72.
38. Roosevelt, *Rough Riders*, 138.
39. Roosevelt, 140; and Wheeler, *Santiago Campaign*, 74.
40. Roosevelt, *Rough Riders*, 140–41; and Roosevelt to Lodge, July 19, 1898, in Theodore Roosevelt, *The Selected Letters of Theodore Roosevelt*, edited by H. W. Brands (Lanham, MD: Roman & Littlefield, 2001), 200.

41. McGinty, *Oklahoma Rough Rider*, 29.
42. Roosevelt, *Rough Riders*, 140–41; and Roosevelt to Lodge, July 19, 1898, in Roosevelt, *Selected Letters*, 200.
43. Davis, *Cuban and Porto Rico Campaigns*, 212–13.
44. Roosevelt, *Rough Riders*, 142.
45. Roosevelt, 142; and Roosevelt to Lodge, July 19, 1898, in Roosevelt, *Selected Letters*, 200.
46. Roosevelt, *Rough Riders*, 144.
47. Roosevelt, 142–45.
48. Roosevelt, 145.
49. Roosevelt, 145–46.
50. Richard Harding Davis, *Notes of a War Correspondent* (New York: Scribner, 1912), 96.
51. Roosevelt, *Rough Riders*, 146–47.
52. Thomas, *War Lovers*, 323.
53. Thomas, 323.
54. Thomas, 324.
55. Roosevelt, *Rough Riders*, 146–47.
56. *New York Journal*, July 4, 1898.
57. Roosevelt, *Rough Riders*, 150–52.
58. Roosevelt, 150.
59. Roosevelt, 152–54.
60. Thomas, *War Lovers*, 326.
61. *New York Times*, August 28, 1898.
62. Roosevelt, *Rough Riders* 155–56.
63. Morris, *Rise of Theodore Roosevelt*, 654.
64. Thomas, *War Lovers*, 328.
65. Thomas, 329.
66. Robert K. DeArment, *Man-Hunters of the Old West* (Norman: University of Oklahoma Press, 2017), 196; Roosevelt, *Rough Riders*, 173.

Chapter 17. The Darkest Day of the War

1. Harlan C. Herner, *The Arizona Rough Riders* (Tucson: University of Arizona, 1965), 151.
2. Arthur Lubow, *The Reporter Who Would Be King: A Biography of Richard Harding Davis* (New York: Scribner, 1992), 187–88.
3. Paul Sorrentino, *Stephen Crane: A Life of Fire* (Cambridge, MA: Belknap Press of Harvard University Press, 2014), 292.
4. Lubow, *Reporter Who Would Be King*, 187–88.
5. John Fox Jr., Augustus Thomas, Theodore Roosevelt, and Gouverneur Morris, *R. H. D.: Appreciations of Richard Harding Davis* (New York: Scribner, 1917), 66.
6. Thedore Roosevelt, *The Rough Riders* (New York: Fall River, 2014), 181; and Charles Johnson Post, *The Little War of Private Post: The Spanish-American War Seen Up Close* (Lincoln: University of Nebraska Press, 1999), 203.
7. Roosevelt, *Rough Riders*, 182.

8. Roosevelt, *Rough Riders*, 181–82; and Billy McGinty, *Oklahoma Rough Rider: Billy McGinty's Own Story*, edited by Jim Fulbright and Albert Stenho (Norman: University of Oklahoma Press, 2008), 38.
9. Herner, *Arizona Rough Riders*, 151.
10. Roosevelt, *Rough Riders*, 189.
11. Roosevelt, 189.
12. Fox et al., *R. H. D.*, 65.
13. *Richmond Item* (Indiana), July 8, 1898.
14. William Loren Katz, *Eyewitness: The Negro in American History* (New York: Pittman Publishing, 1967), 383–84.

After T. C. Butler entered the blockhouse at El Caney and took down the Spanish flag, an officer in the 12th Infantry ordered the buffalo soldier to hand him the flag. Butler complied but not before tearing off a piece of the flag to commemorate the accomplishment of his fellow buffalo soldiers in the 25th Infantry.

15. *Richmond Item* (Indiana), July 8, 1898.
16. *Richmond Item* (Indiana), July 8, 1898.
17. James Creelman, *On the Great Highway: The Wanderings and Adventures of a Special Correspondent* (Boston: Lothrop, 1901), 211–12. See also *Richmond Item* (Indiana), July 8, 1898.
18. Creelman, *On the Great Highway*, 212.
19. *Richmond Item* (Indiana), July 8, 1898; and Creelman, *On the Great Highway*, 213.
20. Stylograph, July 1, 1898, Joseph Wheeler Papers, Alabama Department of Archives and History.
21. Herner, *Arizona Rough Riders*, 152; and Edward Marshall, *The Story of the Rough Riders* (New York: G. W. Dillingham Co., 1899), 212.
22. Roosevelt, *Rough Riders*, 181.
23. Joseph Wheeler, *The Santiago Campaign* (Port Washington, NY: Kennikat, 1971), 45.
24. Stylograph, July 2, 1898, Joseph Wheeler Papers.
25. Wheeler, *Santiago Campaign*, 50.
26. Roosevelt, *Rough Riders*, 194; and *New York Times*, August 28, 1898.
27. McGinty, *Oklahoma Rough Rider*, 34.

The following account of McGinty's disposition toward Roosevelt and relationship with Wheeler is drawn from McGinty, *Oklahoma Rough Rider*, 40, 95.

Billy McGinty always liked Roosevelt, writing that "Colonel Roosevelt . . . was kind and considerate under all kinds of conditions. He had a way about him that would make a tramp or a millionaire feel at home in his presence." However, it was Fighting Joe Wheeler who would have a greater impact on McGinty. Joining Buffalo Bill's Wild West in February 1899, when the troop re-created the charge up San Juan Hill in April 19 and 20, 1899, in Washington, D.C., McGinty played Major General Joseph Wheeler.

28. Roosevelt, *Rough Riders*, 181.
29. Fox et al., *R. H. D.*, 4.
30. Lubow, *Reporter Who Would Be King*, 189.
31. Marshall, *Story of the Rough Riders*, 212.

32. Lubow, *Reporter Who Would Be King*, 188–89.
33. Theodore Roosevelt, *Theodore Roosevelt: An Autobiography* (New York: Da Capo, 1985), 249; and Wheeler, *Santiago Campaign*, 46.
34. Wheeler, *Santiago Campaign*, 46; and Evan Thomas, *The War Lovers: Roosevelt, Lodge, Hearst, and the Rush to Empire, 1898* (New York: Back Bay Books, 2010), 339.
35. Letter from Theodore Roosevelt to Henry Cabot Lodge, 3 July 1898, Lodge-Roosevelt Correspondence, 1884–1924, Massachusetts Historical Society.
36. Lubow, *Reporter Who Would Be King*, 189.
37. *New York Herald*, July 7, 1898.
38. *New York Herald*, July 7, 1898.

Chapter 18. Citizen Hearst

1. David Nasaw, *The Chief: The Life of William Randolph Hearst* (New York: Mariner Books, 2001), 139.
2. *Semi-Weekly Times-Democrat* (New Orleans), July 1, 1898.
3. William Randolph Hearst, *William Randolph Hearst: A Portrait in His Own Words*, edited by Edmond D. Coblentz (New York: Simon and Schuster, 1952), 59.
4. A. B. Feuer, "Spanish Fleet Sacrificed at Santiago Harbor," *Military History*, June 1998, 57.
5. G. I. A. O'Toole, *The Spanish War: An American Epic, 1898* (New York: Norton, 1984), 328–29.
6. Evan Thomas, *The War Lovers: Roosevelt, Lodge, Hearst, and the Rush to Empire, 1898* (New York: Back Bay Books, 2010), 341.
7. O'Toole, *Spanish War*, 331.
8. O'Toole, 330–32.
9. O'Toole, 333–34.
10. Hearst, *William Randolph Hearst*, 64.
11. O'Toole, *Spanish War*, 334.
12. O'Toole, 335.
13. O'Toole, 336.
14. O'Toole, 336.
15. *Topeka State Journal*, July 5, 1898.
16. O'Toole, *Spanish War*, 335–36.
17. O'Toole, 335, 338.
18. Stylograph, July 3, 1898, Joseph Wheeler Papers, Alabama Department of Archives and History.
19. *Boston Globe*, July 6, 1898.
20. Hearst, *William Randolph Hearst*, 65.
21. *Boston Globe*, July 6, 1898.
22. Hearst, *William Randolph Hearst*, 65.
23. Hearst, 65–67.
24. Edward G. Longacre, *A Soldier to the Last: Major General Joseph Wheeler in Blue and Gray* (Washington, DC: Potomac Books, 2007), 228.

25. Arthur Lubow, *The Reporter Who Would Be King: A Biography of Richard Harding Davis* (New York: Scribner, 1992), 189–90.
26. *New York Times*, July 7, 1898.
27. *San Francisco Call*, July 6, 1898.
28. *San Francisco Call*, July 8, 1898; and *Salt Lake Herald*, July 11, 1898.
29. Kenneth Whyte, *The Uncrowned King: The Sensational Rise of William Randolph Hearst* (New York: Counterpoint, 2009), 440–41; and Hearst, *William Randolph Hearst*, 63.
30. Longacre, *Soldier to the Last*, 228; Billy McGinty, *Oklahoma Rough Rider: Billy McGinty's Own Story*, edited by Jim Fulbright and Albert Stenho (Norman: University of Oklahoma Press, 2008), 47; and Loretta Gillespie, "Miss Annie Wheeler remembered during National Military Appreciation Month," *Moulton Advertiser* (Alabama), May 23, 2019.

The following account of Annie Wheeler in Cuba is drawn from Charles Johnson Post, *The Little War of Private Post: The Spanish-American War Seen Up Close* (Lincoln: University of Nebraska Press, 1999), 282.

Charles Johnson Post never forgot catching sight of Annie Wheeler. "Miss Wheeler, daughter of Major General 'Fighting Joe' Wheeler . . . wore a stiff-brimmed, light straw sailor hat with a black velvet ribbon around it. Her shirt-waist, with its full sleeves, was immaculate and crisp; and her long, ankle-length skirt was of a soft gray. She was the first American woman, not counting Clara Barton, that we had seen since we left Port Tampa. . . . She was utterly lovely."

31. Joseph Wheeler to children, July 15, 1898, Joseph Wheeler Papers.
32. Longacre, *Soldier to the Last*, 228–29.
33. Thomas, *The War Lovers*, 351.
34. Nasaw, *The Chief*, 142.
35. Charles Michelson, *The Ghost Talks* (New York: Putnam, 1944), 90.
36. Michelson, *Ghost Talks*, xiv–xv.
37. WRH to PAH, undated, George and Phoebe Apperson Hearst Papers: Correspondence, 1864–1921, Bancroft Library, University of California.
38. Paul Sorrentino, *Stephen Crane: A Life of Fire* (Cambridge, MA: Belknap Press of Harvard University Press, 2014), 294–95.
39. Sorrentino, *Stephen Crane*, 298.
40. Sorrentino, *Stephen Crane*, 298.
41. Sorrentino, 303; and Linda H. Davis, *Badge of Courage: The Life of Stephen Crane* (Boston: Houghton Mifflin, 1998), 271–73.
42. Davis, *Badge of Courage*, 274.
43. Sorrentino, *Stephen Crane*, 303.
44. Whyte, *Uncrowned King*, 442–43.
45. Nasaw, *The Chief*, 147.
46. Nasaw, 148.
47. Menu and Invitation for 93rd Annual Festival of the New England Society in the City of New York, Joseph Wheeler Papers. Although the dinner should have been a triumphant affair for Wheeler, he was haunted by the drowning of his youngest son,

Tom, along with a friend while the two were "surf bathing" on Montauk Point on September 7, 1898.

48. *Morning News* (Savannah, Georgia), December 23, 1898.
49. *Morning News* (Savannah, Georgia), December 23, 1898.
50. Longacre, *Soldier to the Last*, 231–33.
51. *Brooklyn Citizen*, January 15, 1898.

The following account concerning Roosevelt's continued bitterness toward Crane is drawn from Sorrentino, *Stephen Crane*, 291.

While Davis painted Roosevelt as a hero, Crane took the opposite tack. In a collection of war stories he called *Wounds in the Rain*, Crane criticized the press for the attention it had paid to Roosevelt's Rough Riders at the expense of the other American heroes. Sometime later Roosevelt noticed his secretary, George B. Cortelyou, reading *Wounds in the Rain*. Shortly afterward Roosevelt confronted Jimmy Hare about Crane. "You knew this fellow Crane rather well, didn't you, Jimmy?" Roosevelt asked. Hare replied in the affirmative, but it doesn't seem that Roosevelt was really interested in conversation. "I remember him distinctly myself," Roosevelt stated. "When I was Police Commissioner of New York I once got him out of serious trouble." When Hare said Crane was simply doing research in the Tenderloin for his articles, Roosevelt let him know he didn't buy it. "He wasn't gathering any data!" Roosevelt exclaimed. "He was a man of bad character and he was simply consorting with loose women!"

52. John Fox Jr., Augustus Thomas, Theodore Roosevelt, and Gouverneur Morris, *R. H. D.: Appreciations of Richard Harding Davis* (New York: Scribner, 1917), 55–56.
53. *Marshall County Independent* (Indiana), July 21, 1899.
54. *Marshall County Independent* (Indiana), July 21, 1899; and Richard Harding Davis, "Our War Correspondents in Cuba and Puerto Rico," *Harper's New Monthly Magazine*, May 1899, 938–48.
55. Nasaw, *The Chief*, 151.
56. Nasaw, 152.
57. Hearst, *William Randolph Hearst*, 266.
58. Hearst, 48.
59. Hearst, 67.

Epilogue. Retrospective

1. John L. Offner, *An Unwanted War: The Diplomacy of the United States & Spain over Cuba, 1895–1898* (Chapel Hill: University of North Carolina Press, 1992), 229–30.
2. David Nasaw, *The Chief: The Life of William Randolph Hearst* (New York: Mariner Books, 2001), 81.
3. Gerald Langford, *The Richard Harding Davis Years: A Biography of a Mother and Her Son* (New York: Holt, Rinehart and Winston, 1961), 101.
4. Ernest Hemingway, *Green Hills of Africa* (London: Jonathan Cape, 1936), 29.
5. Robert W. Merry, *President McKinley: Architect of the American Century* (New York: Simon and Schuster, 2017), 382.
6. *Selma Times* (Alabama), November 10, 1900.

7. *Selma Times*, November 10, 1900.
8. Doris Kearns Goodwin, *The Bully Pulpit: Theodore Roosevelt, William Howard Taft, and the Golden Age of Journalism* (New York: Simon & Schuster, 2013), 232.
9. Upton Sinclair, *The Industrial Republic: A Study of the America of Ten Years Hence* (New York: Doubleday, Page, 1907), 209–10, 192.
10. *Bridgerton Pioneer* (New Jersey), July 6, 1899; and Goodwin, *Bully Pulpit*, 257–58.
11. Goodwin, *Bully Pulpit*, 258.
12. Theodore Roosevelt, *The Rough Riders* (New York: Fall River Press), 255.
13. Frederick J. Turner, *The Frontier in American History* (New York: Henry Holt, 1921), 219.
14. Theodore Roosevelt, *The Selected Letters of Theodore Roosevelt*, edited by H. W. Brands (Lanham, MD: Roman & Littlefield, 2001), 196.
15. Goodwin, *Bully Pulpit*, 292.
16. Theodore Roosevelt, *Letters and Speeches*, edited by Louis Auchincloss (New York: Penguin Putnam, 2004), 503–4.
17. William J. Clinton, "Remarks on Presenting the Medal of Honor, January 16, 2001," The American Presidency Project, https://www.presidency.ucsb.edu/documents/remarks-presenting-the-medal-honor.

Postscript

1. Edward J. Renehan Jr., *The Lion's Pride: Theodore Roosevelt and His Family in Peace and War* (Oxford: Oxford University Press, 1999), 222.

BIBLIOGRAPHY

Archives

George and Phoebe Apperson Hearst Papers: Correspondence, 1864–1921. Bancroft Library, University of California, Berkeley.
John Davis Long Papers, 1820–1943. Massachusetts Historical Society, Boston.
Joseph Wheeler Papers. Alabama Department of Archives and History, Montgomery.
Lodge-Roosevelt Correspondence, 1884–1924. Massachusetts Historical Society, Boston.
Presidential Speeches: Grover Cleveland Presidency. Miller Center, University of Virginia, Charlottesville.

Newspapers

Alabama Enquirer (Hartselle)
Atchinson Daily Patriot (Kansas)
Atlanta Constitution
Birmingham News (Alabama)
Boston Globe
Bridgerton Pioneer (New Jersey)
Brooklyn Citizen
Brooklyn Daily Eagle
Brooklyn Journal
Buffalo Courier
Buffalo Enquirer
Buffalo Evening News

Buffalo Morning Express
Chattanooga Daily Times
Choctaw Advocate (Butler, Alabama)
Commercial Appeal (Memphis)
Courier-Louisville (Kentucky)
Courtland Enterprise (Alabama)
Critic (Washington, DC)
Daily News (London)
Daily Star (Fredericksburg, Virginia)
Delaware County Daily Times (Pennsylvania)
Democrat and Chronicle (Rochester, New York)
El Paso Herald
Evening Journal (New York City)
Evening Star (Washington, DC)
Evening Sun (New York City)
Evening Times (Washington, DC)
Evening World-Herald (Omaha, Nebraska)
Florence Herald (Alabama)
Franklin Times (North Carolina)
Gadsden Times-News (Alabama)
The Gazette (Cedar Rapids, Iowa)
Greenleaf Sentinel (Kansas)
Harrisburg Evening News (Pennsylvania)
Henderson Gold Leaf (North Carolina)
Herington Tribune (Kansas)
Idaho Statesman (Boise)
Independence Daily Reporter (Kansas)
Indianapolis Journal
Inter Ocean (Chicago)
International Gazette (Black Rock, New York)
Iola Farmer's Friend (Kansas)
Kansas City Journal
Kansas City Star
Lansing State Journal (Michigan)
Leighton News (Alabama)
Limestone Democrat (Athens, Alabama)
Los Angeles Herald
Marshall County Independent (Indiana)
Marshall Messenger (Texas)
Metro Jacksonville
Montgomery Advertiser (Alabama)
Morning News (Savannah, Georgia)
Moulton Advertiser (Alabama)

New Decatur Adviser (Alabama)
New York Herald
New York Journal
New York Press
New York Recorder
New York Sun
New York Times
New York Tribune
New York World
Oakland Tribune (California)
Philadelphia Enquirer
Philadelphia Times
Pittsburg Post
Richmond Climax (Kentucky)
Richmond Enquirer (Virginia)
Richmond Item (Indiana)
Saint Paul Globe (Minnesota)
Salt Lake Herald
San Antonio Light
San Francisco Call
San Francisco Examiner
Santa Cruz Sentinel
Santa Fe New Mexican
Scottsboro Citizen (Alabama)
Seattle Post-Intelligencer
Selma Times (Alabama)
Semi-Weekly Messenger (Wilmington, North Carolina)
Semi-Weekly Times-Democrat (New Orleans)
Sheffield Weekly Enterprise (Alabama)
Standard Union (Brooklyn)
Stevenson Chronicle (Alabama)
The Tennessean (Nashville)
Topeka Daily Capital
Topeka State Journal
Washington Times
Weekly Advertiser (Montgomery, Alabama)
Weekly Times-Democrat (Greenville, Mississippi)

Books and Articles

Abbot, Willis J. *Watching the World Go By*. Boston: Little, Brown, 1933.

Auchincloss, Louis. *Theodore Roosevelt: The 26th President, 1901–1909*. The American Presidents. New York: Henry Holt, 2001.

Auster, Paul. *Burning Boy: The Life and Work of Stephen Crane*. New York: Henry Holt, 2021.

Bergad, Laird W. *Cuban Rural Society in the Nineteenth Century: The Social Economic History of Monoculture in Matanzas.* Princeton, NJ: Princeton University Press, 1990.

Bernstein, Matthew. *George Hearst: Silver King of the Gilded Age.* Norman: University of Oklahoma Press, 2021.

Bierce, Ambrose. *A Sole Survivor: Bits of Autobiography.* Edited by S. T. Josshi and David E. Schultz. Knoxville: University of Tennessee Press, 1998.

Bigelow, Poultney. *Seventy Summers*, Vol. 1. London: Edward Arnold, 1925.

Bloom, Harold. *Stephen Crane.* Bloom's Modern Critical Views. New York: Bloom's Literary Criticism, 2009.

Blow, Michael. "One Learns Fast in a Fight." *MHQ: The Quarterly Journal of Military History* 7, no. 4 (Summer 1995): 20–29.

Buk-Swienty, Tom. *The Other Half: The Life of Jacob Riis and the World of Immigrant America.* New York: Norton, 2008.

Bullard, F. Lauriston. *Famous War Correspondents.* Boston: Little, Brown, 1914.

Byrnes, Thomas F. *Professional Criminals of America.* New York: Cassell & Company, 1886.

Caldwell, Robert Granville. *The Lopez Expeditions to Cuba, 1848–1851.* Princeton, NJ: Princeton University Press, 1915.

Campbell, W. Joseph. "Not a Hoax: New Evidence in the New York Journal's Rescue of Evangelina Cisneros." *American Journalism* 19, no. 4 (Fall 2002): 67–94.

———. *The Year That Defined American Journalism: 1897 and the Clash of Paradigms.* New York: Routledge, 2006.

———. *Yellow Journalism: Puncturing the Myths, Defining the Legacies.* Westport, CT: Praeger, 2001.

Canfield, Michael R. *Theodore Roosevelt in the Field.* Chicago: University of Chicago Press, 2015.

Cashin, Herschel V. *Under Fire with the Tenth U.S. Cavalry.* Niwot: University of Colorado Press, 1993.

Chaffin, Tom. *Fatal Glory: Narciso López and the First Clandestine U.S. War against Cuba.* London: University of Virginia Press, 1996.

Choate, Judith, and James Canora. *Dining at Delmonico's: The Story of America's Oldest Restaurant.* New York: Stewart, Tabori & Chang, 2008.

Cisernos, Evangelina, and Karl Decker. *The Story of Evangelina Cisneros.* New York: Continental Publishing, 1897.

Clare, Israel Smith. *Library of Universal History.* New York: Union Book Company, 1906.

Clark, Leslie Eaton. *George Bronson Rea, Propagandist: The Life and Times of a Mercenary Journalist.* Madison, NJ: Fairleigh Dickinson University Press, 2017.

Conangla, Josep. *Memoir of My Youth in Cuba: A Soldier in the Spanish Army during the Separatist War, 1895–1898.* Tuscaloosa: University of Alabama Press, 2017.

Colvert, James B. *Stephen Crane.* New York: Harcourt Brace Jovanovich, 1984.

Crane, Stephen. *Active Service.* New York: Frederick A. Stokes, 1899.

———. *The New York City Sketches of Stephen Crane and Related Pieces.* Edited by R. W. Stallman and E. R. Hagemann. New York: New York University Press, 1966.

———. "The Open Boat." *Scribner's Magazine.* June 1897.

———. *Stephen Crane: Letters.* Edited by R. W. Stallman and Lillian Gilkes. New York: New York University Press, 1960.

———. *The War Dispatches of Stephen Crane.* Edited by R. W. Stallman and E. R. Hagemann. New York: New York University, 1964.

———. "War Memories." *Anglo-Saxon Review,* December 1899.

Creelman, James. *On the Great Highway: The Wanderings and Adventures of a Special Correspondent.* Boston: Lothrop, 1901.

Davis, Jefferson. *The Papers of Jefferson Davis: July 1846–December 1848.* Edited by James T. McIntosh. Baton Rouge: Louisiana State University Press, 1981.

Davis, Linda H. *Badge of Courage: The Life of Stephen Crane.* Boston: Houghton Mifflin, 1998.

Davis, Richard Harding. *Adventures and Letters of Richard Harding Davis.* Edited by Charles Belmont Davis. New York: Cosimo, 2005.

———. *The Cuban and Porto Rican Campaigns.* New York: Scribner, 1898.

———. "Our War Correspondents in Cuba and Puerto Rico." *Harper's New Monthly Magazine,* May 1899.

———. *Richard Harding Davis' War in Cuba & Spanish-American War: The Articles, Letters & Experiences of One of America's Finest War Correspondents.* Oakpast Ltd., 2021.

———. "The Rocking Chair Period of the War." *Scribner's Magazine,* August 1898.

———. *A Year from a Reporter's Note-Book.* New York: Harper & Brothers, 1898.

DeArment, Robert K. *Man-Hunters of the Old West.* Norman: University of Oklahoma Press, 2017.

Drabelle, Dennis. *The Great American Railroad War.* New York: St. Martin's, 2012.

DuBose, John Witherspoon. *General Joseph Wheeler and the Army of the Tennessee.* New York: Neale Publishing, 1912.

Duke, Thomas S. *Celebrated Criminal Cases of America.* San Francisco: James H. Barry, 1910.

Duffus, Robert L. "The Tragedy of Hearst." *World's Work,* October 1922.

Dunn, Arthur Wallace. *Gridiron Nights.* New York: Fredrick A. Stokes, 1915.

Dyer, John P. *From Shiloh to San Juan: The Life of Fightin' Joe Wheeler.* Baton Rouge: Louisiana State Press, 1941.

Feuer, A. B. "Spanish Fleet Sacrificed at Santiago Harbor." *Military History,* June 1998.

Fox, John, Jr., Augustus Thomas, Theodore Roosevelt, and Gouverneur Morris. *R. H. D.: Appreciations of Richard Harding Davis.* New York: Scribner, 1917.

Freeland, David. *Automats, Taxi Dances, and Vaudeville: Excavating Manhattan's Lost Places of Leisure.* New York: New York University Press, 2009.

Gardner, Mark Lee. *Rough Riders: Theodore Roosevelt, His Cowboy Regiment, and the Immortal Charge Up San Juan Hill.* New York: William Morrow, 2016.

Goodwin, Doris Kearns. *The Bully Pulpit: Theodore Roosevelt, William Howard Taft, and the Golden Age of Journalism.* New York: Simon & Schuster, 2013.

Hearst, William Randolph. *William Randolph Hearst: A Portrait in His Own Words.* Edited by Edmond D. Coblentz. New York: Simon & Schuster, 1952.

Hemingway, Ernest. *Green Hills of Africa.* London: Jonathan Cape, 1936.

Herner, Harlan C. *The Arizona Rough Riders.* Tucson: University of Arizona, 1965.

Hutchisson, James M. *Poe.* Jackson: University Press of Mississippi, 2005.

Hymel, Kevin. "Black Jack in Cuba: General John J. Pershing's Experience in the Spanish-American War." The National Army Historical Foundation. https://armyhistory.org/black-jack-in-cuba-general-john-j-pershings-experience-in-the-spanish-american-war/.

Katz, William Loren. *Eyewitness: The Negro in American History.* New York: Pittman Publishing, 1967.

Keeler, Frank, and Carolyn A. Tyson, eds. *The Journal of Frank Keeler, 1898.* Marine Corps Letter Series No. 1. Washington, DC: Marine Corps Training and Education Command, 1967.

Kennedy, Samuel V., III. *Samuel Hopkins Adams and the Business of Writing.* Syracuse, NY: Syracuse University Press, 1999.

Koenig, Louis W. *Bryan: A Political Biography of William Jennings Bryan.* New York: Putnam, 1971.

Lane, Jack C. *Armed Progressive: General Leonard Wood.* Lincoln: University of Nebraska, 1978.

Langford, Gerald. *The Richard Harding Davis Years: A Biography of a Mother and Her Son.* New York: Holt, Rinehart and Winston, 1961.

Leech, Margaret. *In the Days of McKinley.* New York: Harper & Brothers, 1959.

Leuchtenburg, William E. "The Needless War with Spain." *American Heritage* 8, no. 2 (February 1957). https://www.americanheritage.com/needless-war-spain.

Longacre, Edward G. *A Soldier to the Last: Major General Joseph Wheeler in Blue and Gray.* Washington, DC: Potomac Books, 2007.

Lubow, Arthur. *The Reporter Who Would Be King: A Biography of Richard Harding Davis.* New York: Scribner, 1992.

Lundberg, Ferdinand. *Imperial Hearst: A Social Biography.* New York: Random House, 1936.

Lytle, Andrew Nelson. *Bedford Forrest and His Critter Company.* Nashville: J. S. Sanders, 1984.

Marshall, Edward. *The Story of the Rough Riders.* New York: G. W. Dillingham, 1899.

McCullough, David G. *The Johnstown Flood.* London: Hutchinson, 1968.

McElrath, Joseph R., and Jesse S. Crisler. *Frank Norris: A Life.* Urbana: University of Illinois Press, 2006.

McGinty, Billy. *Oklahoma Rough Rider: Billy McGinty's Own Story.* Edited by Jim Fulbright and Albert Stenho. Norman: University of Oklahoma Press, 2008.

McNeese, Tim. *Time in the Wilderness: The Formative Years of John "Black Jack" Pershing in the American West.* Lincoln: University of Nebraska Press, 2021.

Merry, Robert W. *President McKinley: Architect of the American Century.* New York: Simon & Schuster, 2017.

Michelson, Charles. *The Ghost Talks.* New York: Putnam, 1944.

———. "Introduction." In Stephen Crane, *Midnight Sketches and Other Impressions,* xi–xv. New York: Knopf, 1926.

Milton, Joyce. *The Yellow Kids: Foreign Correspondence in the Heyday of Yellow Journalism.* New York: HarperCollins, 1989.

Morris, Edmund. *The Rise of Theodore Roosevelt.* New York: Random House, 1979.

Moskowitz, Sam. *The History of the Movement: From 1854 to 1890.* West Kingston, RI: Donald M. Grant, 1980.

Muir, John. *A Thousand-Mile Walk to the Gulf.* Boston: Houghton Mifflin, 1916.

Nasaw, David. *The Chief: The Life of William Randolph Hearst.* New York: Mariner Books, 2001.

O'Brien, Frank M. *The Story of the Sun.* New York: George H. Doran, 1918.

Offner, John L. *An Unwanted War: The Diplomacy of the United States & Spain over Cuba, 1895–1898.* Chapel Hill: University of North Carolina Press, 1992.

Osborn, Scott C. "Stephen Crane and Cora Taylor: Some Corrections." *American Literature.* 26, no. 53 (1954): 416–18.

Osborn, Scott Compton, and Robert L. Phillips Jr. *Richard Harding Davis.* Boston: Twayne, 1978.

O'Toole, G. I. A. *The Spanish War: An American Epic, 1898.* New York: Norton, 1984.

Paine, Ralph D. *Roads of Adventure.* Boston: Houghton Mifflin, 1922.

Pascal, Janet B. *Jacob Riis: Reporter and Reformer.* New York: Oxford University Press, 2005.

Post, Charles Johnson. *The Little War of Private Post: The Spanish-American War Seen Up Close.* Lincoln: University of Nebraska Press, 1999.

Powers, Ron. *Mark Twain: A Life.* New York: Free Press, 2005.

Procter, Ben. *William Randolph Hearst: The Early Years, 1863–1910.* Oxford: Oxford University Press, 1998.

Rea, George Bronson. *Facts and Fakes about Cuba.* New York: G. Munroe's Sons, 1897.

Renehan, Edward J., Jr. *The Lion's Pride: Theodore Roosevelt and His Family in Peace and War.* Oxford: Oxford University Press, 1999.

Robertson, Michael. *Stephen Crane, Journalism, and the Making of Modern American Literature.* New York: Columbia University Press, 1997.

Roosevelt, Theodore. *Letters and Speeches.* Edited by Louis Auchincloss. New York: Penguin Putnam, 2004.

———. *Ranch Life and the Hunting-Trail.* New York: Century Co., 1888.

———. *The Rough Riders.* New York: Fall River, 2014.

———. *The Selected Letters of Theodore Roosevelt.* Edited by H. W. Brands. Lanham, MD: Roman & Littlefield, 2001.

———. *Theodore Roosevelt: An Autobiography.* New York: Da Capo, 1985.

Samuels, Peggy, and Harold Samuels. *Teddy Roosevelt at San Juan: The Making of a President.* College Station: Texas A&M University Press, 1997.

Santella, Andrew. *Roosevelt's Rough Riders.* Minneapolis, MN: Compass Point Books, 2005.

Scharnorst, Gary. *Julian Hawthorne: The Life of a Prodigal Son.* Urbana: University of Illinois Press, 2014.

Schoultz, Lars. *That Infernal Little Cuban Republic: The United States and the Cuban Revolution.* Chapel Hill: University of North Carolina Press, 2009.

Sewall, William Wingate. *Bill Sewall's Story of T.R.* New York: Harper & Brothers, 1919.

Sinclair, Upton. *The Industrial Republic: A Study of the America of Ten Years Hence.* New York: Doubleday, Page, 1907.

Sorrentino, Paul. *Stephen Crane: A Life of Fire.* Cambridge, MA: Belknap Press of Harvard University Press, 2014.

Stallman, R. W. *Stephen Crane: A Biography.* New York: George Braziller, 1968.

Stevens, John D. *Sensationalism and the New York Press.* New York: Columbia University, 1991.

Swanberg, W. A. *Citizen Hearst: A Biography of William Randolph Hearst.* New York: Colliers, 1961.

Thomas, Evan. *The War Lovers: Roosevelt, Lodge, Hearst, and the Rush to Empire, 1898.* New York: Back Bay Books, 2010.

Thomas, Hugh. *Cuba or the Pursuit of Freedom.* New York: Harper and Row, 1971.

Tone, John Lawrence. *War and Genocide in Cuba, 1895–1898.* Chapel Hill: University of North Carolina Press, 2006.

Turner, Frederick J. *The Frontier in American History.* New York: Henry Holt, 1921.

Trask, David F. *War with Spain in 1898.* Lincoln: University of Nebraska Press, 1996.

Walker, Dale L. *Rough Rider: Buckey O'Neill of Arizona.* Lincoln: University of Nebraska Press, 1975.

Wendell, Evert Jansen. *New York Athletic Club of the City of New York: Constitutional By-Laws, Rules, and Alphabetical Lists of Members.* Cambridge, MA: Harvard College Library, 1918.

Wertheim, Stanly, and Paul Sorrentino. *The Crane Log: A Documentary Life of Stephen Crane, 1871–1900.* New York: G. K. Hall, 1994

Wheeler, Joseph. *A Revised System of Cavalry Tactics: For the Use of the Cavalry and Mounted Infantry, C.S.A.* Mobile: S. H. Goetzel, 1863.

———. *The Santiago Campaign.* Port Washington, NY: Kennikat, 1971.

Wheeler, Joseph, and Charles H. Grosvenor. "Our Duty in the Venezuelan Crisis." *North American Review* 161, no. 468 (November 1895): 628–33.

Whyte, Kenneth. *The Uncrowned King: The Sensational Rise of William Randolph Hearst.* New York: Counterpoint, 2009.

INDEX